# European Readmission Policy

# Immigration and Asylum Law and Policy in Europe

VOLUME 16

Editors

Elspeth Guild
*Kingsley Napley Solicitors, London,*
*Centre for Migration Law, Radboud University Nijmegen*

Jan Niessen
*Migration Policy Group, Brussels*

The series is a venue for books on European immigration and asylum law and policies where academics, policy makers, law practitioners and others look to find detailed analysis of this dynamic field. Works in the series will start from a European perspective. The incresed co-operation within the European Union and the Council of Europe on matters related to immigration and asylum requires the publication of theoretical and empirical research. The series will contribute to well-informed policy debates by analysing and interpreting the evolving European legislation and its effects on national law and policies. The series brings together the various stakeholders in these policy debates: the legal profession, researchers, employers, trade unions, human rights and other civil society organisations.

*The titles published in this series are listed at the end of this volume.*

# European Readmission Policy

## Third Country Interests and Refugee Rights

*by*

Nils Coleman

MARTINUS
NIJHOFF
PUBLISHERS

LEIDEN • BOSTON
2009

This book is printed on acid-free paper.

ISSN: 1568-2749
ISBN: 978 90 04 16554 0



http://www.brill.nl



PRINTED IN THE NETHERLANDS.

# Table of Contents

# Acknowledgements

Relying on a passion for migration and refugee law to sustain me, I started this book supposing it would more or less write itself if I simply invested the hours every day. A wildly naïve assumption, but one necessary to convince myself that voluntary exposure to many years of doctoral research – arguably one of the most lonely and frustrating occupations ever conceived – was really a good idea. But as it turned out I was not that far from the truth.

A stubborn insistence on this simplistic philosophy was helpful in mustering the required patience and discipline and in making those years enjoyable and fulfilling, the inevitable academic rough patches notwithstanding. This is in no small measure due to the unique setting and intellectual environment afforded by the European University Institute. I am indebted to the law department of the EUI for allowing me to pursue my academic interests with such freedom, and for the unforgettable experience of living in Tuscany. Special thanks in this regard are owed to Bruno de Witte of the EUI, who supervised the research on which this book is based. I benefited greatly not only from his expert legal and academic guidance over the years, but also from being given opportunity to engage in other research projects in the margins of the doctorate. I am hugely grateful in particular to my co-supervisor Thomas Spijkerboer of the Free University of Amsterdam, whose expertise in migration and asylum law, selfless investment of time, and constant reassurances and confidence-boosting in drafting this book were invaluable.

I am also grateful to Rosemary Byrne and Marise Cremona for their insights and comments on the work, to Kees Groenendijk for advising me at an early stage to focus on the versatile topic of readmission agreements, and to Elspeth Guild for showing a constant interest in the research and facilitating its publication in this series.

This book has been shaped to an important degree by an internship in 2003/2004 at the immigration and asylum unit of the Directorate General Justice, Freedom and Security of the European Commission. I was fortunate enough to spend five months at the very source of the common readmission policy. As a researcher, this period provided me with an understanding of the field and its context that would have been impossible to attain as an outsider. On a more personal level, it considerably broadened my professional interests. I would like to thank in particular Jean-Louis De Brouwer,

Sandra Pratt, Martin Schieffer and Peter Bosch for generously including me in a variety of aspects of their work, providing me with information, and trusting me to use that information with appropriate discretion.

Lastly, for lending the necessary moral support, I would like to thank my grandparents Simon and Mary Schaafsma, my parents Philip and Loes Coleman, brother Tim Coleman, and, further, Florence Lec, Ali Ahmad Nobil, Mario Mendez, Olivia Rutazibwa, Mehreen Afzal, Dragana Marjanovic, and Morag Goodwin.

# I Introduction

This introduction explains the genesis of the book, defines its scope and object of research, and clarifies its title. It also outlines the main sources which have been used in preparation of this book, explains its structure, defines its policy context, and comments on related terminology.

## I.i Genesis, scope and title

Readmission agreements facilitate the expulsion of unauthorised immigrants by establishing obligations and procedures regarding readmission between the contracting parties. Agreements of this kind have been concluded by European States since the early nineteenth century. They have however gained in number, importance and visibility especially since the early nineties. More than two hundred bilateral readmission agreements were concluded world-wide during the nineties alone, a large number of which by the current European Union (EU) Member States.[1] The proliferation of this type of agreement has since continued unremittingly.

Not only do the Member States continue to conclude readmission agreements, the European Community (EC) in May 1999 gained competence in the area of readmission with the entry into force of the Treaty of Amsterdam. Agreements are now being brokered with non-EU Member States – third countries – at the Community level, each facilitating the expulsion of unauthorised immigrants from a block of at least twenty-four Member States.[2] In addition, the EC since 1995 incorporates so-called readmission *clauses* into other agreements with third countries. These clauses also regulate the readmission of unauthorised immigrants, albeit in a less detailed manner.

When this research project was conceived in 2001, I was attracted to readmission agreements as typically European and slightly enigmatic instruments that allegedly

1 Estimate taken from a study in the context of the Intergovernmental Consultations on Asylum, Refugee and Migration Policies in Europe, North America and Australia (*IGC Report on readmission agreements*, 1999, IGCARMP, Geneva), cited in Noll 2000, n. 592.

2 Denmark does not participate in Community readmission agreements, and participation of the United Kingdom and Ireland depends on an opt-in.

enabled the swift and efficient expulsion of immigrants and refugees. I was uncertain as to how exactly, but knew that because of this capacity readmission agreements were both highly desired (by EU Member States) and strongly criticised (by civil society and in academia). The European Commission had just started negotiating the first Community readmission agreements with third countries, so the developing readmission policy at the EC level seemed an appropriate angle from which to approach the issue.

Initially, I was driven by three questions: are Community readmission agreements compatible with international obligations of refugee protection; (how) will the European Community manage to persuade third countries to accept these agreements which are clearly not to their advantage; and, (how) do readmission agreements work in practice?

The first question was my primary motivation for undertaking this research, having a certain background already in international refugee law, and having an avid interest in particular in the workings of the principle of non-refoulement. The second question, which is related to the involvement of third countries in EC immigration and asylum policies and the power relations that determine this process, I found fascinating but difficult to answer, lacking a relevant background. Answering this question was made possible by an internship from October 2003 until February 2004 at the immigration and asylum unit of Directorate-General Justice and Home Affairs of the European Commission (DG JHA, which changed its name to DG Justice, Freedom and Security (DG JFS) in November 2004). As a kind of "participant observer", I was able to gather the necessary information and gain insight into the negotiation of Community readmission agreements and readmission clauses, the flanking measures and institutional arrangements that underpin these negotiations, and the policy context in which they operate.

Unfortunately, the development of the third question, regarding the application of readmission agreements by the EU Member States in practice, had to be scaled down considerably. I lacked the means, special competencies, and time to do the necessary qualitative and quantitative research. Unfortunate, while it is the general lack of information concerning the manner and frequency of actual application of readmission agreements, which is in large part responsible for their enigmatic character. The question of how readmission agreements work, and the implications they may be expected to have in practice, is still addressed by this book as an important side issue, but primarily from a theoretical perspective.

The scope of this book is thus mainly determined by two questions, which may be phrased as follows:

> Are Community readmission agreements compatible with relevant international obligations of refugee protection?
>
> How does the European Community attempt to persuade third countries to accept readmission agreements and readmission clauses, and is this strategy successful?

The answer to the first question focuses to a large degree on the relation between readmission agreements and so-called safe third country policies – whereby protection seekers are expelled to a country which is not the country of origin[3] – and the international obligations which are relevant to this context. The answer to the second question, although phrased from the perspective of the Community, analyses not only the negotiating means used by the Community, but also the interests and negotiating position of third countries.

In pursuing these questions, a general objective of this book is to examine and lay bare the prevailing views that readmission agreements raise issues of international refugee law, and, that the conclusion of readmission agreements is an example of the European Community exploiting its political and economic power to the detriment of lesser developed and submissive third countries.

Both questions are reflected in the subtitle of this book. "Third country interests" is a reference to the central issue of incentives, or compensation, offered to third countries in the negotiation of readmission agreements and clauses. "Refugee rights" is a reference to the international protection obligations which are relevant to the application of readmission agreements.

Further with regard to the title, the broad term "*European* readmission policy" should be understood as reflecting the object of research as being readmission policy at the European Community level, but with reference also to readmission policies at the national Member State level. Member State readmission policies are not addressed specifically in this book. The relationship, however, between readmission policies at the Member State and the Community level, both in an historical and a current sense, is addressed. The Community's competence in the area of readmission is arguably the product of the conclusion of readmission agreements by European States, dating back to the early nineteenth century. Furthermore, the Member States continue to pursue individual readmission policies in parallel with the EC's policy, which influences the development of the latter.

The term used throughout this book when referring specifically to policy at the EC level is *common* readmission policy, while this is the term used by the European Commission and the Council of Ministers of the European Union. To my knowledge, the institutions have never sought to define this term or justify its use. Avoiding a discussion of the characteristics which would be required to merit qualification as a common policy, this book is premised on the following understanding of what constitutes the common readmission policy: the conclusion of Community readmission agreements with third countries, the incorporation of readmission clauses into other agreements with third countries, and the whole of flanking measures designed to support these two activities. It should be noted in this regard that readmission clauses are included in the scope of the research, but only as a subsidiary element. The great majority of the analy-

3 When used in the context of safe third country policies, the term "third country" refers first and foremost to a country which is not the country of destination, or the country of origin of a refugee. Such a country may also be, but is not necessarily, a "third country" in the sense of not being an EU Member State.

sis concerns readmission agreements. These impose far more intrusive obligations and are therefore at the centre of the debate regarding the impact on refugee protection, as well the impact on third countries which sign such agreements.

### I.ii Sources

The sources which have been used for this book are relevant literature, articles and newspaper clippings; international conventions; primary and secondary EU legislation; Community readmission agreements and Member State readmission agreements; official documents of the European Commission, Council of Ministers, and European Parliament; case law, primarily of the European Court of Human Rights, and to a lesser degree of the European Court of Justice and national courts; interviews with Commission and Council officials; and an interview with an official of the Dutch Immigration and Naturalisation Service.[4]

Considering the literature of main importance to the development of this book, the following can be noted. With regard to questions of refugee protection in the context of readmission and safe third country policies, several publications are fundamental to the analysis in this book.[5] This literature provides theses or makes claims that I either support or disagree with, both being equally valuable to the shaping of own views and ideas.

Remarkable is that the majority of publications in this area fails to draw a clear distinction between readmission agreements and safe third country policies when discussing their impact on refugee protection, or their relation with international refugee law.[6] The added value of this book in relation to the existing body of literature is that it does make this necessary distinction. It singles out the specific impact of readmission agreements on refugee protection from a legal perspective, thereby enhancing the general understanding of this instrument. Through a multi-layered analysis, incorporating national law of the Member States as well as secondary EU legislation relevant to safe third country policies, this book arrives at conclusions regarding the compatibility of Community readmission agreements with international refugee law and European fundamental rights law.

With regard to the discussion of the impact of readmission agreements on third countries, and the type of behaviour these agreements are expected to trigger from States, I was greatly helped along by publications in particular by Byrne, Noll and

4 *Immigratie- en Naturalisatiedienst (IND).*

5 Achermann and Gattiker 1995; ECRE 1995; Kumin 1995; Marx 1995; Byrne and Shacknove 1996; Noll 1997; Fernhout 1999; Abell 1999; Landgren 1999; Lavenex 1999; Spijkerboer and Vermeulen 1999; Vedsted-Hansen 1999; Noll 2000; De Witte 2000; Noll 2001; Crosland and Morrison 2001; Van Selm 2001; Hathaway 2003; Legomsky 2003; Zwaan 2003; Kuijper 2004; Human Rights Watch 2005b; Battjes 2006.

6 See, in particular, Achermann and Gattiker 1995; Marx 1995; Abell 1999; Landgren 1999; Lavenex 1999; Crosland and Morrison 2001; Van Selm 2001; Hurwitz 2002; Byrne, Noll and Vedsted-Hansen 2002; Bouteillet-Paquet 2003; Legomsky 2003; Human Rights Watch 2005b.

Vedsted-Hansen,[7] and several civil society organisations.[8] Compared to this literature, I place the issue of readmission agreements firmly within the much broader perspective of EU cooperation with third countries in the fields of migration and asylum, and draw attention to the technical limitations of readmission agreements in effecting returns. Furthermore, I question common assumptions by emphasising, not the disadvantages of readmission, but the calculating and strategic approach which third countries take towards concluding readmission agreements, considering the inherent benefits which can be gained from this process.

Finally, with regard to the process of negotiation of Community readmission agreements, the amount of publicly available information in Community documents and selected publications is limited.[9] After the aforementioned five-month internship at the immigration and asylum unit of DG JFS of the European Commission, I was however able to complement this information and provide the, to date, first comprehensive overview and analysis of the readmission negotiations at EC level.

During this internship, I fulfilled a number of tasks in relation to the common readmission policy, the common return policy, and external EC immigration and asylum policies more generally. I attended, *inter alia*, negotiations of the Community readmission agreements with Albania, Russia, and Ukraine, and preparatory meetings for negotiations with other countries.[10] I also attended discussions of the readmission negotiations in informal expert groups, the Migration/Expulsion Working Group of the Council, the Strategic Committee on Immigration, Frontiers and Asylum (SCIFA), and the Justice and Home Affairs Council. I was furthermore present at meetings of the High Level Working Group on Migration and Asylum (HLWG), where relevant legislation[11] and Council conclusions[12] were being prepared at the time. I also conducted numerous interviews with Commission, Council, and Member State officials during this period.

Having access to such an abundance of first-hand information, and being actively involved in the development of the common readmission policy at its very source, has shaped the content and partially determined the direction of this book. Some parts would not have been written. Analysing the negotiation process and related external

7 Noll 1997; Byrne, Noll and Vedsted-Hansen 2002.

8 Kumin 1995; FFM 1997; FFM 2000; Human Rights Watch 2005b.

9 Council doc. 12625/02; MEMO/05/351; Schieffer 2003; Kruse 2004; Peers 2004; Peers and Rogers 2006.

10 In the course of the book, I may refer to the negotiations of Community readmission agreements with third countries simply as "the readmission negotiations"; and to the total of third countries involved as "the readmission countries".

11 Regulation of 10 March 2004 establishing a programme for financial and technical assistance to third countries in the areas of migration and asylum, also referred to as the *Aeneas* Regulation, *OJ L 80*, 18.3.2004, p. 1.

12 Council Conclusions on the monitoring and evaluation mechanism of cooperation of third countries in the field of the fight against illegal immigration, Council Doc. 15292/03, 25 November 2003.

immigration and asylum policies in such detail would not have been possible, without this experience. In this regard, I should note that I have sought to confirm the information of an informal kind which I gathered during this internship (for example by attending meetings or through internal documents) in official Community documents or other written sources.

The analysis and opinions forwarded by this book are entirely my own and do not necessarily reflect the views of the European Commission. Nevertheless, I am aware of the risk of socialisation when submerged in the environment one is researching. I accept the possibility that my research would therefore show a degree of predisposition towards the perspective of the Commission, as opposed to that of, for example, the Council, the Member States, or the third countries involved in the readmission negotiations. In writing this book, I have however carefully guarded my objectivity. Any emphasis on the perspective of the Commission should be understood as the result of my particular familiarity with the position and role of the Commission in the development of the common readmission policy, and not as partisanship.

I also appreciate the difficulty and disadvantages of researching a moving target. The common readmission policy and other external EC immigration and asylum polices are continuously in development. When I started my research in 2001, the common readmission policy was in its early stages, and the Commission had only just started negotiating readmission agreements with a handful of countries. By the time I completed the relevant research (the bulk of which was done in the period October 2003-February 2004), the strategy and direction of the common readmission policy had changed several times, negotiation of a number of agreements had been completed, and several had entered into force. To avoid an endless cycle of updating chapters already written, it was necessary to set a general cut-off date. Excepting newly signed Community readmission agreements, of which a cursory update was included at a later stage, Community documents and other written sources with a publication date have been incorporated up until January 2006.

### I.iii Structure

This book consists of an introduction, nine chapters divided into sections and subsections, and a set of conclusions. The chapters of main importance to the two research questions, formulated above, are chapters 7 and 9. Chapter 7 analyses the process of negotiation of Community readmission agreements. Chapter 9 concerns the relation between Community readmission agreements and relevant international obligations of refugee protection. The remaining chapters are generally of a preparatory or background nature, building up to, and necessary for a full understanding of these two chapters and the underlying issues.

Chapter 1 places the common readmission policy in its historical context, providing an overview of the conclusion and characteristics of European readmission agreements through time since the early nineteenth century. Chapter 2 places the common readmission policy in the context of general international law. It looks at readmission obligations existing under general international law, which is an important factor in the negotiation of Community readmission agreements. This chapter is also relevant to the relation between readmission agreements and the implementation of safe third country policies.

Chapter 3 considers the *raison d'être* of the common readmission policy, which is the fact that the European Community has a greater negotiating weight than individual Member States. It also looks at the objectives which the Community arguably wishes to achieve in pursuing a readmission policy. This involves *inter alia* a discussion of the implications and effects which readmission agreements are generally expected to have in practice. Chapter 3 furthermore introduces the wider external policy context in relation to migration and asylum, and further explains the relation with safe third country policies.

Chapter 4 analyses the legal basis for concluding Community readmission agreements with third countries. It also describes the debate regarding the nature of the Community's competence in this area, which is a disputed issue between the European Commission and the Member States. This chapter provides necessary background information regarding the constitutional and institutional arrangements underpinning the common readmission policy, as well as a later discussion in chapter 7, concerning the friction arising from parallel negotiations of readmission agreements at the Community- and the national level.

Chapter 5 analyses the technical content of Community readmission agreements, as well as certain procedural and institutional factors which are relevant to this content. This chapter makes clear what is demanded of third countries which conclude a readmission agreement with the Community. It also highlights the limits of what these agreements may be expected to achieve in terms of overcoming obstacles to return, and securing the cooperation of third countries.

Chapter 6 discusses the integration of the issue of readmission into the external relations of the EU, which is essentially an outline of the flanking measures designed to support the common readmission policy. These are measures which provide leverage in the negotiation of Community readmission agreements, and this chapter is therefore important for explaining the policy measures with which the EC persuades third countries to conclude such agreements.

Chapter 7 is however the central chapter with regard to this question. This chapter comprehensively discusses the selection of and negotiations with the different third countries. It reveals the counter-demands which have been made by these countries, and the additional policy measures which have been taken by the EC in response to those demands. It also evaluates and makes general observations regarding the negotiation process and its implications, and judges whether the EC's approach and strategy have thus far been successful.

Chapter 8 concerns readmission clauses. The discussion of this other element of the common readmission policy has been deliberately placed after the analysis of Community readmission agreements, while bearing similar characteristics. This chapter is thus able to provide a concise and supplementary discussion of the content, negotiation, practical meaning, and further implications of readmission clauses.

The final chapter 9 details the compatibility of Community readmission agreements with international obligations of refugee protection. Based on the literature, it identifies the main refugee protection concerns in relation to readmission agreements, as being the facilitation of expulsion of protection seekers to safe third countries, in addition to a handful of further concerns. After establishing the relevant international legal framework, it determines whether these concerns raise any legal issues in light of this framework; an analysis which includes a review of safe third country policy under EC law.

### I.iv Policy context and terminology

A final word on the direct policy context of the common readmission policy and some related terminology. The common readmission policy is a component of the wider common *return* policy.

The chronology of policy developments in this area is somewhat odd, while policy at the Community level related to readmission precedes the development of a general policy framework for the return of unauthorised immigrants by a number of years. The Commission presented a green paper on return policy in 2002.[13] At that point, readmission was subsumed into the common return policy, "return" being, according to the Commission, "the genus of the policy field".[14]

This book is strictly limited to the readmission component, and does not pertain to developments in the broader area of return such as, for example, the Council Directives on the mutual recognition of decisions on the expulsion of third country nationals,[15] assistance in cases of transit for the purposes of removal by air,[16] and the organisation of joint flights for removals of third country nationals;[17] the proposal for a directive on minimum standards for return procedures,[18] which at the time of writing is under negotiation in the Council; the EU Return Action Programme;[19] the EU Plan for return to Afghanistan;[20] or the Preparatory Actions on Return programmed for 2005 and 2006.[21] Although some of these instruments bear some relation to the common readmission policy, a discussion of general EC return policy has not been included while it proved

13 COM(2002) 175 final.

14 COM(2002) 175 final, annex.

15 Council Directive 2001/40/EC of 28 May 2001 on the mutual recognition of decisions on the expulsion of third country nationals, *OJ* L 149, 2.6.2001, 34.

16 Council Directive 2003/110/EC of 25 November 2003 on assistance in cases of transit for the purposes of removal by air, *OJ* L 321, 6.12.2003, p. 26.

17 Council Decision 2004/573/EC of 29 April 2004 on the organisation of joint flights for removals from the territory of two or more Member States, of third country nationals who are subjects of individual removal orders, *OJ* L 261, 6.8.2004, p. 28.

18 Proposal for a Directive of the European Parliament and of the Council on common standards and procedures in Member States for returning illegally staying third-country nationals, COM(2005) 391 final, 1 September 2005.

19 Council Doc. 14673/02, 25 November 2002.

20 Council Doc. 15215/02, 4 December 2002.

21 Council Doc. 10375/04, 9 June 2004; see also the website of the Irish Presidency: www.eu2004.ie.

difficult to incorporate into the structure of the book, and was moreover not necessary for answering its questions. Hence, I only mention return policy here as part of the introduction.

I will, however, borrow from the context of EC return policy to clarify the use of certain terminology. The field of return shows a variety of partially overlapping terms, which are moreover interpreted differently between administrative- and judicial authorities of the Member States. The Commission has therefore sought to establish a set of common definitions. A first set was presented in the green paper on Community return policy,[22] which was modified to form a second (and in the absence of further specification still current) set in an ensuing Commission Communication on the same topic.[23] The relevant set of definitions is as follows:

| | |
|---|---|
| Readmission | Act by a state accepting the re-entry of an individual (own nationals, third-country nationals or stateless persons [sic.]), who has been found illegally entering to, being present [sic.] in or residing in another state.[24] |
| Return | Comprises the process of going back to one's country of origin, transit or another third country, including preparation and implementation [sic.]. The return may be voluntary or enforced. |
| Repatriation | Return to the country of origin, in both voluntary or [sic.] forced situations. |
| Voluntary return | The assisted or independent departure to the country of origin, transit or another third country based on the will of the returnee. |
| Forced return | The compulsory return to the country of origin, transit or another third country, on the basis of an administrative or judicial act. |
| Expulsion | Administrative or judicial act, which states – where applicable – the illegality of the entry, stay or residence or terminates the legality of a previous lawful residence [...]. |
| Removal | Act of enforcement, which means [sic.] the physical transportation out of the country. The English word "deportation" is also used in this context.[25] |

These definitions are clearly politically tainted. Alongside the effort to capture their objective or legal meaning, they have been formulated in accordance with policy objectives of the Community in the field (which will be detailed in the course of this

22 COM(2002) 175 final, annex.

23 COM(2002) 564 final, p. 11 and annex.

24 The initial definition of the green paper had simply been: "Decision by a receiving state on the re-entry of an individual".

25 COM(2002) 564 final, p. 11 and annex; COM(2002) 175 final, p. 12 and annex.

book). This explains the strained construction of some of the definitions, the specification of categories of persons within the definition of "readmission", and the repeated reference to transit countries. In addition, the definition of "return" is too wide. The literal meaning of the term – "to come or go back to a place"[26] – indicates that a person must have been physically present in a country before being able to return there. The phrase "another third country" should therefore have read "residence".

Whilst bearing in mind these comments, however, the above definitions do convey the general meaning of these terms and the differences between them, which I will adhere to throughout this book.

26 Oxford Advanced Learner's Dictionary of current English, fourth edition, Oxford, Oxford University Press, 1989.

# Chapter 1 History of readmission policies in Europe

The heredity of the common readmission policy dates back to the nineteenth century. A bird's eye view of the history of European readmission agreements shows that European States concluded numerous agreements in the period roughly from the early nineteenth century until the Second World War.[1] In the immediate post-war period, European States concluded bilateral agreements to deal with the readmission of persons, who were displaced during the war.[2] The Second World War is also a turning point in that earlier readmission agreements largely concentrated on the readmission of own nationals, whilst later agreements increasingly included the readmission of third country nationals.[3] The next period of particular activity in the conclusion of readmission agreements is the 1950s and 60s. During this period, Western European States regulated the migration of persons between each other's territories by means of readmission agreements. The readmission of persons was especially topical in light of Benelux integration.[4] After a subsequent lull, a renewed interest in readmission agreements of lasting significance surfaced in the early nineties, during which time readmission policy at the European level also started taking shape.

In the following, we will highlight some of the early nineteenth and twentieth century European readmission agreements, and the particulars of the conclusion of readmission agreements in the 1950s/60s, and the 1990s. This will be followed by an outline of early common readmission policy. For the purpose of this chapter, early common readmission policy refers to policy in the area of readmission up until the advent of European Community competence to conclude readmission agreements with third countries with the entry into of the Treaty of Amsterdam on 1 May 1999.

1 Krabbe 1912, p. 86-126; Van Eysinga 1916, 116-117, 154-156; Hailbronner 1997, p. 6-7, 15-18; Davy 2004, p. 235.

2 Hailbronner 1997, p. 6.

3 Hailbronner 1997, p. 25.

4 Swart 1978, p. 49-58, 312-313; Denoël 1993, p. 636-642; Fernhout 1999, p. 1, 84-86; Lavenex 1999, p. 22, 79; Hurwitz 2002, p. 3; Bouteillet-Paquet 2003, p. 359; Zwaan 2003, p. 82-83.

## 1.1 Early European readmission agreements

In the early nineteenth century, European States started to move towards a practice of cooperation regarding the expulsion of persons, rather than implementing expulsion unilaterally. Territorial sovereignty is generally considered to imply the competence to determine the entry and presence of aliens, which includes the competence to expel aliens whose presence is undesirable.[5] The latter competence is in principle unlimited, a legal viewpoint which States have only gradually surrendered in favour of a more practical approach.[6] In order to be effective, the implementation of expulsion presupposes readmission by another State, allowing at least entry to its territory.[7] Unilateral expulsion, removing an undesirable person across the border into another State without the consent of the latter, is conducive to interstate conflict. It is moreover likely to meet with a similar response, thus not providing a durable solution. Davy notes:

> Die Praxis der "Problemabschiebung" wurde fragwürdig, als die Zahl der "Unerwünschten" unbekannte dimensionen annahm under die von einem Schubtransport betroffenen Staaten begannen, einen Schubtransport mit einem Schubtransport zu beantworten. "Um [...] zwischenstaatlichen Streitigkeiten abzustellen, "waren die Staaten zu begin des 19. Jahrhunderts bereit, die Lasten auf bestimmte Weise zu fixieren".[8]

The earliest examples of specific bilateral arrangements concerning readmission are a series of agreements concluded in 1818 and 1819 between Prussia and other German States on the "wechselweitiger Übernahme der Vagabunden und Ausgewiesenen".[9] Prussia also concluded the first multilateral treaty on readmission a number of years later, in 1851, known as the Treaty of Gotha.[10] Other relevant agreements, concluded

5 "Chaque Etat est maître, et libre de fixer les conditions d'entrée et de séjour d'étrangers sur son territoire. Le droit de non admission ou d'exclusion est une consequence directe de la souverainité territoriale", Bonfils 1905, cited in: Krabbe 1912, p. 79.

6 "Zu Beginn des 19. Jahrhunderts war noch völlig unbestritten, dass Staaten die weitgehend schrankenlose Befugnis besaßen, verarmte order straffällige Personen über ihre Grenzen abzuschieben", Davy 2004, p. 235. See also *infra*, n. 14.

7 The necessary complement of effective expulsion would in principle be admission. The emphasis in practice is however on *re*admission, while invariably concerning a national of the receiving State, or an alien who has previously resided or at least been present on the territory of the receiving State. Although it cannot be excluded that States would admit aliens, expelled from another State, without such a previous connection to their territory, this is not general practice.

8 Davy 2004, p. 235. See in the same vein Van Eysinga 1916, p. 155.

9 Cited in Davy 2004, p. 235. I am indebted to Kees Groenendijk for a series of references pertaining to early nineteenth and twentieth century readmission agreements.

10 Vertrag zwischen Preußen und mehreren anderen deutschen Regierungen wegen gegenseitiger Verpflichting zur Übernahme der Auszuweisenden vom 15.7.1851, cited in Davy 2004, p. 235. See also Hailbronner 1997, p. 6.

between European States in the nineteenth century, pertained to the mutual settlement or establishment of nationals abroad, in light of which the contracting parties would include provision for expulsion and readmission.[11] One such agreement, the treaty on establishment between the Netherlands and Germany of 7 November 1906,[12] deserves special mention, while its provisions on readmission bear a large resemblance to those of contemporary readmission agreements.

The Dutch-German treaty on establishment of 1906 was considered a milestone, firstly, while arguably codifying a developing principle under public international law that States must open their territories to aliens, as adhered to between "civilised States".[13] Secondly, while it revolutionised Dutch expulsion practice, which had been to simply remove aliens across the border to a country of their choice.[14] Providing a right to establishment, the 1906 Dutch-German treaty on establishment served primarily to circumscribe the previously unlimited competence to expel Dutch nationals from Germany, and *viceversa.* It prescribed readmission as the method of expulsion, detailing a procedure similar to provisions in contemporary readmission agreements. The readmission of nationals and former nationals of one of the contracting parties was arranged by an exchange of letters. Procedural requirements included the prior notification of an intended expulsion, after which the other party would approve or deny readmission based on examination of supporting circumstances and documents. Additionally, the treaty provided for the informal readmission of third country nationals[15] in specific cases.[16]

11 Krabbe 1912, p. 84-124; Hailbronner 1997, p. 6, 16, 25.

12 Outlined in Krabbe 1912, p. 86-124; and Van Eysinga 1916, p. 155.

13 Krabbe 1912, p. 86.

14 Krabbe 1912, p. 110. Krabbe's doctoral thesis of 1912 offers further insight into the then common practice of unilateral expulsion. One the one hand, this practice was informed by absolute interpretations of State sovereignty, national self-interest, and the general lawlessness of aliens. Another reason, however, which initially prevented a transition to a more cooperative approach to expulsion, was a concern that the introduction of readmission agreements would lead to circumvention of the more arduous extradition process. In answering questions in parliament on whether the transfer of persons under the Dutch-German treaty on establishment would entail such a risk, the Dutch Minister of foreign affairs relied on the good faith of the contracting parties. He moreover considered that an individual would be more likely to inform the authorities of his or her involvement in criminal activity when faced with transfer to the authorities of another contracting party under a readmission agreement. To this day, readmission agreements do not generally provide explicit safeguards preventing their misuse for extradition purposes, arguably for the same reasons, Krabbe 1912, p. 73-83, 110, 115-116.

15 In a readmission context, a "third country national" is a person who does not hold the nationality of any of the contracting parties to a readmission agreement. This should not be confused with the term "third country national" as typical to the EU context, referring to a national of any country that is not an EU Member State.

16 This readmission obligation was limited to persons travelling by train, intercepted at the first train station after the border, Krabbe 1912, 110-118.

Another remarkably "modern" provision of the 1906 Dutch-German treaty on establishment concerns the transit of persons across the territory of the other contracting State for the benefit of expulsion to third countries. This provision determined *inter alia* that the costs of transport would be borne by the expelling State, and required the prior consent of the third country to admit the individual in question. These are still common requirements for transit arrangements in readmission agreements. A salient detail is that the Dutch delegation had attempted to negotiate a provision whereby the other contracting party would simply readmit the expellee, and take responsibility for onward expulsion to the third country involved. This unsuccessful attempt was characterised as an "impossible wish" during the discussion of the treaty in the Dutch parliament. "Surely", Krabbe adds in this regard, "one could not require Germany to bear the costs of measures, taken by and in the interest of the Netherlands".[17] An important objective of contemporary readmission agreements is precisely to create this possibility, to expel persons to transit countries where direct expulsion to the country of origin is not possible, or too costly.

Further readmission agreements and treaties on establishment were concluded in the nineteenth and early twentieth century by Belgium, Denmark, France, Germany, Italy, the Netherlands, Russia, and Switzerland.[18] A characteristic of the conclusion of readmission agreements during this period is that it served primarily to enable the expulsion of undesirable persons – vagrants, persons constituting a threat to public order or national security – to their countries of nationality, or former nationality. The conclusion of readmission agreements for the purpose of regulating migration flows more generally started in the 1950s and 1960s.

## 1.2 European readmission agreements in the 1950s and 1960s

The literature tends to refer to the conclusion of readmission agreements as a phenomenon beginning in the 1950s and 1960s.[19] This is inaccurate, considering the previous section. The 1950 and 60s, however, were a highly relevant period in the development of European readmission agreements. There was a peak in the conclusion of readmission agreements between European States in this period, which intended to regulate the migration of persons between each other's territories. As such, the conclusion of readmission agreements in the fifties and sixties reflects more closely the contemporary purpose of these treaty instruments. Furthermore, the most relevant activity in terms of readmission in this period took place in the context of the Benelux. The Benelux

17 " [...] een 'onmogelijken wensch'. Men kan Duitschland toch niet vergen, dat het de kosten draagt van maatregelen door en in het belang van Nederland genomen", Krabbe 1912, p. 119.

18 Krabbe 1912, p. 87; Van Eysinga 1916, p. 155-156; Hailbronner 1997, p. 6, 15-18.

19 Fernhout 1999, p. 79; Lavenex 1999, p. 79; Landgren 1999, p. 22; Hurwitz 2002, p. 3; Bouteillet-Paquet 2003, p. 359. Bouteillet-Paquet refers to readmission agreements concluded in the 1960s as the "first generation" of these agreements (also Fernhout 1999, p. 84; and Zwaan 2003, p. 82).

arguably served as a laboratory for cooperation at the wider European level, also in relation to readmission.

The 1958 Treaty establishing the Benelux Economic Union entered into force in 1960. It created rights for the nationals of Belgium, the Netherlands and Luxemburg to establishment in one of the other contracting States, and to free movement within the Benelux area.[20] To this end, the Benelux States concluded a subsequent agreement that lifted internal border controls on persons, including third country nationals, and transferred the control of persons to the external borders of the Benelux area.[21] This agreement impacted upon the expulsion and readmission of third country nationals in several ways. The agreement provided for the readmission of third country nationals between Benelux States internally.[22] This provision was further detailed in Decision M/P (67) 1 on the removal and readmission of persons, taken by the Ministerial working group in charge of implementing the agreement.[23] In addition, Decision M/P (67) 1 regulated the removal of third country nationals to countries outside the Benelux area.[24] The Benelux furthermore concluded readmission agreements with France in 1964, Austria in 1965, and Germany in 1966, facilitating the expulsion of nationals of these countries, as well third country nationals.[25]

In the case of the Benelux, these detailed arrangements did not prove to be a guarantee for an orderly traffic and transfer of immigrants. The Benelux has a history of "Problemabschiebung",[26] which illustrates how slow and uneven the change from unilateral removal to interstate cooperation on the expulsion and readmission of persons has been in Europe. A common practice of the Dutch authorities was to expel immigrants, who were not entitled to residence in a Benelux country and whose identity and nationality could not be established, using the so-called Roosendaal method. The Roosendaal method consisted of placing immigrants on a train in Roosendaal, a city on the border with Belgium, heading for France. This was a purported attempt

20 Swart 1978, p. 49-50; Denoël 1993, p. 636-637.

21 This agreement – "Overeenkomst inzake de verlegging van de personencontrole naar de buitengrenzen van het Beneluxgebied" – was concluded in April 1960, and entered into force on 1 July 1960, Swart 1978, p. 49.

22 Swart 1978, p. 51.

23 "Beschikking M/P (67) 1 van de Ministeriële Werkgroep voor het personenverkeer betreffende de verwijdering en de overname van personen", 28 July 1967, *Trb.* 1978, 171 (hereinafter Decision M/P (67) 1). For a broader outline of this decision, see Denoël 1993, p. 638-640.

24 Articles 15 and 16 of Decision M/P (67) 1. Article 15 determines that aliens, whose presence is undesired is one of the Benelux States, would be removed across the external border of the Benelux area, unless another Benelux State is obliged to readmission or another Benelux State has granted the person admission to its territory. Article 16 provides for transit across the territory of another Benelux State for the purpose of removal to a third country.

25 Swart 1978, p. 312; Denoël 1993, p. 640-642; Fernhout 1999, p. 79, 84-86.

26 *Supra*, at n. 8.

at removal to a country outside the Benelux area, but was to all intended purposes a unilateral act of removal across the border with Belgium. The Dutch authorities did not seek permission for transit across Belgian territory, nor secured readmission to France. The unescorted immigrants would often disembark at one of several stops at stations in Belgium. They would find their way back to the Netherlands, either of their own accord or at the hands of the Belgian authorities, only to be expelled in the same manner, *etcetera*. This resulted in cases of repeated expulsion of immigrants – also referred to as migrants "in orbit" – between the Netherlands and Belgium, and the necessary tension in Dutch-Belgian relations.[27] The Dutch authorities finally ceased using the Roosendaal method in 1993, a few weeks prior to a ruling by the Supreme Court, which found it in breach of Benelux law.[28]

Considering, finally, some general characteristics of readmission agreements as concluded by European States in the fifties and sixties, we should firstly mention that their practical meaning was limited. This was due to problems in fulfilling the evidence requirements for establishing readmission obligations. Obligations to readmit were typically dependent on evidence of an unauthorised border crossing between the contracting parties, which was difficult to provide in practice.[29] Procedural requirements, such as short time limits for requesting readmission upon detecting the presence of a person without a residence title, also proved obstacles to effective implementation.[30] Secondly, although the conclusion of readmission agreements during this period already reflected their more contemporary purpose of regulating migration flows, a difference is that migration was not yet perceived as a problem.[31] The conclusion of readmission agreements was thus not considered quite as essential as it would from the early nineties onwards.

## 1.3 European readmission agreements in the 1990s

The early nineties saw a veritable *renaissance* of European readmission agreements. This had several reasons. Firstly, the Member States lifted visa requirements for nation-

---

27 See Denoël 1993, p. 640; Spijkerboer and Vermeulen 1999, p. 209-210; and in particular the annotation by Vermeulen to Benelux Gerechtshof 15 April 1992, *RV* 1992, 65.

28 HR 11 June 1993, *RV* 1993, 63, annotated by Vermeulen. The High Court ruling was based on answers to prejudicial questions submitted to the Benelux Court (Benelux Gerechtshof 15 April 1992, *RV* 1992, 65, annotated by Vermeulen). The Benelux Court considered the rules on removal and readmission to third countries as established by Decision M/P (67) 1 to imply a safeguard for individuals that a Benelux State (*in casu*, the Netherlands) would indeed exercise expulsion in accordance with those rules. It therefore deemed the Roosendaal method, which was inconsistent in particular with Article 16 of Decision M/P (67) 1 (*supra*, at n. 24), as impermissible.

29 Lehngut 1997, p. 162-163; Noll 1997, p. 420-421; Lavenex 1999, p. 79-81.

30 Fernhout 1999, p. 86.

31 Fernhout 1999, p. 79.

als of a number of Central European countries.[32] A common expectation or concern is that the lifting of visa requirements may lead to an increase in unauthorised entry and residence. When visa requirements were lifted for nationals of several Central European countries, readmission agreements were therefore concluded in parallel as a compensating safeguard.[33] Meanwhile, the acceptance of bilateral readmission obligations by Central, as well as Eastern European countries towards the Member States was also linked implicitly to the preparation of these countries for EU membership.[34] In addition, the readmission of persons gained a new significance due to the advance of European market integration, and the increase in migration pressure on Western Europe.

During the run-up to the entry into force of the Treaty on European Union (TEU), the creation of an area of free movement of persons as part of the internal market was in full swing. The perspective of abolishing internal border controls, and exclusive reliance on control of the external EU border, changed the landscape of European immigration and asylum policies and required new migration control measures.[35] In a common area where persons move freely, including aliens who are not nationals of one of the participating States, the outlook of readmission policies also changes. We saw this above, in the case of the Benelux. The focus of the Member States in the early nineties changed to expulsion and readmission to countries outside the common area on the one hand, and to equitable distribution of the so-called immigration "burden" within the common area, on the other hand. Along these lines, the Schengen Convention (SC)[36] required the expulsion of third country nationals, present without a residence title in any of the contracting parties, to a third country.[37] In order to facilitate expulsion to third countries, the Member States concluded a large number of bilateral readmission agreements.[38] Within the Schengen context, the Member States furthermore signed the

32 Fernhout 1999, p. 80. See also the European Commission, SEC(91) 1855 final, para. 9; and SEC(91) 1857 final, annex, para. 7.

33 The most notable example in this regard is the Schengen-Polish Accord relating to the readmission of persons in irregular situations of 29 March 1991, concluded in connection with the lifting of Schengen visa requirements for Polish nationals, Fernhout 1999, p. 80; Lavenex 1999, p. 80, 91; Bouteillet-Paquet 2003, p. 364.

34 Bouteillet-Paquet 1997, p. 37; Bouteillet-Paquet 2003, p. 364; Hurwitz 2002, p. 3.

35 For literature on the development of immigration and asylum policies at the European level during this period, see *inter alia* Callovi 1992; Guild and Niessen 1996; and Lavenex 2001.

36 Convention of 19 June 1990 applying the Schengen Agreement of 14 June 1985 between the governments of the States of the Benelux Economic Union, the Federal Republic of Germany and the French Republic, on the gradual abolition of checks at their common borders.

37 Article 23 SC.

38 An estimated 220 bilateral readmission agreements were concluded during the nineties world-wide, a large number of which was between European States, Noll 2000, p. 203, n. 592.

Dublin Convention (DC),[39] a multilateral readmission agreement intended to distribute responsibility for protection seekers evenly between the Member States.

Fuelling these developments further was the significant rise in the numbers of protection seekers and immigrants without a residence title arriving in Western Europe.[40] The negotiation of readmission agreements with Central and Eastern European countries (CEECs) by the Member States was a way to deflect some of this immigration influx into the wider European region.[41] Regarding protection seekers in particular, the Member States introduced safe third country policies, which gave yet additional impetus to the negotiation of readmission agreements.

The general aim of safe third country policies is to enable the rejection of protection seekers, who have either already found protection in a third country, or who have travelled through a third country where it would have reasonably been possible to seek protection. The steep rise in protection claims filed in the Member States in the early nineties made minimisation of the number of persons within the asylum procedure a priority. To this end, the Member States started sifting out protection seekers, who could be expelled to a third country, as early in the procedure as possible.[42] The practice of expulsion to third countries had until then concentrated on persons, who were recognised as refugees after a substantive examination of their protection claim. The emphasis shifted, however, to expulsion without status determination under the influence of EU[43] and Schengen[44] regulation.[45] In order to secure the cooperation of third countries in receiving back protection seekers rejected pursuant to safe third country policies, the Member States relied on readmission agreements.[46]

The readmission agreements concluded in the nineties between the Member States and third countries, which were mainly CEECs, were different from earlier European readmission agreements in several respects. Firstly, they were not concluded between countries of immigration of comparable economic status, seeking to regulate migration and expulsion between their territories on a reciprocal basis. The Member States sought readmission agreements with typical countries of origin and/or transit of migration, implying the expulsion and readmission of migrants in a one-way direction away from the EC. Secondly, in order to optimise the deflection of the immigration burden, it was fundamental to establish responsibility for transit migration in Central and Eastern

39 Convention determining the State responsible for examining applications for asylum lodged in one of the Member States of the Community, signed in Dublin on 15 June 1990.

40 Fernhout 1999, p. 80.

41 Landgren 1999, p. 22; Byrne, Noll and Vedsted-Hansen 2002, p. 383-385; Bouteillet-Paquet 2003, p. 359.

42 Collinson 1996, p. 79-80.

43 Resolution on a harmonised approach to questions concerning host third countries, London, 30 November and 1 December 1992.

44 In particular, the Schengen Convention and the Dublin Convention, *supra*, n. 36 and 39.

45 Spijkerboer and Vermeulen 1999, p. 273-274; Zwaan 2003, p. 6, 55-56, 59, 62-63.

46 Lavenex 1999, p. 76-82, 89.

Europe. A heavier emphasis was therefore placed on the inclusion of readmission obligations regarding third county nationals.[47] Thirdly, evidence- and procedural requirements were changed to remedy some of the pitfalls of the agreements of the fifties and sixties, and to attempt to make the implementation of readmission more effective.[48] Readmission agreements since the early nineties have removed the need to demonstrate the time and place of an unauthorised border crossing for establishing a readmission obligation. Upon detecting a person residing without authorisation, evidence of a previous presence in the other contracting party is generally sufficient.[49] In addition, readmission agreements introduced more elaborate means of evidence of nationality and travel routes, and more flexible time limits for submitting readmission requests.

### 1.4 Early common readmission policy

The early nineties also saw the beginning of a policy at the EU level regarding the readmission of third country nationals. Considering that the European Community did not yet have competence in this area, this early common policy concentrated on stimulating the conclusion of bilateral readmission agreements by the Member States with third countries.[50] The principal objectives of EC measures during this period were to incentivise third countries to accept readmission obligations, and harmonise the content of bilateral Member State agreements.

The European Council in Luxembourg in June 1991 instructed the Ministers responsible for immigration to produce a report on the measures required for harmonising Member State policies on immigration and asylum.[51] In order to provide an input into this process, the Commission adopted Communications on immigration[52] and on "the right of asylum".[53] The Communication on immigration contained a first call for the development of a common policy on the return and readmission of third country nationals, residing without authorisation in the Member States, to countries outside the EC.[54]

The Ministers responsible for immigration submitted their report on the harmonisation of immigration and asylum policies to the European Council in Maastricht in December 1991.[55] The report had a strong external dimension, calling on the (at that time twelve) Member States to control immigration in cooperation with third countries, and to alleviate the root causes of migration from lesser-developed countries. Secur-

47 Lehngut 1997, p. 162-169.

48 Lehngut 1997, p. 163-169.

49 Noll 1997, p. 420-421.

50 Peers and Rogers 2006.

51 Presidency Conclusions of the European Council in Luxembourg of 28 and 29 June 1991, Annex I.

52 SEC(91) 1855 final, 23 October 1991.

53 SEC(91) 1857 final, 11 October 1991.

54 SEC(91) 1855 final, para. 54.

55 SN 4038/91 (WGI 930).

ing the cooperation of third countries on readmission was part of both these elements. In order to counter unauthorised immigration, the Ministers considered cooperation on readmission with source and transit countries of migration essential.[56] The Ministers furthermore found that increasing developmental, economic, social, financial and political cooperation with third countries, as required for alleviating root causes of migration, should be conditional upon the conclusion of readmission agreements.[57]

The next significant policy document was the Declaration on principles of governing external aspects of migration policy, adopted by the European Council meeting in Edinburgh of 12 December 1992.[58] This Declaration committed the Member States to conclude readmission agreements with third countries. It also considered the strategy by which third countries would be persuaded to engage in cooperation on readmission, and on the management of migration flows in general. In this regard, the European Council recognised the potential of linking foreign and economic policies to immigration and asylum policies. Regarding readmission in particular, the European Council linked general international relations to the readiness of third countries to receive back own nationals:

> [I]n their relations with third countries, they [the Community and its Member States, NC] will take into account those countries' practice in readmitting their own nationals when expelled from the territories of the Member States.[59]

The first ever meeting of the Justice and Home Affairs Council on 29 and 30 November 1993 further explored this idea of linking immigration and asylum policy objectives to other policy fields. The JHA Council referred specifically to the "external agreements of the Union". It considered using beneficial agreements, in fields such as development- or economic cooperation, to extract cooperation from third countries on controlling migration and readmitting migrants.[60]

In addition, the JHA Council approved a set of "guiding principles" for the conclusion of readmission agreements with third countries. This was a first effort at directing, and establishing a degree of harmonisation between the readmission policies of the Member States. The Council agreed guiding principles *inter alia* on the identification of third countries relevant to unauthorised immigration into the EC, and on

56 SN 4038/91 (WGI 930), p. 5, 30.

57 SN 4038/91 (WGI 930), p. 6-7, 21-24.

58 *Declaration on principles of governing external aspects of migration policy*, Presidency Conclusions, European Council, Edinburgh, 12 December 1992, Annex 5 to part A; Peers 2004, p. 206.

59 *Declaration on principles of governing external aspects of migration policy*, Presidency Conclusions, European Council, Edinburgh, 12 December 1992, Annex 5 to part A, principle 7.

60 PRES/93/202; PRES/93/209.

technical issues such as the determination of Member State authorities responsible for implementing readmission agreements.[61]

A general lack of follow-up to the above policy papers and statements led the Commission to launch a renewed attempt at developing an EC immigration policy in 1994. The 1994 Communication on immigration and asylum policies[62] referred to the conclusion of readmission agreements as a means to overcome practical obstacles in the expulsion of immigrants to countries of origin and transit. In order to persuade third countries to conclude and implement such agreements, it insisted on the coordination of external action. Reiterating the above JHA Council meeting, the Commission suggested to "establish[...] a link, wherever practicable, between readmission agreements and practices on the one hand and the external agreements of the Community and its Member States on the other".[63]

The 1994 Communication drew attention to the disadvantageous consequences of readmission agreements for third countries. Regarding countries of origin specifically, the Commission acknowledged that "the re-integration of [...] own nationals may put additional strains on the national labour market or government assistance schemes".[64] Regarding transit countries, the Commission considered that "they will have to take charge of the repatriation of the persons concerned".[65] The Commission therefore called for an active EU policy of support and assistance,[66] implying the use of compensating measures in order to facilitate the conclusion of readmission agreements.

After the 1994 Commission Communication, the Council adopted a series of measures. Firstly, the Council took further steps towards harmonising Member State readmission agreements with third countries. In November 1994, it adopted a Recommendation concerning a specimen bilateral readmission agreement between a Member State and a third country.[67] This was followed in July 1995 by a Recommendation on the guiding principles to be followed in drawing up protocols on the implementation of readmission agreements.[68] Assessments in the literature of the impact of these instruments have differed. Noll has emphasised a lack of harmonising effect on the content of Member State agreements, whereas Bouteillet-Paquet has found that the

61 PRES/93/202; PRES/93/209; COM(94) 23 final, para. 114, and Annex II, p. 5.

62 COM(94) 23 final, 23 February 1994. See also Council. Doc. 9809/98, para. 4.

63 COM(94) 23 final, para. 115.

64 COM(94) 23 final, para. 116.

65 COM(94) 23 final, para. 116.

66 COM(94) 23 final, para. 116.

67 Council Recommendation of 30 November 1994 concerning a specimen bilateral readmission agreement between a Member State and a third country, Council Doc. 396Y0919(07); *OJ* C 274, 19 September 1996.

68 Council recommendation of 24 July 1995 on the guiding principles to be followed in drawing up protocols on the implementation of re-admission agreements (*OJ* C 274, 19 September 1996, p. 25).

1994 model exerted a great influence over national policies, and was "largely followed in practice".[69]

Secondly, the Council implemented the idea of linking objectives in the field of immigration and asylum to other policy fields. In a first tangible venture of an EC immigration measure into the external field, the Council decided that readmission "clauses" should be incorporated into Community and mixed agreements, and adopted a standard text for such clauses.[70] Readmission clauses, as we will discuss in chapter 8, commit the contracting parties to the readmission of own nationals. In addition, they generally contain a political commitment to concluding a fully-fledged readmission agreement, covering also third country nationals and stateless persons, if requested by one of the contracting parties. The European Community today incorporates these commitments into agreements with third countries in the areas of, for example, development assistance, or economic cooperation, as a matter of *quid pro quo*.

The following relevant development took place in 1998. The Austrian Presidency submitted a controversial strategy paper on immigration and asylum to the Council.[71] In this document, the Presidency analysed the, in its view, structural failure to implement EU policy in the fields of immigration and asylum since the Commission's 1994 Communication.[72] Regarding the expulsion and readmission of third country nationals, it named the establishment of "the widest possible network of readmission agreements" as one of the unachieved objectives of the Community, and considered steps taken in this direction as "strikingly unsuccessful".[73] The Presidency also felt that "a problem hardly referred to [...] was the increasing refusal of a growing number of States to take back their own nationals from the country they had entered illegally".[74] Viewing readmission agreements as the best solution to this problem, it advised the EU "as an entity [...] to use its international and political muscle to persuade [...] States to adopt such an agreement".[75] The Presidency finally outlined measures and actions as part of an EU strategy on immigration and asylum. Relevant to readmission, this strategy would have committed the EU to:

> (k) [Establish a] complete system of deportation agreements with States of transit and origin including ensuring [sic.] that persons whose identity and nationality is established by an EU document are taken back

69 Noll 2000, p. 206; Bouteillet-Paquet 2003, p. 363-4. For further indication of the degree to and manner in which the Member States have employed the 1994 model, see an assessment of the Council in Council Doc. 7668/1/99, 14 June 1999.

70 Council Doc. 12509/95, 8 December 1995; and Council Doc. 4272/96, 22 January 1996.

71 Draft strategy paper on immigration and asylum, Council. Doc. 9809/98, LIMITE, CK4 27, ASIM 170, 1 July 1998 (available on: www.proasyl.de).

72 *Supra*, n. 62.

73 Council. Doc. 9809/98, para. 19.

74 Council. Doc. 9809/98, para. 19.

75 Council. Doc. 9809/98, para. 108; cited in FECL 1998a, p. 3.

(l) [The] linking of bilateral agreements in connection with [sic.] the relaxation of visa requirements, the reduction of border controls, transport links as well as economic cooperation with repatriation agreements and migration control obligations[76]

Due to the strong public reaction to and criticism of the Austrian strategy paper, the Council never adopted it.[77] It is nevertheless necessary to include the strategy paper as part of the history of the common readmission policy, while it was considered at the time to be generally representative of views and policy tendencies at the European level.[78] The Austrian strategy paper furthermore placed immigration and asylum policies firmly on the agenda of the EU, and did influence their direction and content. Moreover, the failure of the Austrian strategy paper was instrumental to the creation of the High Level Working Group on Asylum and Migration (HLWG), a Council body relevant to the further development of the common readmission policy.

Keen to deflect the Austrian strategy paper yet preserve some its content, the Council launched the HLWG in December 1998, following a proposal from the Netherlands.[79] Explaining the creation of this new Council body, the General Affairs Council stated that "the problem of mass influxes of asylum seekers and illegal immigrants raised the need to establish a common, integrated, cross-pillar approach targeted at the situation in the most important countries of origin".[80] The HLWG is a unique attempt at placing civil servants from the policy fields of home affairs, trade, development, and foreign affairs together in an institutional setting to address migration issues. The initial mandate of the HLWG was to draw up "action plans" regarding third countries relevant to immigration into the EC.[81] This mandate was later expanded to encompass a broader set of tasks in the development of immigration and asylum policies in the external field.[82] In general, the work of the HLWG was supposed to concentrate on the alleviation of the root causes of migration. However, the European Parliament,[83] civil society and international organisations,[84] and implicated third countries[85] soon

76 Council. Doc. 9809/98, section 5.4.

77 Van Buuren and van der Schans 1999, p. 10.

78 FECL 1998b, p. 4;Van Buuren and van der Schans 1999, p. 1, 11. The content of the strategy paper was not solely attributable to Austria, which was drafted with assistance from the "task force" of the General Secretariat of the Commission dedicated to justice and home affairs, and the Presidential Troika, Van Buuren and van der Schans 1999, p. 1.

79 Van Buuren and van der Schans 1999 p. 10; Peers 2004, p. 11.

80 Press: 431 Nr: 13677/98.

81 Press: 431 Nr: 13677/98.

82 Council Doc. 9433/02.

83 European Parliament Resolution of 30 March 2000, *OJ* C 378, 29.12.2000, p. 75. See also the underlying report by rapporteur Mollar, 29 February 2000, A5-0057/2000, PE 285.869/ DEF.

84 On criticism from ECRE and UNHCR, see Hurwitz 2002, p. 14-15.

85 Council Doc. 13993/00, paras. 53-54; Hurwitz 2002, p. 14.

criticised it for overly focusing on the extension of migration control measures to third countries, and on readmission obligations.[86]

Following its initial mandate, the HLWG drew up six action plans for Albania, Afghanistan, Iraq, Morocco, Somalia, and Sri Lanka.[87] The action plans *inter alia* examined the scope for the return and readmission of migrants to these countries, and evaluated the implementation of any existing readmission agreements. The action plans also explored the possibilities for concluding readmission agreements. Accordingly, the HLWG made recommendations to negotiate readmission agreements *inter alia* with Albania, Pakistan,[88] Morocco, and Sri Lanka, which the Council would later follow.

During the run-up to the Treaty of Amsterdam (ToA), the Member States intensified the pursuit of their common interest in the readmission of third country nationals. Within the Council, the Member States started negotiations for two relevant instruments. The first was a standard agreement on readmission between the collective Member States and a third country.[89] The second was the Initiative of the Republic of Finland with a view to the adoption of a Council Regulation determining obligations as between the Member States for the readmission of third country nationals.[90] Both these negotiations were overtaken by the advent of a Community competence to conclude readmission agreements with third countries with the entry into of the ToA on 1 May 1999.

The initiative by Finland concerned an instrument for the readmission of non-protection seeking third country nationals between the Member States. This would have complemented the Dublin Convention, which arranged the internal readmission of protection seekers. The Council discontinued the negotiation of the Finnish initiative during the following Portuguese Presidency for unclear reasons. Peers and Rogers claim that negotiations were abandoned with a view to the forthcoming conclusion of

86 See also Bouteillet-Paquet 2003, p. 373.

87 Council Doc. 6101/99 (Specimen action plan plus annexes), Council Doc. 11424/99 (Action Plan for Afghanistan), Council Doc. 11425/99 (Action Plan for Iraq), Council Doc. 11426/99 (Action Plan for Morocco), Council Doc. 11427/99 (Action Plan for Somalia), Council Doc. 11428/99 (Action Plan for Sri Lanka), Council Doc. 7886/1/00 (draft Action Plan for Albania). See also Council Doc. 13993/00, para. 1; and Council Doc. 8939/00, para. 2.

88 The conclusion of a readmission agreement with Pakistan was recommended in the action plan for Afghanistan, Council Doc. 11424/99, para. 138c.

89 Council Doc. 10338/3/1998. The drafting of this instrument took place under the third pillar in accordance with Article K.1(3)(c) of Title VI of the TEU. This provision lists, as a common interest of the Member States regarding which to develop joint action, "immigration policy and policy regarding nationals of third countries [including] combating unauthorised immigration, residence and work by nationals of third countries on the territory of Member States". To be sure, this instrument was not a third pillar treaty, but a reference text; ready to use in case the Member States decided to collectively conclude a readmission agreement with a third country.

90 *OJ* C 353, 7 December 1999, p. 6.

Community readmission agreements with third countries, which were also to address internal readmission.[91] This is an unsatisfactory explanation. The Finnish initiative and Community readmission agreements would both indeed have addressed the allocation of responsibility for third country nationals between the Member States.[92] The rules established by Community readmission agreements in this regard, however, apply only to a limited number of cases in practice. Arguably more to the point is that the compatibility of the Finnish initiative with the Schengen Convention was questionable.[93]

The discontinuation of negotiations for a reference text for a readmission agreement between the collective Member States and a third country was related more clearly to the introduction of Community competence in the area of readmission. With the entry into force of the ToA, the readmission of immigrants to third countries became a first pillar, instead of a third pillar affair. The Council therefore transferred this instrument to the first pillar, where negotiations continued under the heading of a standard text for a readmission agreement between the European Community and a third country.[94] Chapter 5 below outlines the content of Community readmission agreements, as partially determined by this standard text.

After the entry into force of the Treaty of Amsterdam, the Tampere European Council in October 1999 invited the Council to conclude readmission agreements with

91 Peers and Rogers 2006.

92 The purpose of the Finnish initiative was to determine the Member State responsible for the expulsion of a third country national, found present in one of the Member States without a residence title, to a third country. The regulation provided for readmission to the territory of the responsible Member State in case the third country national had been apprehended in another Member State. Community readmission agreements in this regard are limited to allocating responsibility for a third country national between the Member States for the purpose of readmission from a third country into the EC (see, for example, Article 5(3) of the Community readmission agreement with Albania, *OJ* L 124, 17 May 2005, p. 22, Annex; and *infra*, subsection 5.3.4, at n. 38).

93 Contrary to the Finnish initiative, namely, Article 23 SC expressly determines that a third country national without a residence title should be expelled to a third country by the Member State which apprehended him or her. As a side note, we can add that, notwithstanding the incompatibility with the GC, a Regulation on the internal readmission of third country nationals would have been useful in practice. The readmission of third country nationals between the Member States is common practice, especially where regarding apprehension at internal Schengen borders (see CIVIPOL 2003, Council Doc. 11490/1/03, p. 19). The Netherlands, for example, operate an extensive practice of apprehension and expulsion of immigrants at the Dutch-German border, based on mostly informal application of the Benelux readmission agreement with Germany, interview, M. Rietbergen, Dutch immigration and naturalisation service (IND), 16 April 2003 (hereinafter interview IND, 16 April 2003). The Finnish initiative would have regulated these Member State practices.

94 Council Doc. 10338/3/98.

third countries.[95] Chapter 7 describes how the Council proceeded by selecting the third countries with which to conclude Community readmission agreements, as well as the further continuation of the development of the common readmission policy.

## 5.5 Conclusion

This chapter outlined the history of readmission policies in Europe. It presented the conclusion of readmission agreements in Europe as a phenomenon starting early in the nineteenth century, contrary to the literature which mostly describes European readmission agreements as appearing in the 1950s and 60s.

This chapter discussed the main characteristics of readmission agreements as concluded by European States, respectively, in the early nineteenth century, the 1950s and 60s, and the 1990s. In the early nineteenth century, readmission agreements first appeared as European States started to move towards a practice of cooperation regarding the expulsion of persons, rather than unilateral implementation. In 1950s and 60s, the conclusion of readmission agreements between European States peaked in an effort to regulate the unauthorised movement of persons between their territories. The evidence- and procedural requirements of these agreements, however, limited their practical meaning.

In the 1990s, the emphasis shifted to the readmission of migrants to transit countries outside the European Community. The EC Member States concluded a large number of readmission agreements with third countries, primarily in Central and Eastern Europe, establishing obligations to readmit also third country nationals – persons with the nationality of neither the requesting nor the requested State. Evidence- and procedural requirements were changed to remedy some of the pitfalls of the agreements of the fifties and sixties, and make the implementation of readmission more effective.

This chapter, finally, provided an outline of early common readmission policy, as developed at the EU level before the advent of Community competence in the area of readmission.

95 Presidency Conclusions, Tampere European Council of 15 and 16 October 1999, para. 27.

# Chapter 2 International law obligations to readmit persons

The objective of this chapter is to identify which obligations to readmit persons exist under general international law, and how these relate to the conclusion of readmission agreements. In case of a lack of a pre-existing obligation under general international law, readmission agreements may be considered to be constitutive of that obligation. To the extent that an obligation to readmit under general international law would exist already, it is necessary to examine in which manner readmission agreements, which reiterate that obligation, relate to that international norm.

The European Community regularly claims that general international law requires States to readmit own nationals.[1] The EC has not supported this claim with legal arguments, or specified the source from which this readmission obligation would arguably derive.[2] Claims to further international readmission obligations are not commonly made by the EC or by States in general.

The question of readmission obligations under international law, and their relation to readmission agreements, has received little specific attention in academic literature. By far the most elaborate study to date is by Hailbronner, which identifies *inter alia* customary international law as a source of readmission obligations.[3] This chapter analyses the obligations under international law to readmit persons, based on this study, several earlier scholarly reflections, careful consideration of readmission practice, and the role and influence of readmission agreements.

1 Tampere European Council of 15 and 16 October 1999, Presidency Conclusions, para. 26; COM (2001) 672 final, p. 24; COM (2002) 175 final, p. 22; Proposal for a comprehensive plan to combat illegal immigration and trafficking of human beings in the European Union, *OJ* C 142, 14.6.2002, p. 23, paras. 71, 76, 77; draft Council Conclusions on intensified cooperation on the management of migration flows with third countries, 14 November 2002, Doc. 13894/02; Proposal for a return action programme, Doc. 14673/02, para. 64; COM (2004) 412 final, p. 14.

2 Peers 2004, p. 208.

3 Hailbronner, K., "Readmission agreements and the obligation on States under public international law to readmit their own and foreign nationals", *Zeitschrift für ausländisches öffentliches Recht und Völkerrecht*, Band 57 (1997), p. 1-49.

When considering readmission obligations under international law, it is useful to distinguish between the following categories of persons: own nationals, third country nationals,[4] former nationals, and persons formally recognised as refugees[5] or stateless persons. The readmission agreements which the Community is asking third countries to conclude cover all these categories of persons, implicitly or explicitly. In the following, we will discuss these categories separately, although focussing mainly on the obligations to readmit own nationals and third country nationals.

## 2.1 Own nationals

Subsection 2.1.1 analyses the right to return to one's country and the right of States to expel aliens, which arguably provide a basis in international law for the obligation to readmit own nationals. This obligation is presumed to be part of international customary law. Subsection 2.1.2 continues by discussing possible challenges to the customary nature of this obligation.

### *2.1.1 The right to return and the right to expel*

A legal basis in general international law for the readmission of a State's own nationals is generally found in the fundamental right to return to one's country, and the sovereign right to expel aliens.

The right to return as the legal basis of a State obligation to readmit nationals is uncontested. Fundamental rights catalogues relevant to the EC Member States including a right to return[6] are the Universal Declaration of Human Rights,[7] the International Covenant on Civil and Political Rights,[8] the International Convention on the elimination of all forms of racial discrimination,[9] and Protocol No. 4 of the European Con-

4 For the purpose of the present chapter, use of term "third country national" refers to its meaning within a readmission context, i.e. a person who does not hold the nationality of any of the contracting parties to a readmission agreement. This may also be, but is not necessarily, a person who is not a national of an EU Member State.

5 Hailbronner also discusses the readmission of "ex"-refugees; persons whose cause of flight no longer exists (Hailbronner 1997, p. 40-44). The repatriation of such persons is politically important, and States have concluded specific international agreements for this purpose. While implying the readmission of nationals, however, we will not consider this category separately.

6 Notably, the right to return (and to leave) one's country has not been explicitly included in the Charter of Fundamental Rights of the European Union. It is arguably subsumed, however, within Article 45, which grants freedom of movement and residence within the territory of EU Member States to EU citizens and long-term resident third country nationals.

7 Article 13(2): "Everyone has the right to leave any country, including his own, and to return to his country".

8 Article 12(4): "No one shall be arbitrarily deprived of the right to enter his own country".

9 Article 5(d)(ii): "The right of everyone [...] to equality before the law [...] in the enjoyment of [t]he right to leave any country, including one's own, and to return to one's country".

vention for the protection of human rights and fundamental freedoms.[10] The generally accepted argument is that while the right to return would only be meaningful when coupled with a corresponding State obligation to readmit, this obligation is implied.

The State obligation to readmit as derived from the right to return is firstly held towards the individual, who is the beneficiary of that right. It has been suggested that the right to return would also create an interstate duty.[11] This implies that the individual as well as the State in which s/he is present would be able to assert the individual's "right to readmission",[12] and invoke the resulting obligation to readmit on the part of his or her own country.[13]

It arguably follows from the concept of nationality that the obligation to readmit a person rests with his or her country of nationality. Weis explains:

> Nationality in the sense of international law is a technical term denoting the allocation of individuals, termed nationals, to a specific State – the State of nationality – as members of that State, a relationship which confers upon the State of nationality [...] rights and duties in relation to other States.[14]

Oppenheim further clarifies that the *right* of a State in this regard is to protect its nationals abroad, while its *duty* is to receive "such of its nationals as are not allowed to remain on the territory of other States".[15]

There is some question as to whether, in addition to nationals, States would also be held to readmit permanent residents. This question depends on the personal scope of the right to return. Academic discussion regarding this question has focused on Article 12(4) ICCPR and the meaning of the words "his own country", which would appear wider in scope in comparison with the clear choice for restriction to nationals in Protocol 4 of the European Convention.[16] It has on occasion been argued that Article 12(4) ICCPR would include long-term resident non-nationals as beneficiaries, as well as persons with a "genuine link" to the country.[17] This is especially relevant, considering that

10 Article 3(2): "No one shall be deprived of the right to enter the territory of the State of which he is a national".

11 Hailbronner 1997, p. 1-4. See also Weis 1979, p. 46.

12 For a similar argument in the context of refugee protection, see Grahl-Madsen 1972, p. 325; *infra*, section 2.4, at n. 110.

13 It is not clear whether the State of residence would do so *on behalf of* the individual, or whether to invoke another country's readmission obligations would be an independent entitlement of the State of residence. The underlying assumption of the latter possibility is that an international fundamental right, agreed upon between States by convention to the benefit of individuals, would be able to generate entitlements of which another State is the beneficiary, which is debatable.

14 Weis 1979, p. 59.

15 Oppenheim 1992, p. 857.

16 *Supra*, n. 8 and 10, respectively.

17 Lawand 1996, p. 547-558.

the possession of, for example, a residence permit or visa issued by a particular country is commonly a criterion for establishing a readmission obligation under readmission agreements. It would appear, however, that such treaty provisions do not find a basis, or confirmation, within general international law. Hailbronner concludes that neither the general consensus in the literature, nor State practice indicates a right to return for permanent residents.[18]

A possible second basis for an interstate obligation to readmit nationals is the sovereign right of States to regulate the entry and presence, and thus also the expulsion of aliens. A recurring argument in the literature is that the refusal of a State to readmit a national who is expelled from the territory of another State would infringe upon the latter State's territorial sovereignty.[19] Territorial sovereignty gives the right to States to decide which aliens to allow on their territory. An infringement of this sovereignty would occur when a State is forced to keep on its territory an alien, whose residence it has the right to end. Exercising territorial sovereignty by way of expulsion of an alien whose residence is no longer allowed would thus imply another State's obligation to readmit that alien, lest a State's "right to expel" would be effectively void.[20] The State responsible for readmission would again be the State of nationality.[21]

An unresolved matter is the effect which an unlawful expulsion by a State of residence would have.[22] Relevant examples are cases where expulsion is exercised arbitrarily,[23] or where expulsion is not in accordance with the 1951 Convention relating to the status of refugees,[24] fundamental rights conventions, or the domestic legislation of States regulating the residence of aliens. The admission and expulsion of aliens as expressions of territorial sovereignty are within state discretion, and subject only to overriding norms of international law, or limitations agreed by treaty.[25] An expulsion contrary to a State's own domestic legislation would thus not affect interstate readmission obligations. In case of violation of international obligations, however, the State of residence would not have a valid claim to the sovereign right to expel. It would in that case seem arguable that the country of nationality would be relieved of the obligation

18 Hailbronner 1997, p. 3.

19 Goodwin-Gill 1978, p. 136-7; Weis 1979, p. 45-7; Hailbronner 1997, p. 6-12; Lehnguth 1997, p. 161. The same reasoning applies in case a State would seek to expel one of its own nationals, Weis 1979, p. 47.

20 Hailbronner 1997, p. 8, 11-12.

21 *Supra*, at n. 14-15.

22 Goodwin-Gill 1978, p. 136.

23 Oppenheim 1992, p. 940.

24 Convention Relating to the Status of Refugees, adopted by the United Nations Conference of Plenipotentiaries on the Status of Refugees and Stateless Persons on 28 July 1951 (hereinafter referred to as the Geneva refugee Convention, or GC). All references are to the Geneva Refugee Convention as modified by the Protocol relating to the status of refugees of 31 January 1967.

25 Weis 1979, p. 45.

to readmit its national, while refusing readmission would not violate the sovereignty of the State of residence.[26]

State sovereignty as a legal basis for an interstate duty to readmit nationals, who are expelled from other countries, is not uncontested. A controversial detail, considering the position of the European Community on the readmission of nationals under international law,[27] is that the Legal Service (LS) of the Council of Ministers adheres to a different view:

> It is doubtful whether, in the absence of a specific agreement [on readmission] between the States concerned, a general principle of international law exists which would oblige those States to readmit their own nationals if they do not wish to return to their country of origin.[28]

The LS appears to contrast the readmission of involuntary returnees with the readmission of voluntary returnees, considering only the latter an obligation under international law incumbent on countries of origin. It would thus appear that views differ at the EU level insofar as regarding a possible international obligation to readmit involuntary returnees. Controversy regarding an obligation to readmit nationals was also noted by the Nordic Joint Advisory Group on Refugee Policy in an analysis of readmission agreements in 1999, submitted for discussion in the Migration/Expulsion Working Group of the Council.[29] "There seems to be consensus as to the presence of a 'moral' obligation in that respect", only, the Nordic Joint Advisory Group concluded.[30] Furthermore, Noll has pointed to a possible counterargument, finding that an obligation under international to readmit involuntary returnees would prima facie frustrate the right to leave one's country.[31]

---

26 The practical relevance of this argument is limited to cases where expulsion would infringe an international obligation of the State of residence, and the State of origin would have no interest in receiving a person back. One could think of the expulsion of dissidents who are at risk of persecution in a country of origin which has no interest in receiving them back. Another example are specific cases of inhuman or degrading treatment within the meaning of Article 3 of the European Convention of Human Rights, such as the unavailability of essential medical treatment in a country of origin, featuring in *D. v. United Kingdom* (30240/96 [1997] ECHR 25, 2 May 1997).

27 *Supra*, at n. 1.

28 Council Legal Service Opinion, Council Doc. 6658/99; cited in Statewatch 2000a.

29 Nordic Joint Advisory Group 1999, Council Doc. 7707/99.

30 Nordic Joint Advisory Group 1999, Council Doc. 7707/99, p. 6.

31 Noll 1997, n. 7. The right to leave is guaranteed by Article 12(1) of the International Covenant on Civil and Political Rights, Article 13(2) of the Universal Declaration of Human Rights, Article 5(d)(ii) of the International Convention on the elimination of all forms of racial discrimination, and Article 2(2) of Protocol No. 4 of the European Convention for the protection of human rights and fundamental freedoms.

Nevertheless, there are overriding arguments to accept an obligation to readmit nationals who are expelled from other countries. It is arguable that the international legal order seeks to ensure that at least one State is responsible for each person. Weis remarks that a persistent refusal of expelled persons by their countries of nationality "would necessarily lead to a disruption of orderly, peaceful relations between States within the community of nations".[32] Similarly, Hailbronner notes that "international order presupposes that each state should at least take care of its own nationals";[33] a duty which exists regardless of whether return is forced or voluntary.

In the absence of an international norm guaranteeing a responsible State in expulsion cases, expellees could be rendered stateless. Furthermore, expellees would risk ending up as migrants "in orbit". This term refers to a continuous shuttling of migrants between States, without any State accepting responsibility and granting durable access to territory. Such situations have proven to sour international relations. Additionally, certain fundamental rights arguably call for a readmission guarantee for nationals in expulsion cases, considering that situations of migrants "in orbit" have in the past raised a fundamental rights issue.[34]

It is therefore doubtful that, as the Council LS seems to suggest, the obligation to readmit nationals would apply only to voluntary returnees. Where an alien is willing to return, the right to return implies a readmission obligation on the part of the country of nationality. Considerations regarding State sovereignty to administer the entry, presence and expulsion of aliens, orderly international relations, and the protection of underlying fundamental rights, however, indicate that interstate obligations to readmit nationals also exist independently of an individual's willingness to return.

In sum, it can be concluded that States are under duty to readmit voluntary returnees, as well as "such of its nationals as are not allowed to remain on the territory of other States,"[35] provided, arguably, that expulsion by the State of residence is in accordance with its international obligations.

With regard to the nature of this duty under international law, authoritative references are often vague. Goodwin-Gill refers to the obligation to readmit nationals as "firmly fixed within the corpus of general international law".[36] Similar pronouncements by Weis are with regard to a "generally accepted" and "universally recognised" State obligation.[37] A common reference in the literature is the *van Duyn* case, where

32 Weis 1979, p. 47.

33 Hailbronner 1997, p. 7, 11, 19-20.

34 In particular under the prohibition of inhuman or degrading treatment as contained in Article 3 of the European Convention for the Protection of Human Rights and Fundamental Freedoms, Council of Europe, 4 November 1950 (hereinafter European Convention, or ECHR). We will elaborate on the problem of migrants "in orbit" below in subsections 5.3.5.5 and 9.2.3.3.2.

35 Oppenheim 1992, *supra*, n. 15.

36 Goodwin-Gill 1978, p. 137.

37 Weis 1979, p. 47-48.

the European Court of Justice speaks of "a principle of international law" precluding a State from refusing the right of entry or residence to its own nationals.[38]

Hailbronner is more precise, and argues that the obligation to readmit nationals is customary international law.[39] The following analysis continues on the basis of this presumption.

### 2.2.2 *Possible challenges to the customary rule to readmit own nationals*

Instead of a detailed analysis determining whether the obligation to readmit own nationals fulfils the requirements of customary international law,[40] this subsection focuses on three possible challenges to the customary nature of this obligation. These are: practical and procedural obstacles to readmission imposed by requested States, the proliferation of readmission agreements reiterating the obligation to readmit own nationals, and the fact that readmission agreements are concluded on the basis of *quid pro quo*.

#### 2.1.2.1 Practical and procedural obstacles to the readmission of own nationals

States rarely refuse the readmission of their own nationals, provided nationality is uncontested.[41] Problems in practice, regarding the return and readmission of migrants to countries of origin, concentrate on insufficiently documented migrants coupled with an "uncooperative" attitude on the part of requested States. Whereas no State would explicitly oppose a rule obliging to the readmission of own nationals,[42] this rule is easily circumvented in practice.

A rule that States must readmit their nationals depends on the ability to demonstrate nationality, and therefore to a great degree on the documents which a migrant carries. In the absence of sufficient documentation, this dependency shifts to the willingness of requested States to accept a suspicion of nationality, or different means of evidence, and issue the required documents for admission to their territory. It is here that requesting States may experience what they perceive as a lack of cooperation. Requested States can impose requirements and procedures for the identification of their nationals and the issuing of documents, which in practice are significant and time-consuming obstacles to readmission. It is necessary to examine whether requested States hereby contradict the obligation of States to readmit their own nationals, and thereby prevent that obligation from having customary status.

States commonly assert the rule that States must readmit their nationals when requesting readmission in an individual case, or when inviting another State to enter

38 Case 41/74 *van Duyn v Home office*, [1974] ECR 1337, 1351; cited in Goodwin-Gill 1978, p. 137; Lawand 1996, p. 552; Hailbronner 1997, p. 13; Bouteillet-Paquet 2003, p. 361.

39 Hailbronner 1997.

40 The requirements for formation of a rule of customary international law are: fundamentally norm-creating character, generality of practice, uniformity and consistency of practice, and *opinio juris*, see Article 38(1)(b) of the statute of the International Court of Justice; and *North Sea Continental Shelf* cases, Judgement, ICJ Reports 1969.

41 Bouteillet-Paquet 2003, p. 361.

42 Fernhout 1999, p. 83.

into a readmission agreement. Such expressions of *opinio juris* invariably originate from requesting States with a primary interest in the existence of such a rule. Requested states, however, generally do not express disagreement on the matter; the basic premise being that abstaining from protest denotes tacit acceptance.[43] One could argue that to impose procedures for establishing nationality and issuing documents would imply disagreement. However, the fact that requested States resort to such procedures when confronted with a person holding insufficient documentation (instead of simply refusing readmission) would sooner point to the contrary. Even where the lengthy and bureaucratic nature of readmission procedures may pose obstacles or effectively block readmission, States do thereby formally examine whether a readmission obligation exists, which may arguably be considered an indicator of *opinio juris*.

The imposition of lengthy or bureaucratic procedures for establishing nationality and issuing documents could furthermore be of relevance to the requirement of uniformity and consistency of practice. The question is whether procedural obstacles could be considered in breach of the rule that a State must readmit its nationals. Breach of a rule, namely, may render practice inconsistent, thereby indicating the absence (or demise) of a customary norm.

A breach in the present case is not apparent. It is clear that procedural obstacles to readmission may reflect a reluctance to receive back own nationals. A prerequisite for a breach of the obligation to readmit nationals, however, presupposes that the nationality of the person involved would be definitely established. Unless requesting and requested State have concluded an agreement regarding the evidencing of nationality, the establishment of the nationality of a potential readmittee is a matter firmly within the domestic legal order of the requested State.[44] As a result, a breach of the obligation to readmit a national is difficult to distinguish as long as the requested State contests the nationality as suggested by the requesting State. Clearly, States hold a strong sovereignty card when requested to readmit an alleged national.

In addition, the odds that a breach of a rule would imply a lack of uniformity or consistency are limited given the current state of international law. Following relevant ICJ case-law, inconsistency of practice as a result of a breach of a rule is difficult to

43 On the role of protest and tacit acceptance in the formation of customary law, see Meijers 1979, p. 14-15, 22-23; Villiger 1985, p. 16-20; Brownlie 1990, p. 6, 10; ILA Statement of principles of customary international law 2000, p. 15.

44 International law places certain limits on State jurisdiction regarding nationality. In the *Nottebohm* case, the ICJ defined the concept of nationality in international law (*Liechtenstein v. Guatemala* [1955] ICJ Rep. 4, cited and discussed in Lawand 1996, n. 96). Whereas the ICJ hereby provided a normative definition of nationality, however, the means of evidence by which to indicate fulfilment of that norm remain within State discretion. Regarding evidence, Hailbronner notes that "State practice [...] is not sufficiently uniform to enable the establishment of detailed rules about which documents constitute acceptable proof or about which form readmission procedures should take", Hailbronner 1997, p. 14.

establish. Referring to the *Nicaragua*[45] case, even large-scale breach of the rule that States must readmit their own nationals would not necessarily exclude a customary status. According to the ICJ, namely, international law dictates that where States seek to justify certain behaviour on their part a rule exists, irrespective of the validity of the justification.[46] Legally relevant is therefore any attempt at justification. Contesting the nationality of a returnee, or insisting on the necessity of requirements or procedures to establish nationality or issue documentation, can be considered such an attempt. An "uncooperative" attitude on the part of requested States, in other words, may be construed as a permissible exception that does not contradict, but confirms the existence of a customary rule to readmit nationals.

In sum, practical or procedural obstacles to the readmission of nationals, imposed by requested States, do not present an *opinio juris* or practice contrary to the customary norm.

#### 2.1.2.2 The proliferation of readmission agreements

This subsection considers the importance of readmission agreements in practice, and their possible influence on the customary obligation to readmit nationals.

Readmission agreements typically establish an obligation to readmit nationals,[47] a list of means of evidence obliging a requested State to recognise nationality,[48] and an

45 *Military and Paramilitary Activities in and against Nicaragua*, Judgement, ICJ Reports 1986.

46 In considering the requirement of uniformity or consistency of practice for the formation of international custom, the ICJ finds that "[i]f a state acts in a way *prima facie* incompatible with a recognised rule, but defends its conduct by appealing to exceptions or justifications contained within the rule itself, then whether or not the State's conduct is in fact justifiable on that basis, the significance of that attitude is to confirm rather than weaken the rule", *Military and Paramilitary Activities in and against Nicaragua*, ICJ Reports 1986, p. 98. Attempts at justification may similarly point to the existence of an *opinio juris* concerning a given rule, Goodwin-Gill 1996, p. 168-169.

47 An example is Article 2 of the readmission agreement between the Community and Albania: "Albania shall readmit [...] nationals of Albania." A corresponding obligation concerning nationals of EC Member States is contained in Article 4. For the text of the agreement, see *OJ* L 124, 17 May 2005, p. 22.

48 See, for example, Article 8 in conjunction with Annex 1 and Annex 2 of the Community readmission agreement with Albania. One should bear in mind that readmission agreements do not present a clear-cut solution to the problem of *un*documented migrants. The aim of lists of evidence for the substantiation of nationality, which contemporary readmission agreements typically provide, is firstly to secure acceptance of as wide a variety of documents as possible. In addition to travel documents, lists may include seaman's passes, military service books, driving licences, insurance documents, as well as items such as cinema tickets or shopping receipts. In order to enable readmission in case of a complete absence of paper-based evidence, lists would need to include oral evidence, provided by the readmittee or third persons, or language analysis as evidence of nationality. We will elaborate on this point below in subsection 5.3.5.2.

obligation to issue a travel document within a certain time limit.[49] They are thus a clear bid to overcome practical and procedural obstacles to readmission, which result from insufficiently documented migrants and uncooperative requested States.

From the previous subsection, it followed that an obligation for States to readmit their own nationals may well exist, but that it presupposes the ability to distinguish who is a national of a requested State to the satisfaction of that State, without which the practical meaning of the obligation is restricted. States which seek to expel aliens find it necessary to conclude readmission agreements in order to address this loophole and effect expulsion. In the course of this book, we will on occasion touch upon the degree to which readmission agreements may actually be considered to solve problems of readmission practice.[50] Relevant to the present context is that States with an interest in expulsion profess readmission agreements to be indispensable in this regard, and aim to have as many agreements in place as possible.

Hundreds of interstate relations pertaining to the readmission of own nationals are now governed by readmission agreements, rather than customary law. Chapter 1 discussed the conclusion of readmission agreements in Europe from the 19th century until the late nineties.[51] The importance which States assign to readmission agreements as a solution to practical problems in the return and readmission of migrants has caused these treaties to proliferate. There has been a rise in the negotiation and conclusion of readmission agreements especially since the early nineties. An estimated 220 readmission agreements were concluded world-wide during the nineties alone, a large number of which involved European States.[52] The pursuit of readmission agreements, emanating from the European continent and especially the European Union, has since continued relentlessly.

The late 1990s saw the advent of Community readmission agreements with third countries, negotiated on behalf of what became a block of 27 States on 1 January 2007.[53] Furthermore, the number of bilateral agreements concluded by EU Member States continues to rise with no indication of abating, considering the number of agreements still under negotiation. All of the 15 "old" Member States pursue a policy of concluding readmission agreements, with many of the "new" Member States following suit. These European States have concluded agreements amongst each other, but have also extended their interests beyond the European continent. In parallel with activity at the EC level, the Member States have concluded agreements with third countries along

49 Article 2(2) of the draft agreement with Albania provides for the issue of a travel document "without delay", and the acceptance of the EU standard travel document after expiry of a period of 14 calendar days.

50 See in particular *infra*, subsections 3.2.1, and 5.3.5.2.

51 Hailbronner 1997, p. 6-9.

52 Estimate taken from a study in the context of the Intergovernmental Consultations on Asylum, Refugee and Migration Policies in Europe, North America and Australia (*IGC Report on readmission agreements*, 1999, IGCARMP, Geneva), cited in Noll 2000, n. 592.

53 *Supra*, introduction, n. 2.

transit routes[54] and in regions of origin. The negotiating activity of the Community and its Member States furthermore acts as a catalyst for the conclusion of readmission agreements amongst third countries, creating a ripple-effect eastwards into Asia and southwards into sub-Saharan Africa.[55]

It is necessary to consider whether this strong expansion of treaty law could dispute the (continued) existence of an obligation under customary international law to readmit own nationals. In this regard, it should firstly be emphasised that codification of a rule in treaty law does not *prima facie* contradict a customary status.[56] A rule may exist under treaty law and customary international law simultaneously, as long as practice continues to be accompanied by an *opinio juris*. Secondly, considering the specific importance of readmission agreements in relation to the customary obligation to readmit nationals, Hailbronner refers to readmission agreements as "confirming",[57] and "putting into concrete terms"[58] international law. It is indeed arguable that readmission agreements reaffirm, as well as specify the international obligation of States to readmit their own nationals. The proliferation of readmission agreements therefore does not constitute *prima facie* evidence contrary to the customary status of the international obligation to readmit own nationals.

#### 2.1.2.3 Readmission agreements and *quid pro quo*

The previous section has determined that readmission agreements confirm and specify the obligation of States to readmit their own nationals. However, a relevant question is still whether practice, regarding the readmission of own nationals, as established by these agreements is accompanied by an *opinio juris*. In case of a lack of *opinio juris*, the large and growing number of readmission agreements concluded between States may arguably be an indicator of the absence of a customary norm. This subsection considers, in particular, whether the manner in which readmission agreements are *negotiated* precludes an *opinio juris* regarding the readmission of own nationals.

---

54 An agreement concluded with a typical transit country – the primary interest of which would be to enable the readmission of third country nationals – will often also include the readmission of own nationals. Readmission agreements that exclusively address the readmission of third country nationals are rare.

55 Kumin 1995, p. 4. Hailbronner 1997, p. 8, 31-32; van Selm 2001, p. 32; Bouteillet-Paquet 2003, p. 364-368. See also in general Lavenex 1999; and Byrne, Noll and Vedsted-Hansen 2002. The Community and its Member States expressly stimulate this development, which is further discussed below in subsections 3.2.3 and 7.2.

56 It is also possible for custom to evolve from or be evidenced by a treaty obligation. The landmark *North Sea Continental Shelf* case concerned a custom, which was rooted in a treaty obligation. (Judgement, ICJ Reports 1969), Villiger 1985; p. 192; Brownlie 1990, p. 13.

57 Hailbronner 1997, p. 8.

58 Hailbronner 1997, p. 14. See also Schieffer 1997, p. 100; and Nordic Joint Advisory Group 1999, Council Doc. 7707/99, p. 7.

It is a common practice of requesting States to withhold explicit compensatory benefits in exchange for readmission agreements insofar as pertaining to own nationals. The negotiating position of requesting States is generally that the readmission of own nationals is an existing obligation under general international law, which is therefore unconditional and "non-negotiable".[59] The underlying reasoning is that requested States should not benefit from implementing what is an existing international obligation. In addition, refusing compensating benefits is considered necessary to prevent the international norm from becoming conditional upon such benefits, and to ensure its continued existence.

For this reason, individual EC Member States generally refrain from granting benefits in exchange for the readmission of own nationals, with the exception of Italy.[60] The European Community institutions also appear to recognise the tension in granting benefits in exchange for the implementation of an existing obligation under international law. The Council has stated to be cautious to negotiate readmission agreements with third countries without "jeopardising the fundamental legal position, that the readmission of own nationals is a non-negotiable obligation incumbent on any State".[61]

Nevertheless, the negotiating position at the EC level remains somewhat ambiguous in this regard. In addition to an obligation to readmit own nationals, every Community readmission agreement includes an obligation to readmit third country nationals. The readmission of third country nationals is not generally considered required by general international law,[62] and therefore mostly compensated by certain benefits. This makes it difficult to determine whether benefits, offered in exchange for a Community readmission agreement, provide an incentive for the readmission of third country nationals, own nationals, or both. In addition, the EC appears to allow occasional exceptions. In exchange for concluding a readmission agreement, the EC granted a request by Sri Lanka for increased law enforcement cooperation.[63] Sri Lanka is purely a country of origin, so one may consider this as a benefit in exchange for the readmission of own nationals.

Regardless of whether the EC is consistent or not in refusing benefits in exchange for the readmission of own nationals, it is clear that concluding a readmission agreement always represents interests, other than the innate conviction of following an obligation of law to readmit own nationals. It is arguable that a readmission agreement between the EC, or an EC Member State, and a third country inevitably implies certain benefits for that third country. The question is whether this would preclude an *opinio*

59 See, in this regard, the proposal for a return action programme of the Council, *supra*, at n. 1; Hailbronner 1997, p. 48-49; and Nordic Joint Advisory Group 1999, p. 14.

60 COM(2004) 412 final, p. 14. Italy offers explicit incentives in exchange for the readmission of nationals, or the conclusion of agreements for that purpose, in particular in the form of labour agreements and immigration quota.

61 Proposal for a return action programme, Doc. 14673/02, para. 64.

62 *Infra*, section 2.2.

63 *Infra*, subsection 7.2.4.

*juris*, and prevent extrapolation of a norm concerning the readmission of own nationals, beyond the treaty obligations which readmission agreements establish.

In accordance with the traditional drafting style of these treaties, readmission agreements are almost invariably drawn up in a reciprocal manner.[64] On paper, the contracting parties accept mutual and equal obligations regarding the readmission of their nationals. The readmission of migrants under agreements, concluded between countries of comparable economic status (such as for example the agreements between Western European States of the 1950s and 1960s[65]) is likely to be balanced in practice. Such agreements could therefore be considered as expressions of a mutually felt legal obligation regarding the readmission of migrants.

The reciprocal wording of more contemporary readmission agreements, however, is often not reflected in practice. Readmission agreements, as concluded since the early nineties, are instruments which typically regulate the readmission of migrants, one-way from countries of destination to countries of origin.[66]

The fact that requesting States and requested States do not generally share a common interest in the return and readmission of migrants suggests that requested States have an *alternative* interest in the conclusion of a readmission agreement. Requested States frequently demand explicit benefits in exchange for a readmission agreement. Even when not demanding explicit compensation, or in case such a demand is rejected, requested States take account of the fact that cooperating on readmission may have certain implicit benefits. The conclusion of a readmission agreement results in improved international relations, which may lead to further benefits politically and economically.[67] Deciding not to cooperate on readmission, by contrast, may have the opposite effect. Requesting States, on their part, bank on the fact that requested States expect to receive, or fear being denied, such implicit benefits to successfully complete

64 Noll refers to two agreements, between Germany and, respectively, Algeria and Vietnam, as exceptions in this regard, Noll 1997, p. 417.

65 *Supra*, section 1.2.

66 The European Commission has recognised the disparity in readmission levels between contracting parties as a main difficulty in the negotiation of readmission agreements with third countries. See COM(2002) 175 final, p. 22; COM(2002) 564 final, p. 24; COM(2003) 323 final, p. 14.

67 Illustrative in this regard is the aforementioned analysis of the Nordic Joint Advisory Group on Refugee Policy, which advised the Migration/Expulsion Working Group of the Council that "[i]t may be useful to analyse the incentives of the country of origin to enter into readmission agreements. They may include a desire to achieve and maintain international recognition as a reliable collaborator. This desire may be based on expectations of entering into international collaboration fora or obtaining financial gains, for example, in the form of trade agreements, agreements on reintegration aid or other financial assistance. Finally, a country of origin may obtain real and concrete advantages such as visa exemption", Nordic Joint Advisory Group 1999, Council Doc. 7707/99, p. 18; *supra*, subsection 2.1.1, at n. 29.

negotiations.[68] The conclusion of readmission agreements, in other words, implies an inevitable element of *quid pro quo*.

However, *quid pro quo*, arguably, does not *ipso facto* preclude a requested State from having an *opinio juris* regarding the readmission of own nationals when concluding a readmission agreement. Readmission agreements not only codify an obligation to readmit nationals, but also make this obligation more concrete by establishing a procedure, evidence, and time-limits relevant to its implementation. This is a limitation of the sovereignty and related administrative discretion, which a requested State normally enjoys in readmitting persons to its territory. Any benefits, which a requested State receives in exchange for concluding a readmission agreement, may be considered to compensate for this particular consequence of the agreement.[69] Therefore, when concluding readmission agreements codifying the existing international obligation to readmit own nationals, requested States are not necessarily precluded from acting out of *opinio juris*.

From this perspective, it is possible that the care, taken by EC Member States and the Council to refuse *explicit* benefits in order to safeguard the customary norm, is not necessary. All benefits awarded for concluding a readmission agreement, whether implicit or explicit, could be interpreted as compensation, not for the obligation to readmit own nationals itself, but for the added administrative limitations these agreements entail. As such, granting benefits would not contradict or endanger the customary status of the obligation to readmit own nationals.

There are, however, indications that the conclusion of readmission agreements is becoming incentive-driven to a degree, which could eventually challenge the customary norm. A relevant example is that the Former Republic of Yugoslavia (FRY) in 1999 explicitly refused the readmission of own nationals from the UK *until* a readmission agreement would be concluded for this purpose.[70] This appears to have been an isolated incident, related to the specific circumstances of FRY at the time. However, the push by the EC and its Member States towards a predominantly treaty-based readmission practice, which relies heavily on providing third countries with incentives, clearly has certain risks.

Already in 1999, the Nordic Joint Advisory Group on Refugee Policy observed that "[a]n increasing number of countries can refer to a specific readmission agree-

---

68 The transfer of competence in the area of readmission to the Community is an example in this regard. The main motivation for developing a common readmission policy was to amplify, through the Community label, the political appeal for third countries to conclude readmission agreements, and thus achieve a higher success-rate in negotiations, *infra*, subsection 3.1.

69 This would arguably apply, also in the case where a requested State would fear being denied certain benefits for not cooperating. Such a concern may be considered to enforce the bureaucratic facilitation created by a readmission agreement, rather than the core obligation to readmit nationals itself.

70 See the comment by the UK regarding the Former Republic of Yugoslavia in Council Doc. 7609/1/99, 3 May 1999, p. 7.

ment to avoid the readmission of own [...] nationals".[71] It furthermore warned that "[e]nforcement of the principle of readmission under international law can become difficult if concrete readmission agreements become normative".[72]

As readmission agreements become more prolific, requested States increasingly regard the conclusion of readmission agreements as an opportunity to further their interests in other policy fields.[73] As a result, more States might start insisting on a formal agreement before cooperating on the readmission of their nationals in order to become eligible for the accompanying benefits. Such a development would clearly challenge the customary status of the obligation to readmit nationals under international law. It follows that, in order to avoid undermining the unconditionality, as well as the customary status of the international obligation to readmit nationals, prudence in granting explicit benefits for the readmission of own nationals continues to be necessary.

In sum, the explosive development of treaty law since the early nineties, regulating the readmission of own nationals, arguably represents a practice which is in support of a customary norm. Trends in the negotiation of readmission agreements may be pointing away from a customary obligation to readmit nationals, but it is too early to draw definite conclusions in this regard. For the time being, therefore, the customary nature of the international obligation to readmit own nationals must be presumed to persist.

### 2.2 Third country nationals[74]

This section first examines in subsection 2.2.1 whether the principle of neighbourliness could provide a legal basis for the readmission of third country nationals under general international law. It then considers in subsection 2.2.2 whether general international law requires the readmission of a special category of third country nationals – protection seekers – in light of the proliferation of safe third country policies and readmission agreements.

#### *2.2.1 The principle of neighbourliness*

The existence of a general international law obligation to readmit third country nationals is generally rejected. One author, Hailbronner, has argued in favour of deriving such an obligation from the principle of neighbourliness, and considered whether it has customary status.[75]

The UN Charter refers to the principle of neighbourliness in Article 74, which reads:

---

71 Nordic Joint Advisory Group 1999, Council Doc.7707/99, p. 13.

72 Nordic Joint Advisory Group 1999, Council Doc.7707/99, p. 13.

73 The manner in which third countries use the conclusion of readmission agreements to their advantage is discussed below in sections 3.2.2, and chapter 7.

74 *Supra*, n. 4.

75 Hailbronner 1997, p. 25-37. In support of the principle of neighbourliness as a legal basis for the readmission of third country nationals, see also Schieffer 1997, p. 103.

> Members of the United Nations [...] agree that their policy in respect of the territories to which this Chapter applies, no less than in respect of their metropolitan areas, must be based on the general principle of good-neighbourliness, due account being taken of the interests and wellbeing of the rest of the world, in social, economic, and commercial matters.

Hailbronner finds that the principle of (good) neighbourliness "under international law is considered to be universally accepted", suggesting customary status.[76] Specific literature on the issue does not entirely support this finding. There is general agreement that the principle of neighbourliness – also referred to as the principle of *bon voisinage*[77] or (good) neighbourship, or as neighbourship law[78] – is a political principle. Whether it would qualify as law (for example as customary international law), has been questioned, as well as its usefulness in solving actual disputes between States.[79] Nevertheless, the principle of neighbourliness does appear to be legal in nature.

The principle of neighbourliness places limits on the exercise of territorial sovereignty when impinging upon other States, closely related to the concept of abuse of rights and the principle of *sic utere tuo ut alienum non laedas* ("use your own so as not to injure another").[80] The principle of neighbourliness is applied in international environmental law in relation to disputes between States, arising, for example, from the pollution of international waterways, and detrimental cross-border effects of nuclear testing.[81] In this context, a United Nations conference on the human environment in 1972 in Stockholm proclaimed the responsibility of all States "to ensure that the activities within their jurisdiction and control do not cause damage to the environment of other States or areas beyond the limits of national jurisdiction".[82] The International Court of Justice has made similar pronouncements.[83] These are indications that the principle of neighbourliness is indeed a legal principle, which is most likely part of customary international law.

Drawing an implicit parallel with cross-border environmental damage, Hailbronner considers the principle of neighbourliness applicable to international migration

76 Hailbronner 1997, p. 34.

77 Malanczuk, P., *Akehurst's modern introduction to international law*, seventh revised edition, London, Routledge, 1997, p. 246; Schachter, O., *International law in theory and practice*, Dordrecht, Martinus Nijhofff Publishers, 1991, p. 363.

78 Lammers, J.G., *Pollution of international watercourses*, The Hague, Martinus Nijhofff Publishers, 1984, p. 563-569.

79 Lammers 1984, p. 563-569; Schachter 1991, p. 363-365; Malanczuk 1997, p. 246-247.

80 Lammers 1984, p. 566.

81 Outside the field of environmental law, it has also been mentioned in relation to danger for other States arising from military activities, and mine fields in frontier areas, Lammers 1984, p. 564.

82 Cited and discussed in Lammers 1984, p. 362-363.

83 *Advisory opinion on the legality of the threat or use of nuclear weapons*, ILM 35 (1996), 809; cited in Malanczuk 1997, p. 246.

flows, establishing responsibility for uncontrolled transit migration as well as a readmission obligation regarding third country nationals. Paraphrasing his reasoning, the principle of neighbourliness would arguably require States to prevent the transit of migrants across their territory towards neighbouring countries, considering the harmful impact of unauthorised immigration on the latter. In other words, the principle of neighbourliness would arguably give rise to a positive obligation to exercise border and migration control, held towards a neighbouring State. A third country national entering a neighbouring State without the required documentation indicates that a transit State has failed to adhere to that positive obligation. This, in turn, would create an obligation on the part of transit States to make repair by readmitting third country nationals who have entered neighbouring States *via* their territory.[84]

Such penalisation of a failure to control migration by way of an obligation to readmit persons is reflected in contemporary readmission agreements. Evidence of transit through the territory of the requested State is generally sufficient to establish a readmission obligation under agreements concluded since the early nineties. The readmission agreements currently concluded between the European Community and third countries also contain this provision. For this reason, Hailbronner regards readmission agreements as evidence of growing recognition in the international community of an obligation to readmit third country nationals, based on the principle of neighbourliness.[85] In conclusion, he recognises that a lack of general practice and *opinio juris* prevent the existence of a customary norm at present, but suggests that an obligation to readmit third country nationals between neighbouring States may be developing.

To be sure, when inviting third countries to enter into readmission agreements, the European Community does not claim that the readmission of third country nationals is required by international law.[86] There is, however, manifest endorsement in political discourse, policies, legislation and treaties of the EC and the Member States of the premise that countries should control transit migration and readmit persons who manage to enter a neighbouring territory, and thus of the interpretation of the principle of neighbourliness forwarded by Hailbronner. Examples include European Council conclusions,[87] the Dublin Convention[88] and its successor in EC secondary law the Dublin Regulation,[89] readmission agreements with third countries, as well as, argu-

84 Hailbronner 1997, p. 32-34.

85 Hailbronner 1997, p. 25-28, 31-37.

86 Determining its negotiation position, the European Community does assert the existence of an international obligation of States to readmit their own *nationals*, see *supra*, n. 1.

87 Declaration on principles of governing external aspects of migration policy, Conclusions of the Presidency, European Council, Edinburgh, 12 December 1992, Annex 5 to part A, principle 6. See also Hailbronner for declarations by Member States relating readmission to neighbourship, Hailbronner 1997, p. 31-6.

88 Convention determining the State responsible for examining applications for asylum lodged in one of the Member States of the Community, signed in Dublin on 15 June 1990.

89 Regulation 343/2003 of 18 February 2003 establishing the criteria and mechanisms for determining the Member State responsible for examining an asylum application lodged

ably, the European Neigbourhood policy (ENP).[90] Given the vigour with which the EU is seeking to establish responsibility for transit migration in third countries, it is important to determine the validity of Hailbronner's reasoning, which would provide a readmission obligation regarding third country nationals.

One can raise several objections against the proposed application of the principle of neighbourliness to international migration flows. Firstly, it is too broad. Whereas the principle of neighbourliness indeed places limits on the exercise (or, in the present case, *non*-exercise) of sovereignty, the extent of these limits is not clearly defined. It is recognised that the principle of neighbourliness may limit the sovereignty of States where inflicting *physical* damage upon another State, such as some cases of environmental damage. Despite the explicit reference in Article 74 of the UN Charter to "social, economic, and commercial matters", however, it is doubtful that the principle of neighbourliness would extend to economic, social or political damage, such as might result from an influx of undocumented immigrants.[91] In addition, it is questionable whether this principle would be able to create *positive* State obligations such as the exercise of migration or border control. Lammers, for one, notes the following:

> It is generally argued that neighbourship law in principle involves an obligation for a State to *abstain* from conduct – or to take such positive action as is necessary to convince private persons or entities in its territory to abstain from conduct [...]. It purports to enable neighbouring States to *coexist* by setting certain limits to the exercise and enjoyment of their territorial sovereignty and it does not in principle compel them to undertake positive action for the benefit of other States or to *improve* their mutual condition through co-operation.[92]

This passage furthermore indicates a second objection. Lammers emphasises that the essence of the principle of neighbourliness is to enable States to "coexist".[93] This specifies the principle's content. On the one hand, neighbourliness limits the enjoyment of sovereignty which is at the detriment of other States. On the other, however, it also implies "a duty to *tolerate* to a certain extent harmful effects caused by activities not in themselves unlawful, undertaken in neighbouring States".[94] The principle of neigh-

in one of the Member States by a third-country national, *OJ* L 50, 25 February 2003, p. 1 (hereinafter Dublin Regulation).

90 The central purpose of the ENP, which includes return and readmission cooperation with third countries neighbouring the EC, has been defined as providing "assistance [...] for the development of an area of prosperity and good neighbourliness", Proposal for a Regulation laying down general provisions establishing a European Neighbourhood and Partnership instrument, COM(2004) 628, 29 September 2004, Article 1. For more details regarding the ENP, see *infra*, subsection 6.2.4.

91 Lammers 1984, p. 564-565.

92 Lammers 1984, p. 568.

93 *Ibid.*

94 Lammers 1984, p. 568.

bourliness arguably aims to achieve harmonious reciprocal relations between States, consisting of corresponding obligations and rights. It is therefore unlikely to support an allocation of responsibility for migrants which is necessarily unbalanced, while determined by travel routes and the geographical location of countries in relation to regions of origin.

Thirdly, although above we confirmed that the principle of neighbourliness is indeed of a legal nature, its proposed application in the field of migration is decidedly political. Requesting States, seeking to expel immigrants to redirect migration pressure away from their territories, have a clear interest in interpreting the principle of neighbourliness as requiring the readmission of third country nationals. They emphasise that transit States, which do not control the movement of migrants across their territory, damage neighbouring States which unwillingly host these migrants. Taking the opposite perspective, however, one could equally argue that the expulsion of aliens to transit States of which they are not a national imposes an immigration burden, which impinges upon the sovereignty of these States and is damaging. Defining what constitutes good neighbourly conduct in relation to cross-border migration is prone to political or subjective interpretation, and therefore unsuitable as a basis for establishing related international obligations.

Fourthly, it is arguably incorrect to consider readmission agreements as evidence of recognition of the principle of neighbourliness. To find that "the obligation to readmit nationals of third States [...], as contained in modern readmission agreements, has its roots in the principle of neighbourliness"[95] disregards the negotiation practice of such agreements. Readmission agreements which provide for the readmission of third country nationals are generally negotiated on a strictly *quid pro quo* basis. Considering that a readmission agreement is likely to lack reciprocity in practice, typically requested States receive some form of compensation. The readmission of third country nationals is generally exchanged with explicit benefits, which precludes requested States from acting out of a conviction of good neighbourly conduct.

It follows from the above that the principle of neighbourliness does not provide an arguable basis for an obligation to readmit third country nationals under international law. Nor can it be said that such an obligation is a norm of customary international law *in statu nascendi*.

### *2.2.2 Protection seekers*

Under certain circumstances, international law requires States to *admit* protection seekers to their territories.[96] This is a claim under international refugee law or fundamental rights law, however, which is unrelated to physical contact with the territory of a State at a previous point in time, and as such unrelated to *re*admission. The specific issue of the readmission of protection seekers would in fact, and in law, be indistinguishable from the readmission of third country nationals in general, if not for safe third country policies. Safe third country policies may be considered a bid for creating a separate

95 Hailbronner 1997, p. 31.

96 *Infra*, subsections 9.2.2.4 and 9.2.3.5.

subcategory regarding the readmission of protection seekers. We will briefly consider whether this distinction has any basis in international law.

Safe third country policies have been adopted unilaterally as well as multilaterally. The only example of the latter to date is the 1990 Dublin Convention, which was succeeded by the Dublin Regulation.[97] The general aim of safe third country policies is to enable the rejection of protection seekers who have already found protection in a third country, or who have travelled through a third country where it would have been possible to seek protection while considered "safe". The effective implementation of expulsion pursuant to such policies requires a readmission component, which the Dublin Regulation provides. In order to secure the cooperation of transit countries following the application of *unilateral* safe third country policies, States have relied on the conclusion of readmission agreements.

A legal basis for safe third country policies under international law is not definitely established.[98] Hailbronner has proposed the principle of neighbourliness as a potential legal basis. In his view, the notion that States are responsible for migration movements across their territory would include the uncontrolled migration of persons seeking protection. This would imply a readmission obligation incumbent on transit States with regard to this group.[99] We refer to the objections listed above in subsection 2.2.1, which apply *mutatis mutandis*, and reject this proposition.

Considering briefly a possible customary status, Hailbronner has concluded that despite the development of the Dublin Convention "it remains impossible to derive recognition of the "first-country concept"[100] from customary international law".[101] We can add that readmission agreements would not constitute evidence towards a customary rule of this content, either. In practice, readmission agreements are used to facilitate the expulsion of protection seekers pursuant to safe third country policies. Generally, however, readmission agreements do not refer to protection seekers as an explicit or separate category. The readmission of protection seekers is implemented under the

97 *Supra*, n. 88-89.

98 On Article 31(1) of the Geneva refugee Convention as the disputed legal basis of safe third country policies, see Zwaan 2003, p. 22-30; van Selm 2001, p. 47-50; Vedsted-Hansen 1999, p. 277-278.

99 Hailbronner 1997, p. 39.

100 This is a reference to the "first country of asylum" concept, which Hailbronner considers as an obligation for persons to seek protection in the first eligible country they encounter after fleeing their country of origin. In this understanding, it is synonymous with the concept of "safe third country". There also exists a different reading of the first country of asylum concept, according to which first countries of asylum are a subcategory of safe third countries, referring in particular to countries where a protection seeker has already found some form of protection, Legomsky 2003, p. 570-571. It is in this latter sense that the first country of asylum concept has been incorporated into EC legislation, as demonstrated by Article 25(2)(b) in conjunction with Article 26 of the Directive on minimum standards on procedures in Member States for granting and withdrawing of refugee status, *OJ* L 326, 13 December 2005, p. 13.

101 Hailbronner 1997, p. 39.

terms agreed for third country nationals in general. Readmission agreements, including those concluded by the Community, are therefore not able to reflect a legal conviction in support of safe third country policies.

In sum, treaty law and EC secondary law (the Dublin Convention and the Dublin Regulation) have provided a specific legal basis for the readmission of protection seekers. The readmission of protection seekers to transit countries is however not required by general international law.

### 2.3 Former nationals

In a readmission context, one can divide stateless persons[102] into three subgroups. These are firstly stateless persons formally recognised under the 1960 Convention relating to the status of stateless persons. Readmission obligations concerning this subgroup are identical to readmission obligations concerning recognised refugees, which we will discuss jointly in the next section. The second subgroup consists of persons who lost their nationality *before* entering a requesting State, regarding which no particular readmission obligations can be identified under general international law. Readmission agreements often arrange for the readmission of this subgroup under the same terms as third country nationals,[103] *i.e.* requesting States generally attempt to remove these persons to transit States.[104] The third subgroup concerns persons who lost their nationality *after* entering a requesting State, which we discuss in this section. These persons are usually referred to as former nationals, regarding whom explicit readmission obligations can be identified in general international law as well as treaty law.

In subsection 2.1.1, it was argued that the international legal order seeks to ensure that at least one State is responsible for each person. In this vein, international law determines that a State assumes responsibility for a person, who has lost his or her nationality, through naturalisation. The allocation of responsibility in the period between a loss of nationality and the possible acquisition of another nationality, however, is not clearly defined.

There appears to be agreement in the literature that States are not able to escape readmission obligations regarding their nationals abroad by means of unilateral deprivation of nationality. It has been argued that to deprive nationals of their nationality in order to avoid readmission obligations[105] would impinge upon the territorial sovereignty of other States, violate the good faith of other States, constitute an abuse of

102 For the purpose of this chapter we consider as a stateless person anyone who does not hold a nationality, following the definition of the term under Community readmission agreements. See, for example, Article 1(e) of the agreements with Hong Kong (*OJ* L 17, 24.1.2004, p. 25), and Albania (*OJ* L 124, 17 May 2005, p. 22).

103 An example is the readmission agreements concluded by the Community, which establish a standard readmission obligation pertaining to third country nationals and stateless persons jointly.

104 Hailbronner 1997, p. 18.

105 Regarding State practice of depriving nationals of nationality for the purpose of preventing readmission, see Schieffer 1997, p. 102-103.

rights, and violate the individual's fundamental right to return.[106] In addition to own nationals, States are thus arguably held to readmit former nationals, who were deprived of their nationality involuntarily.

Hailbronner argues that readmission obligations could not be thwarted by voluntary renunciation of nationality, either. Considering that a readmission obligation "depends to a large extent on considerations towards the other State",[107] he argues that the means by which the release from nationality has taken place is immaterial. There is however no apparent basis for this argument. In case of voluntary renunciation of nationality one cannot rely on the above arguments concerning sovereignty, good faith, or an abuse of right, which pertain exclusively to State interaction. Nor is it possible to appeal to the fundamental right to return, which the individual must be considered to have relinquished along with his or her nationality. Although an unsatisfactory conclusion, implying that aliens would be able to frustrate expulsion by renouncing their nationality, the legal basis for a readmission obligation under international law appears to be unclear in this case.

Some readmission agreements arrange specifically for the readmission of former nationals. Examples are the agreements negotiated by the Community, which expressly treat the readmission of former nationals on the same terms as own nationals, regardless of whether nationality was lost involuntarily or voluntarily.[108] This provision aims to prevent States of origin from circumventing readmission obligations by depriving their nationals abroad of their nationality, which confirms general international law. This provision also prevents individuals from frustrating expulsion by renouncing their nationality, which arguably fills a gap in international law.

### 2.4 Persons formally recognised as refugees or stateless persons

The Geneva Refugee Convention provides for the readmission of persons to a State where they have been formally recognised as a refugee. The 1960 Convention relating to the status of stateless persons provides for the readmission of recognised stateless persons in the same manner.[109] In particular, a State must readmit refugees and stateless persons to whom it has issued a travel document within the meaning of Article 28 of these conventions. Not only the person in question, but also the State in which they are

106 Weis 1979, p. 54-58, and n. 123. Hailbronner 1997, p. 17-24, 45, 47; Lawand 1996, p. 555, 566. See also Lehnguth 1997, p. 161.

107 Hailbronner 1997, p. 22-23.

108 See Article 2(1) of the Community agreements with Hong Kong (*OJ* L 17, 24.1.2004, p. 25), Macao (*OJ* L 143, 30.4.2004, p. 99), and Albania (*OJ* L 124, 17 May 2005, p. 22). Exceptionally, a provision to this effect was not negotiated with Sri Lanka (*OJ* L 124, 17 May 2005, p. 43). In defining a "stateless person", Article 1(e) of this agreement moreover expressly excludes persons who have renounced, or have been deprived of their nationality. For further examples of agreements arranging for the readmission of former nationals, see Hailbronner 1997, p. 15-19.

109 Grahl-Madsen 1972, p. 325-326.

present may invoke this obligation.[110] In principle, the readmission obligation lasts for the duration of the validity of the document.[111] Similar arrangements regarding persons recognised as refugees or stateless persons were included in a number of multilateral and bilateral agreements in the 1950s and 1960s, providing interstate readmission claims.[112] More contemporary readmission agreements do not, in general, refer to this category of persons explicitly, but do provide for their readmission implicitly.[113]

Notwithstanding occasional allusion in the literature to "a generally accepted rule",[114] obligations to readmit formally recognised refugees or stateless persons are not considered to extend beyond the above treaty law.

### 2.5 Conclusion

Considering the above findings, we can conclude that general international law provides a legal basis for an obligation to readmit own nationals, which probably has customary status. General international law offers at least a partial basis for an obligation to readmit former nationals, namely regarding those who involuntarily lost their nationality. General international law does not provide a legal basis for an obligation to readmit third country nationals (including protection seekers), nor for persons formally recognised as refugees and stateless persons. These obligations only exist in treaty law, or EC secondary legislation.

Relating this state of law to the conclusion of readmission agreements, we can conclude the following. Where providing for the readmission of own nationals, readmission agreements confirm and specify general international law. Regarding third country nationals, readmission agreements establish a legal basis which is not present in general international law. Where referring explicitly to former nationals, readmission agreements confirm and specify an existing obligation of international law insofar as concerning persons who lost their nationality involuntarily. Insofar as concerning persons who relinquished their nationality voluntarily, readmission agreements establish a legal basis for readmission, which may possibly fill a gap in general international law. Regarding formally recognised refugees and stateless persons, finally, readmission agreements do not generally establish an explicit readmission obligation. Their readmission is subsumed under the general terms of readmission for third country nationals, which means no specific conclusion can be drawn regarding the relation of

110 Grahl-Madsen 1972, p. 325. Hailbronner 1997, p. 37.

111 For specific circumstances under which the individual's right to readmission would arguably exceed this period, see Grahl-Madsen 1972, p. 304-311.

112 Grahl-Madsen 1972, p. 326; Hailbronner 1997, p. 37.

113 Community readmission agreements, for example, provide for the readmission of stateless persons under the same terms as third country nationals, which may include the specific subgroup of persons formally recognised under the Convention relating to the status of stateless persons. The terms of readmission for third country nationals also cover persons, recognised as a refugee in another State.

114 Grahl-Madsen 1972, p. 326.

readmission agreements with general international law where concerning this category of persons.

Regarding in particular the negotiation of Community readmission agreements, it should be borne in mind that this state of law partially determines the respective negotiating positions of the Community, and of the third countries involved. Insofar as the obligations imposed by Community readmission agreements confirm general international law, the position of the Community is relatively strong, and demands of compensation from third countries have little to stand on. This is the case for obligations to readmit own nationals and former nationals who lost their nationality involuntarily. Insofar as the obligations imposed by Community readmission agreements do not exist under general international law, the position of the Community is relatively weak, and third countries have a strong case for demanding compensation. This is the case for obligations to readmit third country nationals, and former nationals who relinquished their nationality voluntarily.

# Chapter 3 The reasons for a common readmission policy

This chapter analyses the motivation of the Member States for pursuing a common policy on the readmission of third country nationals to third countries. It will in particular determine what the Member States perceived as the added value of concluding readmission agreements with third countries at the Community level, as opposed to the national level. The second part of this chapter will then determine and evaluate the objectives which the Community wishes to achieve with the common readmission policy.

## 3.1 The motivation for having a *common* policy on readmission

Subsection 3.1.1 first discusses an apparently obvious reason for taking a common approach to the readmission of immigrants to third countries, but which did not motivate the Member States. We will demonstrate that the free movement of persons between Schengen States and within the internal market did not directly influence the decision to introduce a Community competence to conclude readmission agreements. Regarding what *did* motivate the Member States, subsection 3.1.2 argues that the main motivation was to extract a greater degree of cooperation from third countries on readmission, using the negotiating weight of the Community.

### *3.1.1 The relation between the common readmission policy and the free movement of persons*

The abolition of internal border controls, following Schengen cooperation and the creation of the internal market, is arguably a strong motive for concluding readmission agreements at the EC level. It makes less sense for the Member States to pursue individual readmission policies in an area where persons are able to travel across internal borders unchecked. Persons who fear expulsion to a certain third country could theoretically move to another Member State without a readmission agreement with that country. Individual Member State readmission policies would hereby be circumvented, and moreover affect other Member States. The conclusion of readmission agreements at the Community level would arguably reduce the potential for internal movements and imbalances in the distribution of immigrants between the Member States. There are however a number of indications that the direct motivation of the Member States to transfer competence to the Community in the area of readmission was unrelated to the free movement of persons.

Shortly after the entry into force of the ToA, the Council determined that the conclusion of Community readmission agreements was not relevant to the Schengen *acquis*. The background of this decision is as follows. The introduction of a Community competence to conclude readmission agreements in 1999 required the Council to determine which Council configuration would be responsible for preparing the negotiation directives for these agreements.[1] In particular, the Council had to determine whether this would take place within the Mixed Committee. The Mixed Committee includes Iceland and Norway, and involves these countries in Schengen-related issues considering their association to the Schengen *acquis*.[2] Initially, the negotiation directives for Community readmission agreements were discussed within the Mixed Committee of the Migration and Expulsion Working Group.[3] A meeting of the COREPER on 15 March 2000,[4] however, decided that Community readmission agreements did not constitute part of the Schengen *acquis*, as incorporated into the EU framework with the Treaty of Amsterdam.[5] Accordingly, the preparation of the negotiating directives was relocated to the Migration and Expulsion Working Group proper.[6] This decision discontinued the association of Iceland and Norway, which are effectively Schengen States, with the development of the common readmission policy. Additionally, it excluded Denmark, which is within the internal market, from participating in Community readmission agreements.[7]

1 The conclusion of Community readmission agreements takes place pursuant to the procedure laid down in Article 300 TEC. Accordingly, following a recommendation from the Commission, the Council adopts decisions authorising the Commission to start the negotiation of a Community readmission agreement with a particular third country, which are also known as negotiating directives or mandates.

2 See the Agreement of 18 May 1999 between the European Union and Iceland and Norway concerning the latters' association with the implementation, application and development of the Schengen *acquis*, *OJ* L 176, 10 July 1999, p. 36; and Council Decision 1999/437/EC of 17 May 1999 on certain arrangements for the application of this Agreement, *OJ* L 176, 10 July 1999, p. 31.

3 Council Doc. 11042/99, 23 September 1999, para. 2.

4 Council Doc. 6720/00; Council Doc. 7637/00; and SI(2000) 249, 17 March 2000, cited in Schieffer 2003, p. 352.

5 The Treaty of Amsterdam integrated the Schengen *acquis* into the framework of the European Union, see Protocol 2 annexed to the TEC and the TEU.

6 The COREPER did determine that Iceland and Norway would be given regular updates on the conclusion of readmission agreements. It also decided to add a standard declaration to each Community readmission agreement, creating an opening for the negotiation of a readmission agreement on the same terms between the third country in question and Iceland and Norway. This declaration is further discussed below, in subsection 5.3.15.

7 Article 5 of the protocol annexed to the TEC and the TEU on the position of Denmark leaves Denmark the possibility of an "opt in", determining its participation in Council decisions concerning legislative proposals under Title IV TEC, and proposals building

The reasoning of the COREPER is difficult to follow. Under the terms of association of Iceland and Norway with the Schengen *acquis*, the negotiating directives for Community readmission agreements should arguably be prepared within the Mixed Committee.[8] Furthermore, finding that Community readmission agreements lack Schengen relevance appears inconsistent with the fact that Schengen cooperation since the early nineties has produced several instruments relating to readmission, including the Schengen Convention itself.[9] The decision of the COREPER is moreover inconsistent with previous appraisals within the Council context.[10] The decision does make clear, however, that the Member States were unconcerned by the impact of the free movement of persons on the implementation of the common readmission policy. A consequence of this decision is namely that third country nationals can evade the field of application of Community readmission agreements by entering the territories of Iceland, Norway or Denmark. These are gaps within the common readmission policy,[11]

---

upon the Schengen *acquis*. The finding that Community readmission agreements were not part of the Schengen *acquis*, therefore excluded Denmark from participating.

8 Article 1(C) of Council Decision 1999/437/EC (*supra*, n. 2) refers to proposals and initiatives concerning the expulsion of illegal residents, and the free movement of third country nationals, as subject to association with Iceland and Norway.

9 Article 23 SC relates to expulsion and readmission to third countries, and specifically refers to readmission agreements concluded by the Schengen States as implementing measures in this regard. Furthermore, the collective Schengen States concluded a readmission agreement with Poland in 1991. In 1997, the Schengen States drafted a standard readmission agreement between a Schengen State and a third country, although this instrument was never adopted while overtaken by the advent of Community competence in this area (Council Doc. 7669/99, 26 April 1999, p. 3). Additionally, the catalogue of recommendations for the correct application of the Schengen *acquis* and best practices, which assists Acceding Member States in meeting the requirements of the *acquis*, includes rules on removal and readmission (Council docs. 12790/3/01; 5018/02).

10 The Mixed Committee was engaged in the negotiation of the standard agreement on readmission between the collective Member States and a third country (Council Doc. 10338/3/1998 (*supra*, section 1.4, at n. 89) prior to the entry into force of the Treaty of Amsterdam. Relevant, furthermore, is a discussion which took place in the Council in 1999, regarding the competent body for negotiating the Finnish Initiative regarding a Regulation on the readmission of third country nationals between the Member States (*supra*, section 1.4, at n. 90). At the time, the "vast majority" of the Member States within the Expulsion Working Party favoured discussion in the Mixed Committee "because this matter is covered by Article 23 [GC], and because it is a prerequisite to the effective functioning of an agreement with a third country", Council Doc. 11042/99, 23 September 1999, point 3.

11 The forthcoming Directive on common standards and procedures in Member States for returning illegally staying third-country nationals may possibly contribute to plugging these gaps. Article 16 of the original Proposal of the Commission for this Directive (COM(2005) 391 final, 1 September 2005) provides for unauthorised immigrants, who are subject to a return decision or removal order in a Member State, but are apprehended in another Member State. The Proposal gives that other Member State several options, one of which is to request the first Member State to take back the third country national in question. The

which indicate that free movement within the Schengen area and the internal market did not inform the transfer of competence to the EC to conclude readmission agreements.

A second indication in this regard is the fact that the competence to conclude readmission agreements with third countries is shared between the Community and the Member States.[12] Accordingly, the Member States continue to operate individual readmission policies, despite the free movement of persons. The genesis of this competence division, moreover, explicitly confirms that free movement did not underpin the common readmission policy. The Legal Service of the Council produced a legal opinion concerning the nature of the competence to conclude readmission agreements at the time of the entry into force of the ToA.[13] In this document, the LS requested the Council to judge politically whether the conclusion of readmission agreements should be a purely Community affair, or shared with the Member States, and formulated a criterion for this purpose. The Council was to judge whether:

> readmission agreements are inseparably bound up with the achievement of the Community's immigration policy objectives, so that it should not be possible for one or more Member States alone to continue to conclude such agreements with third countries, on account of the potential resulting distortions for other Member States in the context of an area without internal border controls;[14]

This passage may be interpreted as follows. The LS asked the Council to consider the relationship between the conclusion of readmission agreements with third countries, and the free movement of persons with the Schengen area and the internal market. It considered this relationship decisive for determining the nature of Community competence to conclude readmission agreements. In particular, the LS considered that bilateral policies within an area of free movement of persons, as a result of competence sharing, could lead to "distortions" for other Member States. We may assume that these distortions refer to internal movements of third country nationals to Member States with more favourable readmission policies, as noted above. That the possibility of such internal movements would exist is clear; hence, the LS asked the Council for a political, and not a factual judgement. In other words, the LS was asking the Member States whether they were willing to take the risk of such possible distortions for the preservation of their national readmission policies.

---

Proposal for this Directive is considered a development of the Schengen *acquis* (Preamble, recital 21, COM(2005) 391 final), meaning that Norway and Iceland are associated, and that Denmark may decide to opt in.

12 We will discuss the nature of this Community competence in detail below, *supra*, section 4.2.

13 Council Doc. 6658/99, 10 March 1999; Migration News Sheet 1999, p. 1. See also Noll 2000, p. 207-208.

14 Migration News Sheet 1999, p. 1.

Responding to the legal opinion of the LS, the JHA Council meeting of 27 and 28 May 1999 decided that the competence to conclude readmission agreements with third countries would be shared.[15] The Member States made a clear choice to retain their national readmission policies, notwithstanding possible implications for other Member States in light of the free movement of persons. This would confirm the conclusion that the free movement of persons within the Schengen area and the internal market did not motivate the Member States to introduce a Community competence to conclude readmission agreements.

### *3.1.2 Using the negotiating weight of the Community*

Peers has noted that in the field of migration policy, and readmission in particular, the Member States have readily allowed the Community to exercise its competencies.[16] We mentioned in chapter 1 that the Member States in the mid-nineties started to exploit the resources of the Community in the external field in order to extract readmission obligations from third countries. The Council introduced a policy of incorporating readmission clauses into Community- and mixed agreements in 1995, predating first pillar competence relating to readmission.[17] The idea behind this policy was to make use of the Community's external powers in fields such as trade and development, and the significant accompanying budgets, to forward Member State interests in the field of readmission.[18] The same idea was expanded and deepened in 1999 with the decision to conclude fully-fledged readmission agreements with third countries at the Community level.

The Council has determined that the conclusion of a Community readmission agreement with a third country must present an added value in comparison with the conclusion of bilateral Member State agreements.[19] Relevant to what might constitute this added value, the Council has stated that "[t]he EU should [...] use its political weight to encourage third countries which show a certain reluctance to fulfil their readmission obligations".[20] Regarding the readiness of the Member States to recur to Community action, a Commission official, involved in the negotiation of Community readmission agreements, furthermore observed that:

15 Justice and Home Affairs Council meeting of 27-28 May 1999, Conclusions on "re-admission agreements – consequences of the entry into force of the Amsterdam Treaty", Press release 168 – Nr: 8654/99.

16 Peers 2004, p. 194, 213.

17 *Supra*, section 1.4, at n. 70.

18 Noll 2000, p. 206.

19 Council Doc. 7990/02, 16 April 2002; Proposal for a comprehensive plan to combat illegal immigration, *OJ* C 142. 14 June 2002, para. 75; see also Schieffer 2003, p. 348.

20 Proposal for a Comprehensive Plan to combat illegal immigration, *OJ* C 142, 14 June 2002, para. 76. The Commission had suggested this strategy earlier in identical wording, see COM(2001) 672 final, p. 25.

> conviction had gained momentum that individual Member States were no longer able to react appropriately to the increasing difficulties [...] in the field of return [...] linked [...] to the fact that return measures always require the cooperation of another State. [...] Some third countries [...] refuse to cooperate for political reasons or – openly or covertly – make readmission contingent upon, e.g., visa facilitation or financial considerations.[21]

In other words, the Member States transferred competence to the Community, expecting that the political and economic weight of the Community would increase the readiness of third countries to enter into readmission agreements. The point was to gain footing in the negotiation of readmission agreements which the Member States were unable to muster individually.

The EC Member States have generally sought readmission agreements with third countries from which they experience an influx of migrants, and/or receive an unsatisfactory level of cooperation on readmission. Some third countries have a reputation as "problem States"[22] or "difficult clients" in this regard. Individually, the Member States are typically unable to persuade such countries to accept formal readmission obligations, or improve the level of practical cooperation on readmission received from them. The communitarisation of readmission agreements was masterminded in order to gain a more dominant negotiating position especially *vis-à-vis* such problematic countries.[23]

Regarding large and politically significant "problem States", such as for example Russia or China, the Community level was expected to provide more clout in negotiations while levelling the playing field politically and geographically. Regarding smaller and less influential yet problematic countries, such as for example Morocco or Pakistan, the Community was expected to reach agreements faster and negotiate more favourable terms of readmission. The Member States were relying in particular on the fact that third countries would expect the conclusion of a readmission agreement with the Community to create prospects for approximation to the EU. The Member States estimated that political and tacit incentives, concerning the association process or even EU membership, would provide a significant stimulus to cooperation on readmission with third countries.

In sum, the Member States perceived the greater negotiating weight of the Community as *the* added value of concluding readmission agreements at the Community level, as opposed to the national level. In the face of failing individual attempts at concluding readmission agreements with third countries, the Member States considered

21 Schieffer 2003, p. 343.

22 Council Doc. 9808/98, para. 133.

23 As illustrated by the fact that in order to decide with which countries to conclude the first Community readmission agreements, the Council took stock of the third countries posing the most problems to the Member States in the readmission of immigrants, Council Doc. 13888/99, 7 December 1999, annex. We will discuss this selection process below in subsection 7.1.

the political, economic and financial resources of the European Community as a means to increase the success-rate of negotiations and negotiate better deals.

## 3.2 The objectives of the common readmission policy

This section identifies the objectives of the common readmission policy. These objectives are related to the general expectations of readmission agreements as instruments for the return of immigrants, and as vehicles for the establishment of wider international relations and cooperation concerning migration.

The objectives of the common readmission policy as identified here are to fight unauthorised immigration by facilitating the return of third country nationals without a residence title, to establish a cordon of third countries responsible for transit migration around the EU, to stimulate the negotiation of readmission between third countries, to complete safe third country policies, and to expand the number of countries that are able to receive immigrants.

### *3.2.1 Fight unauthorised immigration by facilitating return*

The so-called "fight against illegal immigration" has been high on the political agenda of the EU since the introduction of first pillar competence in the fields of immigration and asylum.[24] The political climate regarding immigration and asylum has since then generally become more restrictive and control-oriented. Policy regarding (unauthorised) immigration is now an important electoral issue in many of the Member States. A marked increase in attention for unauthorised immigration followed the incident in Dover in July 2000, where a group of Chinese immigrants suffocated in a lorry attempting to enter the UK. This incident, widely publicised as one of many, influenced in particular the development of immigration policy at the Community level and pushed it towards a greater emphasis on restriction and control.[25] The attacks by Al Qaeda in New York, Washington and Pennsylvania in September 2001 further strengthened this development at the EC as well as national level.[26] Overall, the adoption of measures under Title IV TEC has been characterised by an emphasis on control measures, in which the Member States are important stakeholders.

Community policy documents regularly call attention to the number of third country nationals, residing in the Member States without a residence title, and the number of yearly new arrivals.[27] The return of these persons to a country outside the EC is a pivotal element of Community immigration policy for a variety of reasons. In the view of the European Commission, an effective return policy undermines the activities of

24 Community competence in the fields of immigration and asylum is determined by Title IV TEC.

25 COM(2000) 757, p. 6; Statewatch, June-August 2000b, p. 8; Statewatch, November-December 2000c, p. 6.

26 Regarding the emphasis on security and control in European immigration and asylum policies post-9/11, see in general Brouwer, Catz and Guild 2003.

27 See, for example, Council Doc. 9809/98, 1 July 1998, para, 21; and COM(2000) 757, p. 13.

criminal networks involved in the smuggling and trafficking of persons.[28] In addition, the Commission considers that implementing returns prevents immigration by sending a dissuasive signal to third country nationals that stable residence in the EU is difficult to attain. More profoundly, the Commission posits return as a precondition for safeguarding the credibility and integrity of immigration and asylum policies.[29] This, in turn, is necessary according to the Commission for maintaining public support for immigration, and a climate that allows for the integration of long-term resident third country nationals.[30] Furthermore, the Member States within the Council generally posit control over unauthorised immigration, and thus an effective return policy, as a prerequisite for allowing more labour immigration. In other words, the political interest in realising an effective return policy is considerable.

The importance of measures against unauthorised immigration, in particular return policy, reflects directly upon the conclusion of readmission agreements. Readmission agreements are generally considered important instruments for implementing the return of immigrants without a residence title. For this reason, readmission agreements have been presented as the central instrument of the Community's return policy.[31] As noted in chapter 2, a main problem hampering the return of immigrants is a lack of cooperation on readmission from third countries. Readmission agreements are deemed to acquire that cooperation by spelling out readmission obligations, a procedure, means of evidence, and time limits. The expectation is that the conclusion of readmission agreements would therefore lead to the implementation of more returns.

There are reasons to doubt whether readmission agreements do indeed have such a vital effect on return practice. Firstly, there are cases where requested States have continued to provide limited cooperation on readmission, despite the existence of a readmission agreement.[32] Conclusion of a readmission agreement is not always followed by cooperation on its implementation. This could be attributed to the general

28 COM(2002) 175 final, p. 23; COM(2003) 323 final, p. 8; Schieffer 2003, p. 344.

29 COM(2000) 755 final, p. 10-11; COM(2001) 672 final, p. 8, 25; COM(2002) 175 final, p. 8; COM(2002) 564 final, p. 4, 8; and most recently, COM(2003) 323 final, p. 8. See also Nordic Joint Advisory Group on Refugee Policy 1999, Council Doc. 7707/99, p. 4. The UNHCR has expressed a similar opinion, see UNCHR 2001a and UNHCR 2001c.

30 SEC(91) 1855 final, para. 27, 31; COM(2004) 412.

31 Justice and Home Affairs Council meeting of 27-28 May 1999, Conclusions on "re-admission agreements – consequences of the entry into force of the Amsterdam Treaty", Press release 168 – Nr: 8654/99; Proposal for a Comprehensive Plan to combat illegal immigration and trafficking of human beings in the European Union, *OJ* C 142, 14 June 2002; Proposal for a return action programme, Doc. 14673/02; COM(2002) 175 final; COM(2002) 564 final.

32 An inventory of problems experienced by the Member States in the expulsion of immigrants to certain third countries, undertaken within the context of the Council in 1999, reveals several of such cases, Council Doc. 7609/1/99, 3 May 1999.

problem of enforcement of treaties.[33] Where concerning readmission agreements, however, it also appears to be a matter of negotiation. Requested States tend to be more cooperative on readmission when compensated. The mere conclusion of a readmission agreement may prove insufficient for certain countries, requiring the provision of benefits to secure implementation.[34] One could therefore argue that not readmission agreements, but the provision of incentives are the essential instrument for attaining the cooperation of third countries.

Secondly, there are technical and practical limits to the implementation of readmission agreements. Readmission agreements dating from the fifties and sixties are used only sparingly due to impracticable evidence- and procedural requirements.[35] Readmission obligations are relatively easier to establish under agreements dating from the early nineties onwards, but important practical limitations persist. Perhaps the most significant obstacle that States face in the practice of return is the lack of cooperation of returnees, and the lack of documentation in their possession. Readmission agreements require requested States to issue travel documents to an undocumented person whom they are obliged to readmit. In order to establish that readmission obligation, however, the requesting State will first need to demonstrate at least nationality and/or the travel route of the person concerned. This remains problematic in case an undocumented migrant of unknown identity and origin is unwilling to cooperate by providing information that may facilitate expulsion, with or without a readmission agreement. The more recent agreements do attempt to address this problem by including a wide range of means of evidence, including oral evidence and language analysis. The added practical value of such provisions, however, is arguably limited.[36]

Thirdly, the EC institutions have posited readmission agreements as the single most important return instrument, but without providing any data regarding the frequency with which the Member States actually use them in practice. The frequency as well as the manner of application of Member State readmission agreements would merit scrutiny.

There is at least one Member State making only limited use of the readmission agreements at its disposal. Referring to the Netherlands, the Dutch authorities do not use the majority of the readmission agreements available to them. Excluding Memoranda of Understanding and other less formal bilateral arrangements, the readmission

33 Some of the more recent readmission agreements do attempt to strengthen their enforcement by establishing a joint committee to oversee implementation. We will discuss the competences and tasks of joint readmission committees as established by Community readmission agreements below, in subsection 5.3.10.

34 A case in point is Nigeria, which has readmission agreements with both Ireland and Italy. Ireland has not received adequate cooperation from the Nigerian authorities in implementing the readmission of Nigerian nationals under their bilateral agreement. Italy, on the other hand, combined its readmission agreement with Nigeria with an agreement on labour migration, and is receiving satisfactory cooperation on the readmission of Nigerians.

35 *Supra*, section 1.2.

36 We will further elaborate this point below, *infra*, subsection 5.3.5.2.

agreements relevant to Dutch return practice have mostly been concluded at the Benelux level. The Benelux has readmission agreements with Austria, Bulgaria, Croatia, Estonia, the Former Republic of Yugoslavia, France, Germany, Latvia, Lithuania, Rumania, Slovakia, Slovenia, and Switzerland. Also relevant is the regulation of readmission between the Benelux States.[37] The Dutch authorities regularly apply only the agreements with Bulgaria, France, Germany and Rumania, and the internal Benelux rules. Application of the remaining agreements is negligible. In addition, the manner of application is often informal, that is, outside the terms of the agreement.[38]

The application of readmission agreements for the expulsion of immigrants from the Netherlands concentrates on countries bordering the Netherlands and/or the Benelux area, *i.e.* Belgium, France and Germany. This includes an extensive practice of apprehension and expulsion at the Dutch-German border, involving informal application of the Benelux-German readmission agreement.[39] Of the available readmission agreements with countries which are further away, only the agreements with Bulgaria and Rumania serve a purpose in practice. The Netherlands have established an effective informal cooperation with these countries, based loosely on the readmission agreements concluded in the Benelux context. Bulgaria and Rumania readmit to their territory respective groups of X persons of unknown identity but of suspected Bulgarian or Rumanian nationality, which the Netherlands return by charter flight. Contrary to the terms of the available readmission agreements, procedures for establishing identity and nationality are undertaken *after* readmission and under the responsibility of the requested State. According to the Dutch authorities, part of the success of this practice lies in the availability of a readmission agreement as a fallback option, in case cooperation from Bulgaria or Rumania would falter.[40]

It is not possible to draw general conclusions based on the practice of one Member State. The Dutch example, however, gives reason to wonder whether the European Community is not overestimating or overplaying the importance of readmission agreements, and calls for examination of the practice of other Member States. In Dutch practice, only a minority of available readmission agreements is used, the majority is surplus. Moreover, the primary value of the agreements that *are* used is arguably as a catalyst of informal practices, and not the obligations, procedures, means of evidence, and time limits they establish. Before declaring readmission agreements as pivotal return instruments and dedicating considerable financial and human resources to their negotiation, it would have been pertinent for the EC institutions to investigate Member State practices.

37 Decision M/P (67) 1, *supra*, section 1.2, n. 23.

38 This reflects the state of affairs of Dutch return practice up until April 2003, interview IND, 16 April 2003.

39 This informal practice concerns an unknown but large number of immigrants, probably accounting for the majority of yearly expulsions carried out by the Dutch authorities, interview IND, 16 April 2003.

40 Interview IND, 16 April 2003.

### *3.2.2 Establish migration control in third countries*

The EU Member States generally attempt to conclude agreements providing for the readmission of nationals, as well as third country nationals. Given the lack of a basis in international law, negotiating the readmission of third country nationals is difficult and not always successful. Nevertheless, the numerous readmission agreements concluded between the Member States and CEECs in the nineties mostly cover this group of persons. The readmission of third country nationals is also a standard provision of Community readmission agreements.

The general purpose of negotiating the readmission of third country nationals is to expand return options beyond the country of origin. To this end, readmission agreements attempt to establish responsibility for the readmission of third country nationals based on a possible visa or residence permit, issued by another country. Above all, however, readmission agreements attempt to establish responsibility for readmission based on transit through the territory of other countries. This enables the return of immigrants to third countries through which they travelled, covering immigrants who did not arrive by air or sea directly from the country of origin. Return and readmission to transit States is advantageous for requesting States. It provides an alternative in case expulsion to the country of origin is difficult for technical, practical or legal reasons. It also creates a perspective for the expulsion of persons whose identity and nationality cannot be established, provided that past transit through a third country *can* be substantiated. Furthermore, expulsion to a transit State can be considerably less costly, which makes it an attractive option in general.[41]

In addition, obligations to readmit third country nationals are considered to extract a higher degree of migration control from requested States. A current priority of the Community is to establish a "buffer zone"[42] of countries assuming responsibility for transit migration around the EU. The ultimate buffer, of course, consists of countries which not only readmit immigrants, but also block or intercept immigrants *en route* to the EU. Readmission agreements, which provide for the readmission of third country nationals, are generally assumed to persuade neighbouring third countries to do also the latter.

The reasoning behind this assumption, which has also taken hold at the EC level,[43] is as follows. It has been argued that by signing a readmission agreement obliging to the readmission of transit migrants, a State takes responsibility for "the consequences

41 Some readmission agreements oblige requesting States to prioritise expulsion to countries of origin. This is intended to limit the readmission of third country nationals to transit States for reasons of convenience or cost reduction. Some of the third countries with which the Community is negotiating readmission agreements have insisted on stipulations to this effect.

42 Another common reference in this regard is "*cordon sanitaire*", see, for instance, Landgren 1999, p. 41; Crosland and Morrison 2001, p. 37.

43 The EU Schengen catalogue of recommendations on removal and readmission, for example, posits that "[r]eadmission makes the Member States and the third States responsible for controlling their borders efficiently", EU Schengen Catague 2002, p. 55.

of failures in the control of migration flows".[44] Faced with the possible readmission of transit migrants, this State would arguably seek to prevent this consequence by controlling migratory movements into and across its territory.[45] In other words, this State would try harder to block the entry of immigrants at its borders, or intercept them while passing through.

The accuracy of this reasoning is questionable. Firstly, it appears only partially sound in theory. A transit country's reaction to the conclusion of a readmission agreement in terms of migration control is likely to be determined by cost estimation. From this perspective, it is possible that a transit country would indeed prefer to block the entry of an immigrant at its borders sooner, rather than run the risk of readmission later. Readmitting a transit migrant presents a country with a generally unattractive and potentially costly situation. Its options would be to detain readmittees with a view to onward expulsion, grant them residence, tolerate their presence, or declare them present "illegally" with an order to leave the country. Reducing the number of transit migrants – potential later readmittees – by exercising more border control may therefore be relatively advantageous. There is less reason to believe however that a risk of later readmission would lead transit countries to intercept migrants in-country or exercise exit control. Once an immigrant has successfully evaded border controls and entered, interception in-country or during exit would result in the same situation as created by readmission. In such cases, the transit State would arguably be more inclined to accept the risk of readmission, the occurrence of which is after all not certain, even with a readmission agreement in place.

Secondly, it is difficult in practice to corroborate whether readmission agreements induce border and migration control. There is a degree of factual basis for assuming that a relation exists between the two, at least insofar as concerning migration control *capacity*. While negotiating readmission agreements, some requested States agree to, or even request assistance to protect borders and police immigration. There are numerous examples of readmission agreements which have been combined with extensive financial and technical assistance to this effect.[46] Bearing in mind that increased capacity does not necessarily imply an increase in actual *control*, there have also been States which have visibly stepped up the interception of transit migrants after concluding a

44 Denoël 1993, p. 636. See also the discussion of the principle of neighbourliness above, in subsection 2.2.1.

45 Noll 1997, p. 419; Noll 1998, p. 33; Lavenex 1999, p. 82; Bouteillet-Paquet 2003, p. 364-365.

46 Common examples are the financial assistance offered by Germany to Poland and Czech Republic in connection with readmission agreements, see *infra*, subsection 3.2.5, at n. 74. Offering assistance to build border and migration control capacity in combination with a readmission agreement is a common practice of the Member States, which the European Commission has also adopted, COM(2004) 412, p. 14. The Commission was given a larger budget for this purpose with the adoption of the Regulation of 10 March 2004 establishing a programme for financial and technical assistance to third countries in the areas of migration and asylum (Aeneas), *OJ* L 80, 18 March 2004, p. 1.

readmission agreement.[47] However, such behaviour on the part of requested States is determined by a number of different factors, besides a possible concern for the readmission of transit migrants.

Requested States may have ulterior motivations for requesting financial or technical assistance to build border and migration control capacity. Negotiating a readmission agreement with the Community, Ukraine, for example, has requested EC assistance to demarcate and strengthen the control of its borders with Russia, Belarus and Moldova. Transit migrants enter relatively easily through these borders whilst exiting across Ukraine's Western borders into EC Member States is significantly more difficult. A number of migrants is thus left stranded, a problem which could be aggravated by the readmission of third country nationals under a Community readmission agreement. Preventing an additional increase in immigration pressure would be reason to strengthen Ukraine's control of its more porous Eastern, Southern and Northern borders.[48] A prerequisite for controlling these borders, however, is their proper demarcation, which is still pending after the collapse of the Soviet Union. This happens to be also of strategic importance to Ukraine in its relations with Russia.

Another example relates to the fact that assisted capacity building in the area of migration control often involves the supply of border surveillance equipment.[49] This includes hardware such as airplanes, helicopters, speedboats, jeeps, night-vision goggles, and infrared-, and radar-systems, which are generally attractive assets for countries, and bear a recognised risk of so-called "dual-use".[50] This implies that requested States, which ask for such equipment in exchange for a readmission agreement, might want it for purposes other than migration control.

In addition, there are ulterior outside influences pushing requested States to increase their migration and border control, certainly in the case of third countries bordering the EU. In addition to the conclusion of readmission agreements, the EC pushes for the introduction of control measures by way of the above-mentioned political dia-

47 Poland is again an example, which concluded a readmission agreement with the Schengen States in 1991. During the nineties, Poland increased the control of its borders, as well as the number of checks on and arrests of immigrants in-country, FFM 1997, p. 9-14; FFM 2000, p. 4-5; Byrne, Noll and Vedsted-Hansen 2002, p. 58-59. NGOs furthermore observed a spill-over effect within the region. As Poland increased its control measures, migration routes towards the EU shifted *inter alia* to the Czech Republic. Increased political pressure on the Czech Republic to address this situation led to a number of reforms and new control measures also in that country, FFM 1997, p. 9-14; FFM 2000, p. 4-5.

48 Kruse 2004, p. 23-28.

49 COM(2004) 412, p. 14. Recently, Libya was provided with such equipment in an attempt by the EC, spearheaded by Italy, to stem immigration flows through this country towards Northern Mediterranean Member States, see NRC Handelsblad 2004a, NRC Handelsblad 2004b, NRC Handelsblad 2004c, La Repubblica 2004.

50 In supplying third countries with equipment for the purpose of border and migration control, the Council has stated to be careful to include "safeguards regarding [...] potential dual-use", GAERC Conclusions of 19 May 2003 on migration and development, Council Doc. 8927/03, para. 8.

logue, the association- and accession process, and external assistance programmes. Yet additional spheres of influence are the intergovernmental Budapest process and the Council of Europe.[51] These are all strong parallel incentives. It is thus unclear whether third countries bordering the EU would increase their migration control for the specific reason of concluding a readmission agreement with the Community (or one of the Member States).

In sum, one cannot think of the relation between readmission agreements and responsibility for transit migration in the broad sense in an isolated manner. The existence of a direct relation between readmission agreements and the introduction of more stringent control measures by requested States is doubtful. A possible concern for preventing the later readmission of transit migrants is only one of a complex of reasons, which stimulate third countries to reduce immigration pressure on the EU. Parallel incentives provided, for example, by cooperation and association agreements, or the enlargement process, are arguably more important determinants of third countries' choices in this area.

### *3.2.3 Stimulate the negotiation of readmission between third countries*

A major concern of third countries bordering the European Union is to become a bottleneck for transit migrants, who are unable to secure durable entry into the EU. The conclusion of a readmission agreement with the Community, providing for readmission of third country nationals, amplifies this concern. Possible returns resulting from such an agreement are an additional immigration burden. On the part of the EU, the return and readmission of migrants to countries right outside its borders bears an inherent risk of re-entry.[52] These respective concerns of incurring a greater immigration burden versus the risk of re-entry are common to each conclusion of a readmission agreement. The contracting parties thus always share an interest in onward expulsion of readmitted migrants to elsewhere.

From a strategic perspective, readmission negotiations offer the EU several options for reducing the risk of re-entry. The Community could conclude readmission agreements with countries of origin or with third countries that are further away. The Community is currently concentrating on third countries bordering the EU, but concluding agreements with other third countries and countries of origin does form part of its strategy. An inherent downside, however, is that implementing returns to such countries is more costly, and, especially in the case of further away transit countries, more problematic.[53] An alternative is therefore to stimulate neighbouring countries, with which the Community is negotiating readmission agreements, to conclude readmis-

51 FFM 1997, p. 3-7, 10. Regarding the influence of EU membership perspectives, and regional, sub-regional and bilateral forms of intergovernmental cooperation on decisions of CEECs in the area of migration, see Byrne, Noll and Vedsted-Hansen 2004.

52 Kumin 1995, p. 3, 4; Bouteillet-Paquet 2003, p. 366.

53 Noll points to problems of procedure and evidence regarding expulsion to transit countries. As time and distance lapses, it is increasingly difficult to prove transit through a requested State, Noll 1998, p. 34.

sion agreements of their own. This creates a framework for onward expulsion, which implies less implementation costs for the Member States and offloads implementation problems on to the EU's neighbours. Having readmission agreements at their disposal, which facilitate expulsion, may also increase the readiness of neighbouring third countries to intercept transit migrants in-country.

The accumulation of stranded transit migrants in third countries bordering the EU creates a favourable climate for prompting the conclusion of further readmission agreements. In the nineties, the Member States successfully exercised pressure on Central and Eastern European countries to conclude readmission agreements with their Eastern neighbours.[54] The result was a network of readmission agreements between CEECs, and between CEECs and other third countries as well as source countries.[55] There are indications that the more recent negotiation of Community readmission agreements has a similar effect. Community readmission agreements represent potential returns of transit migrants from at least 24 Member States,[56] which multiplies the concerns of requested States accordingly. It comes as no surprise that the negotiation of Community readmission agreements has triggered neighbouring third countries to initiate or intensify their own readmission policies.

Russia has expressed far-reaching ambitions in this regard. It intends to create a continent-spanning readmission "zone" or "territory" around its borders, including also major countries of origin. It has recently concluded a number of readmission agreements, and is exploring possibilities for further agreements with countries of the CIS and in Asia.[57] Ukraine has similar visions of a "single readmission area" or "common readmission space", and aims to sign readmission agreements with Russia, Belarus and Asian source countries in sink with the agreement with the Community.[58] Albania is another example. The Commission granted an Albanian request to delay the implementation of readmission of third country nationals under the agreement with the Community. This delay is intended *inter alia* to give it time to conclude readmission agreements with source countries.[59] Morocco is also noteworthy. In order to counter its slow transformation into a country of destination for nationals of Sub-Saharan

54 Byrne, Noll, and Vedsted-Hansen 2002, p. 383-385.

55 Kumin 1995, p. 5; Hailbronner 1997, p. 8, 31-32. Bouteillet-Paquet 2003, p. 364-368. See also in general Lavenex 1999; and Byrne, Noll and Vedsted-Hansen 2002.

56 Denmark does not participate in Community readmission agreements; the UK and Ireland participate on an "opt-in" basis.

57 See news reports Pravda 2002, Pravda 2003, and Itar-Tass 2004.

58 Kruse 2004, p. 27; RFERL 2004. For a list of Ukrainian activity in the conclusion and negotiation of agreements on readmission up until December 2003, see the website of the Mission of Ukraine to the EC: www.ukraine-eu.mfa.gov.ua.

59 Kruse 2004, p. 22; COM(2004) 92 final, p. 3. Regarding the Western Balkan region, Albania wants to go further than the mere establishment of readmission relations. It is in favour of creating an area of free movement of goods and persons between Western Balkan countries, based on the Schengen and EC model, Institute of European Affairs 2004.

countries,[60] Morocco has set its sights on the conclusion of readmission agreements to facilitate return to Sub-Saharan source countries of migration. For similar reasons, Turkey has sought to stall the negotiation of a readmission agreement with the Community to conclude agreements with other countries first.[61]

The Community purposely stimulates these developments. The negotiation process provides certain indirect stimuli. The negotiation of Community readmission agreements familiarises third countries with the negotiation and content of contemporary readmission agreements, both of which are increasingly technical. This enhances their expertise in the drafting of agreements and the conducting of negotiations with other countries. Furthermore, the Commission offers technical and/or political assistance to the readmission negotiations of third countries. Possible assistance ranges from reviewing the text of draft agreements and exchanging information relevant to negotiations, to providing political encouragement of other countries to reach agreement with the Community's readmission partners. Additionally, recent EC legislation – the so-called Aeneas Regulation – explicitly enables the Community to fund projects, providing technical or financial support to third countries' readmission negotiations.[62]

One may reasonably expect that the conclusion of a readmission agreement between a third country and a "fourth" country would in turn encourage also the latter to adopt a readmission policy, and so on and so forth. The conclusion of readmission agreements has a clear ripple effect, promoting the creation of chains of consecutive readmission agreements. One can conclude that by stimulating the establishment of readmission agreements between countries along the travel routes of migrants, the EU is actively seeking to improve the capacity of third countries to deflect migration flows away from the EU and back towards regions of origin.

### *3.2.4 Complement safe third country policies*

In practice, States may use readmission agreements to facilitate the expulsion of rejected protection seekers. Readmission agreements, including those concluded by the Community, generally do not refer to protection seekers or refugees explicitly. In the application of readmission agreements, rejected protection seekers are treated simply as immigrants without a residence title. In this manner, States may apply readmission agreements to any rejected protection seeker in order to facilitate expulsion

---

60 Kruse 2004, p. 28. This development is partially explained by the level of development of Morocco in comparison with Sub-Saharan countries. It is however also due to the fact that control of Spain's maritime borders has intensified in recent years.

61 Kruse 2004, p. 35; Kirişci 2004, p. 8.

62 Article 2(2)(j) of the Regulation of 10 March 2004 establishing a programme for financial and technical assistance to third countries in the areas of migration and asylum, also referred to as the Aeneas Regulation (*OJ L 80*, 18.3.2004, p. 1). For details of funding under this regulation, see *infra*, subsection 6.2.2.2.

to the country of origin or a third country, regardless of the grounds for rejection.[63] The application of readmission agreements within the context of asylum is however associated primarily with the expulsion of protection seekers rejected on safe third country grounds. Considering that international law does not provide a basis for the readmission of third country nationals, readmission agreements may be considered to complement safe third country policies.

Safe third country policies are unilateral policies under national law (and under European law[64]). This is contradictory, considering that the implementation of these policies is dependent on the cooperation of implicated third countries. A State may declare a third country "safe" under national law, and accordingly reject protection seekers who travelled through that country. Without the third country's consent to allow those persons on its territory, however, such a policy is clearly ineffective. As mentioned in section 1.3 above, the Member States introduced safe third country policies during the early nineties to cope with the rising number of arriving asylum seekers. "The Member States hereby unilaterally incorporated third countries [...], such as the CEECs, into their system of redistribution for handling asylum claims".[65]

Subsequent implementation, however, proceeded with difficulty, while implicated third countries in Central and Eastern Europe were unwilling to receive protection seekers back. This was a reason for the Member States to seek readmission agreements with these countries, securing a legal basis for the readmission of third country nationals.[66] The cooperation of third countries is a *sine qua non* for the implementation of safe third country policies, and the conclusion of readmission agreements is a means by which to acquire it (albeit implicitly, considering that readmission agreements do not generally mention protection seekers or refugees in the text).

It should be emphasised that the efficacy of readmission agreements for implementing the expulsion of protection seekers to third countries is largely subject to the same technical and practical limits outlined earlier.[67] Protection seeking and non-protection seeking migrants often travel together, using the same migration facilitators as well as the same strategies to reach a chosen destination, and thwart possible expulsion to a third country.[68] Finding the necessary evidence for establishing a readmission obligation on the part of a transit State may therefore be problematic. Fernhout has noted an additional complication regarding asylum cases, which is that the length of asylum procedures may prevent the use of readmission agreements for implementing

63 Regarding related concerns for the international protection of refugees, see *infra*, subsection 9.3.2.2.

64 *Infra*, at n. 71.

65 Lavenex 1999, p. 76.

66 Lavenex 1999, p. 78-82, 89.

67 *Supra*, subsection 3.2.1.

68 On the mixed nature of migration flows, see Hailbronner 2000, p. 162-163; Noll 2000, p. 109-110, 490; Gortezar 2001, p. 122; Morrison and Crosland 2001, p. 16-19, 25-27; UNHCR 2001d; UNHCR 2001e.

expulsion after rejection.[69] Readmission agreements contain a time limit for submitting a readmission request upon detection of an unauthorised immigrant, ranging from six months to one year. A requesting State would therefore be required to complete the examination of the "safety" of a third country for a particular protection seeker within this period. Given the widespread use of accelerated procedures and general, instead of individual safety examinations, however, one would not expect this to be a significant limitation.

In 2000, the European Community started developing a common safe third country policy, based on a Commission proposal for a Directive on minimum standards on procedures in Member States for granting and withdrawing of refugee status.[70] The Directive on minimum standards on procedures in Member States for granting and withdrawing of refugee status was finally adopted on 1 December 2005.[71] Before the adoption of this directive, Community readmission agreements were able to facilitate the expulsion of protection seekers to third countries based on national Member State policies. At present, one may consider that Community readmission agreements complement a common safe third country policy.

### *3.2.5 Build reception capacity in third countries*

As noted above, the Community combines the conclusion of readmission agreements with promoting border and migration control, and promoting the negotiation of further readmission agreements by third countries. In addition, the conclusion of Community readmission agreements may be supported by building reception capacity.

Building reception capacity has been a necessary complement of concluding readmission agreements since the early nineties. The CEECs with which the Member States concluded agreements in the nineties had not been countries of immigration or transit in their recent past. Institutional experience, administrative capacity, immigration and asylum legislation laying down procedures and substantive criteria, and the infrastructure required for receiving immigrants, were therefore lacking. This lacuna was especially pressing with regard to the reception of protection seekers and the handling of their claims, regarding which relatively more expert knowledge and care is required.[72]

In addition to the efforts of international organisations and NGOs,[73] the Member States attempted to improve this situation. Commonly cited examples in this regard are the agreements on "cooperation regarding the effects of migratory movements", which Germany concluded with Poland in 1993 and Czech Republic in 1994 after designating them as safe third countries. They were linked explicitly to a 1991 readmission agree-

69 Fernhout 1999, p. 86, 87.

70 For the text of the original proposal, see COM(2000) 578 final, 20 September 2000.

71 Council Directive 2005/85/EC of 1 December 2005 on minimum standards on procedures in Member States for granting and withdrawing refugee status, *OJ* L 326, 13 December 2005, p. 13.

72 Kumin 1995, p. 3-4; Lavenex 1999, p. 85-90.

73 Kumin 1995, p. 4.

ment between Poland and the Schengen States, and a 1994 readmission agreement between Germany and the Czech Republic. The agreements on migration cooperation provided Poland and Czech Republic with financial assistance amounting to 120 and 60 million DM, respectively. These were lump sums intended for the improvement of migration control, and for the building of infrastructure for receiving protection seekers.[74] The EC Member States set up several more of such support programmes during the nineties, all intended to compensate for the consequences of readmission agreements and safe third country policies.[75]

It is still common practice to seek readmission agreements with countries that are ill-equipped institutionally and financially to receive immigrants. There are several examples amongst the third countries selected for Community readmission agreements, of which we will briefly highlight the case of Albania. During the negotiation of a Community readmission agreement, Albania argued its lack of capacity to handle the readmission of transit migrants and protection seekers. It requested a delay of the readmission of third country nationals under the agreement of five years to enable appropriate capacity building,[76] with the Commission finally agreeing to a period of two years. During this time, in addition to the negotiation of readmission agreements as noted above, Albania will improve its legislative, institutional and administrative structures for the reception, detention, and processing of immigrants.

These improvements are part of a general process of legislative reform in Albania, assisted by the EU through the Stabilisation and Association Process (SAP)[77] and specific Justice and Home Affairs cooperation.[78] This assistance was reinforced in light of the readmission agreement. The Thessaloniki European Council of 19 and 20 June 2003 explicitly earmarked part of the SAP budget for building readmission capacity. In addition, the Commission included readmission capacity building in Albania as an objective of the B7-667 budget-line,[79] enabling the procurement of specific projects to this effect.

74 Schieffer 1997, p. 104, 106; Landgren 1999, p. 28; Lavenex 1999, p. 82; van Selm 2001, p. 34; Byrne, Noll and Vedsted-Hansen 2002, p. 56-59; Bouteillet-Paquet 2003, p. 365. The agreements on migration cooperation were presented as instruments for building refugee protection structures. Germany's main interest was however in the control measures of its neighbours, as clearly illustrated by the allocation of funding under the agreements. The majority of the budget of the German-Polish agreement went towards border control (49%) and capacity building of the Polish policy force (38%), leaving only a small percentage for protection infrastructure, Lavenex 1999, p. 84, 88. Bouteillet-Paquet notes that the budget of the German-Czech agreement showed a similar allocation, cited in Hurwitz 2002, n. 34.

75 Lavenex 1999, p. 87.

76 Kruse 2004, p. 22.

77 COM(2003) 339, p. 29.

78 COM(2002) 703 final, p. 54.

79 The B7-667 budget-line finances projects regarding "cooperation with third countries in the field of migration", see *infra*, subsection 6.2.2.1.

The case of Albania illustrates that the EU improves reception capacity in third countries through a variety of measures. B7-667 and other budget-lines within the field of Justice and Home Affairs[80] have regularly funded projects during the last few years. This funding now continues under the Aeneas Regulation, which created a multi-annual assistance programme succeeding B7-667. The association- and accession process, and the Community's external assistance programmes also invest in upgrading the conditions of reception, detention and processing of immigrants in third countries.[81]

The European Commission draws from some of these financial resources to support its readmission negotiations with neighbouring third countries. As an incentive, the Commission offers assistance in building reception capacity in compensation for the conclusion of Community readmission agreement.[82] This is a negotiating tool, which clearly serves also the wider EU agenda for external immigration and asylum policies. Building reception capacity improves the ability of third countries to absorb readmitted transit migrants as well as incoming migration flows. It also improves the viability of safe-havens for refugees in countries outside the European Union, which benefits the implementation of safe third country policies. It moreover potentially increases the sustainability of return and readmission, which may reduce the risk of re-entry into the European Union after readmission.

One should of course keep sight of the fact that reception capacity is only one, and an arguably less important factor determining a country's suitability as a host country. Short of a significant economic development, the third countries with which the Community has concluded or is negotiating readmission agreements – like Albania, Algeria, Morocco, Ukraine, Russia and Turkey – will remain unattractive countries for migrants to settle in. The lack of durable solutions for immigrants in third countries neighbouring the EU impedes an efficacious common readmission policy and related "export" of enforcement and control measures. A cause for concern is that this perspective is unlikely to direct EU external policy towards improving general conditions in neighbouring countries or, indeed, the alleviation of root causes of migration. In the short- to medium term, it is more likely to focus EU support to third countries on border control, and detention capacity with a view to onward expulsion.

## 3.3 Conclusion

This chapter has made clear that the motivation underpinning the common readmission policy is directly related to the purported negotiating power of the European Com-

80 For a detailed overview of Community budgeting in this field, see COM(2002) 703 final, annex 2bis.

81 Byrne, Noll and Vedsted-Hansen rightly stress that such incentives should be seen within a wider context of European cooperation. Raising the standards of treatment of protection seekers in CEECs, for example, is a continuous and accumulative process of interrelated bilateral, sub-regional and regional frameworks, in addition to the enlargement and external policies of the EC, Byrne, Noll and Vedsted-Hansen in "Understanding refugee law in an enlarged European Union", *ejil* (2004), Vol. 15 No. 2, p. 355-379.

82 COM(2004) 412, p. 14.

munity. The Member States expected that conducting negotiations at the Community level would be more effective in persuading third countries to accept readmission obligations. Whether this approach has produced the expected result will be discussed in chapter 7.

Regarding the objectives of the common readmission policy, the Community considers readmission agreements to be essential instruments for implementing the return of third country nationals without a residence title, including protection seekers. We have highlighted some doubts concerning the efficacy and degree of application of readmission agreements. This chapter has however made clear that the common readmission policy serves multiple objectives. Readmission agreements are attractive instruments for the Community beyond their direct purpose of enabling returns. Regardless of whether these doubts would be warranted, therefore, the Community and its Member States have an interest in pursuing a common readmission policy.

Further to the objectives of the common readmission policy, we have inserted some reasonable doubt into the assumption of a direct correlation between readmission agreements and the introduction of control measures in third countries. This is without prejudice to the fact that readmission negotiations are an opportunity to offer third countries Community assistance in the improvement of border and migration control, reception conditions, and the negotiation of agreements of their own. The common readmission policy may therefore be considered a vehicle for the establishment of wider cooperation between the EC and third countries concerning migration and asylum.

# Chapter 4 The competence to conclude Community readmission agreements

This chapter discusses the competence of the European Community to conclude agreements with third countries on the readmission of unauthorised immigrants. The EC attained this competence with the entry into force of the Treaty of Amsterdam on 1 May 1999, although the Treaty does not contain an explicit legal basis. Section 4.1 determines the manner in which this legal basis is derived from Title IV TEC implicitly. Section 4.2 then discusses the controversy over the nature of the Community's competence in the area of readmission. After establishing that the Community's competence is in practice shared, section 4.3 considers whether the common readmission policy complies with the principle of subsidiarity. Section 4.4, finally, identifies the rules which govern the division of competence between the Community and the Member States.

## 4.1 The legal basis in EC law

The draft Constitutional Treaty,[1] signed in Rome on 29 October 2004, contains an explicit legal basis for concluding readmission agreements with third countries. Article III-168 reads:

> the Union may conclude readmission agreements with third countries for the readmission of third country nationals residing without authorisation to their countries of origin or provenance[2] [...].

At the time of writing of this book, it is uncertain whether the Constitutional Treaty will enter into force, and if so, in which form. Ratification by the Member States has been suspended after rejection of the Constitutional Treaty by referenda in France and the Netherlands. We will therefore only consider the current legal basis for the conclusion of readmission agreements under the Treaty of Amsterdam (ToA).

---

1 Draft Treaty establishing a Constitution for Europe, 18 July 2003, 2003/C 169/01.

2 The addition of the word "provenance" is curious, being a synonym of "origin". At first sight, readmission to (third) countries of transit would therefore appear excluded from this legal basis.

The European Council in Tampere in October 1999 confirmed that "the Amsterdam Treaty conferred powers on the Community in the field of readmission", and invited the Council to conclude readmission agreements.[3] The ToA transferred competence from the third to the first pillar concerning visas, asylum, immigration and other policies related to the free movement of persons. The Community's powers in these fields are determined by Title IV of the EC Treaty. It would however appear that the drafters of the TEC did not anticipate the development of a common readmission policy. Title IV does not provide for the conclusion of treaties with third countries[4], nor does it refer to "readmission" of unauthorised immigrants. The European Court of Justice has determined that in the absence of express external Community powers it may be possible to derive implied external powers from the treaties.[5] A Treaty provision is thus required, which establishes relevant competence in the internal sphere, implying a competence to conclude agreements on readmission with third countries.

Given the lack of reference to "readmission" in either the TEC or TEU, the competence to conclude readmission agreements has been derived from the term "repatriation" in Article 63(3)(b) of the TEC. This article reads as follows:

> The Council [...] shall [...] adopt [...] measures on immigration policy within the [area of] illegal immigration and illegal residence, including repatriation of illegal residents.

In May 1999, the Council explicitly linked the conclusion of readmission agreements to the "Community objective of 'repatriation of illegal residents'", thereby determining Article 63(3)(b) as the relevant legal basis.[6] Readmission agreements are instruments that may facilitate the repatriation of unauthorised residents, and can therefore be considered to be authorised by Article 63(3)(b). Repatriation, however, is a technical term, referring specifically to "return to the country of origin".[7] In order to account for the full personal scope of the readmission agreements as concluded by the Community, it would therefore be necessary to adopt a broad interpretation of the term repatriation, or to consider Article 63(3)(b) in its entirety.

3 Presidency Conclusions, Tampere European Council of 15 and 16 October 1999, para. 27.

4 We should note that the Protocol on the position of Denmark, which is annexed to the Treaty of Amsterdam and determines Denmark's participation in measures adopted under Title IV TEC, refers in Article 2 to international agreements concluded by the Community. The conclusion of treaties pursuant to Title IV was therefore foreseen, even if not explicitly provided for.

5 Case 22/70, *Commission v. Council* (ERTA) [1971] ECR 263; Craig and De Búrca 1998, Second Edition, p. 116; Peers and Rogers 2006.

6 Justice and Home Affairs Council meeting of 27-28 May 1999, Conclusions on "re-admission agreements – consequences of the entry into force of the Amsterdam Treaty", Press release 168 – Nr: 8654/99.

7 COM(2002) 175 final, annex.

In addition to the readmission of persons to their countries of origin, Community readmission agreements also provide for the readmission of persons to transit countries, extending beyond the narrow meaning of repatriation. This incongruity can be partially remedied by arguing that readmission to a third country which is not the country of origin would amount to indirect repatriation, and therefore be covered by Article 63(3)(b). The very term repatriation would however still exclude stateless persons, whose return to the country of origin is impossible. It would also exclude protection seekers and refugees, whose expulsion to the country of origin in any manner, directly or indirectly, would violate international law.

A better solution is therefore to consider Article 63(3)(b) in its entirety, disconnecting the legal basis to conclude readmission agreements from the narrow objective of repatriation. Considering the text of Article 63(3)(b), the word "including" indicates that "repatriation of illegal residents" is not an exhaustive indication of Community measures falling under this provision. Insofar as providing for return to transit countries beyond the definition of repatriation, readmission agreements would still qualify as a "measure [...] in the area of illegal immigration and illegal residence" under the terms of this provision.[8] Article 63(3)(b) would in this manner provide an implied legal basis for the full personal scope of the readmission agreements currently concluded by the Community.

### 4.2 The controversy over the nature of the competence

The nature of the Community's competence to conclude readmission agreements with third countries is a source of lingering disagreement between the European Commission on one side, and the Member States and Council on the other. At the time of the entry into force of the ToA, the Commission claimed exclusive Community competence to negotiate and conclude readmission agreements.[9] The Justice and Home Affairs Council in May 1999 took a different position, deciding that this competence would be shared with the Member States.[10] The issue is still formally unresolved. The Commission has tacitly accepted shared competence for the time being, in order not to hinder the development of the common readmission policy,[11] but has not withdrawn its claim to exclusivity.

The Commission has not motivated its position in any public access document. From selected publications we can deduce that the Commission seems to be aiming for exclusive power, while "a workable policy at Community level on repatriation of

8 The Legal Service of the Council has interpreted Article 63(3)(b) in a similar vein, Council Doc. 6658/99, 10 March 1999.

9 Council docs. 5677/99, 8265/99 and 13757/99; cited in Peers and Rogers 2006. For a detailed argument in favour of exclusive competence in the area of readmission, reflecting the position of the Commission, see Kuijper 2004, p. 617-619.

10 Justice and Home Affairs Council meeting of 27-28 May 1999, Conclusions on "re-admission agreements – consequences of the entry into force of the Amsterdam Treaty", Press release 168 – Nr: 8654/99.

11 Schieffer 2003, p. 350-351.

third State nationals illegally resident in the Community cannot be achieved without agreements with third States on readmission".[12] One can furthermore not suppress the possibility of political motivations on part of the Commission, which has a general interest in strong Community powers for developing the common immigration and asylum policy.

It is possible that there is internal disagreement within the Commission, especially between the Commission's Legal Service and the Commission services responsible for the readmission negotiations. Exclusivity would have significant consequences for the workload of the Commission. The Member States would no longer be allowed to negotiate agreements with third countries, at least not without first seeking the explicit consent of the Council.[13] From a practical point of view, it is doubtful whether the Commission, as the sole party in the EC negotiating readmission agreements with third countries, would be able to satisfy the needs of the Member States. This would in any case require a substantial increase in the human and financial resources currently dedicated to readmission negotiations at the EC level. In addition, exclusive competence would imply the inefficient and undesirable task of replacing all bilateral Member State agreements with Community agreements.[14]

The view of the Member States and Council that the conclusion of readmission agreements is a shared competence requires elaboration. In March 1999, the Council's Legal Service (LS) produced an opinion[15] on the impact of the entry into force of the Treaty of Amsterdam on the draft standard readmission agreement between the collective Member States and a third country.[16] The purpose of this Council LS opinion was *inter alia* to help settle the competence debate that had ignited after the Commission asserted exclusive competence in the area.

According to the Council LS, the nature of the Community competence to conclude readmission agreements with third countries hinged on two criteria:

1. assessment by the Council (and if need be by the Court of Justice) of whether readmission agreements are *inseparably bound up* with the achievement of the Community's immigration policy objectives, so that it should not be possible

12 Kuijper 2004, p. 818; Schieffer 2003, p. 350. Pieter Jan Kuijper is a senior advisor in the Commission's Legal Service. Martin Schieffer was for a number of years involved in the readmission negotiations on behalf of DG JFS of the Commission.

13 Schieffer 2003, p. 350.

14 Schieffer 2003, p. 350; Kuijper 2004, p. 618-619.

15 Council Doc. 6658/99, 10 March 1999. Considering that Council Legal Service opinions are confidential documents, the analysis of this document is based largely on an outline published in Migration News Sheet 1999. See also Noll 2000, p. 207-208.

16 As noted above, the Member States were negotiating this third pillar instrument within the Council at the time of the entry into force of the ToA. The interim result was transferred to the first pillar with the advent of Community competence, where negotiations continued under the heading of a standard Community readmission agreement, *supra*, section 1.4, at n. 89, 94.

for one or more Member States alone to continue to conclude such agreements with third countries, on account of the potential resulting distortions for other Member States in the context of an area without internal border controls; [Italics added, NC]

2. whether or not there are any internal Community rules on repatriation which might be affected by a Member State's conclusion of a readmission agreement with a third country.[17]

The first criterion is presumably based on *Opinion 1/94*,[18] in which the ECJ determined that the conclusion of an agreement with third countries concerning the establishment and access to service markets of third country nationals (GATS) was not subject to exclusive Community competence, while not "*inextricably linked*" to the attainment of the Community objectives of freedom of establishment and the freedom to provide services for EU nationals.[19] The second criterion is based on the *ERTA* ruling,[20] in which the ECJ interpreted the concept of exclusive competence as meaning that whenever the Community acts to implement a common policy under the Treaty, the Member States no longer have the right to take external action which would affect that common policy.[21]

With regard to the first criterion, we refer to our earlier discussion of possible distortions within the internal market resulting from individual Member State readmission policies in light of the free movement of persons, which the LS hereby left to the Council to assess.[22] Regarding the second criterion, we should firstly note that, despite using the phrase "internal Community rules on *repatriation*" [Italics added], the LS must have been referring to EC rules on the readmission of third country nationals, not nationals, between the Member States. In this context, the LS reviewed Article 23 of the 1990 Schengen Convention, considering that the Treaty of Amsterdam had incorporated this particular element of the Schengen acquis into Community law.[23] Article 23(2) SC requires aliens who have a title to residence in one of the Schengen States to enter the territory of that State, implying a corresponding obligation to readmit. Paragraphs 3 and 4 of Article 23 concern the expulsion of unauthorised immigrants within the Schengen area to non-Schengen States, referring explicitly to the use of readmission agreements by the Schengen States. The LS rightly did not see any friction between these provisions and Member States' bilateral readmission agreements.

Not yet on the books at the time was the Initiative of the Republic of Finland with a view to the adoption of a Council Regulation determining obligations between

17 Migration News Sheet 1999, p. 1.

18 *Opinion 1/94,* [1994] ECR I-5267.

19 *Opinion 1/94*, [1994] ECR I-5267, para. XV.

20 Case 22/70, *Commission v. Council* (ERTA) [1971] ECR 263.

21 Craig and De Búrca 1998, Second Edition, p. 116.

22 *Supra*, subsection 3.1.1, at n. 13-14.

23 Migration News Sheet 1999, p. 1.

the Member States for the readmission of third country nationals.[24] This regulation, which was never adopted, would arguably not have been affected by the conclusion of bilateral Member State readmission agreements. Member State agreements would rather have been complementary instruments, given that the purpose of the regulation was to determine the Member State responsible for expulsion to a third country. Similarly, the Community had not yet acted upon Article 63(1)(a) concerning criteria and mechanisms for determining which Member State is responsible for considering an application for asylum submitted by a national of a third country in one of the Member States. At the time, the 1990 Dublin Convention did not conflict with bilateral Member State agreements, considering that Article 3(5) DC explicitly allowed for expulsion to third countries. The same provision was later included in the Dublin Regulation.[25] In sum, internal Community rules on readmission that might be affected by Member State readmission agreements with third countries were (and are still) not present. The nature of the Community's competence therefore depended entirely on the Council's assessment of the first criterion, which was taken up by the JHA Council meeting in May 1999.

The relevant part of the JHA Council conclusions of May 1999 reads as follows:

> The Community objectives in the field of immigration policy include the repatriation of persons residing unlawfully in a Member State (Article 63(3) of the EC Treaty). Readmission agreements constitute a valuable instrument of an active expulsion policy. The Council will in suitable cases authorise the Commission to conduct negotiations with third States on readmission agreements.
>
> Community agreements are not, generally speaking, *indissolubly linked* with the achievement of the Community objective of "repatriation of illegal residents". Whether this is so must be assessed in each individual case. This also applies to the question of whether distortions can arise for other Member States through a Member State's bilateral readmission agreement with a third State. [...] The Community's responsibility is therefore not exclusive.[26] [Italics added, NC]

The Council made sure to link Community readmission agreements to the Community objective of repatriation, sufficiently to safeguard a legal basis in Article 63(3)(b), but not to the degree of resulting in exclusive competence. In the political assessment of the Council, the link between Community readmission agreements and the objective

24 *OJ* C 353, 7.12.1999, p. 6, *supra*, section 1.4, at n. 90-93.

25 Article 3(3) of the Regulation 343/2003 of 18 February 2003 establishing the criteria and mechanisms for determining the Member State responsible for examining an asylum application lodged in one of the Member States by a third-country national, *OJ* L 50, 25.2.2003, p. 1.

26 Justice and Home Affairs Council meeting of 27-28 May 1999, Conclusions on "re-admission agreements – consequences of the entry into force of the Amsterdam Treaty", Press release 168 – Nr: 8654/99.

of repatriation of unauthorised immigrants was in general not considered "indissoluble", and the competence to conclude readmission agreements therefore shared. The Member States hereby retained the right to conclude agreements with third countries on a bilateral basis, implicitly accepting, as noted in subsection 3.1.1, the risk of distortions within the internal market in light of the free movement of persons.

Rather puzzling is the Council's apparent differentiation between individual cases, suggesting that readmission agreements with some third countries may be indissolubly linked with the objective of repatriation, requiring an exclusively common approach, whereas others are not, allowing individual Member State action. Given the free movement of persons, however, the Community and individual Member States would arguably have a relevant interest in every Community- or Member State readmission agreement concluded with a third country.[27] It is unclear what possible criteria for differentiation the Council had in mind here.

The limited progress thus far in the negotiations of Community readmission agreements[28] makes it unlikely that the Commission would challenge the Council's assessment, and assert exclusive competence before the ECJ, at least for the time being. Should such a challenge ever arise, the literature proposes different views as to its possible outcome. Peers and Rogers have argued in favour of a shared competence, citing ERTA and several ECJ opinions.[29] Schieffer, a Commission official involved in the negotiation of Community readmission agreements, estimates that the Court would lean towards exclusive competence.[30] Kuijper is a fervent proponent of exclusive competence.[31]

As noted above, Kuijper appeals in particular to the necessity of readmission agreements for achieving Community objectives in area of repatriation of unauthorised residents.[32] Although securing the cooperation of third countries is indeed essential for the successful implementation of expulsion, it was argued in subsection 3.2.1 that the purported necessity of readmission agreements in this regard is subject to debate. Kuijper's case for exclusivity is in other words based on a questionable empirical assumption.

An arguably stronger argument in favour of exclusivity is provided by the free movement of persons within the internal market and Schengen area.[33] In an area without internal border controls individual Member State readmission policies may be circumvented by secondary movements of unauthorised immigrants to another Member State. The Council in May 1999 made a political assessment of the risk of such dis-

27 *Supra*, subsection 3.1.1.

28 *Infra*, section 7.2.

29 Peers and Rogers 2006.

30 See Schieffer, citing case C-466/98, Commission v. UK [2002] ECR I-09427 in the field of civil aviation, Schieffer 2003, p. 351.

31 Kuijper 2004, p. 617-619.

32 *Supra*, n. 12.

33 *Supra*, subsection 3.1.1.

tortions if Member States continue to conclude readmission agreements with third countries, and decided this risk was acceptable. A (legal) assessment by the Court on this point might have a different outcome. Until the Court is solicited to decide this point, however, the Community's competence in the area of readmission will in practice remain shared.

### 4.3 The principle of subsidiarity

The previous section determined that the *status quo* in the competence debate in the area of readmission is that the Community's competence to conclude readmission agreements with third countries is not exclusive. Even though usually related to internal policies, and not to external EU action, it is arguably necessary to establish whether the Community's competence in the area of readmission complies with the principle of subsidiarity of Article 5 TEC:

> [...] In areas which do not fall within its exclusive competence, the Community shall take action, in accordance with the principle of subsidiarity, only if and in so far as the objectives of the proposed action cannot be sufficiently achieved by the Member States and can therefore, by reason of the scale or effects of the proposed action, be better achieved by the Community. [...]

With regard to "the objectives of the proposed action", the common readmission policy arguably has several different objectives, as discussed in chapter 3. The general objective of the common readmission policy, relevant here, is to facilitate the readmission of third country nationals, who are present without a residence title in one of the Member States, to third countries. The question is whether this objective is "better achieved by the Community", considering the motivation of the Member States to conclude readmission agreements at the Community level, as opposed to the Member State level.

Section 3.1 demonstrated that the Community competence to conclude readmission agreements was not conceived with the free movement of persons in mind. The principal motivation of the Member States for transferring competence to the Community in the area of readmission was to gain more resources and bargaining power, enabling the conclusion of more, and more favourable readmission agreements. Arguably, compliance with the principle of subsidiarity must therefore be assessed in this light.

A suitable yardstick for this assessment is the main problems that States experience in practice in the readmission of migrants. As an authoritative source, the UNHCR has summarised these problems as follows:

1 Logistical problems in enforcing returns, including transit through third countries
2 Disappearance/failure to report of the persons concerned
3 Bureaucratic delays
4 Lack of financial resources to cover the return travel
5 Non-issuance of travel documents by the country of origin

6 Staggering of returns required by the country of origin
7 Denial or non-recognition of citizenship
8 Inadequate reception/re-integration facilities in the country of origin.[34]

Readmission agreements generally attempt to alleviate problems 1, 3, 5, 6, and 7, which is also true for Community readmission agreements.[35] Under complementary actions, Community resources are used to finance returns[36] and stimulate reception and reintegration in third countries,[37] thus alleviating obstacles 4 and 8. In other words, expanding the amount of resources and negotiating power, dedicated to the conclusion of readmission agreements and related measures, potentially addresses the majority of return problems as listed here. Based on this assessment *a priori*, the common readmission policy arguably complies with the principle of subsidiarity. After assessing the actual results of negotiating readmission agreements at the Community level in section 7.2, we will briefly revisit the issue of subsidiarity.

## 4.4 The rules governing the sharing of competence

Since the entry into force of the ToA, the EC institutions and the Member States have in practice acted upon a shared competence to conclude readmission agreements with third countries. A number of rules exist which govern this sharing of competence between the Community and the Member States. These rules may be derived from the opinion of the Legal Service of the Council, and the JHA Council meeting of May 1999, cited in the section 4.2.

In considering the consequences of the entry into force of the ToA, the Council LS argues that the Member States are no longer allowed to collectively conclude a readmission agreement with a third country. Doing so would circumvent the EC Treaty, in particular Article 300 thereof.[38] Article 300 TEC lays down the general procedure by which the EC institutions conclude Community agreements with third countries, to which also Community readmission agreements are subject. Article 300 TEC *inter alia* requires a Commission recommendation for a negotiating directive which is adopted by the Council, the appointment of a committee to supervise the negotiations, which are conducted by the Commission, and consultation of the EP. Conclusion of a readmission agreement between the collective Member States and a third country, instead of a Community agreement, would circumvent these requirements. It is arguable that such a course of action would be contrary to the duty of sincere cooperation of Article 10 TEC.[39]

34 UNHCR 2001a.

35 For a detailed content of Community readmission agreements, see *infra*, section 5.3.

36 "Framework Preparatory Action on Return", Council Doc. 6144/04, 10 February 2004; see also the website of the Irish Presidency: www.eu2004.ie.

37 *Infra*, subsection 6.2.1 and 6.2.2.

38 Migration News Sheet 1999, p. 1.

39 Schieffer 2003, p. 350-351.

The implications of this finding are arguably limited, while the conclusion of readmission agreements by the collective Member States is not very common. The only example to date is the 1991 readmission agreement concluded between the collective Schengen States and Poland. This agreement, concluded outside the Community context, was left unaffected by the entry into force of the ToA. The Member States had begun to show an interest in concluding more agreements collectively, illustrated by the development of a standard reference text for an agreement on readmission between the collective Member States and a third country.[40] With the advent of first pillar competence, however, this third pillar instrument was simply abandoned.

It should be emphasised that the conclusion of readmission agreements with third countries by a subgroup of Member States has remained compatible with the TEC. Readmission policies of subgroups of EC Member States are more common. The Benelux States have had a common readmission policy since the early sixties. More recently, the group of Member States constituting the so-called "G5" – Italy, France, Germany, Spain, and the UK – expressed discontent with the progress of readmission negotiations at the EC level, and an intent to therefore jointly conclude readmission agreements with third countries of mutual interest.[41] Such action, though politically controversial, would not in of itself imply a conflict with EC law.

The JHA Council meeting of May 1999 agreed on a series of further rules governing the continued conclusion of readmission agreements by the Member States. We already touched upon one of these in the previous subsection. The JHA Council determined that the question of an "indissoluble link" with the objective of repatriation, and the question of whether distortions can arise for other Member States through a Member State's bilateral agreement with a third country, must be assessed on a case-by-case basis.[42] This would arguably imply a requirement to notify the Council before concluding a bilateral agreement with a third country, enabling it to undertake that assessment. To the knowledge of the present author, such a procedure was never consistently implemented. A possible reason for the Council's lack of enforcement of this requirement is its unclear underpinning. We noted earlier that it is difficult to discern a reason for differentiation between readmission agreements concluded with third countries.[43] Nevertheless, notification of the Council is arguably a formal requirement to which the Member States should adhere.

The JHA Council conclusions of May 1999 furthermore include the following passage:

---

40 *Supra*, section 1.4, n. 89, 94.

41 Statements at subsequent meetings of the G5 in La Baule and Garmisch-Partenkirchen, see the press reports "Die Runde der Fünf, Die großen EU-Mitglieder koordinieren ihre innere Sicherheit", *Frankfurter Algemeine Zeitung*, 22 October 2003; "Absprachen der großen Fünf", *Frankfurter Algemeine Zeitung*, 18 February 2004.

42 *Supra*, section 4.2, at. n. 26.

43 *Supra*, section 4.2, at n. 27.

> A Member State can continue to conclude readmission agreements with third States provided that the Community has not concluded an agreement with the third State concerned or has not concluded a mandate for negotiating such an agreement. In individual cases Member States may also conclude bilateral agreements after the conclusion of a Community agreement or after the opening of negotiations, for instance where the Community agreement or the negotiating mandate contains only general statements on readmission but one or more Member States require more detailed arrangements on the matter. The Member States may no longer conclude agreements if these might be detrimental to existing Community agreements.

One can identify three further rules in this passage. The first concerns a general condition relating to shared competence and the conclusion of agreements with third countries. A Member State may only conclude a readmission agreement with a third country insofar as the Community has not yet exercised its power to do so. From the moment the Council adopts a negotiating directive concerning a readmission agreement with a particular third country, readmission relations with that third country may be considered "communitarised". In conformity with the duty of sincere cooperation under Article 10 TEC, the Member States are from that moment required to refrain from or cease any ongoing negotiations.[44] Shared competence leaves space for the Member States, only regarding third countries with which the Commission is not or not yet in the process of establishing readmission relations on behalf of the Community.

The Council immediately established an exception in this regard, which may be considered as the second rule contained in the above passage. The Council found that the Member States may establish more detailed arrangements, if so required, for instance in case the Community agreement or the negotiating mandate would contain only general statements on readmission. The content of Community readmission agreements, as well as the negotiating directives adopted by the Council, is very detailed. Nevertheless, in translation of this rule, Community readmission agreements provide explicitly for the possibility of the conclusion of separate implementing Protocols between the Member States and the third country in question.[45] These protocols arrange details such as the designation of authorities responsible for receiving and submitting readmission requests, and border crossing points for the physical transfer of readmittees.

Finally, the Council determined that the Member States may not conclude readmission agreements insofar as these might be detrimental to existing Community agreements. This is once again a translation of the duty of sincere cooperation of the Member States under Article 10 TEC. The Council did not elaborate on the meaning of "detrimental", which appears open to broad interpretation. Moreover, the term "existing Community agreements" should arguably also be read broadly, including Community agreements that are still under negotiation in addition to already concluded agreements. A Member State should therefore refrain from negotiation or conclusion of readmission agreements with third countries, which might be detrimental to the

44 Schieffer 2003, p. 350.

45 *Infra*, subsection 5.3.11.

implementation of a Community readmission agreement, or to readmission negotiations conducted at the EC level.

In summary of the above, we can list five rules to which the Member States must adhere in their continued conclusion of readmission agreements with third countries after the entry into force of the Treaty of Amsterdam:

1. The Member States collectively may not conclude readmission agreements with third countries;
2. A Member State must notify the Council of its intention to negotiate a readmission agreement with a third country;
3. A Member State may negotiate or conclude a readmission agreement with a third country only insofar as the Council has not (yet) adopted a negotiating directive for a Community agreement concerning that country;
4. Regarding third countries for which the Council has adopted a negotiating directive for a Community readmission agreement, a Member State may exceptionally conclude an agreement containing more detailed arrangements, if required;
5. A Member State may not negotiate or conclude a readmission agreement in case this might be detrimental to the implementation of a Community agreement, or to readmission negotiations conducted at the EC level.

These rules divide between the Community and the Member States the competence to conclude readmission agreements with third countries. It would however appear that neither party is satisfied with this division. The above rules endorse shared competence in the area of readmission, where the Commission has aspired to exclusive Community competence. Although this *status quo* clearly retains power at the national level, it appears insufficient to meet the needs of the Member States. Individual Member States have tested, and even directly challenged the above rules in the negotiation or conclusion of readmission agreements of their own with third countries.[46] Whether such challenges merit an infringement procedure is debatable. However, should the Commission decide to bring the latent competence debate before the ECJ, it is likely to do so in an infringement procedure against a Member State defying the above rules.

## 4.5 Conclusion

This chapter confirmed that Article 63(3)(b) provides an implicit legal basis for the conclusion of Community readmission agreements. Insofar as providing for return to transit countries beyond the ordinary meaning of the term "repatriation", referred to in Article 63(3)(b), it was argued that Community readmission agreements should be considered as "measures [...] in the area of illegal immigration and illegal residence". In this interpretation, Article 63(3)(b) covers the full personal scope of Community readmission agreements.

This chapter furthermore discussed the controversy over the Community's competence in the area of readmission, outlining the disagreement between the Commission, Council, and the Member States on whether this competence is exclusive or shared. It

46 These cases are discussed below, *infra*, subsection 7.3.6.

was noted that since the entry into force of the Treaty of Amsterdam, the Community competence to conclude readmission agreements with third countries has in practice been shared, although the debate is still formally undecided.

Given this *status quo*, it was considered whether this competence is in accordance with the principle of subsidiarity. Considering the motivation for having a *common* readmission policy as discussed in chapter 3, it was argued that as a matter *a priori* the conclusion of readmission agreements by the Community complies with the principle of subsidiarity. The issue of subsidiarity will be revisited below in chapter 7, after an assessment of the actual results of the readmission negotiations at the EC level thus far.

Finally, this chapter formulated a set of five rules, which have in practice governed the division of competence in the area of readmission between the Community and the Member States. These rules will serve as the basis for a discussion in chapter 7 of several cases of infringement of these rules by the Member States.

# Chapter 5 The content of Community readmission agreements

This chapter analyses the content of Community readmission agreements with third countries, as well as several procedural and institutional factors which are relevant to this content. Section 5.1 describes how the EC institutions and the Member States jointly determine the content of the draft text of the agreements, based on which the Commission negotiates with third countries. Section 5.2 highlights an internal debate within the Commission concerning the Community's responsibility for persons, who are readmitted to third countries. Proposals to include certain safeguards in this respect in the text of Community readmission agreements were eventually discarded. Section 5.3, finally, provides an annotated outline of the technical content of Community readmission agreements.

## 5.1 Negotiating directives and the informal standard draft agreement

The content of Community readmission agreements is to a large degree determined by the negotiating directives of the Council, and by an informal standard draft agreement, which was adopted within the framework of the Council after the entry into force of the Treaty of Amsterdam.

Following a recommendation from the Commission, the Council adopts decisions authorising the Commission to negotiate a Community readmission agreement with a particular third country.[1] These negotiating directives, or negotiating mandates, are not published. The directives in question prescribe in considerable detail the substantive elements that must be included in the agreement. This delimits the Commission's flexibility to compromise on the technical content of the agreement during negotiations. The Council's directives may also authorise the Commission to offer a third country a specific incentive, providing negotiating leverage. The negotiating directives follow a uniform format and use almost identical wording. Their content has remained largely unchanged since the Commission received the first directives after the entry into force of the Treaty of Amsterdam. Community readmission agreements are thus constructed around a set of detailed generic elements that is basically identical.

1 Article 300 TEC.

In the negotiation of Community readmission agreements, the Commission makes use of an informal standard draft agreement. This draft text is not published, either, and is continuously modified in accordance with ongoing readmission negotiations. The initial standard text for a Community readmission agreement was developed within the context of the Council in the course of 2000, based on a proposal by the Commission.[2] After its completion, the Commission formally transmitted identical draft agreements to the first set of targeted countries through diplomatic channels in April 2001. Every transmission of a draft readmission agreement includes a request to enter into negotiations, and an informal document – a so-called "non-paper" – outlining and explaining the main purpose and elements of the agreement.

The Commission takes a standardised approach to the negotiation and conclusion of Community readmission agreements with third countries. To the extent possible given the volatile nature of negotiations, the Commission attempts to ensure homogeneity between agreements concluded with different countries. An important element of this approach is the continuous modification of the informal standard draft agreement by the Commission in cooperation with the Member States. The Commission holds periodic informal meetings with Member State experts during which all parties may suggest amendments to the standard text. Such amendments mostly result from negotiations with a particular third country. In case the negotiation of an individual agreement requires a substantial amendment, the Commission will first seek the approval of the Member States. Whenever considered beneficial to the general position of the Community, the same amendment will be inserted into ongoing negotiations with other countries, and into the standard draft agreement. In this manner, negotiations with new countries start on the basis of the most recently modified text. The standard draft text is however also a flexible instrument, meaning that provisions may be added or left out to fit a particular country and the type of problems it poses. It should be borne in mind that the informal standard draft agreement is unilateral. It represents the content which the Community attempts to persuade third countries to accept, forming the starting point of negotiations.

In addition to aiming for homogeneity between agreements and optimising negotiation results, this informal drafting process between the Commission and the Member States fulfils several further functions. It has firstly allowed the Commission to tap into the experience of the Member States in concluding readmission agreements. When Community competence in this field was established (in 1999), Commission officials largely lacked the necessary technical expertise to conclude readmission agreements, and Member State experts were a valuable resource in this regard. Secondly, these meetings serve a distinctly political purpose. On the part of the Commission, they provide a forum for seeking support for its readmission negotiations. The Commission requires approval of particular negotiation strategies or incentives from higher political levels within the Council, in particular from the Migration/Expulsion Working Group,[3]

2 Council Doc. 10338/3/1998; *supra*, section 1.4, at n. 89, 94.

3 In October 2002, the Migration-Expulsion working group was appointed as the consultative body within the Council, guiding the Commission in the negotiation of readmission

which refers to the SCIFA or Coreper in case of a lack of consensus. The meetings with Member State experts allow the Commission to insert issues at the working level, and rally support from the bottom up. On the part of the Member States, these meetings enable a degree of control over the content of Community readmission agreements, as well as their negotiation, throughout the entire process.

## 5.2 Discarded content – Community responsibility for readmittees

The involvement of the Community in the readmission of immigrants to third countries sparked an internal debate within the Commission concerning the responsibility for readmittees, that is, the fate of readmitted persons once they have left the territory of the EU. In this section, we briefly outline this debate between, in particular, the Directorate Generals of Justice, Freedom and Security[4] (JFS) and External Relations (RELEX).

The introduction of first pillar competence required determining which Commission service would be responsible for the negotiation of readmission agreements. The choice was between DG JFS and DG RELEX. The readmission of unauthorised immigrants falls within the general policy domain of DG JFS, which is where the technical expertise concerning readmission agreements is present. DG RELEX controls the EU's diplomatic contacts with and has diplomatic representations in third countries. DG RELEX also has a larger budget than DG JFS, which is relevant in terms of the travel expenses which negotiations require. A compromise was reached making seemingly optimal use of the resources of both DGs. DG RELEX was appointed *chef de file*. The geographical desk of DG RELEX, relevant to the third country with which negotiations are taking place, therefore heads the Commission delegation that prepares and conducts those negotiations. An official of DG JFS contributes the required technical expertise to this delegation.[5]

The collaboration between DG JFS and DG RELEX revealed strongly diverging views concerning the Community's involvement in the readmission of unauthorised immigrants. DG JFS has a political and pragmatic approach to the development of the common readmission policy, which concentrates on fulfilling the Council's negotiating directives as swiftly and effectively as possible. In the view of DG JFS, the common readmission policy should concentrate on reaching agreement with third countries on a technical level, and on attaining sufficient political and substantive negotiating leverage to complete negotiations. In the view of DG RELEX, however, the development of a common readmission policy should also include responsibility for the treatment of readmittees. At the onset of European Community competence in the area of readmission, DG RELEX initiated an internal debate between the affected Commission services. It advocated *inter alia* the incorporation of fundamental rights guarantees, safeguards for the implementation of return in a humane fashion, and a system for

agreements with third countries, Council Doc. 13609/02, 29 October 2002.

4 DG Justice and Home Affairs changed its name to DG Justice, Freedom and Security in November 2004.

5 Schieffer 2003, p. 352.

post-return monitoring of readmittees. In this context, DG RELEX also made proposals regarding the content of Community readmission agreements, none of which survived inter-service consultations and which were thus never included.

DG RELEX had suggested including a general reference to the essential importance of democratic principles, respect for human rights, and the rule of law in the text of the (informal) standard draft Community readmission agreement. Secondly, where applicable, it had proposed including a reference to a human rights clause in a partnership, cooperation or equivalent agreement with the third country concerned. It is unclear whether the latter reference would have implied the possibility of suspension of a Community readmission agreement in case of human rights violations, or a lack of respect for democratic principles or the rule of law in the third country. Whether intended as such, or merely as a political statement, referring to a human rights clause in a readmission agreement would have been partially out of place. Human rights clauses are generally included in agreements that are beneficial to third countries, while exercising a potentially preventative effect only if a third country has something to lose. Inserting a human rights clause, or a reference of similar effect, into a readmission agreement would be inconsequential from this perspective, as suspension would not disadvantage the third country. However, it would have provided the Council with the possibility to suspend the agreement in light of situations affecting the safety of return. A provision for the suspension of a Community readmission agreement is currently not included in the standard text, which only offers the possibility of termination (on unspecified grounds).[6]

We should note that the general view of DG RELEX concerning the common readmission policy is supported by the European Parliament. Considering the procedure of Article 300 TEC, the first occasion for the EP to comment on the development of the common readmission policy was in a report on the signing of the first Community readmission agreement with Hong Kong.[7] The EP addressed the Council and Commission in the following way:

> The Union and the Member States must base their policies on respect for fundamental rights, and this applies in particular to binding measures concerning the movement of persons, such as those governing voluntary or forced repatriation to countries of origin. How do the Commission and the Council intend to ascertain that these rights are respected in the event of repatriation, especially on a massive scale? What joint monitoring mechanisms are to be set up with the countries with which readmission agreements or clauses have been negotiated? What criteria are applied to ascertain whether a country to which it has been decided to repatriate one or more people is "safe"?[8]

6 *Infra*, subsection 5.3.14.

7 European Parliament, session document A5-0381/2002 final.

8 European Parliament, session document A5-0381/2002 final, p. 9.

Curiously, the Commission initially appeared to be more sensitive towards potential implications in the fundamental rights context. The 2001 Commission Communication on illegal immigration reflected concerns in this regard, and proposed a relatively tentative approach to the readmission of unauthorised immigrants.[9] In particular, the Commission stated that before deciding to negotiate a readmission agreement, the political- and human rights situation in the targeted third country should be taken into account. It also called for evaluation and assessment of the implementation of the first readmission agreements.[10] Assurances of this kind were not repeated in further policy documents of the Commission in the field.[11]

This apparent change in the position of the Commission might be explained firstly by the fact that the Council did not endorse a fundamental rights-oriented approach to the common readmission policy.[12] Secondly, the Commission was unable to agree internally on the responsibility of the Community for readmittees, and the related assurances contained in the 2001 Communication. DG JFS, in particular, regarded a Community-funded system of post-return monitoring as inoperable and unfeasible, considering that the Member States generally do not systematically monitor persons and their well-being after return due to the practical difficulties and high costs thereof. In line with its general view regarding the common readmission policy described above, DG JFS would rather emphasise the quality of the investigation of conditions in a third country before expulsion.

Outside pressure to achieve more progress in the negotiations of Community readmission agreements finally decided the debate between Commission services in favour of DG JFS. Several concerned Member States issued a warning during the JHA Council meeting of 2 and 3 October 2003 in Rome, threatening to withdraw the negotiating directives if the Commission would not achieve a higher success rate. The "G5" also issued statements to this effect at a meeting in La Baule during the same period.[13] The fact that the Commission was being held politically accountable for a lack of negotiation results seemed to unite the Commission services sufficiently to adopt a political and pragmatic approach to the development of the common readmission policy.

## 5.3 Annotated content of Community readmission agreements

Notwithstanding the use of a standard draft agreement, actual negotiations obviously lead to differences in the content of Community readmission agreements, depending on the third country. The negotiation of Community readmission agreements has thus far been difficult.[14] Difficult negotiations generally lead to a larger degree of variation

9 Peers 2004, p. 207.

10 COM(2001) 672 final, p. 50.

11 Peers 2004, p. 208.

12 As illustrated by the subsequent Proposal for a comprehensive plan to combat illegal immigration and trafficking of human beings in the European Union, *OJ* C 142, 14 June 2002.

13 Frankfurter Algemeine Zeitung 2003.

14 COM(2002) 175 final, p. 23; COM(2002) 564 final, p. 24; COM(2002) 703 final, p. 25.

in wording and substance between agreements. Nevertheless, Community readmission agreements are still rather homogeneous, sufficiently so to discuss their content generally without too much need for specification by agreement.

The annotated outline in this chapter is based on the texts of four Community readmission agreements with Albania,[15] Hong Kong,[16] Macao,[17] and Sri Lanka.[18] Given the continuous modification of the standard text according to developments in the negotiations, the outline in this section of the general content of Community readmission agreements is based primarily on the most recently concluded agreement in this list, which is the agreement with Albania. Differences in content with other agreements will be indicated only where relevant. The numbering of articles is also based on the agreement with Albania. The text of this agreement has been included in Annex 1.

Besides the Preamble and a first article on definitions, Community readmission agreements are divided into eight numbered and titled sections. Section I contains the readmission obligations of the third country. Section II lays down the readmission obligations of the Community.[19] Section III contains the readmission procedure. Section IV concerns transit operations for the purpose of return to a further country. Section V is on costs. Section VI is titled "data protection and non-affection clause". Section VII regards the "implementation and application" of the agreement. Section VIII contains final provisions. Each agreement also has a number of standard annexes and joint declarations attached to it.

### *5.3.1 Preamble*

The Preamble of Community readmission agreements with third countries explains the objective of the agreement, stating that its general objective is to strengthen cooperation in order to combat illegal immigration more effectively. Its specific objective is

15 For the final text of this agreement, see *Agreement between the European Community and the Republic of Albania on the readmission of persons residing without authorisation - Declarations*, *OJ* L 124, 17 May 2005, p. 22 (full text included in Annex 1).

16 *Agreement between the European Community and the Government of the Hong Kong Special Administrative Region of the People's Republic of China on the readmission of persons residing without authorisation*, *OJ* L 17, 24.1.2004, p. 25.

17 *Agreement between the European Community and the Government of the Macao Special Administrative Region of the People's Republic of China on the readmission of persons residing without authorisation*, *OJ* L 143, 30.4.2004, p. 99.

18 For the final text of this agreement, see *Agreement between the European Community and the Democratic Socialist Republic of Sri Lanka on the readmission of persons residing without authorisation - Declarations*, *OJ* L 124, 17 May 2005, p. 43. For a comparison between the text of the agreements with Hong Kong, Macao and Sri Lanka, see Peers and Rogers 2006.

19 The readmission agreements with Ukraine and Russia are constructed differently. These agreements include the reciprocal obligations of the contracting parties under the same section. Instead of referring to the obligations of the Community on the one hand, and the third country in question on the other, these agreements use the terms requesting and requested State.

to establish rapid and effective procedures for the identification and return of persons without a residence title, and the facilitation of transit for return purposes. The Preamble also states that the contracting parties wish to regulate readmission on the basis of reciprocity, and in a "spirit of cooperation".

### *5.3.2 Definitions*

Article 1 is a list of definitions of terms used throughout the agreement. Generally included are definitions of the terms "Member State", "national" regarding each of the contracting parties,[20] "third country national",[21] "stateless person", "visa", and "residence authorisation". Noteworthy is the latter definition of what constitutes a residence authorisation. We will see below that a residence authorisation issued by a contracting State is a factor establishing a readmission obligation. Article 1 explicitly excludes "temporary permissions to remain [...] in connection with the processing of an asylum application" from being considered as a residence authorisation under the terms of the agreement.[22] We can therefore deduce that the European Community has so far not succeeded in formally extending criteria for responsibility for protection seekers – akin to the current Dublin Regulation – to third countries.

### *5.3.3 Readmission of nationals and former nationals*

Section I, listing the readmission obligations of the third country,[23] determines in Article 2(1) that the requested State shall readmit its own nationals "without any formalities other than those provided for" in the agreement. Subject to readmission are unauthorised immigrants, in particular "all persons who do not, or who no longer, fulfil the conditions in force for entry to, presence in, or residence on, the territory of the requesting [...] State". The readmission obligation regarding nationals is conditional upon proof, or a valid assumption based on "prima facie evidence", of nationality (the meaning of these different categories of evidence will be explained further below).

The second sentence of Article 2(1) determines that the readmission of persons, commonly referred to as "former nationals",[24] will take place under the same terms

20 The agreements with Hong Kong and Macao, in light of their status as a Special Administrative Region of China, use the term "permanent resident" instead of "national".

21 The agreements with Hong Kong and Macao, in light of their status as a Special Administrative Region of China, use the term "person of another jurisdiction" instead of "third country national".

22 This is contrary to the negotiating directives of the Council, which instruct the Commission to make provision for including asylum applications as such.

23 Considering that obligations under Community readmission agreements are reciprocal as well as for the sake of simplicity, we will use the terms requested and requesting State throughout this section, avoiding the need to continuously differentiate between the Community and the third country.

24 Defined by Article 2(1) as persons who have been deprived of, or who have renounced their nationality after entering the territory of the requesting State.

as nationals.[25] The obligation to readmit a former national is forfeited in case s/he has been naturalised, or promised naturalisation, by the requesting State.[26]

Article 2(2) obliges the requested State to issue a travel document to persons whose readmission it has accepted under Article 2(1), if so required for entering the territory of that State. The Commission always attempts obtain agreement on the use of the EU standard travel document for expulsion purposes[27] here, instead of a national document. If the third country does not agree with this, the EU standard travel document is generally included as a fall-back option. Should the requested State fail to issue a national travel document "without delay", meaning within a period of around 14 calendar days, it will then be deemed to accept the EU document.

### *5.3.4 Readmission of third country nationals and stateless persons*

Article 3(1) of Section I establishes an obligation to readmit third country nationals – persons who do not have the nationality of either of the contracting parties to the agreement – without any formalities other than those specified in the agreement. The readmission of stateless persons is equated with that of third country nationals under this provision. Subject to readmission are unauthorised immigrants, again defined as "all persons who do not, or who no longer, fulfil the conditions in force for entry to, presence in, or residence on, the territory of the requesting [...] State". The obligation to readmit is coupled with an obligation to issue a travel document for the purpose of entry[28] in the same fashion as described above.

The obligation to readmit third country nationals and stateless persons is conditional upon proof, or a valid assumption based on prima facie evidence, of the following. The requesting State must demonstrate that the unauthorised immigrant holds, or held at the time of entry into its territory, a visa or residence authorisation issued by the requested State; or, the requesting State must demonstrate that the unauthorised immigrant entered its territory after having stayed in, or transited through the territory of the requested State. The precise terms of the criterion of previous stay or transit vary between agreements. The standard article, however, specifies that entry into the requesting State must have been "unlawful".[29] At first sight, Community readmission agreements would therefore appear modelled upon the impractical evidence requirements of readmission agreements as concluded in the 1950s and 60s.[30] Further examination of the specific provisions on evidence below will however reveal that

25 *Supra*, section 2.3, at n. 108.

26 Exceptionally, a provision for the readmission of former nationals was not negotiated with Sri Lanka (SEC(2003) 255 final).

27 *OJ* C 274, 19 September 1996.

28 Article 3(3).

29 The agreements with Hong Kong, Macao, Sri Lanka and Russia, and the agreements under negotiation with Ukraine, Russia and Morocco, require an unlawful entry into the requesting State. The agreement with Albania, and the draft agreement with Pakistan, merely requires demonstration of entry, without specification.

30 *Supra*, subsection 1.2, at n. 29.

Community readmission agreements do not actually require evidence of an "unlawful" border crossing as such, and are therefore modelled on readmission agreements as concluded from the early nineties onwards.[31]

Regarding the technical terms of Article 3(1), the Commission is authorised by the Council to offer during the negotiations to limit the readmission obligation, based on a previous stay or transit, to so-called direct arrivals.[32] In case this limitation is incorporated in the text, a readmission obligation only exists regarding persons travelling directly from the requested to the requesting State. The agreement then pertains to third country nationals and stateless persons arriving directly from a third country bordering the EU, as well as from third countries further away in case of direct arrivals by air or by sea. Relevant in this regard is that Article 3(2)(a) determines that airside transit in a third country does not establish a readmission obligation. This is arguably an indication that a journey by air from the requested State, which includes one or several stopovers at airports in third countries, would still constitute a direct arrival.[33] The main consequence of a limitation to direct arrivals is thus that the agreement does not pertain to third country nationals and stateless persons arriving from a third country further away, who travelled by land.

Article 3(2) lists two exceptions to the obligation to readmit third country nationals and stateless persons. The first we just mentioned. The Commission is authorised to exempt "airside transit"[34] or "mere transit without entering"[35] in the requested State from the application of the agreement. The second exception occurs in case the requesting State has issued a visa or residence authorisation to an immigrant before or after entering its territory, unless s/he would be in possession of a visa or residence authorisation of the other contracting party with a longer period of validity.[36] This exception is remarkable while generally excluding visa overstayers from the application of the agreement, who account for a significant proportion of unauthorised immigrants in the

31 *Supra*, subsection 1.3, at n. 48, 49.

32 See, for example, Article 3(1)(b) of the agreements with Hong Kong, Macao and Sri Lanka.

33 This is further supported by the Community readmission agreement with Sri Lanka, which is the only agreement thus far specifying the meaning of a "direct" arrival. Article 3(1)(b) of this agreement states that a direct arrival concerns an arrival by air or ship "without having entered another country in-between". A joint declaration attached to the agreement states that "mere airside transit shall not be considered as having entered another country". As long as transit migrants did not formally enter the territory, therefore, a stopover at an airport in a third country would not preclude a "direct" arrival within the meaning of this agreement.

34 See Article 3(2)(a) of the agreements with Albania, Hong Kong and Sri Lanka.

35 See Article 3(2)(a) of the Macao agreement.

36 In other words, in case, for example, both a Member State and Albania have issued a visa or residence permit to the person involved, the document with the longer period of validity indicates which party is responsible.

EC.[37] In addition, the Commission always attempts to insert a second "unless" clause here, according to which the requested State remains responsible for readmission in case the visa or residence authorisation issued by the requesting State was obtained on the basis of forged or falsified documents.

Articles 4 (nationals and former nationals) and 5 (third country nationals and stateless persons) of Section II of Community readmission agreements list the readmission obligations of the European Community. Considering the reciprocal nature of the agreement, the obligations in sections I and II are identical, except for a specific set of criteria in section II determining the responsible Member State in case of readmission of a third country national or stateless person into the EC.[38]

### *5.3.5 Readmission procedure*

Section III of the agreement establishes different elements of the readmission procedure. Article 6 is entitled "principle", and ensures that the readmission of persons under the agreement is based on prior communication between the contracting parties. Article 7 determines the content of a formal readmission application. Articles 8 and 9 lay down the means of evidence with which the requesting State is able to demonstrate the existence of a readmission obligation on the part of the requested State. Article 10 lays down time limits. Article 11 arranges the physical transfer and transportation of persons who are readmitted under the agreement. Article 12 provides for readmission back to the requesting State in case of errors, also referred to as "re-readmission".

#### 5.3.5.1 Prior communication

Pursuant to Article 6(1), the readmission of a person under the agreement requires the prior submission of a "readmission application" to the competent authority of the requested State. The content of this readmission application is determined by Article 7 and a standard common form, which is annexed to the agreement. The requesting State must firstly provide "the particulars of the person", a non-exhaustive list of personal data including *inter alia* the name, surname, place and date of birth, sex and physical description, nationality and language, possible nicknames, aliases or pseudonyms, and the civil status of the readmittee. Secondly, the requesting State must indicate which means of evidence underpin the readmission application. Thirdly, the requesting State should provide information concerning the readmittee's state of health if calling for help or care during the transfer, provided s/he has explicitly consented to the communication thereof. Fourthly, the requesting State should indicate whether the readmittee is a "particularly dangerous person"[39] requiring protection or security measures, for example while suspected of a serious offence or while displaying aggressive behaviour.

---

37 COM(2004) 412, p. 10, 11.

38 See, for example, Article 5(3) of the Community readmission agreement with Albania.

39 See the common form for readmission applications, annex 5, point B(2).

It should be pointed out that providing the above data is subject to a considerable degree of discretion. The requested State is obliged to provide the information listed on the readmission application only "to the extent possible".[40] This implies *inter alia* that Community readmission agreements do not strictly require identification of a readmittee. In practice, a requested State could insist on identification and dispute whether the requesting State has attempted identification "to the extent possible" under the terms of the agreement. In principle, however, Community readmission agreements allow the readmission of a Mr or Ms "X", provided there is sufficient evidence of nationality, c.q. stay or transit.

If a readmittee possesses a valid travel document or a valid visa or residence authorisation of the requested State, the requirements concerning prior communication between the contracting parties are less strict. Article 6(2) determines that in such a case an informal "written communication" suffices, as long as submitted to the competent authority of the requested State within a reasonable period before the person is transferred. The standard text of this provision previously included an additional requirement, which was removed during the negotiations with Albania. In addition to possessing valid documentation, the person in question had to be "willing to return" before the requesting State could make use of this "lite" readmission procedure.[41] The deletion of this requirement enables the Member States to make use of this procedural option also in cases of forced return where sufficient documentation is available.

#### 5.3.5.2 Means of evidence

Articles 8 and 9 lay down the means of evidence of the conditions establishing readmission obligations under Articles 2 to 5. Article 8 concerns the means of evidence of nationality (or former nationality). Article 9 concerns the means of evidence regarding third country nationals and stateless persons.

The agreement distinguishes between two types of evidence. The first is "proof". Means of evidence constituting proof are accepted by the other contracting party as establishing a readmission obligation, without requiring further investigation or other formalities. The second is "prima facie evidence", which establishes a "valid assumption" of either nationality, or the conditions required for the readmission of third country nationals and stateless persons. Prima facie evidence, unlike proof, is rebuttable. The requested State will accept prima facie evidence as establishing the conditions of readmission under the agreement, unless it can prove otherwise.

Article 8 refers to two lists of documents annexed to the agreement. Annex 1 is a common list of documents constituting proof of nationality. Annex 2 is a list of documents constituting prima facie evidence of nationality. Article 9 also refers to two lists of means of evidence in annex. Annex 3 is a common list of documents constituting proof of the conditions for the readmission of third country nationals and stateless persons. Annex 4 is a common list of documents constituting prima facie evidence of the same. The agreement determines in general that false documents cannot act as

40 Article 7(1) and 7(2).

41 See Article 6(2)(b) of the agreements with Hong Kong, Macao and Sri Lanka.

evidence; documents, of which the period of validity has expired, however, generally can. The Commission of course will always attempt to negotiate as wide a list of means of evidence as possible. The standard lists have widened significantly since the start of the first negotiations.[42]

Annex 1 lists the means of proof of nationality, which are documents of an official nature. Included in the list are passports and identity cards of any kind, service books and military identity cards, seaman's registration books and skippers' service cards, citizenship certificates, and other official documents that mention or indicate citizenship. Annex 2, which lists the means of *prima facie* evidence of nationality, includes firstly photocopies of all the documents listed in Annex 1. It then adds driving licences, birth certificates, and company identity cards, as well as photocopies of any of these documents. Also constituting *prima facie* evidence are statements by witnesses, and statements by the readmittee as well as the language s/he speaks. The Commission always attempts to negotiate the inclusion of the catch-all phrase "any other documents which may help to establish the nationality of the person concerned".[43]

Annex 3, listing the means of proof of the conditions for the readmission of third country nationals and stateless persons, is especially elaborate. Included firstly is proof of entry into or departure from the requested State, such as entry/departure stamps in travel documents. The list then mentions documents, certificates, bills, and tickets of any kind, demonstrating that the person concerned has been present on or has travelled through the requested State. Named as examples in this regard are hotel bills, hospital bills, car rental contracts, credit card receipts, tickets for air, train, coach or boat passages, and evidence of the use of a courier or travel agency. Also included in the list of Annex 3 are official statements by border staff or other witnesses, who testify that the person in question crossed the border into the requesting State. (This particular means of evidence would thus pertain exclusively to neighbouring contracting States.) A final means of proof is any official statement made by the readmittee in judicial or administrative proceedings.

Annex 4, listing the means of prima facie evidence of the conditions for the readmission of third country nationals and stateless persons, is more limited. The list mentions firstly a description by State authorities of the place and circumstances of interception of the person concerned after entering the requesting State.[44] Like the testimony in relation to a border crossing listed in Annex 3, such evidence is again applicable only between neighbouring contracting States. Furthermore included as

42 The lists annexed to the agreements with Sri Lanka and Albania are wider than under the agreements with Hong Kong and Macao, the negotiation of which were completed at an earlier date.

43 See annex 2 of the agreement with Albania, last indent.

44 The Council recommendation of 24 July 1995 on the guiding principles to be followed in drawing up protocols on the implementation of re-admission agreements (*OJ* C 274, 19 September 1996, p. 25) explicitly suggests a separate and accelerated readmission procedure in the case of apprehension after a border crossing. Community readmission agreements have not followed this suggestion.

*prima facie* evidence is information relevant to establishing a readmission obligation provided by international organisations, family members, or travelling companions, and a (unofficial) statement by the readmittee.

Establishing these lists represents one of the primary aims of the agreement. They secure the acceptance by the requested State of a variety of means of evidence establishing a readmission obligation. Community readmission agreements hereby limit the opportunity for requested States as well as individual immigrants to prevent return for technical or practical reasons. It should however be emphasised that Community readmission agreements, and readmission agreements in general, cannot entirely eliminate return problems. Community readmission agreements do make provision for, but cannot guarantee the return of undocumented migrants who are unwilling to cooperate.

In the above lists, we can roughly distinguish three kinds of means of evidence: documents, other paper-based evidence such as bills, receipts and tickets, and oral evidence. Undocumented migrants (or their migration facilitators), who have already hidden or destroyed any travel and identity documents, can do the same with other paper-based evidence and thereby greatly frustrate application of the readmission agreement.

In such a case, readmission as a third country national or stateless person becomes dependent on a possible witnessing of a border crossing and/or interception at the border, the possibility of an international organisation providing relevant information, or the willingness of the readmittee, family members or travelling companions to confess to the travel route.

Readmission as a national or former national becomes dependent firstly on "witnesses" – one would assume again family members or travelling companions – or the readmittee himself confirming his or her nationality. In addition, language analysis may also be used to attempt to identify nationality, bearing in mind that language is an imprecise indicator of nationality and easily rebutted in some cases.[45] Thirdly, in the absence of any of the means of evidence listed in Annex 1 and Annex 2, Community readmission agreements make express provision in Article 8(3) for presenting a person to the diplomatic representation of the suspected State of nationality. The embassy or consulate will then arrange for an interview to establish nationality. This is the common State practice where a readmission agreement is not available. Except for a stipulation in Article 8(3) to make the necessary arrangements "without undue delay", the procedure for establishing nationality will be at the usual discretion of the requested State.

In other words, Community readmission agreements may be expected to limit but not eliminate return problems, while leaving opportunity for both immigrants and

45 Examples in this regard would be persons from border regions where the language or dialect spoken at either side of the border is the same or similar, or persons from ex-Soviet republics where Russian has remained the first language. We recall that language analysis constitutes *prima facie* evidence of nationality under the agreement, and is therefore rebuttable.

requested third countries to frustrate expulsion. Especially where immigrants have disposed of documents and other paper-based evidence and are unwilling to return, "problem" States will be able to continue withholding effective cooperation on readmission. In the implementation of Community readmission agreements, the goodwill of third countries will therefore remain an important factor. This implies that much will depend on the quality of relations of the Community and the Member States with third countries, as well as other incentives for cooperation.

A final observation concerns Article 9(3) on the meaning of an "unlawful" entry under the agreement. We noted above that the standard text of Community readmission agreements in Article 3(1) requires an unlawful entry in order to establish a readmission obligation for a third country national or stateless person.[46] This seems to suggest a dependency on evidence of time and place of an unauthorised border crossing; an evidence requirement which has generally rendered readmission agreements impracticable. Article 9(3), however, makes clear that evidence of a border crossing is not required for demonstrating entry. It states that the "unlawfulness" of entry, presence or residence may be established by the simple fact of the absence of a necessary visa or residence authorisation.[47] Akin to readmission agreements as generally concluded since the early nineties, Community readmission agreements thus equate unauthorised entry with an unauthorised presence or residence.[48] To establish an obligation to readmit a third country national or stateless person under the agreement, it suffices to demonstrate an unauthorised residence on the territory of the requesting State, together with a previous (authorised or unauthorised) stay on or transit through the requested State.

#### 5.3.5.3 Time limits

Article 10 sets a number of time limits for different elements of the readmission procedure. On the one hand, this provision intends to allow the requesting State sufficient time to submit a readmission request, ensuring the efficacy of the agreement.[49] On the other, it intends to limit the discretion of the requested State to impose lengthy bureaucratic procedures for readmission.

Article 10(1) determines that after detection of the unauthorised presence of a person, the requesting State has a maximum of one year to submit a readmission application. This time limit can be extended in case "legal or factual obstacles" prevent a timely application. The agreement does not give examples of such obstacles, nor demand that they be demonstrable.

---

46 *Supra*, subsection 5.3.4, n. 29.

47 The Commission during negotiations always attempt to include, as evidence of an unlawful entry, the *absence* of any travel documents in the possession of the person concerned. See the agreement with Macao, Article 9(3).

48 *Supra*, section 1.3, at n. 48-49.

49 Short time limits for requesting readmission limit the effective implementation of readmission agreements, Fernhout 1999, p. 86.

Article 10(2) requires a reply to the readmission application from the requested State "without undue delay". This means within a maximum of about 14 calendar days, starting with the date of receipt of the readmission application. The agreement fails to require the requested State to send an acknowledgement of receipt of the application, leaving a degree of imprecision here. Article 10(2) further determines that a refusal of a readmission application must be motivated. In addition, expiry of the time limit without a reply has legal effect; the physical transfer of the person to the requested State is then "deemed to have been agreed to". Due to this latter provision, the lack of an acknowledgement of receipt of a readmission application becomes potentially problematic. Means of communication being fallible – one imagines a readmission application would be transferred by fax, e-mail, registered- or courier post – the possibility is not excluded that a person would be transferred pursuant to a request that was never received.

Article 10(3), finally, sets a time limit for the physical transfer of the person concerned. After a positive reply to the readmission application (or expiry of the time limit for reply), transfer must take place "without undue delay". This means within three months, barring extension because of further "practical or legal obstacles".

#### 5.3.5.4 Transfer and transportation

Article 11(1) requires the contracting parties to make arrangements regarding the physical transfer of a readmittee, such as determining the date and place of transfer, and the possible need for escorts. Article 11(2) then determines that any means of transportation, meaning by land, air or sea, may be used for the purpose of transfer. Regarding return by air, it specifically forbids restriction to national carriers of the requesting or requested State, and mentions scheduled as well as charter flights as options. Regarding possible escorts, Article 11(2) allows the use of persons from the requested and requesting State, as well as any other Member State. It should be noted that these terms would permit the use of joint (charter) flights of the Member States pursuant to Decision 2004/573 of the Council.[50]

#### 5.3.5.5 Re-readmission

During the negotiations with Albania, a new Article 12[51] entitled "readmission in error" was added to the standard text of Community readmission agreements. This is also known as a re-readmission clause. Considering that readmission agreements are reciprocal, normally a contracting State would have to reverse the entire readmission procedure for persons it readmits in error. A re-readmission clause firstly provides an additional guarantee that the other party will take the person back, and secondly,

50 Council Decision 2004/573/EC of 29 April 2004 on the organisation of joint flights for removals from the territory of two or more Member States of third-country nationals who are subjects of individual removal orders, *OJ* L 261, 6 August 2004, p. 28.

51 The following numbering of articles is based solely on the agreement with Albania in which a new article 12 on re-readmission was inserted, *i.e.* is no longer in conformity with the numbering of articles in the agreements with Hong Kong, Macao and Sri Lanka.

greatly facilitates the reversal of readmission. Article 12 determines that, if within 3 months upon transfer of a person it becomes clear that the conditions for readmission were in fact not fulfilled, "re-readmission" will take place without delay.

Re-readmission clauses are beneficial to requested States. The Commission therefore uses the possible inclusion of this provision as a negotiating tool, a concession regarding the technical terms of the agreement. Re-readmission clauses however are also an additional safeguard against immigrants "in orbit". "In orbit" refers to the shuttling back and forth of undocumented immigrants between States, each denying responsibility and refusing (re)admission. "In orbit" situations in the past have generally resulted from unilateral acts of removal without the consent of the receiving State. We noted previously that this is ultimately damaging to international relations as well as to the rights of the persons concerned.[52] Readmission agreements mitigate the risk of immigrants ending up in orbit by establishing a procedure, requiring a readmission application and a reply by the requested State. Formal implementation of this procedure should flush out most mishaps (such as miscommunications, procedural errors, or disagreement over evidence between the contracting parties) before the actual transfer of a readmittee, thus precluding the possibility of "in orbit" situations. A re-readmission clause is an additional guarantee against the possibility of ending up in orbit while repairing procedural errors that would come to light after transfer.

Re-readmission clauses are not a new instrument. The Benelux States, for example, already included such a clause in the provisions on readmission in Decision M/P (67) 1.[53] An additional example may be drawn from Dutch readmission practice. The Netherlands presently apply re-readmission clauses, although on an informal basis. In subsection 3.2.1, we noted an informal practice regarding readmission between the Netherlands on the hand, and Bulgaria and Rumania on the other. The Dutch authorities periodically round up groups of persons of suspected Bulgarian and Rumanian nationality, resident without authorisation, which they return by charter flight to Bulgaria and Rumania, respectively.[54] The Bulgarian and Rumanian authorities then take responsibility for establishing identity and nationality of the readmittees. Bulgaria and Rumania accept this particular procedure, which is not in accordance with the procedure established by the readmission agreements between the Netherlands and these countries, because the Netherlands guarantees to take back any person who turns out not to have the Bulgarian or Rumanian nationality. The Netherlands explicitly offers such re-readmission guarantees to facilitate the establishment of informal cooperation on readmission. It should be noted that a Community readmission agreement, which provides a formal re-readmission clause, takes away the negotiating value of informal re-readmission guarantees offered by individual Member States.

52 *Supra*, chapter 1, at n. 7-8, 27 Regarding specific implications in relation to fundamental rights, see *infra*, subsection 9.2.3.3.2.

53 "Beschikking M/P (67) 1 van de Ministeriële Werkgroep voor het personenverkeer betreffende de verwijdering en de overname van personen", 28 July 1967, *Trb.* 1978, 171; see also Denoël 1993, p. 639.

54 Interview IND, 16 April 2003.

### 5.3.6 *Transit for return purposes*

Section IV of the agreement concerns "transit operations", referring to transit across the territory of the requested State for the purpose of return to another country. Providing for an obligation to allow such transit widens the expulsion options of the contracting parties, and is particularly beneficial to expelling States in case direct flights to the intended country are not available, or return by land *via* another country is less costly. Transit arrangements necessarily concern only third country nationals and stateless persons. Section IV consist of two articles: Article 13 entitled "principles" and Article 14 on procedure.

As a general principle, Article 13 determines firstly that the contracting parties "should restrict" the transit of third country nationals or stateless persons to cases where direct return to the State of destination is not possible. This limits, but would not exclude transit requests as a cheaper alternative to an otherwise available direct flight, or journey by sea. Secondly, an obligation to allow transit exists only if readmission by the State of destination, or onward passage through further transit States, is assured.

Article 13(3) then lists several grounds for refusal of a transit request. Transit through the requested State can be refused in case of a risk of persecution, torture or inhuman or degrading treatment or punishment, or the death penalty in the State of destination or a further transit State. All grounds for refusal are discretionary – "transit can be refused" – therefore this provision could not be considered an obligation of the requested State to investigate the (safety conditions of the) onward journey. Transit may also be refused in case the person would be subject to criminal prosecution or sanctions in the requested State or in another transit State. This provision presumably intends to prevent circumvention of extradition procedures. Lastly, transit may be refused on grounds of public health, domestic security, public order, or other national interests of the requested State.

As a matter of procedure, the requesting State must add a declaration to the transit request stating that the onward journey is assured, and that no grounds for refusal "are known of".[55] As a final general principle, Article 13(4) specifies that an authorisation of transit may be revoked should any grounds for refusal arise subsequently, or in case the onward journey is no longer assured. Re-readmission, if necessary, will then take place without delay.

Article 14 on procedure determines the content of the transit request (a common form for transit requests is annexed to the agreement), and sets a time limit of five days for a reply from the requested State. Article 14 also determines that the person concerned and any escorts are exempted from transit visa requirements in case of a transit operation by air. Article 14(4), finally, specifies that the requested State may assist in the transit operation, in particular in the surveillance of the person concerned. Surveillance would presumably be relevant primarily in case transit takes place unescorted. Considering the risk that the person in question might abscond during transit, and re-enter the requesting State or remain unauthorised in the requested State, one would expect the contracting parties to agree on escorted transit and/or strict surveillance.

55 Article 14(1)(d).

### 5.3.7 Costs

Section V concerns costs and consists of a sole Article 15, which allocates all transport costs resulting from the readmission or transit of persons under the agreement to the requesting State. The requesting State does reserve the right to recover these costs from the person concerned or third parties.

### 5.3.8 Data protection

Section VI is titled "data protection and non-affection clause". The objective of Article 16 on data protection is to ensure that the transfer of personal data pursuant to the Community agreement is in accordance with the domestic law of the involved third country, and Directive 95/46 of 24 October 1995.[56]

### 5.3.9 Non-affection clause

Article 17 is a so-called "non-affection clause", which regulates the relation between the agreement and other international obligations as well as other readmission arrangements of the contracting parties.

Article 17(1) starts with the catch-all statement that the agreement shall be without prejudice to the rights, obligations and responsibilities of the Community, the Member States, and the third country "arising from International Law". The article then generally refers to a number of international conventions in particular. The standard draft Community readmission agreement, based on which the Commission starts negotiations, refers to the following list of conventions:

- The Geneva Refugee Convention
- International conventions determining the State responsible for examining applications for asylum
- The European Convention for the protection of human rights and fundamental freedoms
- The Convention against torture and other cruel, inhuman or degrading treatment or punishment
- International conventions on extradition and transit
- Multilateral international conventions and agreements on the readmission of foreign nationals[57]

The non-affection clause as included in the final text of the different agreements however varies considerably. The third countries with which the Commission has negotiated have clearly had different views regarding which international conventions to mention specifically. Hong Kong and Macao were unwilling to include reference to

56 *OJ* L 281, 23 November 1995, p. 31. Brief comments on possible gaps in data protection in light of the directive have been made by Peers, see Peers and Rogers 2006.

57 Council Doc. 14101/02, paraphrased in Peers and Rogers 2006. This list has not changed since the first set of directives in September 2000 in relation to Morocco, Pakistan, Russia and Sri Lanka was given to the Commission.

any specific convention.[58] Sri Lanka preferred a general reference to "any applicable International Convention or agreement".[59] Albania accepted references only to the European Convention of Human Rights, the Geneva Refugee Convention, and international instruments on extradition. There is no legal reason for the reluctance of third countries to refer to any or certain international conventions. Apparently, third countries have been reluctant to include references to conventions of which they are not a party,[60] notwithstanding the fact that such conventions might contain relevant obligations of the Member States. This is difficult to follow while the non-affection clause does not create obligations to which a contracting party is not already bound.

The inclusion of a non-affection clause in (Community) readmission agreements is not strictly required by international law. Readmission agreements and the conventions listed above are treaties, between which there exists no hierarchical relationship under general international law. Nevertheless, the contracting parties to a Community readmission agreement explicitly accept the precedence of other international obligations, thereby providing a conflict rule. This resolves cases where the agreement would conflict with any other treaty obligations of the Community, the Member States, or the third country in question.

Remarkable in this regard is the explicit reference to instruments relevant to international refugee protection – the GC,[61] ECHR[62] and CAT[63] – considering that the text of the agreement applies only to unauthorised immigrants, not mentioning protection seekers or refugees.[64] One could consider this to be an implicit recognition of the fact that application of Community readmission agreements may facilitate the expulsion of protection seekers and refugees. In case of reference to the GC, ECHR or CAT, Article 17(1) confirms that a Member State would not apply the agreement in an individual case if incompatible with international protection obligations.

Article 17(2) states that "nothing in this Agreement shall prevent the return of a person under other formal or informal arrangements". This emphasises the fact that the

58 See Article 16(1) of the agreements with Hong Kong and Macao, which only contains the catch-all reference to rights, obligations and responsibilities "arising from International Law".

59 Article 16(1) of the agreement with Sri Lanka.

60 An example is the negotiation of this clause with Hong Kong, see the report of the European Parliament, session document A5-0381/2002 final, p. 8. We shall see below that this reluctance also influences the content of readmission clauses that are included in Community- or mixed agreements, *infra* section 8.3.

61 Convention Relating to the Status of Refugees, adopted by the United Nations Conference of Plenipotentiaries on the Status of Refugees and Stateless Persons on 28 July 1951.

62 European Convention for the Protection of Human Rights and Fundamental Freedoms, Council of Europe, 4 November 1950.

63 Convention against Torture and Other Cruel, Inhuman or Degrading Treatment or Punishment, adopted by the General Assembly of the United Nations on 10 December 1984.

64 With exception to the definition of a "residence authorisation" in Article 1, which excludes temporary permission to remain in connection with asylum applications.

contracting parties are not obliged, as such, to apply the agreement. The Member States may use other means at their disposal for the expulsion of unauthorised immigrants. This provision safeguards *inter alia* the continued application of a considerable array of informal readmission practices established by the Member States.[65] It should be noted that the stipulation in Article 17(2) is subject to Article 20, which determines the hierarchical relationship between the Community agreement and individual Member State arrangements.[66]

### *5.3.10 Joint readmission committee*

Section VII concerns the "implementation and application" of the agreement, which is supervised by a "joint readmission committee" established by Article 18. In this committee, expert civil servants of the contracting parties provide each other with "mutual assistance in the application and interpretation of the agreement".[67] The Commission represents the Community at committee meetings, assisted by Member State experts.[68] Regarding actual decisions of the committee, however, the position of the Community is determined by the Council, acting by qualified majority on a proposal from the Commission.[69] The committee holds regular meetings every six months, hosted alternately by the Commission and the third country in question. The contracting parties may convene additional meetings whenever necessary.

The joint readmission committee has several tasks intended to ensure the smooth operation of the agreement.[70] The committee monitors the application of the agreement. It also exchanges information on bilateral implementing protocols drawn up between individual Member States and the third country in question.[71] In addition, it may take decisions and make recommendations, based on consensus. Only decisions are binding on the contracting parties. The committee may decide on implementing arrangements necessary for the uniform execution of the agreement, such as common forms in addition to those already provided by the agreement. It may also decide on amendments to the annexes of the agreements. In terms of amending the text of the agreement itself, the committee only has the power to make recommendations. In practice, the committee may be expected to also fulfil a political trouble-shooting function. On the Community side, the Commission, for example, is likely to convene meetings in case the Member States would experience a lack of cooperation on readmission from a third country.

65 Informal cooperation on readmission may be laid down in a Memorandum of Understanding or an exchange of letters between competent authorities, but may also be based on purely *ad hoc* cooperation between diplomatic or consular authorities.

66 *Infra*, subsection 5.3.12.

67 Article 18(1).

68 Article 18(3).

69 See the Council Decision concerning the conclusion of the agreement with Albania, Article 4, Council Doc. 12361/05, 4 October 2005.

70 Listed in Article 18(1)(a) to (e).

71 Pursuant to Article 19 of the agreement, see *infra* subsection 5.3.11.

The joint readmission committee is not subject to democratic or public scrutiny. The EP has no part in determining the position of the EC regarding committee decisions.[72] Meetings are not open to the public, unless the contracting parties would decide otherwise on individual occasions. At its discretion, the committee may hold public briefings or otherwise inform interested members of the public concerning the outcome of meetings. All records and documents of committee meetings are confidential.

This lack of scrutiny is mitigated by the fact that the decision-making power of the committee is limited. It can only take binding decisions concerning certain implementing arrangements, and amendment of the annexes (pertaining to the means of evidence, and the content of the common forms for readmission- and transit applications). The committee cannot autonomously change the content of the main body of the readmission agreement, regarding which it can only make recommendations to the contracting parties.

### *5.3.11 Implementing protocols*

In recognition of the fact that implementation of the agreement may require more detailed arrangements, Article 19 allows the third country concerned and individual Member States to conclude bilateral "implementing protocols". These protocols are intended to work out an explicitly limited number of details insofar as necessary to secure effective implementation of the agreement by a given Member State. Article 19(1) determines that protocols may designate the competent authorities for submitting and receiving readmission applications, as well as contact points within the respective administrations. They may also designate border crossing points to use for the transfer of persons under the agreement, and establish conditions for escorted return or transit. The contracting parties to a protocol may also decide on additional means of evidence for establishing readmission obligations.

Following Article 19(2), the entry into force of an implementing protocol requires notification of the joint readmission committee. Article 19(3) determines that the third country in question will apply any provision of a protocol with one Member State also in its relations with any other Member State, upon request of the latter.

72 *Supra*, n. 71. Article 300(2) TEC does require that "[t]he European Parliament shall be immediately and fully informed of any decision [...] concerning the establishment of the Community position in a body set up by an agreement". This requirement, however, would only apply insofar as "that body is called upon to adopt decisions having legal effects, with the exception of decisions supplementing or amending the institutional framework of the agreement", as specified in the third sentence of Article 300(2) TEC. Considering the tasks of the joint readmission committee listed in Article 18 of Community readmission agreements, decisions of the committee would therefore not involve the EP.

### 5.3.12 *Relation with bilateral Member State readmission agreements or arrangements*

The objective of Article 20 is to clarify the relation of the agreement to bilateral Member State readmission agreements or other readmission arrangements with the same third country, providing explicit conflict rules. It states that the agreement shall take precedence over any bilateral agreement or arrangement on readmission concluded by a Member State with the same third country, as well as over any protocols with that country concluded pursuant to Article 19.[73]

According to this provision, the Member States may continue to apply earlier concluded agreements or arrangements with the same country insofar as these are compatible with the Community agreement. Arguably, this includes the possibility for Member States to apply existing agreements or arrangements that provide more detail than the Community agreement, as long as they stay within the limits of Article 19. It would then be possible for an existing Member State agreement to be considered simply as an implementing protocol. Furthermore, regarding implementing protocols under Article 19, Article 20 confirms that the Community agreement takes precedence in case of conflict, which would ensure that the Member States respect the limits set by Article 19. We recall, finally, that the relation with fully-fledged bilateral readmission agreements concluded after the Community agreement is governed by the division of competence in this area between the Community and the Member States, discussed above in section 4.4.

### 5.3.13 *Territorial application*

Section VIII contains "final provisions". During the negotiations with Sri Lanka, it was considered necessary to clarify the territorial application of the Community agreement. A new Article 21 was inserted into the standard text. Article 21(1) determines that the agreement applies to the territory in which the TEC is applicable, and the territory of the third country in question. Article 21(2) confirms that the agreement does not apply to the territory of Denmark.[74] We discussed the exclusion of Denmark from participation in Community readmission agreements above in chapter 3.[75]

### 5.3.14 *Entry into force, duration and termination*

Article 21 determines that the agreement will enter into force on the first day of the second month, following the date on which each contracting party has notified the other of the completion of national procedures for ratification or approval. The agreement is concluded for an unlimited period. Each party may denounce the agreement by official

73 The standard text of this provision was altered during the negotiations with Albania. The previous text established the precedence of the Community agreement over bilateral relations "insofar as [...] incompatible", see Articles 19 of the agreements with Hong Kong, Macao, and Sri Lanka. This amendment does not make a substantial difference.

74 Denmark is also explicitly excluded from the definition of "Member State" under Article 1 of the agreement.

75 *Supra*, subsection 3.1.1, n. 7.

notification of the other party, six months after which the agreement would cease to apply. Suspension is not a possibility provided for in the terms of the agreement.[76]

### *5.3.15 Annexes and joint declarations*

The last provision of the agreement, Article 23, determines that the standard annexes, concerning the means of evidence and the readmission- and transit application, form an integral part of the agreement. In addition to these annexes, each Community readmission agreement generally attaches a number of joint declarations by the contracting parties.

There are two standard joint declarations, one concerning Denmark in light of its exclusion from the agreement, and one concerning Iceland and Norway in light of their association with the Schengen acquis. The declarations state that it would be "appropriate" for Denmark, respectively, Iceland and Norway, to conclude a bilateral readmission agreement with the third country concerned. They also specify a political commitment to do so on the same terms as the Community agreement. The addition of these joint declarations was a compromise, after the Coreper decided in March 2000 that Community readmission agreements would not form part of the Schengen acquis.[77] As noted, this decision excluded Denmark from participating in Community readmission agreements, and excluded Iceland and Norway from the development of the common readmission policy. It should be stressed that these declarations are purely political gestures. They can therefore not be considered to mitigate the risk that unauthorised immigrants would evade the common readmission policy by moving to the territories of Denmark, Iceland or Norway.

A Community readmission agreement may also carry a number of specific joint declarations, which generally reflect compromises that were reached during the negotiations. A negotiating tool of the Commission is to mention concessions on the part of the Community (which are not, or which the Community does not wish to make legally binding) in political declarations attached to the agreement. We will discuss several of these declarations in the outline of the state of negotiations below.[78]

## 5.4 Conclusion

This chapter has explained the formal and informal procedures by which the Commission, Council and the Member States jointly determine the content of Community readmission agreements, and based on which negotiations with third countries take place. This chapter has furthermore established that the Commission has a political and pragmatic approach to the development of the common readmission policy, which has partially determined the content of the agreements. Proposals to adopt a more funda-

76 Peers and Rogers argue that the non-affection clause in Article 17 provides an implicit obligation for the Council to suspend a Community readmission agreement in case of fundamental rights problems in the third country concerned, see Peers and Rogers 2006.

77 Council Doc. 6720/00; Council Doc. 7637/00; and SI(2000) 249, 17 March 2000, cited in Schieffer 2003, p. 352; *supra*, subsection 3.1.1, at n. 4.

78 *Infra*, section 7.2.

mental rights-oriented approach and include certain rights guarantees in the Community's readmission agreements, originating from the European Parliament as well as within the Commission itself, were unsuccessful.

This chapter has also outlined and discussed the general content of Community readmission agreements as concluded with third countries. Like contemporary readmission agreements in general, their content is highly technical. They facilitate the readmission of unauthorised immigrants based on bilateral cooperation and consent between the contracting parties. Detailed procedural and evidence requirements underpin obligations to readmit nationals and former nationals, and obligations to readmit, or allow the transit for the purpose of onward return, of third country nationals and stateless persons. In addition, Community readmission agreements regulate their relation to other international obligations of the contracting parties, as well as bilateral readmission agreements or other arrangements between individual Member States and the third country in question.

In the analysis of these provisions, it was emphasised that Community readmission agreements may be expected to limit but not eliminate return problems, while leaving opportunity for both migrants and the authorities of third countries to frustrate expulsion. Especially where migrants have disposed of documents and other paper-based evidence and are unwilling to return, so-called "problem" States will be able to continue withholding effective cooperation on readmission. It was argued that the goodwill of third countries will therefore remain an important factor in the implementation of Community readmission agreements, which, in turn, depends on the quality of relations of the Community and the Member States with third countries, as well as other incentives for cooperation.

In light of the discussion of the importance of quid pro quo in the negotiation of readmission agreements in chapter 2, the absence of any reference to compensation in the standard text of Community readmission agreements, or the Council directives for their negotiation, is particularly remarkable. Such concessions are sometimes referred to, but only in joint declarations of the contracting parties attached to individual agreements. The issue of reciprocity, and the use of incentives by the Community to compensate third countries for concluding a readmission agreement, is dealt with extensively in chapter 7.

# Chapter 6 Integrating readmission into EU external relations

As noted in chapter 2, the reciprocity of readmission agreements is generally not reflected in practice. This is also true for Community readmission agreements with third countries, which are clearly to the one-sided benefit of the Community.[1] In addition, the obligations imposed by readmission agreements, including those of the Community, are only partially supported by general international law.[2] This chapter will examine some of the policies and instruments which the European Union has developed to persuade third countries to, nevertheless, conclude these agreements. In particular, it will look at the manner in which the external relations of the European Union are employed to stimulate the negotiation of such agreements.

The integration of immigration and asylum issues into the EU's external relations, aimed at establishing cooperation with third countries for the joint control of migration flows, has been an important policy objective since the early nineties. The best example of the integration of the specific issue of readmission into EU relations with third countries is the inclusion of so-called readmission *clauses* in Community and mixed agreements.[3] We will discuss readmission clauses in a separate chapter further below.[4] The reason why third countries accept readmission clauses is relatively straightforward, as are the related negotiations. In this chapter, and the next, we will first analyse the far more complex process of negotiating fully-fledged readmission agreements.

Integrating migration issues into EU external relations has been a dominant theme within the development of common immigration and asylum policies, especially since the European Council meeting in Tampere in October 1999. In this ongoing process, the EU places particular emphasis on the readmission of unauthorised immigrants. The Commission, in need of leverage for the negotiation of Community readmission agreements, has gradually managed to place the issue of readmission more firmly on the external agenda of the EU. Several flanking measures have been developed to aid

1 *Supra*, subsection 2.1.2.3, n. 66.

2 *Supra*, section 2.5.

3 *Supra*, section 1.4, at n. 70.

4 Chapter 8.

the readmission negotiations. These divide into positive and negative incentives – or "carrots and sticks" to use a term common to international relations discourse. This chapter discusses a number of these incentives under the headings of "support" and "punishment".[5]

Subsection 6.1 provides an overview of the general policy guidelines relevant to the integration of the issue of readmission into the EU's external relations. This overview covers the period from the Tampere European Council until roughly January 2006. Later developments have not been taken into account. Subsection 6.2 discusses a number of specific EU policies, which provide support to third countries requested to enter into a readmission agreement with the Community. These policies mitigate some of the negative consequences of the conclusion of readmission agreements, thereby facilitating their negotiation. Subsection 6.3, finally, considers the degree to which the EU is ready to take punitive measures to persuade unwilling third countries to enter into a Community readmission agreement.

## 6.1 General policy guidelines

The meeting of the European Council in Tampere in October 1999 outlined a 5-year programme for creating a so-called area of freedom, security, and justice in the European Union.[6] This programme provided *inter alia* for the development of a common immigration and asylum policy.[7] The European Council considered the management of migration flows in "partnership" with third countries a key element of this policy, taking its cue from the mandate of the HLWG that was created less than a year before.[8] This was the beginning of a more structured attempt, in comparison with previous years,[9] at integrating migration and asylum issues into the EU's external relations.

As noted earlier, the Tampere meeting also gave the starting signal for the negotiation of readmission agreements with third countries at the Community level.[10] In terms of negotiating strategy, the European Council called for "assistance to third countries of origin and transit [...] to help [...] strengthen their ability to [...] cope with their readmission obligations towards the Union and the Member States".[11] The European Council formally approved the use of supportive measures to help third countries deal

5 Further flanking measures at the disposal of the Commission are detailed in the next chapter, in the discussion of the negotiation process itself.

6 Tampere European Council of 15 and 16 October 1999, Presidency Conclusions on the creation of an area of freedom, security and justice within the European Union.

7 Tampere European Council of 15 and 16 October 1999, Presidency Conclusions, at para. 10.

8 Tampere European Council of 15 and 16 October 1999, Presidency Conclusions, at para. 11. Concerning the creation of the HLWG, see *supra*, section 1.4, at n. 79-88.

9 *Supra*, section 1.4.

10 Tampere European Council of 15 and 16 October 1999, Presidency Conclusions, para. 27.

11 Tampere European Council of 15 and 16 October 1999, Presidency Conclusions, para. 26.

with a possible immigration burden, resulting from a readmission agreement with the Community.[12] Subsection 6.2 below discusses several concrete measures which have resulted from this general mandate.

The Santa Maria de Feira European Council of 19 and 20 June 2000 confirmed intentions to develop an EC immigration and asylum policy with a strong external dimension. It adopted conclusions on "European Union priorities and policy objectives for external relations in the field of Justice and Home Affairs".[13] These listed the conclusion of Community readmission agreements as a priority of external JHA policy. The next relevant European Council meeting, illustrative of a growing commitment to make the Union's external relations "migration-minded", took place in Laeken in December 2001. The European Council stated that the conclusion of readmission agreements should specifically be taken into account when integrating policy on migration flows into the EU's foreign policy.[14]

Spain took over the EU Presidency in January 2002. At the time, Spain was increasingly preoccupied with the rising numbers of unauthorised immigrants, arriving from and through Southern Mediterranean countries. A further cause for concern was Spain's inability to establish cooperation with these countries to manage this problem. An important objective of the Spanish Presidency was to find new ways to harness EU external relations so as to promote the control of migration flows abroad, including the readmission of unauthorised immigrants to third countries.

Against this backdrop, the Presidency submitted draft conclusions in preparation for the Seville summit on 21 and 22 June 2002, titled "cooperation with third countries of origin and transit to jointly combat illegal immigration".[15] The content of the draft conclusions was reminiscent of the 1998 Austrian strategy paper, which therefore drew a fair share of public attention and criticism.[16] The draft conclusions were so controversial that the GAER Council was unable to reach agreement, passing them on to the European Council itself.[17] The Presidency conclusions as eventually adopted were watered down to reach a certain level of "political correctness". The Seville meeting, however, still marked a significant change in strategy by formally approving the possible use of punitive measures against third countries, unwilling to exercise migration control to the benefit of the European Union.

The European Council decided that measures to combat unauthorised immigration should be incorporated into the EU's relations with third countries following

12 A policy long-established at the Member State level, aimed at stimulating the conclusion of readmission agreements, see *supra*, subsections, 3.2.2 and 3.2.5.

13 Council Doc. 7653/00.

14 Presidency Conclusions, Laeken European Council of 14 and 15 December 2001, para. 40.

15 Council Doc. 9917/3/02, 18 June 2002.

16 Peers 2004, p. 209.

17 Council Doc. 9917/3/02; Peers 2004, p. 209.

an "integrated and comprehensive approach".[18] It advocated using "all appropriate instruments" in the field of external relations,[19] and stressed the importance of ensuring the cooperation of third countries on border control, and the readmission of unauthorised immigrants.[20] To this end, the European Council firstly called for more EU resources to provide the necessary technical and financial support.[21] Secondly, it called for a "systematic assessment of relations with third countries which do not cooperate in combating illegal immigration", possibly leading to the adoption of punitive measures.[22] The current state of development of a mechanism for this assessment is discussed below in section 6.3.

It is worth noting that, while the GAER Council was debating the Seville European Council conclusions on migration, drawing the necessary public attention, the *JHA* Council drew up near identical policy guidelines relatively unnoticed. A JHA Council meeting in Luxembourg on 13 June 2002 adopted conclusions on "measures to be applied to prevent and combat illegal immigration and trafficking in human beings by sea".[23] The Council called for the incorporation of migration control into the EU's external relations, devised an "integrated approach" to this end, and listed "measures which should be adopted by countries of boarding, departure or transit". It decided that acceptance of these measures would be a factor determining the quality of relations with the Union, including the use of supportive or punitive measures, depending on a "systematic assessment". Specific emphasis was placed on the acceptance of readmission obligations by third countries. It seems that, in the lee of the Seville European Council, implementation of the new strategy of using "sticks" in addition to "carrots" to extract migration control from third countries had already started within the JHA sub-context.

Following the Seville European Council, the HLWG and Commission were instructed to identify a set of priority countries with which to intensify cooperation on migration matters.[24] "Intensified" cooperation firstly meant that dialogue on migration matters would be initiated or strengthened with these countries.[25] The Council and Commission were to start using every available relation and institutional structure, for example under Cooperation or Association Agreements, to table migration issues and seek cooperation. Secondly, external EU action relating to migration and asylum would focus on this specific set of third countries. They would be prioritised in the allocation of funding for migration-related programmes and projects, but also be the

18 Presidency Conclusions, Seville European Council of 21 and 22 June 2002, para. 33.

19 Presidency Conclusions, Seville European Council of 21 and 22 June 2002, para. 33.

20 Presidency Conclusions, Seville European Council of 21 and 22 June 2002, para. 34.

21 Presidency Conclusions, Seville European Council of 21 and 22 June 2002, para. 34.

22 Presidency Conclusions, Seville European Council of 21 and 22 June 2002, para. 35.

23 Press release 9620/02 (Presse 175), p. 9-12.

24 See the "road map" concerning follow-up to the Seville summit, Council Doc. 10525/1/02, annex, point 17.

25 Council Doc. 13754/2/02.

first to risk possible punitive measures in case of insufficient cooperation, for example on readmission.[26]

In November 2002, the HLWG and Commission finished collecting information on, and mapping existing EU relations with third countries considered the most important in terms of migration flows affecting the EU.[27] The GAER Council subsequently adopted conclusions, listing nine priority countries, as well as the criteria by which they had been selected.[28] These criteria were:

- Nature and size of migratory flows towards the EU
- Geographical position in relation to the EU
- Need for capacity building concerning migration management
- Existing framework for cooperation
- Attitude towards cooperation on migration issues.[29]

The nine third countries, identified as subject to intensified cooperation relating to migration control, were Albania, China, the Federal Republic of Yugoslavia (FRY), Libya, Morocco, Russia, Tunisia, Turkey, and Ukraine.[30] Compared with the set of countries for which the HLWG drew up action plans in 1999,[31] this list illustrates a shift in the agenda. The work of the HLWG initially focused on the alleviation of root causes of migration. The majority of the action plans had thus been directed at source countries of migration. Eight out of the nine countries selected by the HLWG in November 2002 were neighbouring countries of the EU, or would soon become neighbouring countries with the 2004 enlargement. The emphasis of external EC immigration and asylum policies had clearly shifted to cushioning transit migration through States in the direct vicinity of the EU.[32]

The November 2002 list of priority countries also took clear account of the development of the common readmission policy. Six of the selected countries – Albania, China, Morocco, Russia, Turkey, and Ukraine – were subject to a Council mandate for the negotiation of a readmission agreement. Their inclusion in the November 2002 list

26 See below, section 6.3.

27 Council Doc. 10525/1/02, annex, point 17.

28 Council Doc. 13754/2/02.

29 Council Doc. 13754/2/02.

30 In addition, the Council stated that neighbouring countries would be considered when taking relevant action, pursuant to a so-called "regional approach", Council Doc. 13754/2/02, para. 5. This is a typical term of EU migration policy language, referring to the fact that migration flows by definition have a regional impact, which must be taken into account when developing policies. The Community generally takes a regional approach to external migration and asylum policies, including, as we shall see in the next chapter, the common readmission policy.

31 Albania, Afghanistan, Iraq, Morocco, Somalia, and Sri Lanka, *supra*, section 1.4, at n. 81, 87.

32 See also *supra*, subsection 3.2.2.

was *inter alia* intended to support the readmission negotiations. It made it easier for the Commission to address readmission issues, and push for speedy negotiations, in relations with the above countries regarding, for example, trade, economic cooperation, or development cooperation. Furthermore, the additional funding for migration-related programmes and projects, allocated to the above countries under the EU's external assistance programmes, gave the Commission some concrete leverage in the readmission negotiations.

Since the Tampere European Council, the Commission had been investing a great deal of political effort in placing the readmission negotiations more firmly on the external agenda of the EU. It soon became clear to the Commission that it would need more concrete bargaining power to fulfil the Council mandates for the conclusion of readmission agreements. In an attempt to turn the trend of "migration-minded" external relations to the benefit of the common readmission policy, the Commission started issuing increasingly frequent demands for more negotiating leverage.[33]

In December 2002, the Commission published a Communication on "migration and development".[34] The Commission discussed the impact of migration on developing countries, and several related policies, but also pronounced on external EC migration policy more generally. It advocated a more effective use of the EU's external relations to attain migration policy objectives, with particular attention for the conclusion of Community readmission agreements.

The Commission outlined a set of measures considered necessary to ensure successful readmission negotiations, which remains the most elaborate discussion of this topic in a (public[35]) EC document to date. It underlined the negative impact which readmission agreements may have on third countries economically and politically. It confirmed the need for measures, supporting third countries in dealing with these consequences, as well as with immigration generally. The Commission, however, also stressed the need to compensate for the conclusion of readmission agreements in other areas, such as visa policy and labour immigration, in order to negotiate successfully. In line with continuous Council declarations since the early nineties,[36] the Commission

33 The first policy paper in which the Commission unambiguously called for more negotiating leverage, citing a lack of progress in the readmission agreements, was the Green Paper on a Community return policy on illegal residents of 10 April 2002 (COM(2002) 175 final), soon repeated in a Communication on the same issue on 14 October of that year (COM(2002) 564 final).

34 COM(2002) 703 final. "Migration and development" is a policy heading, which addresses different aspects of the relation between migration and the development of countries, such as for example the impact of migrants' remittances, or "brain drain", on developing countries.

35 The Commission later adopted a Communication on the priorities and successful development of a common readmission policy, but classified it confidential: Council Doc. 11505/04 MIGR 63 RESTREINT UE.

36 *Supra*, section 1.4.

requested broad linkage between readmission negotiations and EU external relations policies to allow for a concrete incentive-driven negotiation process.[37]

The five-year Tampere programme for the creation of an area of freedom, security and justice expired in 2004. Continuing this ongoing process, the European Council on 5 November 2004 agreed on a set of policy guidelines for the next five years; the so-called The Hague programme.[38] It is under this general mandate that the EU is currently operating. The Hague programme strengthens the external dimension of EC immigration and asylum policies, elaborating cooperation with origin and transit countries of migration, including the timely conclusion of readmission agreements.[39]

Calling for a "coherent approach" between return policy and all other aspects of the external relations of the Community,[40] the European Council did not announce any new strategic elements for attaining the cooperation of third countries. The Council and Commission in the last few years have repeatedly emphasised migration control as a strategic priority of the external relations of the EU, but the main policy guidelines have remained the same.[41] The EU uses its external relations to attain migration and asylum objectives by steadily expanding dialogue with third countries at every level and every suitable forum,[42] by providing technical and financial support through a variety of means and instruments, and by threatening with possible punitive measures. Special attention is awarded to the readmission of unauthorised immigrants, and the conclusion of readmission agreements with the Community.

The following sections analyse the manner in which the EU deals out support or punishment to third countries, depending on their level of cooperation with the readmission of unauthorised immigrants.

---

37 COM(2002) 703 final, p. 25-26.

38 The Hague Programme for strengthening freedom, security and justice, Council Doc. 16054/04.

39 The Hague Programme, Council Doc. 16054/04, para. 1.6.

40 The Hague Programme, Council Doc. 16054/04, para. 1.6.4.

41 COM(2005) 184 final; COM(2005) 390 final; Council Doc. 14769/05; COM(2005) 621; Council Doc. 15446/05.

42 For an impression of the expansion of migration dialogue between the EU institutions and third countries since Tampere, see Commission staff working paper, SEC(2003) 815 (also available on the website of the Council as Council Doc. 11450/03), which measures progress in the implementation of the November 2002 GAER conclusions. The Commission reported constant discussion of migration issues, including readmission and the progress in negotiating readmission agreements, within the framework of the Association Agreements with Morocco and Tunisia, the Accession Partnership with Turkey, the Stabilisation and Association Process (SAP) involving Albania and the FRY, and the Partnership and Cooperation Agreements (PCA) with Ukraine and Russia. In addition, migration dialogue intensified at the regional level within the framework of the Barcelona Process concerning the Mediterranean, the Stabilisation and Association Process (SAP) concerning the Western Balkans, and the Asia-Europe Meeting (ASEM) concerning Asia.

## 6.2 Readmission and support

Since the Tampere European Council in October 1999, the amount of EU money spent on enhancing third countries' capacity to deal with migration flows has risen significantly. The financial appropriations are increasingly important, and cover a range of actions in the external field. As noted in chapter 3, the EU invests heavily in upgrading transit countries' institutional and technical capacity to exercise migration and border control, and receive, process, and detain immigrants. Less, yet growing investment is aimed at alleviating root causes of migration in countries of origin under policy headings such as that of "migration and development".[43] Promoting the readmission of unauthorised immigrants, *inter alia* through the negotiation of agreements, is a further part of this strongly developing complex of external immigration and asylum policies.

Due to the Member States' interest in expulsion to third countries, and not least the insistence of the Commission, the negotiation of Community readmission agreements is a focal point of EU external expenditure. This section discusses several policies and instruments, which may be considered flanking measures of the common readmission policy. These provide different forms of support to third countries, which the Commission uses as leverage in readmission negotiations.

Subsection 6.2.1 looks at spending on migration-related projects in third countries under EU external assistance programmes, which is of relevance to the readmission negotiations. Subsection 6.2.2 discusses two instruments – the B7-667 budget line, and the Aeneas Regulation – purposely developed within the JHA context to support immigration and asylum objectives in the external field, including readmission. Subsection 6.2.3 concerns a specific policy of the Community under the heading of migration and development, regarding migrants' remittances, and discusses its importance to the readmission agenda. Subsection 6.2.4, finally, considers the relation between the European Neighbourhood Policy (ENP) and the establishment of readmission obligations in countries on the periphery of the EU.[44]

### *6.2.1 External relations assistance programmes*

To a degree, the EU external assistance budget supports the Community in attaining migration-related objectives abroad. Following the Tampere European Council, the Commission has steadily inserted Community interests in the field of migration into external programming and expenditure.

This has not been a straightforward process, considering the traditional differences in approach and political objectives between civil servants working in home- and foreign affairs. At the EU level, the home affairs issues of immigration and asylum have not necessarily been welcomed with open arms by the Commission's external

43 See, for example, COM(2005) 390 final.

44 This book does not include specific analysis of the role of the enlargement process as a means to establish migration control and readmission obligations in acceding countries, which has been elaborately described elsewhere, see Byrne, Noll and Vedsted-Hansen 2002, Byrne, Noll and Vedsted-Hansen 2002.

relations DGs. The rearranging of external priorities in line with migration interests met with a certain resistance, especially in the field of development cooperation.[45] The HLWG, charged with developing external EC migration policies, noted early on that "for the HLWG to operate effectively, a chain of actors must be mobilised in the Member States and in the European Union whose interests do not necessarily coincide or whose support for the objectives defined is unequal".[46] Nevertheless, one can say that most EU external relations policies have gradually acquired a certain migration "profile", which is reflected in strategic priorities as well as budgeting.

EU external assistance is managed with the aid of strategy papers. Regional Strategy Papers (RSP) and, pertaining to individual third countries, Country Strategy Papers (CSP) usually span a period of five to seven years. On the basis of priorities defined in these papers, national indicative programmes (NIP) determine where and how to spend available funds over the next two to three years.[47] The respective strategies are backed up by large budgets, representing significant financial and developmental interests for the countries and regions concerned.

The Commission Directorates General External Relations (DG RELEX) and Development (DG DEV) draft and implement these policy aids. DG DEV manages the strategy papers of ACP countries; DG RELEX covers the rest of the world. Incorporating migration issues into RSPs, CSPs, and NIPs is thus the primary responsibility of these DGs. DG JLS, the competent DG for migration and asylum affairs, however, keeps a close watch and exerts a degree of influence on this process.

In December 2002, the Commission published a Communication which examined the effectiveness of EC financial resources for the development of external immigration and asylum policies.[48] This communication *inter alia* provides a snapshot of the state of integration of migration objectives into relations with third countries. The review of Commission budgeting and expenditure at the regional[49] and national level[50] shows varying results. The fusing of migration issues and external relations at the time was more advanced with regard to the Mediterranean region, the Western Balkans, Eastern Europe, and Central Asia, than with regard to regions further away (Asia, ACP, and Latin America). This imbalance can be explained by differences in migration rel-

45 Pointed to by the HLWG, Council Doc. 8939/00, para. 5, and Council Doc. 13993/00, para. 50-51; also reflected in Presidency Conclusions, Seville European Council of 21 and 22 June 2002, para. 36, and COM(2002) 703 final, p. 21, 26.

46 Council Doc. 13993/00, para. 50.

47 COM(2002) 703 final, p. 40.

48 Commission Communication on integrating migration issues into the European Union's relations with third countries, I. Migration and development, II. Report on the effectiveness of financial resources available at Community level for repatriation of immigrants and rejected asylum seekers, for management of external borders and for asylum and migration projects in third countries, COM(2002) 703 final, 3 December 2002.

49 COM(2002) 703 final, p. 18-20.

50 COM(2002) 703 final, annex 2 bis.

evance,[51] and the availability of existing frameworks for cooperation.[52] In addition, it arguably reflects the prioritisation of action in transit countries over source countries of migration.[53] The emphasis on migration control capacity of third countries close to the EU's external borders is evident in Commission programming at the regional as well as the national level.

The strategy papers, determining EU relations with third countries and related expenditure, are subject to periodic review. The above 2002 Communication announced this so-called mid-term review as an occasion to determine if and where migration objectives could be emphasised more, *inter alia* with a view to encouraging the conclusion of readmission agreements.[54] Anxious to lift the migration profile of EU external relations, DG JLS (then DG JHA) inventoried the results of the mid-term review undertaken by DG RELEX in the course of 2003. It was time to see whether colleagues in the foreign office were sufficiently supportive of the migration agenda, in line with repeated European Council demands.

DG JLS examined the national indicative programmes and 2002-2006 country strategy papers[55] of thirty of the main source and/or transit countries of migration to the EU, as well as the TACIS,[56] CARDS[57] and MEDA[58] strategy papers. The results again varied between regions, but strategic priorities, budget, and expenditure overall showed that the importance of migration issues in the EU's external relations was increasing.

As noted, one of the objectives of the mid-term review was to make the financing of readmission-related projects in third countries more visible in order to encourage

---

51 Influx from Latin America into the EU is limited, for example. Also, the majority of economic migrants arriving in the EU come not from low-income countries, but from middle income countries and countries in economic transition, COM(2002) 703 final, p. 10; Preamble GAERC Conclusions of 19 May 2003, Council Doc. 8927/03.

52 The development of frameworks for cooperation within which to address migration issues with, for example, Asia started relatively recently and is less advanced.

53 *Supra*, at n. 32.

54 COM(2002) 703 final, foreword, and p. 27. Supported by the GAER Council in its related conclusions of 19 May 2003 on migration and development, Council Doc. 8927/03, para. 4, 7.

55 These documents are available on: www.europa.eu.int/comm/external_relations.

56 Technical Assistance to the Commonwealth of Independent States (TACIS) is the Community's assistance programme for Eastern Europe and Central Asia. Its legal basis is Council Regulation No 99/2000 of 29 December 1999, *OJ* L 12, 18 January 2000, p. 1.

57 Community Assistance for Reconstruction, Democratisation and Stabilisation is the Community's assistance programme for the Western Balkans. Its legal basis is Council Regulation No 2666/2000 of 5 December 2000, *OJ* L 306, 7 December 2000, p. 1.

58 The MEDA programme supports the European-Mediterranean Partnership and is the Community's assistance programme for the Mediterranean region. Its legal basis is Council Regulation No 2698/2000 of 27 November 2000, *OJ* L 311, 12 December 2000, p. 1.

the negotiation of Community readmission agreements.[59] Financial appropriations for capacity building projects in third countries have a certain facilitating effect on negotiations. Relevant CSPs and NIPs should therefore give an indication of the degree to which the EU external budget actively supports the development of the common readmission policy.

The CSPs and NIPs of the third countries for which the Commission has received a Council directive to negotiate a Community readmission agreement – the "readmission countries"[60] – do not refer to "readmission" as such. From the viewpoint of increasing the "visibility" of the issue of readmission in EU spending, the mid-term review process was therefore unsuccessful. One should however bear in mind that any increase in a third country's capacity to receive and process immigrants, or to control borders and transit migration flows, can be relevant to readmission. A broad range of migration-related projects is able to mitigate the impact of a readmission agreement with the Community, and thus provide the Commission with leverage in the negotiations. RELEX programming can therefore be considered to support the Commission's readmission negotiations, but it is difficult to determine the degree to which it specifically aims to do so.

In January 2006, the Commission initiated a general overhaul of the EU's external assistance programmes. The objective of this reform is to simplify the legislative framework governing the EU's external actions, *inter alia* by reducing the number of geographical instruments through which assistance is currently channelled. Assistance to separate regions, under programmes such as CARDS, MEDA, TACIS, and ACP, will be regrouped under three new instruments. These will cover, respectively, acceding countries, EU neighbouring countries, and the rest of the world.[61] It may be expected that the attention for migration issues, including readmission and the negotiation of Community readmission agreements, will be maintained under these new geographical instruments.

### *6.2.2 JHA funding of migration cooperation with third countries*

The development of external immigration and asylum policies had a slow start. In part, this was due to a lack of independent financial backing. The action plans, adopted by the HLWG in 1998,[62] had very little impact. Implementation of the plans faltered for several reasons, an important one of which was the absence of a supporting budget.[63] Dependent on bits and pieces from less than forthcoming RELEX and DEV budgets, and Member State contributions, the HLWG was unable to translate the action plans

59 *Supra*, n. 54.

60 At the time of writing, these countries (and entities) are Albania, Algeria, China, SAR Hong Kong, SAR Macao, Morocco, Pakistan, Russia, Sri Lanka, Turkey, and Ukraine.

61 COM(2006) 26 final, p. 3.

62 *Supra*, section 1.4, at n. 81 and 87.

63 See the EP's report on the HLWG action plans, A5-0057/2000, PE 285.869/DEF; HWLG, Report to the European Council in Nice, Council Doc. 13993/00; and Council Doc. 8939/00.

into practice. It became clear that the external dimension of immigration and asylum policies would require a budget of its own in order to be meaningful and effective. The somewhat patchy integration of migration issues into EU external spending, outlined in the previous subsection, further underlines the importance of financing migration cooperation with third countries through specific resources.

Noting the ineffectiveness of external immigration and asylum policies without an appropriate budgetary allocation, the European Parliament in 2000 proposed creating a new budget heading.[64] The Commission subsequently launched the budget-line "cooperation with third countries in the area of migration" (B7-667) in 2001.[65] The financing of migration cooperation with third countries under B7-667 later evolved into the Aeneas Regulation in 2004,[66] and from there into a fully-fledged thematic programme for EU external assistance in 2006.[67] The following subsections will detail the manner of financing cooperation with third countries under the B7-667 budget and the Aeneas Regulation, and analyse the relevance of these instruments to the readmission negotiations.

#### 6.2.2.1 The B7-667 budget-line

The financing of migration cooperation with third countries under B7-667 was included in the overall budget as a so-called "preparatory action". This is common practice when the Community embarks upon a new area of activity. A preparatory action implies an exploratory phase; a period for assessing the appropriateness and effectiveness of a particular Community activity, and for determining whether, and how it will continue. Preparatory actions have relatively modest budgets. The yearly budget for B7-667 increased between 2001 and 2003 from 10 to 12,5 to 20 million Euro; a total of EUR 42,5 million over three years.[68]

Launching the B7-667 budget-line, the Commission stated simply that its "overarching objective will be to influence migratory flows".[69] Initially intended to support implementation of the HLWG action plans, financing under B7-667 soon widened to cover external migration issues more generally as the action plans became obsolete.[70]

The development of B7-667 took place in parallel with the integration of migration issues into RELEX and DEV strategies. Financing of essentially the same type of activity was thus taking place under parallel budgets. The faltering implementation of the action plans justified an additional source of financing in the form of B7-667.

64 European Parliament Resolution of 30 March 2000, *OJ* C 378, 29 December 2000, p. 75, para. 32; Council Doc. 13993/00, para. 60.

65 Framework for preparatory actions B7-667 in 2001, SEC(2001) 1338.

66 Regulation (EC) No 491/2004 of the European Parliament and of the Council of 10 March 2004 establishing a programme for financial and technical assistance to third countries in the areas of migration and asylum (AENEAS), *OJ* L 80, 18.3.2004, p. 1.

67 COM(2006) 26 final.

68 COM(2006) 26 final, p. 6.

69 Framework for preparatory actions B7-667 in 2001, SEC(2001) 1338.

70 Framework for preparatory actions B7-667 in 2002, SEC(2002) 1979.

More importantly, B7-667 was a budget-line belonging to the Justice and Home Affairs field. *Chef de file* was DG JLS (then DG JHA) of the Commission. This enabled more direct control and pursuit of JHA migration interests in the external field, including the readmission negotiations, without depending on the benevolence of policy-makers in external relations policy fields.

B7-667 money was used to procure migration-related projects, which were implemented, or had their effect, in relevant third countries. Each year of preparatory action was preceded by a call for tender, specifying a number of priority actions and priority countries. The Commission adapted the lists of priority actions and target countries each year in accordance with the needs of the Community. Project proposals were welcomed from a range of actors, including government authorities of third countries and Member States, international organisations, and NGOs.

The selection of projects was entirely in the hands of the Commission. DG JLS organised a yearly inter-service consultation for this purpose, which moreover served to ensure that B7-667 financing would not overlap with migration-related actions under RELEX and DEV budgets. After reaching internal agreement, the Commission would convene an informal meeting with interested Member States to discuss the projects, short-listed for procurement. Here, Member States were given opportunity to express their interest in particular projects, and attempt to sway the Commission in its final allocation of the budget of that year.

Regarding the type of projects procured under B7-667,[71] the emphasis of the first call for tender in 2001 was clearly on building migration control- and refugee protection capacity in transit countries. The 2002 and 2003 calls were more balanced, inviting projects in relation to migration control and refugee protection, as well as root causes and labour immigration. Projects, selected for financing, in 2001 and 2002 still favoured migration- and border control measures in transit countries. By 2003, however, the control overtone of funding under the B7-667 budget had diminished, showing a relative increase in spending for action in source countries of migration.

A particular motivation for developing B7-667 was the need to advance the common readmission policy. DG JLS set up B7-667, intending for it to provide leverage in the negotiations, and assist third countries in implementing Community readmission agreements. The first call for tender in 2001 invited projects, which would assist third countries "to cope with their readmission obligations towards the European

71 The detailed overview in annex 2bis of the December 2002 Commission Communication on integrating migration issues in the European Union's relations with third countries (COM(2003) 703 final) gives an impression of the allocation of B7-667 funding. For yearly changes in programming, see the Framework for preparatory actions B7-667 in 2001 (SEC(2001) 1338); the Framework for preparatory actions B7-667 in 2002 (SEC(2002) 1979); and the call for proposals of 2003 (documents available on: www.europa.eu.int/comm/justice_home).

Community and the Member States",[72] and strengthen "flanking measures"[73] for the conclusion of Community readmission agreements. B7-667 thus immediately gave the common readmission policy additional financial backing. Although subject to the constraints of project-based financing, B7-667 widened possibilities for the Commission to pledge financial and technical assistance in dealing with the readmission of unauthorised immigrants.

Express leverage for the readmission negotiations is not apparent from the list of B7-667 projects, funded in 2001 and 2002.[74] The common readmission policy again featured prominently in the 2003 call for proposals. It included all of the readmission countries as priority countries. It moreover invited project proposals for providing "targeted support to capacity-building within the framework of readmission". However, only one such project was eventually selected for funding, with regard to Albania.[75]

As noted above, leverage in the readmission negotiations can also be provided by projects which do not refer explicitly to "readmission".[76] Referring explicitly to readmission in B7-667 calls for tender is relevant mainly insofar as it makes financial assistance to readmission countries clearly visible. This may facilitate negotiations in certain cases, a good example of which is Albania. In substantive terms, "capacity-building within the framework of readmission", as referred to in the 2003 call for proposals, does not have a distinct meaning. It encompasses a range of possible actions aimed at enhancing a country's capacity to receive immigrants, secure documents, detect forgeries, *etcetera*. Many such actions were also included in B7-667 calls for proposals, and could have resulted in potentially useful projects for the Commission in terms of negotiating leverage.

Generally, however, one may question the effectiveness of B7-667 as an instrument for creating leverage in the readmission negotiations. The constraints of project-based financing are considerable in this regard. B7-667 allowed the Commission to channel funds towards the readmission countries, but this depended entirely on the project proposals received each year. The content and originator of projects can be determined only to a limited degree by a call for tender. B7-667 was able to provide direct negotiating leverage, but only if a readmission country would apply for funding. Project proposals by international organisations or local NGOs, impacting upon a relevant third country, also have a certain negotiating value. As it turned out, the Commission hardly received any grant applications from government authorities of third countries, and project proposals by local NGOs were often too unprofessional to be selected for financing. Although the Commission developed B7-667 with the common

72 SEC(2001) 1338 (paraphrasing paragraph 26 of the Tampere Conclusions, *supra*, at n. 11).

73 SEC(2001) 1338.

74 COM(2003) 703 final, annex 2bis.

75 The Commission hereby partly fulfilled its pledge to assist Albania in preparing for the readmission of third country nationals under the agreement with the Community, which had purposely been postponed for a period of two years, *supra* 3.2.5, n. 76-79.

76 *Supra*, subsection 6.2.1.

readmission policy in mind, its impact on the readmission negotiations was arguably limited.

#### 6.2.2.2 The Aeneas Regulation

In 2003, the Commission proposed to extend JHA funding for migration cooperation with third countries, and provide it with a legal basis. Succeeding the B7-667 budget-line, the Council adopted the Aeneas[77] Regulation on 10 March 2004. This legislation establishes a programme for financial and technical assistance to third countries in the areas of migration and asylum for the period 2004-2008. It is supported by a budget of EUR 250 million. With DG JLS again acting as *chef de file*, the Aeneas Regulation represents a significant increase in the impact of external EC immigration and asylum policies.

The manner in which Aeneas funds are dispensed is largely the same as under B7-667: project-based financing, based on a yearly call for proposals.[78] The main difference is that the Member States have a say in which projects are financed. The involvement of the Member States in the yearly programming and project selection was one of the main issues of negotiation in the HLWG, which prepared the final text of the Regulation. Instead of an informal meeting with the Commission to discuss the yearly selection, the Member States and Commission under the Aeneas Regulation form a so-called "management committee". Article 9 of the Regulation determines that this committee will assist the Commission in all aspects of managing and implementing the Aeneas programme in accordance with Council Decision 1999/468/EC.[79] This means that Member State representatives in a committee, chaired by the Commission, shall discuss and vote upon Commission proposals for programming as well as the selection of projects by qualified majority.[80] The sphere of influence of the Member States in determining external EC immigration and asylum policies has thus significantly increased.

The overarching objective of the Aeneas Regulation is formulated as being "a more efficient management of migration flows in close cooperation with third coun-

77 In the press release, announcing its adoption, the Commission explains that the Regulation is named after "the hero of Vigil's Aeneid". Press release of 19 February 2004, IP/04/243. In the epic tale of Aeneid, after the fall of Troy, Aeneas led a band of Trojan refugees to Italy and became the founder of Roman culture. Aeneas arguably symbolises the enrichment and diversity that may result from immigration, as opposed to associations with social and financial burden. Except for the fact that Aeneas was a refugee (which would entitle any instrument dealing with migrants to bear his name), a specific parallel with the present Regulation is difficult to identify. The primary purpose of the Aeneas Regulation is not to stimulate or enable, but rather to prevent the arrival of migrants in the EU, and promote their return to third countries.

78 Article 8(3) of the Aeneas Regulation.

79 Council Decision 1999/468/EC of 28 June 1999 laying down the procedures for the exercise of implementing powers conferred on the Commission, *OJ* L 184, 17 July 1999, p. 23.

80 Article 4 of Council Decision 1999/468/EC.

tries".[81] This is broken down into a set of general objectives, each dividing into a set of specified actions, indicating the kind of projects eligible for financing.[82] The objectives and actions present a reasonable balance between stimulating migration control, border control, and refugee reception in transit countries, and undertaking action regarding root causes of migration in source countries. The development of labour immigration possibilities into the EU, as an objective of the Aeneas Regulation, was thoroughly watered down during negotiations. The Member States clearly wanted to retain control over the financing of action in this area.[83] Stimulating the readmission of unauthorised immigrants, rejected protection seekers, and former refugees to third countries ("in full respect of the law"[84]), is also an explicit objective of the Regulation.

The genesis of the Aeneas Regulation is linked directly to the Commission's need for negotiating leverage in the conclusion of readmission agreements with third countries. Referring to the original proposal for the Aeneas Regulation, the Commission has stated that:

> [t]he general objective of this financial instrument will be [...] to provide a [...] response to the needs of third countries of origin and transit in their efforts to ensure third countries with a stimulus [sic.] in their preparation for implementing existing or future readmission agreements with the Community or to support them in implementation proper.[85]

The negotiations in the HLWG started with the idea of providing additional technical and financial assistance, specifically to third countries which are requested to enter into a Community readmission agreement. The Member States soon widened Aeneas assistance to encompass a more comprehensive set of Community objectives in the fields of migration and asylum. The promotion of the readmission agenda however remains a principal vested interest of this legislation.[86] Bearing in mind the constraints of project-based financing referred to above, the Aeneas Regulation finances certain actions in readmission countries, "subject to progress in the negotiations".[87] This is the leverage function. In addition, the Aeneas Regulation is used to assist third countries,

81 Preamble, Recital 14, Aeneas Regulation.

82 Article 2(1) and Article 2(2) of the Aeneas Regulation, respectively.

83 Article 2(1)(b).

84 Article 2(1)(e).

85 COM(2003) 323 final, p. 13.

86 See Article 1(2) of the AENEAS Regulation, which reads: "The programme is particularly, but not exclusively, intended for those third countries actively engaged in preparing or implementing a readmission agreement initialled, signed or concluded with the European Community". See also Recital 7 of the Preamble, and Article 2 of the Regulation.

87 Reference document for financial and technical assistance to third countries in the area of migration and asylum AENEAS Programme 2004 – 2006 (available on: www.europa.eu.int/comm/).

which have concluded a Community readmission agreement, in the implementation thereof.[88]

It is worth noting that, during the negotiations in the HLWG, one Member State proposed amending the Aeneas Regulation to provide support also to readmission negotiations with third countries at the Member State level.[89] This amendment would have enabled the Member States to promote their individual readmission agendas on the back of the Community budget. Considering the still controversial division of competence between the Community and the Member States in the area of readmission, the amendment was sensitive and did not gain sufficient support. It should however be borne in mind that the management committee, referred to above, enables the Member States to influence Aeneas spending to the benefit of their national agendas. This would include particular readmission interests of individual Member States.

At the time of writing, only one cycle of Aeneas programming has been completed (2004). The project proposals submitted in response to the 2005 call for tender are still under consideration. On the basis of these results,[90] one can conclude that visibility of the issue of readmission, as well as the likely amount of resulting leverage in the readmission negotiations, has increased under the Aeneas Regulation in comparison with B7-667.

"Readmission" is a standard heading in the calls for proposals, divided into a set of detailed actions. Looking at the list of projects selected for funding under the 2004 cycle, it seems the response to the call for proposals was such that the Commission was able to channel a notably larger amount of funding to the readmission countries. Several of those projects moreover explicitly refer to "readmission". Particularly evident is the investment of financial and technical resources in countries with which a Community readmission agreement has been successfully concluded.[91] Regarding the still ongoing negotiations, however, it seems that the Aeneas Regulation has so far provided mainly indirect leverage by funding certain projects of international organisations. The Commission has noted that applications for funding by government authorities of third countries are still very limited.[92] This suggests the same for any direct leverage in readmission negotiations resulting from the Aeneas Regulation.

88 *Ibid.*

89 Following this amendment, the text of article 1(2) would have read: "The programme is particularly, but not exclusively, intended for those third countries actively engaged in preparing or implementing a readmission agreement initialled, signed or concluded with the European Community, *or a Member State*." [Italics added, NC]

90 Aeneas Call for Proposals for 2004; Aeneas Call for Proposals for 2005; Projects selected for co-financing by the European Commission under the 2004 budget for the AENEAS Programme, COM(2006) 26 final, Annex I. See also the Aeneas annual workprogramme, COM(2006) 26 final, Annex II.

91 See projects financed in relation to Albania, SAR Macao, and Sri Lanka, COM(2006) 26 final, Annex I.

92 Reference document for financial and technical assistance to third countries in the area of migration and asylum AENEAS Programme 2004 – 2006 (available on: www.europa.

We referred earlier to the general overhaul of the EU's external assistance programmes, which is ongoing at the time of writing.[93] In addition to the smaller number of geographical instruments under the new regime, the number of thematic programmes will also be reduced. In evidence of the rising importance of migration issues within the EU's external relations, one of the seven new thematic programmes concerns cooperation with third countries in the areas of migration and asylum.[94] The Aeneas programme, covering the period 2004-2008, will be cut short, and succeeded by this thematic programme under the financial perspectives for 2007-2013. Readmission will remain a high-profile issue under this new instrument. The thematic programme will be built on five main "strands", one of which will pertain explicitly to "fighting illegal immigration and facilitating the readmission of illegal immigrants".[95]

### *6.2.3 Migrants' remittances*

Falling under the policy heading of migration and development, migrants' remittances has become a topical issue in recent years. Policy-makers caught on to the role and importance of migrants' remittances as more became known of the dimensions and size of this cross-border flow of private money. Global remittance flows were estimated at US$90 billion in 2003. Remittances are of considerable importance to source countries of migration. For many such countries, the money sent home by their nationals abroad is one of, and in some cases the largest external source of income, outranking exports and foreign direct investment.[96]

Remittances have a significant development potential. Policy makers and development organisations world-wide are currently considering how this potential could be harnessed, considering that remittances are first and foremost private resources. One can trust remittances to raise immediate poverty levels, and in time benefit local economy through increased consumption. In addition, source countries, and now also destination countries, are attempting to channel this money towards the public good and into development projects that would benefit the local community at large. Financial institutions and banks caught on earlier to the magnitude and stability of remittance flows and siphon off a large percentage in transfer costs. A main challenge for policies, currently in development, is to find ways to reduce these transfer costs in order to increase the remittance level which actually reaches recipients.[97]

The Commission has been interested in the issue of remittances since the early nineties, and has regularly flagged their importance in policy documents.[98] In the course of 2003, the Commission started reflecting upon the possibility of a common policy

eu.int/comm/); COM(2006) 26 final, p. 7.

93 *Supra*, at n. 61.

94 Press release IP/06/82; COM(2006) 26 final, *supra*, n. 67.

95 COM(2006) 26 final, p. 9, 11.

96 World Bank 2003.

97 World Bank 2003.

98 See, for example, COM(94) 23 final; and COM(2002) 703 final.

on remittances in the European Union.[99] Since then, the Commission has primarily focused on improving the available data on remittances, on enhancing their development impact, and on reducing transfer costs.[100]

Regarding the JHA domain, stimulating migrants' remittances at the EC level is relevant, firstly, while it arguably alleviates the root causes of migration, thereby contributing to the reduction of immigration into the EU. Secondly, the development of remittance-facilitating policies has a certain negotiation value in the readmission negotiations with third countries.

The larger a country's diaspora; the greater its remittance income. Concluding a readmission agreement, which facilitates the return of a country's nationals residing (without authorisation) abroad, may reduce this income. This is one of the negative consequences that a source country of migration may experience upon concluding a readmission agreement with the Community. Several countries, such as Albania, Algeria and Morocco, have expressed their concern in this regard during readmission negotiations with the Commission. The Commission is now able to mitigate these concerns, at least to a degree, by emphasising the fact that the Community is investing in ways to increase remittances to these countries, generated by their nationals residing in EU Member States *with* authorisation. This is expected to promote progress in the readmission negotiations, as well as in the implementation of eventual agreements.

### *6.2.4 European Neighbourhood policy*

In March 2003, the Commission launched the "Wider Europe, New Neighbourhood policy",[101] which was later renamed the "European Neighbourhood policy" (ENP).[102] The principal objective of the ENP is to avoid new "dividing lines"[103] between the EU and its neighbouring countries after the May 2004 enlargement. To this end, it promotes stability in third countries on the EU's external border by encouraging closer political, security, economic, social, and cultural cooperation with the EU. The ENP is best described as a political process, which assembles under one banner pre-existing as well as new forms of cooperation with EU neighbouring countries in a range of policy fields.

The principal instrument of the ENP is the "action plan", tailor-made for each country included under this policy. Action plans are drawn up by the Commission in collaboration with the third country concerned. They are not international agreements, but politically binding documents, which draw general guidelines for cooperation in

99 GAERC Conclusions of 19 May 2003, Council Doc. 8927/03, para. 9.

100 See COM(2005) 390 final; and Council Conclusions of 21 November 2005 on migration and external relations, Council Doc. 14769/05.

101 COM(2003) 104 final, 11. See also the GAER Council Conclusions of 16 June 2003 on Wider Europe – New Neighbourhood, Council Doc. 10447/03; and the ENP website of the Commission at: www.europa.eu.int/comm/world/enp.

102 COM(2004) 373 final. See also the ENP website of the Commission at: www.europa.eu.int/comm/world/enp.

103 COM(2004) 373 final, p. 3.

different policy areas. So far, action plans have been adopted for Israel, Jordan, Moldova, Morocco, the Palestinian Authority, Tunisia and Ukraine. Further action plans are being developed for Armenia, Azerbaijan, Egypt, Georgia and Lebanon.[104]

The action plans generally address cooperation under six headings: political dialogue and reform; economic and social reform and development; trade issues, market and regulatory reform; transport, energy, information society and environment; so-called "people-to-people contacts", and cooperation in justice and home affairs.[105] The EC objective of creating a "buffer zone" of third countries surrounding the EU, which assume responsibility for transit migration, is clearly reflected in the ENP. The action plans prominently include border- and migration control, coupled with the readmission of unauthorised immigrants, under the heading of JHA cooperation.

The ultimate incentive for third countries to further cooperation with the EU under the ENP, arguably, is the long-term prospect of participating in the internal market and of benefiting from free movement rights. The Commission has formulated the trade-off between benefits and obligations under the ENP banner as follows:

> In return for concrete progress demonstrating shared values and effective implementation of political, economic and institutional reforms, including in aligning legislation with the acquis, the EU's neighbourhood should benefit from the prospect of closer economic integration with the EU. To this end, Russia, the countries of the Western NIS and the Southern Mediterranean should be offered the prospect of a stake in the EU's Internal Market and further integration and liberalisation to promote the free movement of – persons, goods, services and capital [...].[106]

At first sight, the leverage which the ENP presents to the negotiation of Community readmission agreements would thus seem significant. As noted, however, the ENP is a political process, making different forms of cooperation visible under a single banner. Concrete conditionality between certain beneficial forms of cooperation, and the acceptance of readmission obligations, remains subject to Council decisions in relation to the policy fields involved. Rather than a direct trade-off, therefore, the ENP provides a forum in which to promote readmission obligations by emphasising existing linkages with other policy fields,[107] and to stimulate the implementation thereof.

At the time of writing, the EU neighbouring countries are becoming a geographical focal point for EU external assistance. As noted, the EU neighbourhood will be the subject of one of the three geographical instruments under the new external assistance

104 Press release IP/05/1467; SPEECH/06/30.

105 See the text of the action plans for Israel, Jordan, Moldova, Morocco, the Palestinian Authority, Tunisia and Ukraine, available on: www.europa.eu.int/comm/world/enp.

106 COM(2003) 104 final, p. 4.

107 See, for example, the actions plans for Morocco and Ukraine under JHA cooperation, as well as the following speech by the RELEX Commissioner, SPEECH/06/30, 24 January 2006.

regime.[108] This will likely increase the financial resources at the Commission's disposal to facilitate the negotiation of readmission agreements with neighbouring countries of the EU.

### 6.3 Readmission or punishment

In the autumn of 2003, the HLWG prepared not only an instrument intended to support the readmission countries – the Aeneas Regulation – but also laid the groundwork for possible punitive action. Where the Aeneas Regulation provides "carrots", the so-called "monitoring and evaluation mechanism of cooperation of third countries in the field of the fight against illegal immigration",[109] launched in November 2003, prepares for the application of the proverbial "stick". It provides a basis for Council decisions taking action against third countries unwilling to cooperate with the EU's wishes in countering unauthorised migration, including readmission.

The use of punitive measures, or negative incentives, has always hovered beneath the surface of EU discourse regarding external immigration and asylum policies. Instead of the term punishment, which is found only occasionally in EU documents,[110] the Council and Commission have generally preferred the term "linkage". "Linking" migration issues with other policies can imply a number of things, such as the withholding of supportive measures, or the discontinuation of beneficial forms of cooperation, in case of a lack of cooperation on migration. Early references to such "linkage" can be found in the 1992 Edinburgh Declaration on principles of governing external aspects of migration policy, the first meeting of the JHA Council in November 1993, and the 1994 Commission Communication on immigration and asylum policies.[111]

Periodically, the tone of EC external immigration and asylum policies hardens, and calls for punitive measures against uncooperative countries become more explicit. An example in this regard is the 1998 Austrian Strategy paper.[112] The current monitoring and evaluation mechanism is rooted in the proposals and suggestions contained in this paper.[113] The spirit of punishment again rose to the surface at the Seville European Council, which took concrete steps towards developing this mechanism.

---

108 COM(2006) 26 final, p. 3, *supra*, at n. 61.

109 Council Doc. 15292/03, 25 November 2003 (hereinafter referred to as the monitoring and evaluation mechanism).

110 See, for example, the European Parliament, which in a 2000 resolution refers to "punitive action" proposed by the HLWG action plans, European Parliament Resolution of 30 March 2000, *OJ* C 378, 29 December 2000, p. 75, para. 6.

111 See *supra*, section 1.4, at n. 59, 60 and 63.

112 *Supra*, section 1.4, at n. 71.

113 The Austrian Presidency *inter alia* called for a "comprehensive and systematic assessment" of the level at which third countries cooperated on migration issues, as a determining factor for EU relations with these countries, Council Doc. 9809/98, para. 115 and under 5.1.

While clarifying the relation of the monitoring and evaluation mechanism with punitive action, as well as with the common readmission policy, we quote the relevant conclusions of the Seville European Council in full:

> 34. The European Council stresses the importance of ensuring the cooperation of countries of origin and transit in joint management of migration and in border control as well as on readmission. Such readmission by third countries should include that of their own nationals unlawfully present in a Member State and, under the same conditions, that of other countries' nationals who can be shown to have passed through the country in question. Cooperation should bring results in the short and medium term. [...]
> 35. The European Council considers it necessary to carry out a systematic assessment of relations with third countries which do not cooperate in combating illegal immigration. That assessment will be taken into account in relations between the European Union and its Member States and the countries concerned, in all relevant areas. Insufficient cooperation by a country could hamper the establishment of closer relations between that country and the Union.
> 36. If full use has been made of existing Community mechanisms but without success, the Council may unanimously find that a third country has shown an unjustified lack of cooperation in the joint management of migration flows. In that event the Council may, in accordance with the rules laid down in the treaties, adopt measures or positions under the Common Foreign and Security Policy and other European Union policies, while honouring the Union's contractual commitments but not jeopardising development cooperation objectives.[114]

The European Council thus warned of a number of punitive measures that might follow upon a negative evaluation of a third country's cooperation on migration issues. The Council could firstly decide to dismiss the possibility of "closer relations" between that country and the EU. Secondly, the Council could adopt undisclosed measures under the Common Foreign and Security Policy, and other European Union policies. The European Council, however, also set the limits of punitive action: the Council is required to honour the Union's contractual commitments, and refrain from jeopardising development cooperation objectives.

The Thessaloniki European Council subsequently mandated the HLWG to develop the monitoring and evaluation mechanism, indicating a number of criteria based on

114 Presidency Conclusions, Seville European Council of 21 and 22 June 2002, para. 34-36. Previous drafts of the relevant conclusions in notably hasher wording can be found in Council Doc. 9917/3/02, and Council Doc. 9723/02. See also Peers 2004, p. 209. Mentioned as possible "sticks" were certain foreign policy measures, an invitation to the Commission to reduce development aid, and the suspension of cooperation and association agreements.

which third countries should be judged, including cooperation on readmission.[115] The lack of cooperation of third countries in readmitting unauthorised immigrants was clearly an important factor, leading the European Council to take this decision.

Unlike Aeneas, the monitoring and evaluation mechanism does not have a legal basis. The mechanism is outlined in Council conclusions.[116] The purpose of the mechanism is "to monitor the migratory situation in relevant third countries, their administrative capacity to manage asylum and migration, including the actions undertaken in order to tackle illegal immigration".[117] The mechanism must provide "all relevant information" necessary for the systematic assessment and evaluation of the degree of cooperation received.[118] In principle, it may cover "all relevant third countries", although the first year of operation of the mechanism was determined to be a pilot year, pertaining to a limited number of countries in order to test its functioning. Up for evaluation in this pilot year are the priority countries of the November 2002 GAER Conclusions: Albania, China, the Federal Republic of Yugoslavia (FRY), Libya, Morocco, Russia, Tunisia, Turkey, and Ukraine.[119] Turkey was later removed from the list, when it became a candidate Member State.[120]

To gather the necessary information, the Council asked the Commission and the Member States to pool their resources. The Commission compiles the information in annual reports to the Council.[121] The annual reports are drawn up along a "list of indicators", which is drafted by the Commission in conclave with the Member States.[122] This is an extensive checklist that is not made public. It lists the migration policies regarding which third countries are monitored, then evaluated.

The Council conclusions contain a number of recommendations, giving an indication of the general content and nature of the checklist. Subject to scrutiny are *inter alia* national legislation relating to unauthorised immigration, visa policy, reception capacity, the participation of third countries in international instruments relevant to asylum and immigration, and "efforts in" migration management, border control and the interception of unauthorised immigrants.[123] In accordance with the Seville and Thessaloniki conclusions, the issue of readmission is prominently included. Paragraph 5(c) reads:

> Cooperation in readmission/return of their own nationals and of third-country nationals, giving special attention to the readmission of their own nationals without for-

115 Presidency Conclusions, Thessaloniki European Council of 19 and 20 June 2003, para. 19-21.

116 Council Doc. 15292/03, 25 November 2003.

117 Council Doc. 15292/03, para. 4.

118 Council Doc. 15292/03, para. 4.

119 Council Doc. 15292/03, para. 8; *supra*, at n. 30.

120 COM(2005) 352 final, p. 2.

121 Council Doc. 15292/03, para. 5.

122 Council Doc. 15292/03, para. 5.

123 Council Doc. 15292/03, paras. 5(a), (b) and (d).

> malities and providing all necessary documentation, as well as to the conclusion and implementation of readmission agreements with the European Community, its Member States and relevant third countries.

At first glance, one wonders what the novelty of this mechanism is. In addition to the initial selection of the same set of target countries, the information collected for the present mechanism is essentially identical to the information collected under the November 2002 GAER Council conclusions. "Attitude towards cooperation on migration" was moreover already a specific criterion, determining the prioritisation of a third country pursuant to the November 2002 conclusions.[124] The only novelty, arguably, is the change in purpose of this information. Previously intended to promote political dialogue, it will now apparently be used to prepare other Community action against third countries which are uncooperative in stemming migration flows towards the EU. The Council conclusions, outlining the monitoring and evaluation mechanism, however, do not provide any clarification of this aspect.

The Council conclusions on the monitoring and evaluation mechanism explain in detail the "monitoring" element of the mechanism, but reveal very little with regard to the "evaluation" element, and even less with regard to the consequences that may be attached to it. The Council only states that the mechanism should provide information for the systematic assessment and evaluation of third countries' cooperation "as foreseen in the Seville European Council conclusions", and that it "could be of value to the Commission in its programming responsibilities toward relevant third countries".[125]

The Council conclusions have thus not given the monitoring and evaluation mechanism an overtly punitive role. The possibility of punitive Community action in the field of external migration policy remains unspoken. The main association of this instrument is however clearly with the "stick", as opposed to the "carrot". This is apparent from its genesis, and inherent in its purpose of identifying uncooperative, unwilling countries. The idea behind the present mechanism is that it would prepare the "groundwork" for certain decisions of the Council or Commission with a punitive effect. The suggestion is that providing an explicit and seemingly empirical basis for such decisions would increase their legitimacy. This mechanism may thus be considered to bring such decisions a step closer.

With regard to readmission, we noted above that there is a relation between the common readmission policy and the creation of the monitoring and evaluation mechanism. The readmission negotiations partly informed the inception of the present mechanism. Six out of the nine countries that were originally selected for the pilot year of the mechanism are readmission countries. In November 2004, the Council explicitly strengthened this relation. The GAER Council adopted conclusions "on the priorities

124 *Supra*, at n. 29.

125 Council Doc. 15292/03, para. 4.

for the successful development of a common readmission policy".[126] In light of the lack of progress in the readmission negotiations, the Council invited the Commission to:

> [p]ay special attention to the cooperation of third countries in the field of readmission in its yearly assessment. Therefore, the Council invites the Commission to consider extending its yearly monitoring report in the framework of the evaluation mechanism [...] to countries for which the Commission has received a mandate to negotiate a Community readmission agreement. This evaluation should include the negotiating process, as well as the implementation of the readmission agreement in force.[127]

The lack of progress in the readmission negotiations is an important impetus in the development of a Community policy that allows for the use of negative incentives in the area of migration. The threat of punitive Community action, associated with this mechanism, may arguably exercise pressure on third countries to complete negotiations, and cooperate in the implementation of readmission agreements.

Peers and Rogers have called into question the "logic of punishment".[128] According to these authors, undertaking punitive action against a country will ultimately damage EU interests, internally as well as externally. They argue that any action that would further weaken the economy of third countries may lead to an increase in immigration levels into the EU. More persons would depart from countries of origin, and transit countries would have less incentive to halt flows passing through their territory. Furthermore, punitive action sours external relations, which may weaken the EU strategically, and hurt EU business and investment interests.

It is correct to posit that punitive action, which aims to enforce cooperation on readmission specifically or on migration issues generally, risks being ultimately ineffective, or even harmful to EU interests. There indeed exist contradictions between certain external policies of the EU, and the drive towards punitive measures against third countries that do not cooperate on migration issues. For example, the objective of the European Neighbourhood Policy, as discussed in the previous subsection, is to promote the economic and social stability of third countries on the EU's external border.[129] The Commission has recently proposed extending the monitoring and evaluation mechanism to include more ENP countries.[130] Expanding the use of punitive measures to persuade neighbouring countries to sign Community readmission agreements could have a destabilising effect on these countries, which would evidently conflict with the ENP's objectives.

However, it should be borne in mind that the predominant "logic" of punishment, arguably, is that it banks on a preventative effect, precluding the actual taking

126 Council Doc. 13578/04.

127 Council Doc. 13578/04, Conclusion No. 7.

128 Peers and Rogers 2006.

129 *Supra*, subsection 6.2.4.

130 COM(2005) 352 final, p. 10.

of action. When threatening to use negative incentives to further external migration policies, the European Council is inevitably bluffing to a degree. This is especially true where concerning more severe actions, such as the measures under the CFSP and other European Union policies, referred to by the Seville European Council.[131] In case the threat of punitive action by the EU would not persuade a third country to comply, the actual taking of action would moreover highly depend on the circumstances, as well as the strategic importance of the country involved. It is unlikely that the Council would decide on punitive measures and risk souring relations with, for example, Russia or China, over a readmission agreement. (With smaller, less significant countries, though, it might.) In any case, it is the *threat* of punishment which is arguably the principal value of any punitive policy.

Notwithstanding the benefits and downsides of punitive policies, the Community's commitment to overt punishment of third countries for not cooperating in the area of migration is still wavering. As noted, the Council conclusions on the monitoring and evaluation mechanism did not provide any indication of the possible consequences of a negative evaluation under the monitoring and evaluation mechanism. It also remains unclear which procedure the Council would follow upon receiving the Commission's annual report on the evaluated third countries. The report is supposed to be factual, but its content is clearly politically laden considering the consequences it might have. It is submitted to the Council, which would then presumably consider whether to take punitive action in accordance with conclusions 35 and 36 of the Seville European Council. Whether the Commission, independently of the Council, would consider attaching consequences to the report (for example in the exercise of its external "programming responsibilities"[132]) is also unclear, but would in any case depend on the political will of the college of Commissioners.

The Commission published the first annual report, concerning the pilot year of the monitoring and evaluation mechanism, on 28 July 2005.[133] The report consists of a brief overview of cooperation with the EC relating to migration and asylum per target country. It notes achieved progress encouragingly, and identifies areas where more progress is needed, such as the readmission negotiations with China, Morocco, Russia, and Ukraine. Following the November 2004 GAER Council conclusions quoted above,[134] the report mentions the Commission is considering including also the remaining readmission countries, Algeria, Hong Kong, Macao, Pakistan and Sri Lanka, under the mechanism. The report furthermore provides a number of political recommendations to the third countries concerned, the Member States, and the Council, but without ever referring to the possibility of punitive measures. Rather meekly, the Commission limits itself to stating: "It is hoped that this report will assist the Council in assessing the level of cooperation of each country in the fight against illegal immigration as set

131 *Supra*, at n. 114.

132 *Supra*, at n. 125.

133 COM(2005) 352 final.

134 *Supra*, at n. 127.

out in the Seville Council conclusions of 2002."[135] The present author has no information regarding any Council decisions taken with regard to third countries based on the Commission's report.

As argued above, the monitoring and evaluation mechanism may be considered to bring punitive measures in the area of external migration policy a step closer. Taking a different perspective, however, one may doubt whether any more "groundwork" (in terms of providing information and identifying problem countries) is really necessary. The Member States and EU institutions are aware which third countries are persistently uncooperative, having undertaken repeated inventories in the last few years. The necessary information is already present. One could therefore also posit that the creation of the monitoring and evaluation mechanism only postpones the answer to the real question. It remains to be seen whether the political will is present at the EU level to fully implement the Seville European Council conclusions.

One can conclude that punishment, as a flanking measure of the common readmission policy, is still relatively underdeveloped. Excepting a handful of subtle instances of "linkage", which we will discuss in the next chapter, the EU institutions do not yet attempt to persuade third countries to sign readmission agreements with (threats of) punitive measures. For the time being, the extent to which the Community is willing to punish third countries for not cooperating on migration issues remains unclear, and punishment as a flanking measure of the common readmission policy retains a decidedly low profile.

### 6.4 Conclusion

The EU institutions have integrated migration issues into the EU's external relations since the early nineties, a process which intensified after the Tampere European Council in 1999. In relations with third countries, the Council and Commission place specific emphasis on the readmission of unauthorised immigrants, and the conclusion of readmission agreements.

Despite a firm conviction at the EU level of the importance of the external dimension of immigration and asylum policies, integrating migration issues into EU external relations has not been a straightforward process. The reception of migration objectives, including the conclusion of Community readmission agreements, into the different external policies has had varying results.

Nevertheless, a number of flanking measures for the common readmission policy have been developed within the EU's external relations. The most advanced are supportive policies, "carrots", which mitigate the consequences of a readmission agreement with the Community. The Commission has used EU external assistance programmes, and specific budgets within the JHA domain – the B7-667 budget-line and the Aeneas programme – to fund migration-related projects in the readmission countries. Where such projects provide technical and financial support relevant to the implementation of readmission agreements, this funding provides a degree of leverage in the negotiation of such agreements. Furthermore, the developing policy at the EU level, stimulating

135 COM(2005) 352 final, p. 3.

migrants' remittances, has a facilitating effect on the readmission negotiations with certain countries. Finally, the European Neighbourhood Policy may also be considered a flanking measure of the common readmission policy.

A far less advanced flanking measure is the use of punitive measures, negative incentives, or "sticks". Although hovering at the fringes of external EC immigration and asylum policies since the early nineties, overt punitive EU measures against unco-operative third countries still lack the necessary political support.

# Chapter 7 The negotiation of Community readmission agreements

This chapter analyses the negotiation process of Community readmission agreements. At the time of writing, the Commission has received a total of sixteen negotiating directives from the Council. In September 2000, the Council adopted a first set of directives for the negotiation of Community readmission agreements with Morocco, Pakistan, Russia, and Sri Lanka. The Council added directives for Hong Kong and Macao in May 2001 and for Ukraine in June 2002. Directives for Albania, Algeria, China, and Turkey were adopted in November 2002, followed by a final set of mandates for Bosnia and Herzegovina, Macedonia, Moldova, Montenegro, and Serbia towards the end of 2006.

Section 7.1 details the manner in which these third countries were selected for the conclusion of a readmission agreement at the Community level. Section 7.2 discusses the current state of negotiations country-by-country. Section 7.3 then provides several general observations regarding the readmission negotiations.

Most of the research for this chapter was done during an internship at the immigration and asylum unit of DG JFS of the European Commission from October 2003 until February 2004. The description and analysis of developments after February 2004 is thus necessarily less detailed, limited mostly to general updates.

## 7.1 The selection of readmission countries

### *7.1.1 1999 – impromptu selection and political appropriateness*

After the Tampere European Council had invited the Council to start concluding readmission agreements, it was time to start selecting target countries.[1] The first set of third countries, regarding which the Council adopted negotiating directives for Community readmission agreements, was selected with the help of a veritable "hit list".[2]

1 Presidency Conclusions, Tampere European Council of 15 and 16 October 1999, para. 27.

2 Council Doc. 13888/99, annex. For additional Council documents, relevant to the selection of the first target countries, see Peers and Rogers 2006.

In October 1999, the SCIFA undertook an inventory of third countries, which the Member States considered eligible for concluding a Community readmission agreement with. In this manner, the SCIFA hoped to identify a set of countries regarding which there existed a Community-wide interest in the readmission of unauthorised immigrants. A list of 29 pre-selected countries was used as a basis for this inventory. Member States were allowed to cast five votes. The SCIFA subsequently discussed the results of the inventory, counting the number of proposals per country, which were as follows.[3]

| | No. of Proposals |
|---|---|
| China | 7 |
| India | 6 |
| Pakistan, Russia, Turkey | 5 |
| Algeria, Ethiopia, FRY, Nigeria | 4 |
| Iran, Sri Lanka, Ukraine | 3 |
| Albania, Armenia, Bangladesh, Egypt, Moldova, Morocco | 2 |
| Azerbaijan, Belarus, Georgia, Ghana, Lebanon, Mali, Senegal, Sudan, Tunisia | 1 |

The preferences of the Member States were scattered. This might indicate that immigrants of a certain nationality are spread unevenly over the EU Member States. One may however assume that the Member States primarily selected countries with which they had not been able to achieve satisfactory cooperation on readmission.[4] From this perspective, the SCIFA inventory would illustrate that the Member States receive differing degrees of cooperation from third countries.[5] This is not surprising, considering that successful expulsion – presupposing (re)admission by another State – depends greatly on the specific history and quality of relations between two States. Thus, some Member States may receive cooperation on the readmission of unauthorised immigrants, while others experience problems, with the same country.

In any case, it proved difficult to identify a Community interest in readmission to specific third countries, using the "hit list" method. At a subsequent meeting in November 1999, the SCIFA therefore decided to make a selection based on certain additional "factors".[6] Paraphrasing, the SCIFA agreed to take into account also the following:

- The appropriateness of concluding a readmission agreement with a particular country
- Recommendations by the HLWG in its Action Plans

3 Council Doc. 13888/99.

4 *Supra*, subsection 3.1.2.

5 This assumption is confirmed by an earlier inventory (by the Migration/Expulsion Working Group in May 1999) of the problems experienced by the Member States in the expulsion and readmission of immigrants to specific third countries, Council Doc. 7609/1/99.

6 Council Doc. 13888/99.

- Recommendations in the Common Strategy on Russia and the Common Strategy on Ukraine
- The possibility that conclusion of a readmission agreement may be counterproductive in cases where there exists a well-functioning practical cooperation[7]
- The position of individual Member States facing problems with specific third countries
- The availability of a broader political context in which to place, and thereby ease, the negotiation of a readmission agreement[8]

This listing sheds light on the eventual selection of readmission countries by the SCIFA, which is not at all apparent from the above "hit list". In September 2000, the Council authorised the Commission to negotiate readmission agreements on behalf of the Community with Morocco, Pakistan, Russia, and Sri Lanka.[9]

General reasons for singling these countries out were the following. Several Member States were experiencing difficulties in the readmission of nationals and especially third country nationals to Morocco, in some cases even in the presence of a formal agreement.[10] Pakistan was not a priority in terms of numbers of unauthorised immigrants in the EU, but imposed typically lengthy and bureaucratic readmission procedures on requesting Member States. Furthermore, there was a clear interest in increasing the expulsion possibilities for Afghani nationals, previously present in Pakistan.[11] Russia was included as a main source- and transit country of immigration into several Member States. Russia was also known as a notoriously tough negotiator in attempts to reach agreements on readmission by individual Member States. Regarding Sri Lanka, there had been recent signs of improvement in cooperation on the readmission of rejected Sri Lankan protection seekers. To make use of this momentum the SCIFA recommended negotiating a readmission agreement.[12]

Furthermore, in light of the above list of selection "factors",[13] concluding readmission agreements with Morocco, Pakistan and Sri Lanka provided some much needed follow-up to the ineffectual HLWG Action Plans.[14] Concluding a readmission agreement with Russia was one of the recommendations in the 1999 EU common strategy

---

7 See also the opinion of the Nordic Joint Advisory Group on Refugee Policy, Council Doc. 7707/99.

8 Council Doc. 13888/99.

9 Schieffer 2003, p. 344.

10 See the inventory by the Migration/Expulsion Working Group, Council Doc. 7609/1/99, *supra*, n. 5; and the HLWG Action Plan for Morocco, Council Doc. 11426/99.

11 Council Doc. 7609/1/99; EU Action Plan for Afghanistan, Council, Doc. 11424/99.

12 Council Doc. 7609/1/99; EU Action Plan for Sri Lanka, Council Doc. 11428/99.

13 *Supra*, at n. 6, 8.

14 The action plans for Morocco, Afghanistan and Sri Lanka, recommended the conclusion of readmission agreements with, respectively, Morocco, Pakistan, and Sri Lanka. See also *supra*, section 1.4 and subsection 6.2.2.

on Russia.[15] The Partnership and Cooperation Agreement (PCA) with Russia, which entered into force on 1 December 1998, also referred to cooperation on readmission.[16] The PCA moreover provided a political and institutional framework within which to place the readmission negotiations, and discuss matters relating to the implementation of an eventual agreement.

Regarding Pakistan in particular, the prospect of having a similar framework in the near future may have been a relevant factor in this country's selection. At the time, a third generation Cooperation Agreement (CA) between the Community and Pakistan was under negotiation. A joint declaration, attached to this CA, moreover committed to the negotiation of a readmission agreement at the request of one of the contracting parties.[17] Upon further investigation of the list of factors used by the SCIFA, however, the selection of Pakistan is questionable. Negotiating a readmission agreement with Pakistan could arguably not have been considered "appropriate" at the time.[18]

The signing of the CA with Pakistan had been postponed on several occasions, precisely for reasons of political "appropriateness". The CA was initialled in April 1998. The ratification procedures were subsequently suspended several times, however, due to Pakistan's nuclear testing, events in relation to the Kashmir region, and lastly the military coup in October 1999.[19] The coup was condemned by the EU, which did not recognise the new regime headed by Pervez Musharaf. The Council nevertheless ordered the negotiation of a readmission agreement to start in September 2000, which illustrates that a double standard applies where the Community's migration interests are involved. Subsection 7.1.5 will elaborate on this further.

Remarkable in the list of criteria, used by the SCIFA in November 1999 to identify readmission countries, is that it explicitly included political factors, relating to general external relations, next to home affairs interests. Home affairs interests finally trumped considerations of the "appropriateness" of engaging in readmission cooperation, illustrated by the case of Pakistan. When taken into account, political factors may conflict with the establishment of migration cooperation with certain countries. Unsur-

15 Common strategy of the European Union of 4 June 1999 on Russia, *OJ* L 157, 24 June 1999, p. 1.

16 See Article 84 of the PCA with Russia, as well as an attached joint declaration referring to the conclusion of a readmission agreement as "important", *Agreement on Partnership and Cooperation establishing a Partnership between the European Communities and their Member States, of the one part, and the Russian Federation, of the other part*, L/CE/RU/en.

17 Recalled by the HLWG in its Action Plan on Afghanistan, recommending conclusion of a readmission agreement with Pakistan, Council Doc. 11424/99, para. 62 and 138c.

18 The November 1999 SCIFA meeting listed "the appropriateness of concluding a readmission agreement with a particular country" as relevant to selecting readmission countries, Council Doc. 13888/99, *supra*, n. 8.

19 The EU's relations with Pakistan (available on: www.europa.eu.int/comm/external_relations/pakistan, consulted on 18 February 2005); European Parliament, session document PE 311.031.

prisingly, therefore, political factors did not reappear in later sets of criteria, adopted by the Council to select third countries for the conclusion of readmission agreements.

As is apparent from the above, the first set of readmission countries was selected in a haphazard manner. This reflects the initial development of readmission policy following the Tampere European Council, which was generally impromptu. The next negotiating directives for Hong Kong and Macao were adopted by the Council in May 2001 in response to requests for the lifting of visa requirements. The negotiating directive for Ukraine, adopted in March 2002, resulted from a recommendation of the EU common strategy on Ukraine,[20] rather than a specific policy decision. It took some time before an effort was made to direct the common readmission policy on the basis of any real strategy.[21]

### *7.1.2 2002 – first strategic considerations*

The European Council in Laeken in December 2001 determined that the conclusion of further Community readmission agreements should take place "on the basis of a new list of priorities and a clear action plan".[22] The Council's plan on combating illegal immigration, adopted in February 2002, contained only vague references to the development of readmission strategy, but did decide "to identify without delay the third countries generating illegal immigration and negotiate and conclude new readmission agreements with them".[23]

The JHA Council responded with April 2002 conclusions on "criteria for the identification of third countries with which new readmission agreements need to be negotiated".[24] This was a first attempt at formulating an explicit strategy for the development of the common readmission policy, including a new set of selection criteria. As of April 2002, third countries were targeted for the conclusion of a Community readmission agreement, taking account of:

1. The migration pressure exerted by flows of persons from or via third countries, together with the number of persons awaiting return, and relevant obstacles to return
2. The existence of an Association or Cooperation Agreement with the Community
3. Accession negotiations, which should not have started yet

---

20 *OJ* L 331, 23 December 1999, p. 1; Schieffer 2003, p. 346.

21 Despite intentions of the Commission and Council to establish "a coherent EU policy concerning readmission" within two years after the entry into force of the Treaty of Amsterdam, *Action plan of the Council and the Commission on how best to implement the provisions of the Treaty of Amsterdam establishing an area of freedom, security and justice*, Council Doc. 13844/98, quoted in Fernhout 1999, p. 92.

22 Presidency Conclusions, Laeken European Council of 14 and 15 December 2001, para. 40.

23 *OJ* C 142, 14 June 2002, para. 75, 76.

24 Council Doc. 7990/02, 16 April 2002.

4. The geographical position of a third country as adjacent to a Member State
5. The added value in comparison with bilateral Member State agreements
6. Geographical balance and regional coherence[25]

This list shows a clear overlap with the criteria, adopted soon after by the GAER Council in November 2002, determining the third countries with which to intensify migration cooperation.[26]

The first criterion reflects a general objective of readmission agreements, which is to alleviate migration pressure, effect returns, and solve obstacles to returns. The second criterion prioritises associated countries, seeking to make use of readmission clauses that may have been included in relevant Association or Cooperation Agreements. Criterion number three was arguably included out of practical consideration. Negotiating a Community readmission agreement with a third country, which is set to become a Member of the Community, would be largely ineffectual in most cases, and therefore a waste of resources. In relation to Turkey, however, subsection 7.2.10 below explains how this criterion became a highly political issue, as a result of which the Council and Commission may well have regretted including it in this list.

The fourth criterion is a direct translation of the Community objective of creating a "cordon" or "buffer zone" of third countries around the EU, blocking transit migration.[27] Regarding criterion number five, the Council does not explain what could be considered an "added value" of a Community- versus a Member State agreement. This criterion could imply that Community agreements are concluded only with third countries, which pose problems (for example regarding bureaucratic readmission procedures or large numbers of unauthorised immigrants) to a certain minimum number of Member States. "Added value" could however also refer to the dominant negotiating position of the Community, as opposed to individual Member States, identified in section 3.1 above as the main motivation for the pursuit of a common readmission policy.

The sixth criterion stems from the "regional approach" that the Community takes to external migration policies.[28] This policy approach takes account of the fact that migration flows have a regional impact. With regard to readmission policy, this means that, when targeting a third country for a readmission agreement, the Community considers concluding agreements also with other countries in the region. This of course broadens readmission possibilities for the Member States. However, it also avoids the concentration of responsibility for the readmission of persons of an entire region on a single State, considering the obligation to readmit third country nationals. The parallel targeting of additional countries in a region therefore facilitates the negotiation of individual agreements. In addition, the conclusion of agreements with several countries in

25 Council Doc. 7990/02.

26 Council Doc. 13754/2/02, *supra*, section 6.1, at n. 28.

27 *Supra*, section 3.2.2, at n. 42.

28 *Supra*, section 6.1, at n. 30.

a region anticipates, and provides for a possible shift in migration flows to neighbouring third countries, resulting from the conclusion of a readmission agreement.

Furthermore, according to this regional approach, in case of an interest in readmission to a particular country of origin, the Community may decide to negotiate an agreement with a neighbouring third country, instead. This offers a solution in case reaching agreement with that country of origin is particularly difficult, or expulsion to that country is impossible for practical, political or legal reasons. An example in case is Afghanistan, and the negotiation of a readmission agreement with Pakistan to provide for the expulsion of Afghani nationals.

The April 2002 conclusions furthermore requested the Commission to prepare draft negotiating mandates for agreements with Albania, Algeria, China, and Turkey. The Council noted that yet additional mandates would be considered "in due course", though called for restraint in this regard. "In view of the difficulty of negotiating agreements of this kind", the Council stated, "the countries in question need to be identified one by one, drawing upon the results of ongoing negotiations and constantly evaluating [the] practical implementation [of these agreements]."[29]

### *7.1.3 2002 – consolidating the number of directives*

The mandates for Albania, Algeria, China, and Turkey were subsequently adopted by the JHA Council in November 2002.[30] During this Council meeting, the Member States also exchanged views on possible additional negotiating directives for certain ACP countries.[31] A left-over from the Presidency's agenda for the Seville European Council,[32] Spain had launched a bid in September 2002 to adopt directives for ACP countries in Western and sub-Saharan Africa, invoking the readmission clause in the Cotonou Agreement.[33] In line with the restraint advocated earlier, however, the Council decided not to adopt further directives for ACP countries, considering a general lack of progress in the negotiations pursuant to the existing mandates.[34]

Considering the reasons for singling out Albania, Algeria, China, and Turkey, the selection of China was arguably long overdue, considering it came top of the list in

29 Council Doc. 7990/02, para. 3.

30 Press release 14817/02 (Presse 375).

31 Press release 14817/02 (Presse 375).

32 Rather than constrain, the Seville European Council conclusions initially aimed to expand the common readmission policy significantly. The original draft conclusions called upon the EU to make readmission clauses "operational", and to conclude readmission agreements with "all the main transit and origin countries". Council Doc. 9917/3/02. They also referred to readmission agreements in the context of the Cotonou Convention. The conclusions, as finally adopted by the Seville European Council, were limited to calling for the speeding up of ongoing negotiations, and the approval of new briefs for negotiation regarding Albania, Algeria, China, and Turkey. Presidency Conclusions, Seville European Council of 21 and 22 June 2002, para. 30; Council Doc. 10525/1/02, annex, point 4.

33 Council Doc. 14528/02.

34 *Supra*, at n. 29.

November 1999.[35] A number of Member States was experiencing a significant influx of Chinese immigrants. Adding to this problem, China is a traditionally difficult country to approach with regard to migration matters. In the past, it has refused engaging in dialogue on the unauthorised immigration of Chinese nationals into EC Member States, let alone formal agreements regarding migration control or readmission.

Like Russia, China was the archetypal State for the Community to tackle – giant in size and political importance, and problematic in terms of cooperation on readmission. Explaining its belated selection for a negotiation directive, China was unwilling to discuss unauthorised immigration with the EU, until the highly publicised incident in Dover in July 2000.[36] Furthermore, the Commission made a strategic decision to broach the issue of readmitting unauthorised immigrants, firstly, through the negotiation of an agreement relating to tourist visa. The Council mandated the Commission to negotiate an Approved Destination Status (ADS) agreement between the EC and China in September 2002.[37] China regulates outgoing tourism by concluding ADS agreements with selected countries, which provide visa facilitation for groups of Chinese tourists. As a safeguard, the Community insisted on inserting a readmission clause into this agreement, which China accepted. The clause ensures that China will duly readmit any Chinese national who absconds during a tourist visit. In November 2002, the Council and Commission arguably perceived a gathering momentum for approaching China for a fully-fledged readmission agreement.

The remaining countries, Albania, Algeria and Turkey, are typical "cordon" States. Influx into the EC of Albanian nationals, as well as transit migrants coming through Albania, explains the selection of this country. In terms of readmission, Algeria poses problems similar to Morocco. It is a country of origin of unauthorised immigration, and a country of transit of migration from Sub-Saharan Africa. Following Morocco, the targeting of Algeria moreover followed from the regional approach. Turkey, finally, was selected with a view to the presence of unauthorised Turkish immigrants in the EC, as well as a number of rejected, mostly Kurdish, protection seekers. Furthermore, Turkey is known for being a major transit hub, where several smuggling routes come together before entry is attempted into EC territory.

### *7.1.4 2004 – deepening before widening*

The next injection of deliberate strategy into the common readmission policy was not until November 2004. By this time, a political crisis had arisen. Considering the lack of progress in the readmission negotiations, the Member States threatened to withdraw

35 *Supra*, at n. 3.

36 *Supra*, subsection 3.2.1, at n. 25.

37 See the proposals for Council decisions concerning the singing and conclusion of the Memorandum of Understanding between the European Community and the National Tourism Administration of the People's Republic of China on visa and related issues concerning tourist groups from the People's Republic of China, COM(2003) 790 final, 15 December 2003.

the negotiating directives.[38] In an attempt to resolve this crisis, as well as jumpstart the common readmission policy, the Brussels European Council of 16 and 17 October 2003 invited the Commission to produce a report, which would "identify [...] in particular the priorities of a common readmission policy and the measures taken to ensure the successful development of such a policy".[39] The report was labelled as confidential, enabling the Commission to write without the restraint inherent to public access documents. It thus provided a good opportunity to revitalise the common readmission policy, which indeed appeared to be faltering for lack of negotiating results.

The Commission submitted its report to the JHA Council of 19 July 2004.[40] It outlined the state of negotiations, and sought to explain the reasons for the low success rate thus far. The report also suggested possible additional target countries for Community readmission agreements. It did not, however, recommend any new mandates for the time being, at least not until more progress would be achieved. This is understandable, considering that the Commission's resources were spread thinly at the time between eleven mandates. Furthermore, the Commission appeared less than eager to embark upon more negotiations, which would add to its political responsibility to achieve results. Arguably, the Commission considered at the time that the best way of revitalising the common readmission policy was to deepen rather than widen it. It suggested consolidating the Community's negotiating position, before expanding the number of target countries.

The GAER Council subsequently adopted conclusions "on the priorities for the successful development of a common readmission policy" in November 2004.[41] Relevant to the selection of target countries is that the GAER Council prioritised certain of the criteria adopted by the JHA Council in April 2002. As decisive selection criteria, the GAER Council named:

- Migration pressure on particular Member States, as well as the EU as a whole
- The geographical position of countries, including considerations of regional coherence and neighbourhood

The Council considered these "the most important criteria for determining, on a case-by-case basis, with which further countries readmission agreements should be concluded". The Council furthermore mentioned "a country's offer to enter into readmission negotiations with the EU" – a rare occurrence – as a factor to take into account.

38 See, *supra*, section 5.2, at n. 13.

39 Presidency Conclusions, Brussels European Council of 16 and 17 October 2003.

40 Press release 11161/04 (Presse 219); Commission report on the priorities for the successful development of a common readmission policy, Council Doc. 11505/04 MIGR 63 RESTREINT UE. The report was partly declassified in July 2007, see Council Doc. 11505/04, 3 July 2007.

41 Council Doc. 13578/04.

The criterion related to the geographical position of third countries prioritises "buffer zone" or "cordon" States.[42] Especially noteworthy, however, is the criterion regarding migration pressure. This appears to water down, or rather reformulate, the requirement of a Community interest or "added value".

Previously, the Council tended to determine the relevance of a readmission agreement, going by the number of Member States affected by immigration from a certain third country.[43] In November 2004, the Council arguably recognised that migration pressure on individual Member States may also form reason for negotiating an agreement at the Community level. On the one hand, the common readmission policy thus became more accommodating of the interests of single, or small groups of Member States. One the other hand, one could also argue that the Council hereby recognised the relevance of the free movement of persons to the common readmission policy.[44] Concluding a readmission agreement in response to an influx of a particular group of migrants in a single Member State may cause that group to disperse to other Member States, unless the agreement is concluded at the Community level. In this light, a Community interest in concluding a readmission agreement at the EC level is arguably always present.

The November 2004 Council agreed with the Commission, however, not to adopt additional negotiating mandates, until more tangible progress was achieved on the existing eleven. The Council stated that "new authorisations to negotiate with individual third countries will be decided on a case-by-case basis only. To this end the Council invited the Commission to present it with concrete recommendations to negotiate agreements concerning individual third countries, when appropriate." Considering the Commission's position, additional negotiating directives were not adopted until late 2006.

### *7.1.5 2006 – new mandates*

The Council adopted new negotiating mandates for Moldova (an ENP country), Bosnia and Herzegovina, Macedonia, Montenegro, and Serbia (Western Balkan countries) in the fall of 2006.[45] This was a clear reinforcement of the Community's "cordon" policy objective.[46] One may expect the Community to focus on establishing readmission obligations on the part of all EU neighbouring countries before considering additional negotiations with countries further away.

42 *Supra*, subsection 3.2.2.

43 *Supra*, n. 3 and 25.

44 *Supra*, subsection 3.1.1.

45 Commission work-programme 2006, p. 102, 128 (available on: www.europa.eu.int/comm). Council Doc. 13278/06, Council Doc. 15465/06, Council Doc. 16537/06.

46 *Supra*, subsection 3.2.2.

### *7.1.6 The double standard in selecting readmission countries*

At the time of writing, the November 2004 GAER Council conclusions still comprise the principal strategic document for the development of the common readmission policy. As noted above, taking account of political factors is no longer part of the strategy for selecting readmission countries. This is a further illustration of the rising importance of traditional home affairs issues, such as migration, in comparison with general external relations.[47] When destination countries seek partnerships on migration matters, third countries are valued differently than in other policy areas. This is a direct result of the habit of home affairs officials to separate migration matters from external relations proper in order to achieve internal objectives. Foreign affairs officials tend towards the opposite. They view migration as one aspect that should be in conformity with overall relations with a country, but are left with the short end of the stick in the face of the importance of immigration in domestic politics.

As a result, the Community seeks cooperation on migration issues with third countries it would less readily associate itself with in other fields, and which have a doubtful track-record in light of the credo of liberty, democracy, respect for human rights, and the rule of law.[48] One example is the case of Pakistan, mentioned above. Another example is Libya, a "rogue" State until recently, when the EU decided to establish migration cooperation with this country. The need to stem the significant influx of unauthorised immigrants, passing through Libya into the EU, provided a catalyst for the normalisation of international relations with this country.[49] A further example is the list of third countries with which the Community has concluded, or aims to conclude a readmission agreement. This list includes countries associated with a lack of democratic institutions and/or respect for human rights, such as China, Sri Lanka, Russia, Ukraine, and Turkey. Relevant in this regard is the attempt by DG RELEX of the Commission to insert a human rights clause in the text of Community readmission agreements.[50] Arguably, the Community would not have been able to seek readmission cooperation with these countries, had this attempt been successful.

Establishing cooperation on migration issues with countries, regarding which political factors would disadvise the development of relations in other fields, has several perverse effects. The first is purely political. The separation of migration cooperation from general external relations is only of short duration. Migration is increasingly a subject of barter between States. Cooperation on migration comes at a price. Migration and general external relations are quickly reattached by the other negotiating party, which expects some form of quid pro quo in other policy fields. As a result, destination countries develop relations on fronts and with countries, which they would otherwise

47 See also *supra*, section 5.2, and chapter 6.

48 According to Article 6 TEU, the EU is founded on these principles. A lack of respect for these principles on the part of a third country can form grounds for suspension or termination of an agreement with the Community under the standard "human rights clause".

49 For relevant news reports, see NRC Handelsblad 2004a, NRC Handelsblad 2004b, NRC Handelsblad 2004b, and La Repubblica 2004.

50 *Supra*, section 5.2.

not have considered. The negotiation of readmission agreements at the Community level is a case in point, as discussed in the following section.

The second perverse effect has hypothetical legal implications. Countries with poor human rights records, as a rule, produce refugees. Several of the aforementioned countries, in particular China, Russia and Turkey, gave rise to the largest number of new protection claims in 2003.[51] A number of the countries targeted by the Community for their relevance in migration- or readmission terms do not generally feature on "safe third country" lists, either. Due to the different valuing of external relations when concerning migration issues, the Community is nevertheless facilitating expulsion to these countries by negotiating readmission agreements. Hypothetically, therefore, this double standard is relevant to the application of Community readmission agreements in the expulsion of protection seekers to third countries, which is analysed in chapter 9 below.

## 7.2 The state of negotiations

In April and May 2001, the Commission launched negotiations for Community readmission agreements with the first set of readmission countries. Through diplomatic channels, the Commission invited Morocco, Pakistan, Russia and Sri Lanka to commence negotiations. Since then, seven more countries or entities – Hong Kong, Macao, Ukraine, Albania, Algeria, China, and Turkey – have been invited to conclude a readmission agreement with the Community. The following describes the state of negotiations with these countries, following the order of adoption of negotiating directives by the Council.[52]

### *7.2.1 Morocco*

Following official notification of the Community's request to enter into a readmission agreement, Morocco received the draft text in April 2001. A series of informal preparatory meetings, as well as discussion within the EU-Morocco Association Council,[53] was necessary to convince Morocco to commence formal negotiations finally in April

51 UNHCR 2003a, para. 37. Russia, China and Turkey are also in the top 5 countries of origin of protection seekers, which filed claims in industrialised countries in Europe in 2003, See UNHCR 2003b.

52 Main sources used for this section are one of the Commission's regular progress reports on the readmission negotiations, published by the Council in Council doc. 12625/02; an account of the readmission negotiations in Schieffer 2003; and a more recent update of the negotiations, in MEMO/05/351. A source of background information for the negotiations with Albania, Morocco, Turkey, and Ukraine, is Kruse 2004. These publications have been supplemented with personal experiences of the author as an intern at the DG JHA (now JFS) of the European Commission in the period October 2003-February 2004.

53 This institutional framework was set up under the EU-Morocco Association Agreement, signed on 26 February 1996.

2003. By November 2005, a total of eight rounds of formal negotiations had taken place, and agreement on the text was not yet in sight.[54]

The interest of the Community in completing these difficult negotiations is high. Morocco is an important source- and transit country for illegal immigrants, and a "problem country" in terms of cooperation on readmission. In addition, the Community readmission agreement with Morocco is important from a regional perspective.

EC Cooperation on migration issues is relatively less established with countries on the Community's external border in the Southern Mediterranean. In light EU enlargement, the great majority of investment in the recent past has gone towards attempts to seal the Eastern external land border. The securing of the EU's maritime border in the South is now a main priority, especially considering the high number of yearly attempts to cross the Mediterranean Sea into EU territory.[55] Concluding a readmission agreement with Morocco is a relevant part of EU strategy aimed at limiting these crossings.

Furthermore, the conclusion of a readmission agreement with Morocco has become a pivotal case in the development of the common readmission policy regarding the Southern Mediterranean. Once agreement with Morocco is secured, it is expected that other countries in the region would soon follow suit. Finalisation of the negotiation process with Morocco would trigger the start of negotiations with Algeria, the second country in the region for which the Council has adopted a negotiation directive for a readmission agreement. Reaching agreement with Morocco is also expected to pave the way for agreements with countries such as Tunisia and others along the Northern African coast, important to the Community and its objective to seal off the Southern border in cooperation with "cordon" States. Morocco is aware of its function as a model, which strengthens its negotiating position.

It is clear that Morocco's reaction to the Community's invitation to enter into an agreement on readmission has been apprehensive, as illustrated by the belated launch and subsequent course of negotiations. A primary concern on the part of Morocco is that it would incur responsibility for transit migration by accepting an obligation to readmit third country nationals and stateless persons. Morocco fears becoming a gathering ground for migrants originating from Sub-Saharan Africa, who transit its territory in the direction of the Community. A Moroccan counter-proposal, for example, has been to include a provision to the effect of prioritising removal and readmission to ACP source countries over readmission to Morocco.

An important factor is that Morocco is increasingly a country of destination for Sub-Saharan migration. This is partially occurring by default, as the control of Spain's maritime borders has greatly intensified in recent years.[56] It is also due to the improved

54 Press release PRES/05/308.

55 ICMPD has estimated the total number of attempted crossings from the Maghreb region (Morocco, Algeria, Tunisia, Lybia), and to a lesser degree the Mashreq region (Egypt, Lebanon and Syria) at between a 100.000 and 120.000 a year, ICMPD 2004.

56 Council Doc. 11490/1/03, p. 15, 19, 27. Border control in the Mediterranean region was strengthened by the signing of an agreement in January 2004 between Spain and Morocco

level of development of Morocco, especially in comparison with conditions in Sub-Saharan countries such as Chad, Congo, Ghana, Mali, Niger, Nigeria, Senegal, and Sudan.[57]

The change in status from a country purely of emigration to a country also of immigration is a source of domestic concern. Morocco is responding *inter alia* by carrying out more expulsions on an ad hoc basis. In addition, Morocco is considering the development of a readmission policy of its own. It is preparing for the negotiation of readmission agreements with a number of other countries. In this respect, negotiations with the Community are an opportunity for the Moroccan authorities to become yet more familiar with the negotiation of this type of agreement.[58] Agreement on a final text with the Community would also provide Morocco with a blueprint for its own negotiations, and would thus arguably be a handy tool. Morocco has furthermore asked the Community to do more in terms of readmission to Sub-Saharan countries, for example by way of the ACP Cotonou agreement.[59] One such request is the above-mentioned Moroccan counter-proposal to prioritise removal and readmission to ACP countries. Finally, the transitional problems that Morocco is experiencing as a fledgling country of immigration have increased its need for relevant assistance. These factors have provided the Commission with more leverage in the readmission negotiations. Morocco's transformation into a country of immigration is arguably playing into the hands of the Commission in the negotiation of the readmission agreement.

In addition to transit-related concerns, receiving back nationals within a fragile economy with low employment rates is also a concern of Morocco. These emigrants are moreover generating large remittance flows. Remittances have become an important source of income for Morocco that it would not want to see limited by reducing the presence of Moroccan nationals abroad.[60] A Community policy that facilitates and

on the control of their maritime borders and the interception of migrants, see WSWS 2004.

57 The influx into and transit through Northern Africa of Sub-Saharan African nationals has heavily increased in recent years, a trend which is expected to continue with a view to the estimated rise in population in Sub-Saharan Africa over the next 25 years, ICMPD 2004, p. 16-17.

58 Morocco already has readmission agreements with several Member States – Belgium, Germany, Italy, the Netherlands, and Spain. Especially Spain is receiving insufficient cooperation on the implementation of its bilateral agreement, and is therefore eager to explore the Community avenue.

59 The Cotonou agreement contains an elaborate "migration management clause" in Article 13. It commits to cooperation on several migration-related issues between the Community and the ACP countries. It also contains an obligation to readmit nationals, and a political commitment to conclude fully-fledged readmission agreements in future if so requested by one of the contracting parties. For further details, see sections 8.1 and 8.2.

60 Remittances were estimated by the IOM to have accounted for 6.5 % of Moroccan GDP in the period 1975-1998, cited in Kruse 2004, p. 27.

thereby increases migrants' remittances is thus of potential relevance here.[61] The Commission expects that the development of such a policy may offset some of this concern, providing a stimulus to the readmission negotiations.

Another element, noted by the Commission negotiators as beneficial to the negotiations, is the legislative effort of the Community concerning the rights of resident third country nationals. Considering that the position and treatment of its nationals abroad is an important preoccupation of the Moroccan government, it has noted with interest the adoption of the Directives on family reunification and long-term resident third country nationals.[62] The Commission has sought to underline this interest by adding a (strictly political) declaration to the draft readmission agreement, pertaining to the position of legally resident Moroccans in the EU after the adoption of this legislation.[63]

Yet a further factor of relevance is Moroccan public opinion. Expulsion (and thus readmission) may be an important electoral issue in the Member States, Morocco, too, has an electorate to take into account. A repeated argument of the Moroccan authorities is that conclusion of a readmission agreement with the Community would be difficult to sell to the public. To off-set some of this concern, the Commission could offer to adopt a more generic title for the agreement. Examples of titles, which might help to take some of the bite out of public criticism, are "cooperation on the management of illegal immigration", or "cooperation on consular matters". Some of the EC Member States pursue a similar technique by including provisions on the readmission of migrants in bilateral agreements dealing with police cooperation, or cooperation between border guards.[64] Such solutions are however of little interest to Morocco, which approaches the negotiations on a strictly quid pro quo basis.

Morocco has demanded compensation that would not only be substantive, but also clearly visible with a view to its electorate.[65] It should be pointed out that although public opinion may indeed be a factor of importance in such cases, appeals to the electorate or domestic politics also provide a handy vehicle to introduce the issue of quid pro quo into negotiations.

---

61 See also *supra*, subsection 6.2.3.

62 The Council adopted these directives in September and November 2003, respectively. Such legislation is arguably perceived by Morocco as beneficial to remittance levels generated by Moroccan nationals, legally present in the EU (estimated in 1999 at 80% of a total two million Moroccans living abroad, Kruse 2004, p. 28). Government policy is also to maintain close links with Moroccan emigrants in an attempt to attract investment and skill, Kruse 2004, p. 28.

63 The declaration bears the title "déclaration commune sur le statut des ressortissants Marocains qui résident légalement dans l'Union Européenne". It reaffirms the conviction of the contracting parties that cooperation on illegal immigration is beneficial to the position of nationals, legally resident on their respective territories. The declaration furthermore outlines the content of relevant EC legislation insofar as beneficial to the position of Moroccan nationals living in EU Member States.

64 COM(2004) 412 final, p. 14.

65 See also Kruse 2004, p. 31.

Morocco's counter-demands regarding compensation for the conclusion of a readmission agreement with the Community are twofold. They firstly concern technical and financial assistance for border control, and the reception, processing and onward removal of readmitted persons. Morocco largely lacks the infrastructure and funds for performing these functions.[66] A total of 40 million EUR has been reserved under the 2002-2004 MEDA budget for expenditure on Morocco's capacity to "curb illegal emigration".[67] This money could in principle be used to provide for Morocco's needs, provoked by the readmission of unauthorised immigrants to it territory. Rather than a re-labelling of existing money, however, Morocco has insisted on additional funding with an explicit and visible connection to the readmission agreement. The Commission has responded positively in this regard, as confirmed by a further joint declaration, attached to the draft agreement. The declaration contains a political commitment on part of the Community to assist Morocco in the exercise of their "shared responsibility to manage migratory flows" with technical and financial assistance, referring to the Aeneas Regulation.

Morocco's second condition is more controversial. In exchange for the conclusion of a Community readmission agreement, it would like the EC Member States to widen immigration channels for Moroccan nationals. It is difficult for the Commission to respond to this request, while the Community has little power regarding the immigration of third-country nationals for labour purposes. The Member States have carefully guarded their sovereignty in this area.

Since deciding against further labour immigration and introducing so-called "zero immigration" policies in the 1970s, the Member States have been traditionally hesitant to expand immigration, both in terms of numbers and categories of persons. An attempt by the Commission in 2001 to further exercise Community competence under Article 63(3)(a) was unsuccessful.[68] The Commission submitted a proposal to the Council for a Directive on the conditions of entry and residence of third country nationals for the purpose of paid employment and self-employed economic activities.[69] The Commission's proposal was generally considered as going "too far too soon" in comparison with the readiness of the Member States to adopt common legislation in this area. Discussion within the Council was soon suspended indefinitely. Since then, the Com-

---

66 Kruse 2004, p. 31.

67 An additional 5 million EUR is intended to support legal emigration – "movement of persons". Also, 42 million EURO of the same budget pertains to economic development of the Northern provinces of Morocco where most emigrants originate, CIVIPOL 2003, Council Doc. 11490/1/03, p. 84; MEDA NIP Morocco 2005-2006 (available on: www.europa.eu.int/comm/external_relations).

68 Article 63(3)(a) TEC reads: "The Council [...] shall [...] adopt [...] measures on immigration policy within the [area of] conditions and entry of residence, and standards on procedures for the issue by Member States of long-term visas and residence permits, including those for the purpose of family reunion".

69 *OJ* C 332 E, 27 November 2001, p. 248.

mission has attempted to gradually reintroduce the issue of labour immigration on the EU agenda.[70]

Considering the counter-demands of third countries in the readmission context, the Commission would be in favour of introducing a system of immigration quota at EC level. Considering the sensitivity of the area, such a system would need to ensure full Member State control, and limit the involvement of the Commission to a coordinating role. One could imagine a scenario in which the Commission would present the Council with a request for a quota of workers from a particular third country. One or more Member States would then offer maximum quota in accordance with their particular market needs, and authorise the Commission to use this as leverage in the readmission negotiations. This would permit the Member States to retain control over the inflow of labour immigration, whilst creating a concrete perspective for progress in the readmission negotiations.

For the time being, however, it remains unlikely that the Council would consider introducing such a system. The views of the Member States with respect to required levels of immigration differ greatly, and only few would regard benefits in the field of legal immigration (beyond visa facilitation) as a valid instrument to gain third countries' cooperation on readmission. Possibly, the only staunch proponent would be Italy. Italy habitually offers labour immigration quota for low-skilled workers to third countries in return for readmission agreements, and has attempted to introduce a similar strategy at the EC level.[71]

In lieu of adoption of an EC quota system, the Commission expects that a minor, though concrete concession in relation to the immigration of Moroccan nationals would suffice to secure completion of the readmission negotiations. The Moroccan government arguably requires a concession enabling it to present the conclusion of a readmission agreement with the Community as overall beneficial, and demonstrate to the public that it did not "sell out".[72] Extracting the Council's consent for such a gesture however poses a significant challenge. The Member States have been reluctant to agree even to purely political gestures regarding Moroccan immigration in connection with the readmission negotiations.

Late 2003, the negotiations reached a deadlock because Morocco's counter-demands were not being answered. Attempting to unblock the situation, the Commission proposed attaching a joint declaration to the agreement. The title of the declaration

70 Noteworthy in this regard are the Commission's Communication on immigration, integration and employment, COM(2003) 336 final, 3 June 2003; the study on the links between legal and illegal immigration, COM(2004) 412 final, 4 June 2004; and the recent policy plan on legal migration, COM(2005) 669, 21 December 2005.

71 COM(2004) 412 final, p. 8; Central Directorate of Immigration and Border Policy 2004. For the proposal which Italy submitted to the Council, see further below, subsection 7.3.5.

72 Kruse has noted that in view of public opinion it is important to the Moroccan to government to present itself as a negotiating partner of equal status to the EU, and to leave negotiations with a degree of "hard won profit", Kruse 2004, p. 31.

referred to the New Neighbourhood Policy, which foresees eventual participation in the internal market by countries neighbouring on the EU's enlarged external border.[73] In light of this long-term perspective of free movement of persons between the EC and Morocco, as well as aspects of immigration policy that currently feature within the association process, the joint declaration proposed to hold a dialogue on legal migration issues. Ensuring visibility, it was suggested to create a new forum for this dialogue, separate from existing structures under the EC-Morocco Association Agreement. Without entailing any concrete commitment for the Community or the Member States, this ad hoc group – consisting of experts from Morocco and the Member States, and chaired by the Commission – would hold an exchange of views, and explore possibilities of economic immigration between the Community and Morocco.

The Commission discussed the idea with the Member States during one of the regular meetings with readmission experts in December 2003. Although specific to the negotiations with Morocco only (i.e. this joint declaration was not intended for incorporation into the informal standard draft agreement), the reaction of the Member States was generally apprehensive. The Member State experts considered it a considerable change in strategy, and decided it required a decision at the political level. The matter was added to the agenda of the Migration/Expulsion Working Group, scheduled to meet the next day. While concerning strategy, the President of the working group referred it to the SCIFA.

At its meeting on 13 January 2004, SCIFA decided not to approve the Commission's draft joint declaration on the New Neighbourhood Policy.[74] The Member States generally disagreed with the creation of an institutional framework, in addition to that of the Association Agreement. It was moreover felt that such would create unrealistic expectations on the part of Morocco. A further factor of relevance was the fact that a number of Member States already have some sort of arrangement regarding the immigration of Moroccan workers, involving quota or seasonal work. The political support for adding a commitment at Community level to these existing arrangements was absent.

One Member State intervened, objecting to linking benefits with commitments to counter unauthorised immigration. The Member State reasoned that every country is responsible for migration movements emanating from and transiting its territory, independent of compensation. As detailed in chapter 2, such references have been interpreted as supporting the application of the "principle of good neighbourliness" to the area of migration. In an attempt to exert pre-border migration control or cooperation on readmission, destination States commonly invoke the sovereign duty of other States to counter unauthorised immigration. What was extraordinary about this Member State's intervention, however, is that it objected to offering quid pro quo in general.

It is a generally accepted practice to grant benefits in exchange for the control of transit migration, including for a readmission agreement, which imposes an obligation to readmit transit migrants. Morocco's purported responsibility as a sovereign State to

73 See *supra*, subsection 6.2.4.

74 Council Doc. 5455/04.

fight unauthorised immigration does not in general preclude compensating benefits. Indeed, Morocco is already receiving forms of compensation in the form of technical and financial assistance. Present objections within the Council thus appear related specifically to benefits in the field of labour immigration. The SCIFA meeting on 13 January 2004 concluded with yet another appeal from the Commission for at least some form of concession in this field, without which conclusion of the readmission agreement with Morocco was not expected to draw closer.[75] According to a report of the Commission in November 2005, since then progress has been booked, but conclusion of the agreement is still elusive. The Commission summarised the state of negotiations as follows:

> Despite several rounds of negotiations, the EC has not yet been able to agree the text of a readmission agreement with Morocco. Most of the outstanding issues are minor but some, such as the readmission of non-nationals and the forms of evidence to be provided remain problematic.[76]

### *7.2.2 Pakistan*

In subsection 7.1.1 above, we discussed how political factors called for repeated suspension of ratification procedures for a new Cooperation Agreement (CA) between Pakistan and the Community, but did not prevent the Council from adopting a directive for negotiating a readmission agreement.[77] The CA was eventually signed in November 2001, after the Council no longer saw reason for suspension of procedures. The conclusion of the CA, however, was again blocked in light of unfair elections in October 2002, which consolidated the position of Musharaf, and a continuing lack of respect for human rights in Pakistan. This time it was the European Parliament, which suspended ratification procedures.[78]

These difficult relations between the EC and Pakistan compromised the start of the readmission negotiations. Effectively, the Community was unable to invoke the political declaration, attached to the CA, by which the contracting parties agreed to negotiate a readmission agreement, if so requested by one of the contracting parties. We recall that this declaration had informed the selection of Pakistan as one of the Community's first readmission countries.[79] This obstacle did not prevent the Commis-

75 Council Doc. 5455/04. At a meeting of the JHA Council on 6 November 2003, Commissioner Vitorino had already requested the Member States to determine the Commission's room for manoeuvre in granting immigration benefits to Morocco in exchange for readmission. For an outline of the discussion of the JHA Council, see Press release 13747/03 (Presse 308). See also Reuters 2003.

76 COM(2005) 352, p. 5-6.

77 *Supra*, at n. 18, 19.

78 EU's relations with Pakistan (available on: www.europa.eu.int/comm/external_relations/pakistan); European Parliament, session document PE 311.031; European Parliament, session document PE 341.360.

79 *Supra*, n. 17.

sion from pushing for readmission negotiations to commence, which also implies it did not consider the EP's considerations relevant to the readmission context.

The Commission transmitted the draft text of the readmission agreement to Pakistan in April 2001. Despite repeated attempts at the diplomatic level, Pakistan refused to start negotiations for a considerable period.[80] A first preparatory meeting between the two sides finally took place in October 2003, during which Pakistan agreed to start negotiating on the basis of a revised draft text in early 2004. After failing to agree on a date in January 2004, a first round of formal negotiations took place in April 2004.[81]

Motivating its protracted refusal to negotiate a readmission agreement, Pakistan cited the war in neighbouring country Afghanistan in October 2001, and the aftermath thereof.[82] It may however be assumed that the repeated discontinuance of procedures for the conclusion of the Cooperation Agreement also played a crucial role throughout this period, although an explicit link was not established until November 2003. During an official visit to Brussels, the Pakistani Foreign Minister made clear that readmission talks would be possible only once conclusion of the CA would be secured. The EU Ministerial Troïka, visiting Islamabad in February 2004 under the Irish Presidency, received the same message.[83] In April 2004, MEP Cushnahan, the EP rapporteur with regard to the CA with Pakistan, described this linkage as follows:

> This threatening tactic amounts to little more than blackmail, and I would argue that the European Parliament should be wary of compromising its core principles, which are to uphold human rights and democracy, because of the crude threat of non-cooperation on the readmission agreement.[84]

The same report called on the EP to continue withholding its approval of conclusion of the Cooperation Agreement, supported by a strong argument. The CA contains a human rights clause in Article 1, declaring that respect for human right and democratic principles constitute an essential element of the agreement. This provision had underpinned every suspension of procedures towards conclusion of the CA since 1998, and Cushnahan argued that a relevant lack of respect for human rights and democracy persisted in Pakistan.

However, Pakistan's probable argument for refusing to consider concluding a readmission agreement was also strong. Suspending the conclusion of the CA included suspension of the annexed political commitment to negotiate a readmission agreement. This declaration by the contracting parties had constituted an important part of the negotiations, as an obvious demand of the Community in exchange for the trade and

80 Council Doc. 12625/02.

81 Commission reference document for Aeneas 2004 – 2006, para. 5.1.2 (available on: www.europa.eu.int/comm).

82 Schieffer 2003, p. 345.

83 European Parliament, session document PE 341.360; The Dawn 2003.

84 European Parliament, session document PE 341.360, p. 9.

development relations established by the CA. Rather than blackmail, the position of Pakistan may be considered a reminder and confirmation of an existing link, previously established by the Community.

Contrary to Cushnahan's recommendations, the Foreign Affairs Committee of the EP decided to approve the conclusion of the CA with Pakistan. The CA was subsequently concluded in April 2004, the same month, unsurprisingly, in which the readmission negotiations started.[85] In brief, the Foreign Affairs Committee found that while the lack of respect for human rights and democratic principles in Pakistan was still a source of concern, improvements were distinguishable, and the new Cooperation Agreement would provide a further stimulus in the right direction.

It is difficult to draw conclusions regarding the relation between the need for a Community readmission agreement, and the dissolution of political objections to the concluding Cooperation Agreement with Pakistan. It should be remembered that the Council had already lifted its reservations in November 2001, when the CA with Pakistan was signed. Here, one can point to a factor of relevance, other than the readmission negotiations. It is generally recognised that Pakistan's international profile was positively affected by its commitment to the "war on terror", following the Al Qaeda attacks in New York in September 2001. Although international relations remain tense with a view to the dispute in the Kashmir region, Pakistan's WMD capacity, and involvement in nuclear proliferation, its overall profile has changed into that of a viable collaborator in the international field. This was likely the main drive behind political support in the Council to unblock the signing of the CA in 2001, rather than a need to start readmission negotiations.[86]

Pakistan's condition – to start readmission negotiations only once conclusion of the CA was secured – was thus addressed only at the European Parliament. One can only speculate as to the influence of the Community objective to readmit unauthorised immigrants, or of the "war on terror" for that matter, on the decision-making process of the EP and its FA committee in this case. The report by MEP Cushnahan explicitly warned against such influence, but rapporteurs do not necessarily reflect general EP opinion. Regardless, it is certain that the final decision to approve conclusion of the CA enabled the start of, and may exercise a beneficial effect on the course of readmission negotiations with Pakistan.

We briefly discussed the Community's particular readmission interest in Pakistan in subsection 7.1.1. The Community is not necessarily seeking a readmission agreement with this country due to large numbers of illegally resident Pakistani nationals. Pakistani bureaucracy in readmitting its nationals, however, implies a relatively high number of difficult return cases, the UK being the Member State most concerned.

---

85 See Ludford 2004.

86 See the report by rapporteur Cushnahan: "There is a general feeling among certain Member States that Pakistan should be rewarded for its cooperation and support for the international war against terror and that the efforts taken to re-introduce dialogue on Kashmir should also be recognized", European Parliament 2004, session document PE 341.360, p. 9.

The HLWG's recommendation to conclude readmission agreements with Pakistan in its 1999 Action Plan for Afghanistan indicates a further interest.[87] Afghani nationals make up one of the largest groups, resident, or otherwise present in EC Member States. Many of these persons will have previously stayed in neighbouring country Pakistan or Iran, which host the largest numbers of Afghani refugees. Agreement on an obligation to readmit third country nationals with Pakistan would thus broaden the possibilities for expulsion of this group.

In the Action Plan for Afghanistan, however, the HLWG also outlined the point of view of Pakistan regarding such expulsions, which has not changed since. Pakistan is generally unwilling to cooperate on receiving back Afghani nationals from EC Member States that have transited or resided on its territory. Pakistan has repeatedly pointed to the large number of Afghani refugees that it hosts – estimated at 2 million in 1999[88] and at 1.12 million by the end of 2003[89] – next to which the Afghani presence in the EC clearly pales in comparison. Pakistan is thus implicitly arguing for burden sharing.[90]

Accordingly, Pakistan has made clear not to accept a readmission agreement with the Community, which would further increase the Afghani presence on its territory. The Commission had already made a relevant concession by limiting the obligation to readmit third country nationals and stateless persons in the draft agreement to direct arrivals.[91] This means that Afghani travelling *via* smuggling routes by land from Pakistan to EC Member States would not be caught by the agreement, which entails a significant limitation in numbers. It also means that Pakistan would be able to avoid responsibility for the readmission of transit migrants by exercising strict emigration control at its international sea- and airports.

It should be emphasised that Pakistan applied the conclusion of the Cooperation Agreement as leverage only to start negotiations on readmission. In exchange for the actual conclusion of an agreement with the Community on readmission, Pakistan has further conditions. In addition to the perspective of Afghani refugees returning, there is another reason why a readmission agreement would not be to Pakistan's advantage. Also for Pakistan, remittances provide essential revenue. The more Pakistani nationals emigrate, and the fewer are returned, the better it is for Pakistan's GDP, which may clarify the lack of cooperation by the Pakistani authorities in readmitting its nationals. As compensation, Pakistan has requested assistance in relation to counter-terrorism, and border control.

---

87 The HLWG specified that "such agreements should not only cover own nationals but also stateless persons and third country nationals, in particular Afghan nationals who have been living in Pakistan for a substantial period of time", Council Doc. 11424/99, para. 138c.

88 Council Doc. 11424/99, para. 54.

89 UNHCR, 2003 Global refugee trends, p. 3.

90 Council Doc. 11424/99, para. 62, 135.

91 As was done in relation to Hong Kong, Macao and Sri Lanka, see *supra*, subsection 5.3.4, at n. 32.

In principle, the Community would benefit from responding to these counter-demands, also beyond securing agreement on readmission. An improved capacity of Pakistan to undertake counter-terrorism measures, as well as to control its borders, is in line with general Community interests and objectives. A complication is that counter-terrorism measures and border control equipment in the case of Pakistan have a clear link to the conflict in the Kashmir region. This refers to the aforementioned "dual-use" of certain measures and equipment.[92] Granted by the Community as benefits to serve one purpose, such measures may be used in practice also to serve others. Monitoring the actual use of, for example, border control equipment such as helicopters, jeeps and night-vision goggles, once handed over is clearly difficult. There are also clear limits to the degree of safeguards that can reasonably be taken beforehand to prevent dual use from occurring. One thus wonders as to the practical effect of the care taken by the Community in "providing equipment, but with all safeguards regarding potential dual-use", as stated by the Council.[93]

In any case, the state of negotiations with Pakistan at the time of writing is still unclear, indicating that the Council is indecisive in answering to Pakistan's counter-demands.

### *7.2.3* ***Russia***

In general, Russia is of significant strategic interest to the EU, an interest that has gradually increased towards and with enlargement. Russia was already a neighbouring country of the EU, sharing a large land-border with Finland. The enlargement of the Union expanded the shared external border between the EU and Russia, creating direct channels for migrants into EU territory without a need to cross the Baltic Sea.[94] The EU now also borders the Kaliningrad region, which is part of the Russian Federation, but separated from the rest of Russia by Poland and Lithuania.[95] A number of countries – Belarus, Ukraine, Moldova – still separate most of the EU's Eastern external border from Russia, but enlargement since May 2004 has brought Russia significantly closer in geographical, as well as political terms.

In the run-up to enlargement, efforts to strengthen EU-Russia relations were intensified. Migration issues occupy an important position within EC-Russia justice

---

92 *Supra*, subsection 3.2.2, at n. 50.

93 GAERC Conclusions of 19 May 2003 on migration and development, Council Doc. 8927/03, para. 8.

94 It should be noted that the border between Russia and Estonia, Latvia and Lithuania, and thus part of the EU's external border, has not yet been finally demarcated. The ratification procedures for border agreements between Russia and Estonia and Latvia have yet to be completed, The EU's relations with Russia (available on: www.europe.eu.int/comm/external_relations, consulted on 18 February 2005).

95 Regarding Kaliningrad, the EU and Russia reached agreement in November 2002 on a transit regime for persons and goods passing through the countries (now EU Member States) that separate the Kaliningrad region from the rest of Russia, see EU-Russia Joint Statement on Kaliningrad 2003.

and home affairs cooperation. The 1998 Partnership and Cooperation Agreement (PCA) and the TACIS programme have provided large financial injections. The PCA has installed the main institutional framework through which the EU cooperates with, provides support to, and holds dialogue with Russia. In addition, Russia is a prominent subject of the European Neighbourhood Policy.

A recent external policy initiative in relation to Russia is that of the so-called "four common spaces", launched at the EU-Russia summit in St Petersburg in May 2003. Cooperation between the EU and Russia now focuses on four general policy areas, or Common Spaces. The long-term aim is to establish a Common Economic Space, a Common Space of External Security, and a Common Space of Research and Education. The readmission of unauthorised immigrants, and the negotiation of a Community readmission agreement, is part of the establishment of a Common Space of Freedom, Security, and Justice.[96]

The Community's interest in concluding a readmission agreement stems from the fact that Russia is a main country of origin and transit of migrants. In addition, individual Member States have frequently failed to reach agreement on readmission with Russia bilaterally. The negotiation of a Community readmission agreement with this third country is a delicate matter, while Russia is also a main country of origin of protection seekers. Although Russia is not among the top countries of origin of refugees in the world, Russian nationals did file the largest number of new protection claims and appeals in 2003.[97] Whereas by the end of 2003 the number of protection claims received in EC Member States was decreasing, the number of Russian protection seekers was on the rise.[98] Russia is party to the Geneva Refugee Convention and the European Convention of Human Rights, but is not generally considered a "safe third country".[99]

Russia is extremely hesitant to accept an obligation to readmit third country nationals and stateless persons. This hesitation is understandable in light of the migratory flows from Africa, the Middle East, as well Asia that traverse its territory towards the EU and North America. Russia's enormous landmass, porous Southern border, and well-guarded Western border provide further explanation. Migrants from countries further afield, who are apprehended at the EU's Eastern external border, are likely to have passed through Russian territory somewhere along their journey. This means that responsibility for transit migration in the region would largely concentrate on Russia, unless it would also conclude readmission agreements with other countries. We have already discussed Russia's objective of creating a "readmission zone", covering the region with readmission agreements between transit countries, as well as with coun-

96 EU-Russia Joint Statement 2004; Press release IP/03/768. See also the Joint press release of the EU-Russia summit, The Hague, 25 November 2004, Press release 15061/04 (Presse 333).

97 UNHCR 2003 Global refugee trends, para. 37.

98 A large segment of the protection claims received from Russian nationals in the EC is related to the conflict in Chechnya, Europolitque 2003; AP 2004.

99 Lassen and Hughes 1997; Byrne, Noll and Vedsted-Hansen 2002, p. 97.

tries of origin.[100] Russia has asked the Commission for assistance in its negotiation of agreements with other countries. A final problem that Russia has emphasised is with regard to the identification of Russian nationals. Nationals from neighbouring countries often speak fluent Russian, may hold Russian documents, or still be in possession of documents of the ex-Soviet Union. Russia fears that the agreement with the Community would result in the readmission to its territory also of these third country nationals.

In April 2001, the Commission officially presented Russia with the invitation to negotiate a Community readmission agreement, and the draft text thereof. Upon reaching agreement on the Kaliningrad transit regime in November 2002, Russia finally agreed to start negotiating.[101] A first round of formal negotiations was held in January 2003.

The above considerations make clear that Russia does not consider the conclusion of a Community readmission agreement to be in its interest, which caused it to use delaying tactics in the negotiations. In particular, Russia wanted to buy time for the negotiations it is conducting with other countries. Russia is *inter alia* negotiating a readmission agreement with Ukraine, also the target of a Community agreement. The speed at which readmission negotiations between the Commission and Russia progressed has depended to a degree on the course of the negotiations between Russia and Ukraine, as well as the negotiations between the Commission and Ukraine.[102] Delay, respectively progress in the negotiations has furthermore depended on the Community's response to Russia's counter-demands.

Russia requested EC assistance in receiving and processing migrants that Russia would readmit, and in securing its immense Southern border to prevent transit migrants from accumulating on its territory.[103] The Community was already dedicating resources in this regard under the TACIS budget. The Commission was willing to expand this assistance further, considering that enhanced Russian border control is also to the Community's benefit while reducing transit migration towards the EU. In terms of real quid pro quo, Russia has insisted on visa free travel, or, alternatively, visa facilitation for Russian nationals.

100 *Supra*, subsection 3.2.3, at n. 57.

101 EU-Russia Joint Statement on Kaliningrad 2002.

102 *Infra*, subsection 7.2.6.

103 On the website of the Mission of the Russian Federation to the European Communities, the situation is explained as follows: "We are ready to fortify our southern border. A great deal is already being done for this purpose. We have concluded agreements with CIS countries on our joint fight against terrorism, against illicit drug trafficking and against illegal migration. However, we need to cooperate with the EU. Russia's border with Kazakhstan is more than 7,000 kilometers long, and it will be very difficult for us to fortify it alone. Here we need mutual assistance", see Mission of the Russian Federation to the European Communities 2003.

In an interview posted on the website of the Mission of the Russian Federation to the European Communities, a high-ranking Russian official has explained the position of his government as follows:

> [T]he EU insists on the earliest possible signing of a readmission agreement, while trying to postpone the question of visa regime. We do not accept such an approach. Of course, fears exist [...] that Russia might be used as a transit corridor for illegal migration to the West from other countries, primarily Southeast and South Asia. This worries us likewise, and so we are ready to sign an agreement on readmission [...].[104]

The slackening of the EC's visa regime is an important domestic political issue in Russia. The lifting of visa requirements, or even the facilitation thereof, is not a measure that the Community or the Member States would normally consider. The fear of the "the hordes at the border", the purported millions of low-skilled Russians that would seek entry into the West after the lifting of the Iron Curtain arguably never quite dissipated. Added concerns in relation to cross-border crime and considerations of national security explain why visa requirements for Russian nationals have been carefully guarded. Some Member States, which experience an influx of Russian immigrants and protection seekers, such as for example Austria, do not look favourably upon lifting or changing the visa regime vis-à-vis Russia.[105] Others, on the other hand, have recently shown signs of more openness in this regard. In particular, Germany, France and Italy, respectively, initiated dialogue, and signed bilateral agreements on the facilitation of visa issuance to Russian nationals.[106]

The importance of a readmission agreement with Russia for the Community has enabled Russia to force the issue of visa-free travel for Russian nationals as a long-term objective onto the EC's agenda, and to extract a short-term perspective on visa facilitation. The agreement on a transit regime for the Kaliningrad region in November 2002 signalled the start of readmission negotiations, but not without immediate association with the EC's visa regime. The GAER Council of 22 October 2002 had adopted conclusions on Kaliningrad. In response to a "Russian proposal to open discussions on defining the necessary conditions for the eventual establishment of a visa-free regime", the conclusions determined that "discussions on this issue should take place in the PCA [the 1998 Partnership and Cooperation Agreement between the EC and Russia] structures". [107] The GAER Council was careful to stress the strictly long-term perspective of the development of visa-free movement between the EC and Russia. Nevertheless, Russia had attained an important political concession, albeit still tentative.

104 Mission of the Russian Federation to the European Communities 2003.

105 AFP 2003; AP 2004.

106 Subsection 7.3.6 will discuss the implications of these Member State initiatives for the Commission's readmission negotiations, and the possible tension with Community law.

107 Press release 12945/02 (Presse 315).

During the ensuing negotiations of a readmission agreement with the Commission, Russia soon established a strict linkage with the issue of visa. To discuss visa facilitation within the existing institutional framework of the PCA was not to Russia's satisfaction. Its purpose was clearly to use readmission as leverage to attain visa facilitation on the short term, and not to risk a loss of momentum by absorbing the visa issue into the muddle of wider EU-Russia cooperation. Instead, therefore, Russia insisted on discussion of visa facilitation with the Commission, held "back-to-back" with readmission negotiations. This created a complication, while the Commission did not have a mandate to discuss visa matters with Russia as a separate issue, let alone to make relevant concessions. With Russia refusing to continue the negotiation of the readmission agreement, the Commission eventually conceded to Russia's request in October 2003. Initial discussion took place on an ad hoc basis, i.e. without the Council mandate required to for any actual concessions. This process was however soon formalised by the adoption of a Council negotiating directive for an agreement with Russia on visa facilitation.[108]

The linkage with a visa facilitation agreement did not entirely secure the conclusion of the readmission agreement with Russia. The Commission was required to make an additional concession. It agreed to postpone the readmission of third country nationals under the agreement for a period of three years after its entry into force.[109] Similar to the case of Albania,[110] this transitional period will allow Russia to increase its reception and control capacity, assisted by EC funds, and to conclude more readmission agreements with other countries.

Finally, after a total of ten rounds of formal negotiations, the text of the Community readmission agreement was initialled in October 2005 during a meeting of the EU-Russia Partnership Council in Luxemburg.[111] The visa facilitation agreement was also initialled at this occasion. The readmission agreement entered into force on 1 June 2007.[112]

Reaching agreement with Russia on the readmission of unauthorised immigrants may be considered a significant achievement of the common readmission policy, especially considering the difficulties which individual Member States have had in this regard. Equally, however, extracting a visa facilitation agreement from the EC was a considerable result for Russia.

108 Draft negotiating directives for an agreement between the EC and the Russian Federation on the facilitation of the issuance of short-stay visas to Union and Russian citizens (Council Doc. 11071/04) were approved by the COREPER on 30 June 2004, and adopted by the GAER Council on 12 July 2004, Council Doc. 11251/04.

109 Press release IP/05/1263.

110 *Supra*, subsection 3.2.5, at n. 76. See also *infra*, subsection 7.2.7.

111 Press release IP/05/1263.

112 *OJ* L 156, 16 June 2007, p. 37.

### 7.2.4 Sri Lanka

Sri Lanka is a country of origin of unauthorised immigration into the EC, especially of protection seekers.[113] The Member States reject a large percentage of protection claims by Sri Lankan nationals, who are thus eligible for return. In the past, Sri Lankan authorities have not cooperated sufficiently in readmitting returned protection seekers, imposing obstacles by way of document requirements. Subsection 7.1.1 above noted that the HLWG in 1999 signalled a more cooperative attitude on the part of Sri Lanka, deeming the time appropriate for negotiation of a readmission agreement.[114]

Sri Lanka is purely a country of origin; it does not experience transit migration. An agreement concerning an obligation to readmit third country nationals and stateless persons would therefore be inconsequential in practice. For this reason, the Commission proposal for a Council negotiating directive recommended conclusion of a Community readmission agreement pertaining to nationals, only. The Council, however, proved to be inflexible on this point and ordered the Commission to negotiate the standard agreement, including third country nationals.

Needless to say, countries which do not experience transit migration are less concerned by incurring responsibility for the readmission of transit migrants. The readmission negotiations with Sri Lanka were thus completed relatively quickly. The draft text of the agreement and the invitation to start negotiations were transmitted in April 2001. Two rounds of negotiations in July 2001 and March 2002 were sufficient to reach agreement on the text, which was initialed in May 2002. In March 2003, the Commission adopted a proposal for Council decisions on the signing and conclusion of the readmission agreement with Sri Lanka.[115] Considerable delays in the whole process were caused by a reservation of the Dutch parliament on the Council decision to sign the agreement, and by the translation of the agreement into Sinhala and Tamil. The Council adopted its decision on the signing of the agreement in November 2003.[116] After several failed attempts at finding a suitable date and occasion, the signing cer-

113 Interesting to note are occasional reports of sudden influxes of Sri Lankan immigrants into the Member States. An example is Italy, which during a period experienced the arrival of large numbers of Sri Lankan nationals by boat, traveling via the Suez Canal (BBC News 2002; Sunday Observer *Sunday Observer*, "Lankans arrested in Suez Canal deported", available on: www.sundayobserver.lk). Italy has arranged to stem this flow in bilateral cooperation with Egypt, and in consultation with Sri Lanka. Egypt started intercepting vessels carrying Sri Lankan nationals through the Suez Canal after Italy offered to finance the subsequent return by charter flight to Sri Lanka. Cooperation was arguably in the interest of both Egypt and Sri Lanka. In addition to Italy paying for return costs incurred by Egypt (payments amounting to a reported €600.000 by September 2003, CIVIPOL 2003, Council Doc. 11490/1/03, p. 85), both countries have an agreement with Italy on labour immigration quota, which Italy applies in a flexible manner (COM(2004) 412 final, p. 8; CIVIPOL 2003, Council Doc. 11490/1/03, p. 39, 85; Central Directorate of Immigration and Border Policy 2004, p. 3).

114 *Supra*, at n. 12.

115 Council Doc. 7831/1/03.

116 Press release 14492/1/03 REV 1 (Presse 320).

emony took place in Colombo in June 2004.[117] The Council then decided to conclude the agreement, and ratification procedures were successfully completed, allowing the agreement to enter into force in May 2005.[118]

In addition to the absence of issues related to transit migration, a further reason for reaching swift agreement with Sri Lanka on readmission was that its demands for compensation did not pose any difficulties to the Community. Sri Lanka requested closer law enforcement cooperation with the Community, especially on measures concerning the financing of international terrorism.[119] A joint declaration annexed to the agreement on "the facilitation of law enforcement cooperation" reflects the deal that was struck in this regard.[120]

### *7.2.5 Hong Kong and Macao*

This subsection discusses the readmission negotiations with the Hong Kong Special Administrative Region of the People's Republic of China (hereinafter Hong Kong), and with the Macao Special Administrative Region of the People's Republic of China (hereinafter Macao), jointly. The Community readmission agreements with Hong Kong and Macao share the same history, present the same mutual interests, and were negotiated with equal ease.

Hong Kong and Macao are part of the Chinese Republic, but enjoy a degree of autonomy in certain affairs, including immigration. Hong Kong and Macao both approached the Community with a request to lift visa requirements for their permanent residents. The Community agreed to this request, but on the condition of concluding a readmission agreement as a safeguard.

The JHA Council meeting of 1 December 2000 reached political agreement on a new visa regulation, which excluded Hong Kong and Macao from the list of countries that are subject to a visa requirement. In the minutes of this meeting, the Council instructs the Commission to submit recommendations for negotiating directives for readmission agreements with Hong Kong and Macao. The new visa regulation (Council Regulation (EC) No. 539/2001) was formally adopted in March 2001, and entered into force in the following month. The Commission subsequently transmitted draft readmission agreements and accompanying invitations to enter into negotiations to Hong Kong and Macao in July 2001.[121]

The respective negotiation of these two agreements was completed after an informal meeting of technical experts, and one round of formal negotiations. The agreement between the Community and Hong Kong was initialled in November 2001. The Commission submitted proposals for the Council decisions on signing and conclusion of

117 See Government of Sri Lanka 2004. See also the European Parliament report on the conclusion of the agreement, session document A6-0048/2004, p. 6.

118 MEMO/05/351; see also European Parliament, session document A6-0048/2004, p. 6.

119 Schieffer 2003, p. 356.

120 See the text of the agreement in Council Doc. 7831/1/03.

121 SEC(2002) 412, p. 2; COM(2003) 151 final, p. 2.

the agreement in April 2002. Signing and conclusion followed in November 2002 and December 2003, respectively. After receiving notification from Hong Kong in January 2004 of the completion of ratification procedures in accordance with Article 20(2) of the readmission agreement, the agreement entered into force on 1 March 2004.

The agreement between the Community and Macao was initialled in October 2002. In April 2003, the Commission submitted proposals for the Council decisions on signing and conclusion of the agreement, after which signing took place in October. The adoption of a Council decision on conclusion of the agreement followed in April 2004. Having received notification of the completion of Macao's ratification procedures in March 2004, the agreement entered into force on 1 June 2004.

The readmission agreements with Hong and Macao were the first Community readmission agreements to enter into force. The involvement of the Community in the implementation of its readmission agreements is limited to meetings of the joint readmission committee. The first ever meeting of such a joint readmission committee was between the EC and Hong Kong, and took place in Brussels in September 2004.[122]

The agreements with Hong Kong and Macao are of little significance, other than the fact of being the first to enter into force. Their negotiation was relatively easy, as there was a clear interest present at both sides of the negotiating table from the onset. Readmission was a package deal together with the lifting of visa requirements. There was some delay in the completion of relevant procedures towards conclusion of the agreements, but this pertained to technical problems of language translation regarding the agreement with Hong Kong, and a belated EP approval of the agreement with Macao. Hong Kong and Macao are not of real interest to the Community as "countries" of origin or transit of unauthorised immigration.[123] If not for their requests to change the EC visa regime, concluding Community readmission agreements with Hong Kong and Macao would most likely never have been considered.

The agreement with Hong Kong did provide the European Parliament with a first opportunity to express its views on the development of a common readmission policy. Subject to the consultation procedure of Article 300 TEC, the role of the EP is limited.[124] Its approval is required for decisions of the Council on the signing and the conclusion of Community readmission agreements. This means the EP can provide an input only after negotiation of the text of the agreement is already completed, leaving little opportunity for any substantial amendment. This clarifies why the EP report on the signing of the agreement with Hong Kong is more concerned with the common readmission policy in general than with the EC-Hong Kong readmission agreement itself.[125] The EP made use of the occasion to inject its views into the readmission negotiations that were still pending or forthcoming.

122 Press release IP/04/1113.

123 Hong Kong and Macao do not appear on any of the lists that were drawn up at Community level of readmission targets or countries of relevance in the area of immigration, discussed above in subsection 7.1.1.

124 Article 300(3) TEC.

125 European Parliament, session document A5-0381/2002 final.

Commenting on the non-affection clause contained in the EC-Hong Kong agreement, the EP expressed concern regarding a lack of safeguards for the fundamental rights of readmittees, which we quoted earlier.[126] The EP furthermore questioned the effectiveness of the readmission negotiations. It stressed that the negotiations with Hong Kong had been relatively easy, and pointed to the lack of success in other negotiations, as well as the Commission's requests for more negotiating leverage. The EP consequently recommended adoption of a horizontal approach, combining Union and Community policies, and increasing coordination between foreign affairs- and immigration ministers within the Council.[127]

The next occasion for the EP to express its views in a public document was not until two years later, in its report on the signing of the readmission agreement with Macao.[128] The report again contained a number of general considerations. It reviewed the persistent lack of progress pursuant to the Council's negotiating mandates for readmission agreements, identifying the equally persistent lack of available negotiating means as the main cause. The EP also noted the criticism at the address of the Commission for not having achieved a higher success rate. However, the EP did not take a clear position in this dispute between the Commission and the Member States, nor did it present recommendations on improving the development of the common readmission policy. Rather, the EP stressed its limited involvement in the conclusion of Community readmission agreements, with which it distanced itself from the institutional issues raised by the readmission negotiations.[129]

Concerning the level of fundamental rights protection offered by Community readmission agreements, the EP largely repeated its earlier criticism. It still considered the content of the particular non-affection clause insufficient, deploring the lack of reference to instruments such as the Geneva Refugee Convention. As noted in the outline of the standard draft agreement in chapter 5, the text of later Community readmission agreements contains a more elaborate non-affection clause, including a list of references to international conventions.[130] This being the original format as determined by the Council's negotiating directives, it is unlikely that it resulted from the EP's criticism. It would appear that the clause as included in the agreements with Hong Kong and Macao was a particular result of the negotiations with these entities.

### *7.2.6 Ukraine*

The case of Ukraine is similar to that of Russia. The negotiation of Community readmission agreements with these neighbouring countries is closely linked. The parallel targeting of these countries is in accordance with the Community's regional approach to common readmission policy.

126 *Supra*, section 5.2, at n. 8.

127 European Parliament, session document A5-0381/2002 final, p. 8-9.

128 European Parliament, session document A5-0096/2004.

129 European Parliament, session document A5-0096/2004, p. 6-7.

130 *Supra*, subsection 5.3.9.

Like Russia, Ukraine is a country of origin and transit of illegal immigration into the Community, produces refugees, and does not feature on safe third country lists.[131] Regarding relations with the Community, Ukraine concluded a Partnership and Cooperation Agreement in 1998. It is also a beneficiary of TACIS programming and funding, the object of a 1999 EU common strategy, and included in the European Neighbourhood Policy.

Approximation to the EU is an important political issue in Ukraine. The Ukrainian government therefore considers entering into a Community readmission agreement as negotiable, despite domestic political opposition and disapproving public opinion.[132] This does not imply that negotiations have been easy, however.

Ukraine's primary objection to concluding a readmission agreement with the Community is that it would incur responsibility for transit migration. This concern is amplified by the fact that its borders with Russia, Belarus and Moldova are neither properly controlled, nor demarcated. Migrants coming from these directions thus enter easily but find leaving Ukraine to the West much more difficult. As migrants culminate on Ukrainian territory unable to continue their journey, so would responsibility for the readmission of those who do succeed in entering EC Member States after conclusion of an EC-Ukraine readmission agreement.[133] A further concern of Ukraine is with regard to large numbers of Soviet passports that are still in circulation. Ukraine claims that nationals of neighbouring countries such as Moldova and Belarus may still hold such documents with a "Ukraine" stamp on them. Under the terms of the agreement with the Community, this could lead to yet additional requests for readmission to Ukraine.

In an attempt to share responsibility for transit migration with other countries in the region, as well as to create a perspective for expulsion to source countries, Ukraine is negotiating a number of further readmission agreements.[134] The most crucial is the negotiation of an agreement with Russia, with which Ukraine is booking slow and uncertain progress.[135] Like Morocco, Ukraine has requested the inclusion of a provision in the readmission agreement with the Community, which would prioritise removal and readmission to countries of origin.[136] The Commission has tentatively agreed to formulate a joint declaration to this effect, although excluding cases of border apprehension.

It would be in Ukraine's interest to insist also on the prioritisation of removal and readmission to previous transit countries. Let us assume that an EC Member State would apprehend a migrant having travelled through first Russian, then Ukrainian ter-

131 Byrne, Noll and Vedsted-Hansen 2002, p. 97; UNHCR 2003, Global refugee trends.

132 Kruse 2004, p. 23-28.

133 A known route, for example, runs from Russia through Belarus into Ukraine, from where attempted entry into the EC would take place. Ukraine shares an EU external border with Poland, Czech Republic, and Hungary, to which Rumania will be added after the enlargement of the EU in 2007.

134 *Supra*, subsection 3.2.3, at n. 58.

135 Kruse 2004, p. 27.

136 *Supra*, subsection 7.2.1.

ritory. Let us further assume that the Member State is able to prove this transit under the terms of both the Community readmission agreement with Russia, and the agreement with Ukraine. The Member State would have two equal treaty obligations to invoke. Transit through Russia and the triggering of the related readmission obligation having taken place earlier in time, the Member State would possibly direct its readmission request at Russia. The agreements in question, however, do not regulate this relation, and the Member State would not be obliged to proceed in this manner.

The Commission has made clear that in case of apprehension of a transit migrant at the border with Ukraine, readmission to Ukraine would enjoy priority before readmission to the country of origin. This is likely to apply also to previous transit countries. A Member State is furthermore likely to request readmission to Ukraine, because the transfer costs would be lower than sending the person to Russia. Such hypothetical cases arguably encourage Ukraine to conclude a readmission agreement with Russia in order to arrange the allocation of responsibility for transit migrants between them. Clearly, however, avoiding responsibility for such transit cases entirely would be more beneficial. If possible, Ukraine would prefer avoiding the cost of reception and processing migrants, and of possible transfer to Russia pursuant to any future Ukraine-Russia readmission agreement. Inserting a clause into the EC-Ukraine readmission agreement, prioritising readmission to previous transit countries would achieve this goal. It should be emphasised that the responsibility for transit migration in the region would concentrate in any case on Russia, as the main point of entry into the region.

The above makes clear that when considering readmission in a regional context, a number of crosscutting interests appear between countries. As a result, the negotiations between the Community and Ukraine, the Community and Russia, as well as Ukraine and Russia, have fed into each other. In its negotiations with the Community, Ukraine established a link with the EC-Russia negotiations. On its part, Russia established a link with the EC-Ukraine negotiations. This implies that both countries kept abreast of each other's interim results. Progress in the Commission's negotiations with one country became dependent on the results achieved by the other, and viceversa. Ukraine and Russia arguably pursued such a complicating strategy in order to ensure an at least comparable result concerning the readmission of third country nationals and stateless persons. In the same vein, both countries sought to reach agreement more or less simultaneously.[137]

In the meantime, both countries regularly informed the Commission of the course of negotiation of the readmission agreement between them, and of the interests involved. Ukraine even requested the Commission for assistance in its negotiations with Russia. It approached the Commission for advice on the drafting of the agreement, and asked it to encourage Russia to conclude the agreement, as well as finish demarcation of the Russian-Ukrainian border.

Regarding the negotiation of a Community readmission agreement with Ukraine, the following can be noted. Regional considerations, and concerns regarding the readmission of transit migrants, apparently, outweighed Ukraine's desire to approximate

137 See also Kruse 2004, p. 27.

EU membership. Negotiations have been slow and difficult. Ukraine received the draft text of a readmission agreement and invitation to enter into negotiations in August 2002. An informal preparatory meeting followed in March of that year, after which negotiations commenced in November. A second and third round of negotiations was organised in June and September 2003, respectively. After a fourth round in December 2003, agreement on the text was still not in sight. It became clear that concrete concessions would be needed to secure the agreement with Ukraine.

In exchange for concluding a readmission agreement with the Community, Ukraine has requested technical and financial support for the reception of immigrants, and for the demarcation and strengthening of its borders with Russia, Belarus and Moldova. This fits within the broader strategy of EC external immigration and asylum policies, so has formed no obstacle for the Community.[138] Similar to Russia, however, Ukraine has also shown an interest in visa facilitation.

While Ukraine's long-term goal is to attain visa free travel into the EC, the Commission expected a limited degree of visa facilitation would already secure the readmission agreement. Ukraine expressed a particular interest in the facilitation of visa issue to holders of diplomatic- and service passports. While at first glance this would appear a minor concession, there were nevertheless complicating factors. Again, some Member States were not in favour of the facilitation of entry of Ukrainian nationals. Secondly, there are general concerns in relation to this particular visa facilitation. Despite the transition and reforms Ukraine has undergone since its independence in 1991, it is yet to achieve durable political and democratic stability. Widespread corruption and the infiltration of criminal networks in government bodies have affected the Ukrainian administration.[139] One could thus envisage a risk of documents, such as diplomatic- and service passports, falling into the hands of persons, who would benefit from facilitated entry into the EC at the detriment of national security.

Nevertheless, the Commission and Council decided to offer holding visa talks with Ukraine after the text of the readmission agreement would be initialled. This was clearly not considered sufficient by the Ukrainian authorities. On 7 November 2005, the GAER Council agreed to engage in the negotiation of a visa facilitation agreement in parallel with the readmission agreement.[140] Ukraine thus managed to extract the same concession as Russia. Negotiations were finally completed in October 2006, after which the Council decided to sign the agreement in June 2007.[141]

### *7.2.7 Albania*

An important priority of EU external relations is to strengthen the development of the Western Balkans. This process includes ample attention for the building of capacity to

138 COM(2005) 352 final, p. 9.

139 Kruse 2004, p. 24.

140 PRES/05/273; COM(2005) 352 final, p. 9; MEX/06/0201.

141 Council Doc. 9312/07.

control migration and host refugees.[142] For this purpose, the Community injects technical and financial assistance through the Stabilisation and Association Process (SAP), and the supporting CARDS budget. Albania was the first target in this region for a Community readmission agreement because it is a key country of origin[143] and transit of immigration into the Community.[144]

Essential to understanding the negotiation process between the Community and Albania, is that Albania wishes to approximate EU membership. Participation in the Stabilisation and Association Process regarding South East Europe, and the ongoing negotiation of a Stabilisation and Association Agreement (SAA) with the Community, is therefore essential to Albania. In this context, Albania is undergoing an intensive legislative reform, and is adopting a range of legislation in the fields of immigration and asylum. Remarkably, Albania frequently consults the Commission regarding the content of draft legislation in these fields. It is arguably attempting to gain the image of a viable partner and collaborator. Illustrative of its desire to join the EU, Albania is willing to adopt legislation approximating the Community acquis without the status of candidate Member State being even remotely in sight.

The same cooperative and eager attitude has extended to the negotiation of a readmission agreement with the Community.[145] The Commission was able to conduct readmission negotiations with Albania with relative speed and success, including a far-reaching obligation to readmit third country nationals and stateless persons who have transited Albanian territory. This is despite the fact that a readmission agreement with the Community would clearly not be to Albania's (direct) advantage. Remittances are an essential source of Albania's GDP, generated by a large and active diaspora.[146] Albania has nevertheless not only established readmission relations with the Community, but also concluded readmission agreements with Italy, Hungary, Belgium, Switzerland, Bulgaria, Rumania, Germany, Croatia, and the UK. In 2004, Albania was furthermore engaged in readmission negotiations with the Netherlands, Luxembourg, FYROM, Slovenia, Slovakia and Bosnia Herzegovina, and was about to start negotiations with Moldova, Ukraine and Turkey.[147]

After receiving a negotiating directive for Albania, the Commission transmitted a draft readmission agreement and invitation to open negotiations in March 2003. The Commission and Albania met for negotiations in May and September 2003, followed by a third round in November during which negotiation of the text was completed. An initialling ceremony was organised in Brussels on 18 December 2003, after which the

142 See, for example, the Council conclusions on the Western Balkans of 16 June 2003, endorsed by the Thessaloniki European Council on 19 and 20 June 2003.

143 Especially Italy and Greece host large numbers of Albanian nationals without a right to residence or presence, Oxfam GB 2000, p. 37-38.

144 Kruse 2004, p. 18-19.

145 See also Kruse 2004, p. 20-21.

146 Oxfam GB 2000, p. 37-38.

147 SEC(2004) 374/2, p. 31-32.

Community readmission agreement with Albania was submitted to the Council with proposals for decisions on its signing and conclusion. Council decisions to sign and conclude the agreement followed in April and November 2005, respectively.[148] The agreement entered into force on 1 May 2006.[149]

As noted above, the Commission was able to negotiate a far-reaching obligation to readmit third country nationals in the agreement with Albania by agreeing to a two-year transitional period.[150] The obligation will not be implemented until two years after entry into force of the agreement. Albania is in a poor state in terms of capacity to receive and process immigrants, especially where concerning protection seekers. Apparently, the Community expects that two years of targeted support will bring these conditions up to par. Five years, as originally requested by Albania, would undoubtedly have been a more realistic timeframe. Albania, a country which can not sustain its population leading 40% of all men between the age of 19 and 40 to leave and support their families from abroad,[151] is hardly an attractive country of destination for readmitted migrants. Unless over the next two years Albania would attain the resources to implement a rigorous system of detention and onward removal, one would expect most readmissions of third country nationals to be temporary before entry into the EC is re-attempted.

The fact that the Commission was able to offer financial backing for the projected two-year period of capacity building had a beneficial effect on the negotiations. The Commission explicitly earmarked part of the CARDS budget for the strengthening of Albanian "readmission" capacity. In addition, the Commission was able to advertise the forthcoming adoption of the Aeneas regulation.[152] Bearing in mind the limits and constraints of project-based financing, as discussed above, the Aeneas regulation allowed the Commission to pledge further resources for building reception capacity.

Albania also requested assistance in concluding readmission agreements with other countries in the region and countries of origin.[153] The Commission is willing to provide diplomatic support in this regard.[154] Furthermore, in return for its cooperative attitude in concluding the readmission agreement, Albania may look forward to facilitation of the transfer of remittances by Albanian nationals from EC Member States.[155]

A final explanation for the speedy completion of readmission negotiations with Albania is that the Commission established a link with the EC-Albania Stabilisation and Association Agreement.[156] The SAA under negotiation with Albania contains a

148 PRES/05/273.

149 *OJ* L 96, 5 April 2006, p. 9.

150 See *supra*, subsection 3.2.5 at n. 76.

151 Oxfam GB 2000, p. 37. For more statistics, see Kruse 2004, p. 18.

152 *Supra*, subsection 6.2.2.2.

153 SEC(2003) 339, p. 31, 33.

154 COM(2005) 352 final, p. 3.

155 COM(2005) 352 final, p. 3.

156 Kruse 2004, p. 19.

migration management clause, committing to the negotiation of a readmission agreement with the Community or its Member States upon request. Rather than waiting for the SAA to enter into force to invoke this political commitment, the Commission used the SAA negotiations as immediate leverage. It made clear that negotiation of the SAA, which started on 31 January 2003,[157] would not move forward unless readmission negotiations would commence and progress favourably. In other words, the Commission applied a negative incentive to reach agreement with Albania on readmission.

This linkage was an important reason behind the swift completion of readmission negotiations with Albania. In terms of reciprocity, however, it does not appear to have had much of a positive effect on the SAA negotiations. In a 2004 Stabilisation and Association report on Albania, the Commission noted and congratulated Albania with initialling the Community readmission agreement, implying some form of positive impact on Albania's SAP dossier. The Commission however also noted that, after as much as nine rounds of negotiations, completion of the negotiations was not yet in sight, still requiring considerable reform in a number of areas.[158] The SAP negotiations are still ongoing at the time of writing. Completion is expected in the course of 2006.[159]

### *7.2.8 Algeria*

Like Russia and Ukraine, there are strong links between the respective negotiations of Community readmission agreements with Algeria and Morocco. The parallel targeting of these countries again results from the Community's regional approach to readmission. Algeria and Morocco have been selected for the conclusion of readmission agreements for similar reasons. Like Morocco, Algeria is a country of origin of unauthorised immigration into the Community. The number of Sub-Saharan African nationals, departing from its shores towards Spain, France and Italy, or residing on its territory without authorisation, is rising. Morocco and Algeria are both key countries along organised smuggling routes.[160]

At the time of writing, readmission negotiations with Algeria, for which the Commission received a mandate in November 2002, are yet to commence. Algeria has thus far refused to negotiate for two reasons. It firstly wants wait for the entry into force of the 2001 Euro-Med Association Agreement between Algeria and the Community. The negotiating parties initialled the agreement in December 2001, which entered into force towards the end of 2005.[161] Secondly, Algeria has linked the start of readmission negotiations to the outcome of the Commission's negotiations with Morocco.

157 SEC(2004) 374/2, p. 18.

158 SEC(2004) 374/2.

159 Commission work-programme 2006, p. 19 (available on: www.europa.eu.int/comm).

160 ICMPD 2004.

161 PRES/05/308; Presidency conclusions, European Council meeting in Brussels of 15 and 16 December 2005, DOC/05/4, 17 December 2005; see also www.europa.eu.int/comm/external_relations/ euromed/med_ass_agreemnts.htm.

Algeria's objective is to ensure that it achieves agreement on the readmission of persons with the Community on terms, equal to neighbouring country Morocco. One may assume that Algeria would also demand the same degree of compensation. A relevant factor is that a certain political and economic rivalry exists between Algeria and Morocco. Besides such possible sentiments of rivalry, however, Algeria has good reason to view its readmission relations with the Community in tandem with those of Morocco. In light of responsibility for transit migration in a region, establishing readmission relations with the Community that are at least equal to those of neighbouring countries is highly relevant. Smuggling routes into the EU often take migrants through the territories of several countries within the same region, as is the case with Algeria and Morocco. Algeria would therefore seek to avoid accepting the readmission of third country nationals and stateless persons on lighter terms than Morocco.[162] To safeguard its interests in this regards, Algeria could have chosen to conduct negotiations in parallel with Morocco, whilst keeping abreast of Morocco's interim results. This we have seen between Ukraine and Russia. Instead, Algeria has preferred to wait and first examine the technical result of negotiations with Morocco. From a negotiation perspective, this is a highly undesirable situation for the Community, which is discussed further below in subsection 7.3.2.

Subsequent events have underlined the salience of migration issues, and rising tension, in relations between Algeria, Morocco, and the European Community. In September and October of 2005, groups of immigrants repeatedly stormed the fences separating the Spanish enclaves of Ceuta and Melilla from Moroccan territory, resulting in several deaths. During the same period, unable to deal appropriately with the increasing numbers of unauthorised immigrants present on Moroccan territory, the Moroccan authorities took drastic measures. Arguably intended as a deterrent, groups of immigrants were transported to, and abandoned at the border with Algeria in the middle of the dessert.[163] These highly publicised events have raised questions regarding the implications of the EC's external immigration and asylum policies, concerning in particular the intensification of control of the external border in cooperation with EU neighbouring countries.[164] In addition, they have arguably increased the political sensitivity of the negotiation of Community readmission agreements with countries in this region.

### *7.2.9 China*

China is a prime country of origin of illegal immigrants and protection seekers. It has a record of offering limited cooperation on migration matters, whether regarding

162 On the other hand, it is also possible that acceptance of more liberal readmission obligations for third country nationals by Algeria would make it a less attractive transit country and cause a shift in Sub-Saharan migration to neighbouring countries. Such a shift in connection with readmission obligations has been reported, for example, between Tunisia and Libya, see *infra*, subsection 7.3.2, at n. 196.

163 Human Rights Watch 2005a.

164 Spijkerboer 2005.

readmission, or any other form of cooperation regarding the unauthorised immigration of Chinese nationals into EC Member States. Establishing relations with China in the field of external migration and asylum policies therefore poses a significant challenge to the Community. The aforementioned incident in Dover in 2000 created a perspective for EC-China dialogue and cooperation in this area, which has since developed steadily. From the political perspective of the Community, the conclusion of a readmission agreement with China would be a veritable crown on these developments.

The Commission achieved a breakthrough with the inclusion of a readmission obligation in the EC-China ADS agreement signed in February 2004.[165] Chinese nationals are subject to travel restrictions. Travel for tourism purposes is possible only to destinations which have been granted Approved Destination Status (ADS) by the Chinese authorities, and after conclusion of an ADS agreement between China and the country concerned.[166] An ADS agreement provides for visa facilitation for groups of Chinese tourists. In relations with China, agreement on an obligation to readmit any possible escapees – visiting Chinese tourists who overstay their visa – may be considered a success. It was the first time that China accepted such a provision in any of the 23 ADS agreements it has concluded to date.[167]

Having broached the issue of readmission of Chinese nationals, the Commission expects the conclusion of the EC-China ADS agreement to "pave the way" for a fully-fledged Community readmission agreement. Although it received a negotiating mandate in April 2002, the Commission decided for this reason to postpone negotiation of the readmission agreement until negotiation of the ADS agreement was completed. Accordingly, the Commission invited the Chinese authorities to enter into negotiations in January 2004.

In May 2004, China laid down its conditions for the conclusion of a readmission agreement with the Community. Perhaps inspired by the results booked by Russia and Ukraine in this area, China formally requested to commence negotiations for (further) visa facilitation for Chinese nationals in parallel with negotiation of the readmission agreement.[168] The Commission and Council agreed. The first "exploratory discussions", regarding the possibility of exchanging a readmission agreement with visa facilitation for certain categories of Chinese personnel, were held mid-2005.[169]

165 *Supra*, at n. 37. The text of the ADS agreement, which has been drawn up as an MoU, is annexed to the Commission proposals for Council decisions concerning the signing and conclusion of the Memorandum of Understanding between the European Community and the National Tourism Administration of the People's Republic of China on visa and related issues concerning tourist groups from the People's Republic of China, COM(2003) 790 final. For general information, see also Press release IP/04/196; and the report of the EP on the signing of ADS agreement, European Parliament, session document A5-0101/2004 final.

166 COM(2003) 790 final, p. 2-3.

167 COM(2003) 790 final, p. 3; Article 5 EC-China ADS agreement.

168 SEC(2004) 1349.

169 COM(2005) 352 final, p. 4.

At the time of writing, the actual start of readmission negotiations with China remains uncertain, however. The link with visa facilitation has created a concrete opening, but concluding a readmission agreement with this country is likely to remain a slow and time-consuming process.

### *7.2.10 Turkey*

After Algeria and China, Turkey may be considered the most elusive of the readmission countries. After receiving the draft text of a readmission agreement in March 2003, Turkey did not formally acknowledge the invitation to start negotiations until March 2004. This was a clear point of concern for the EU institutions and the Member States. Establishing readmission relations with Turkey is considered essential to the Community's "cordon" policy objective, and the securing of the EU's external border. Turkey is a significant source country of unauthorised immigrants and protection seekers,[170] as well as a bottleneck for smuggling routes into EU territory. Considering also that Turkey was amongst the nine third countries with which the November 2002 JHA Council decided to intensify relations in the area of migration, the lack of headway on the core issue of readmission is a significant political failure.

Turkey became a candidate Member State in 1999, after having applied for EC membership in 1989. The European Council in Nice in December 2000 agreed to an Accession Partnership, which was to form the main element of Turkey's pre-accession strategy. Part of this strategy is to bring Turkey in line with the EU immigration and asylum acquis, which has prominently included strengthening Turkish border control and the countering of unauthorised immigration.[171] Recent years have thus seen intense cooperation in this area involving substantial technical and financial investment. Although assessment of the resulting effect and progress varies between sources, Turkey has generally been found wanting. It has for example been criticised for taking insufficient action against smuggling activities operating on its territory.[172] A 2003 feasibility study on the control of the EU's maritime borders, financed and coordinated in part by the Commission, moreover stated:

---

170 Turkey remains a principal country of origin of protection seekers. In 2003, it produced the fourth largest number of protection claims in Europe. On this list, Turkey is preceded by Russia, Serbia and Montenegro, and Iraq, and followed by China, UNHCR 2003b.

171 COM(2004) 656 final; Kruse 2004, p. 33.

172 The following finding made in a feasibility study on EU maritime border control is especially illustrative: "In spite of the fact that Turkey hopes to develop good relations with the European Union and join eventually, it has not taken any action against people-smuggling, which is regarded as a legitimate business activity there. Statements made to the Greek authorities and by intercepted illegals suggest that unless people-smugglers pose a threat to law and order they are unlikely to meet with difficulties on the Turkish coast", CIVIPOL 2003, Council Doc. 11490/1/03, p. 35. The 2003 regular report of the Commission on Turkey's progress towards accession, by contrast, expresses a more moderate and positive opinion.

> [Turkey] is an official candidate for accession but apparently it is an insufficiently cooperative transit country in the fight against illegal immigration by sea, and it cannot yet be described as safe in terms of political asylum. Some serious work needs to be done with Turkey for it to fully play the role of buffer state before one day potentially becoming a member and manager of the external border.[173]

Efforts by Turkey appear to have since intensified with more success, as indicated by a 2004 Commission report on Turkey's progress towards accession.[174] The Commission remained clearly vexed, however, by Turkey's continued resistance to the negotiation of a readmission agreement. Although abstaining from a formal reply to the invitation to start negotiations, Turkey did detail its position in this regard at several formal and informal occasions.[175]

Turkey's main objection regards the obligation to readmit third country nationals and stateless persons. The key issue in the negotiations is thus yet again the responsibility for transit migration. Turkey accepts the readmission of its nationals,[176] as well as third country nationals holding a Turkish residence permit,[177] but it does not consider the readmission of third country of nationals an obligation of international law. Consequently, Turkey emphasised that it would be ready to conclude a readmission agreement with the Community, limited to nationals and permanent residents.

Further to responsibility for transit migration, Turkey is concerned about becoming a country of destination for migrants, who are unable to reach the EC.[178] It views the conclusion of readmission agreements with other countries as a solution to this problem while distributing the responsibility for transit migration over the region, and creating a scope for return and readmission to countries of origin. The number of countries with which Turkey is seeking readmission agreements is impressive. It already has agreements in place with Syria, Greece, Kyrgyzstan, and Rumania.[179] According to a source dated October 2004, negotiations are underway with Belarus, Bulgaria, Egypt, Kazakhstan, Libya, Lebanon, Macedonia, Sri Lanka, Russia, Ukraine, and Uzbekistan. Furthermore, Turkey is awaiting responses to invitations to negotiate from Algeria,

173 CIVIPOL 2003, Council Doc. 11490/1/03, p. 51.

174 SEC(2004) 1201.

175 One such occasion is a meeting of the EC-Turkey Sub-Committee no. 8 on customs, tax, drugs, and money-laundering in December 2003, Council Doc. 12289/04. This sub-committee is part of the institutional framework of the 1963 EC-Turkey Association Agreement.

176 An obligation to this effect is included in the Turkish Constitution, Council Doc. 12289/04, p. 20.

177 Council Doc. 12289/04, p. 20.

178 Kruse 2004, p. 35; Kirişci 2004, p. 8.

179 Kirişci 2004, appendix: "Turkey's readmission agreements with third countries". Implementation of the readmission agreement between Turkey and Greece is reported to be unsatisfactory, while Turkey rejects a high number of the readmission requests issued by Greece, *Ibid.*, p. 8.

Bangladesh, China, Ethiopia, Georgia, India, Iran, Israel, Jordan, Mongolia, Morocco, Nigeria, Pakistan, Sudan, and Tunisia.[180] In this light, it is likely that Turkey has pursued a delaying tactic in relation to the Community. Before agreeing to the readmission of transit migrants from EC Member States, it has arguably attempted to first secure more readmission obligations from other countries.

The Turkish position involves two more reasoned objections. Turkey has pointed out that its fellow candidate Member States Bulgaria and Rumania have not been approached for the conclusion of a Community readmission agreement. It has appealed to equal treatment, implying that the invitation to negotiate an agreement with Turkey should be either rescinded, or that such invitations should also be issued to Bulgaria and Rumania.[181] The Commission's counter-argument is that there are relevant differences between Bulgaria and Rumania, and Turkey, which preclude equal treatment. During the early nineties, Bulgaria and Rumania concluded readmission agreements with several Member States. Implementation of these agreements progressed satisfactorily, and the EC eventually lifted visa requirements for Bulgarian and Rumanian nationals in 2001. Turkey is still on the visa list. It has established only few readmission relations with Member States, which are moreover not functioning well. Turkey's appeal to equal treatment thus appears unfounded.

Turkey's final objection against the conclusion of a Community readmission agreement, and arguably its strongest card, stemmed from the Community's own readmission strategy as set out in April 2002. The April 2002 Council Conclusions on criteria for the selection of readmission target countries explicitly state: "given the European Union's forthcoming enlargement, countries with which it is negotiating accession agreements should not be included".[182]

Including this criterion was a strategic mistake, considering Turkey. Turkey was not an acceding Member State in April 2002, nor when it received an invitation to enter into a readmission agreement in March 2003, but there was a clear possibility that it would attain that status in the near future. The European Council, meeting in Copenhagen in December 2002, determined that it would decide whether to commence accession negotiations with Turkey in December 2004.[183] In March 2003, Turkey thus knew that if it could push its reply regarding the start of readmission negotiations beyond December 2004, it would have a strong political argument to reject the conclusion of a readmission agreement, assuming that the European Council would indeed decide to start accession talks.

180 Kirişci 2004, appendix. Like the Commission, Turkey has had varying success in establishing such readmission relations. The comparison has been made, however, that "Turkey's performance in terms of number of readmission agreements concluded and being negotiated [sic.] is much better than the performance of the European Commission" Kirişci 2004, p. 7.

181 Council Doc. 12289/04, p. 20.

182 Council Doc. 7990/02, 16 April 2002, para. 2(ii).

183 COM(2004) 656 final, p. 2.

The April 2002 Council conclusions did not leave the Commission with much space for successful counter-arguments. The Commission stressed Turkey's status, for the time being, as merely a candidate Member State. It also noted that actual accession to the EU would be a long-term process, and that a readmission agreement would thus still be required for the interim period. Neither argument was able to trump the fact that Turkey's status as candidate Member State was to all appearances coming to an end, calling for anticipatory application of the April 2002 criterion. The Council's wording of the April 2002 conclusions moreover indicates that duration of actual accession negotiations is irrelevant.

Holding the weaker position in this argument, the Commission resorted to political pressure on Turkey in order to start the readmission negotiations before the December 2004 "deadline". This involved stressing the importance of the start of readmission negotiations at every available instance and level of contact with Turkey. At the initiative of DG JFS, the Commission moreover rallied support internally for the creation of a link with the start of accession talks. To be sure, the start of accession negotiations with Turkey is conditional only upon fulfilment of the Copenhagen criteria.[184] The Commission, however, made clear that a continued lack of response on the readmission issue would reflect negatively upon Turkey's accession dossier. Crucial in this regard is that the decision of the European Council to promote Turkey to the status of acceding Member State in December 2004 would be based on a report and recommendation by the Commission. The Commission's tactic furthermore included gathering political and diplomatic support from the Member States. It repeatedly called upon the Member States to use their bilateral relations and diplomatic contacts to push Turkey for a prompt start of negotiations for a Community readmission agreement.[185]

The exact details of how the situation subsequently unravelled are not clear from public documents of the Council. It would appear, however, that the Commission's tactic was ultimately successful. In March 2004, Turkey reluctantly conceded to the negotiation of a Community readmission agreement, although no precise date or timeframe was agreed.[186] On 6 October of that year, the Commission published its recommendation on Turkey's progress towards accession, which formed the basis for a positive decision of the Brussels European Council of 16 and 17 December 2004 on the start of accession negotiations with Turkey.[187]

At that time, readmission negotiations had however not yet commenced. In the JHA External Relations multi-Presidency programme, presented on 3 January 2005,

184 The accession criteria decided upon by the 1993 Copenhagen European Council.

185 JHA Commissioner Vitorino appealed directly to the Member States in this manner during the JHA Council of 6 November 2003. Relevant passages are included in press release 13747/03 (Presse 308), and the report of a meeting of the HLWG on 6 February 2004, Council Doc. 6293/04.

186 SEC(2004) 1201, p. 139; Kirişci 2004, p. 8.

187 See COM(2004) 656 final for the Commission's recommendation; and Council Doc. 16238/1/04 for the Presidency conclusions of the Brussels European Council meeting on 16 and 17 December 2004.

the new Luxembourg Presidency encouraged Turkey "to build on the substantial progress already achieved and to start negotiating a readmission agreement with the EU".[188] Turkey thus appeared still in need of further persuasion to set a date for a first round of negotiations. At the time of writing, negotiations are reported as "ongoing",[189] but the state of these negotiations is unclear. In any case, the fact that readmission negotiations with Turkey started "under protest" does not bode well for the negotiation process.

### *7.2.11 Western Balkans and Moldova*

After the adoption of negotiating directives for Moldova and the Western Balkan countries Bosnia and Herzegovina, Macedonia, Montenegro and Serbia at the end of 2006, negotiations progressed favourably. Requiring only two rounds of negotiations, the agreements with the four Western Balkan countries were initialled around April 2007. The Commission submitted proposals for decisions to sign these agreements to the Council in July 2007.[190] The state of negotiations between the Commission and Moldova could not be ascertained from public documents at the time of writing.

Explaining these relatively quick results is that, following the precedent of Russia and Ukraine, readmission negotiations were immediately coupled with visa facilitation agreements.[191] The Council has clearly decided to use visa facilitation more broadly to secure readmission agreements with suitable ENP countries and the Western Balkans.

## 7.3 The readmission negotiations – observations

This section provides a set of observations with regard to the readmission negotiations. These observations identify and analyse obstacles to the successful negotiation of Community readmission agreements, attempts at EC level to overcome these obstacles, and the consequences thereof in internal and external policy fields. Observations are also included of the continued pursuit of national readmission policies by the Member States, and the friction this has caused with the readmission negotiations at the EC level, and possibly with EC law.

### *7.3.1 General assessment of the negotiation results*

The original planning of the Commission was optimistic. It expected that negotiating a Community readmission agreement with a given third country would take approximately a year. Since September 2000, the Commission has received directives regarding sixteen countries and completed negotiations with ten of those. Only the negotiations with Hong Kong, Macao,[192] Albania, Bosnia and Herzegovina, Macedonia, Montenegro, and Serbia have gone in accordance with expectations. Others took much longer

188 Council Doc. 5001/05, p. 5.

189 MEMO/05/351.

190 Council Doc. 11998/07, Council. Doc. 12001/07, Council Doc. 12000/07, Council Doc. 12002/07.

191 Commission work-programme 2006, p. 102, 128 (available on: www.europa.eu.int/comm); SPEECH/05/754.

192 Schieffer 2003, p. 345-346.

to complete, are still ongoing, or have yet to even commence. It is clear that the Community has had difficulty to reach agreement with third countries on the readmission of illegal residents, and that this primary function of the common readmission policy has not proceeded as expected.

Agreements with Albania, Hong Kong, Macao, Russia, Sri Lanka, and Ukraine have been signed. Decisions to sign the agreements with Bosnia and Herzegovina, Macedonia, Montenegro, and Serbia are under consideration by the Council. Given the linkage with visa facilitation, there is a perspective for signature also with Moldova on the short term.

When considering these results, it should be borne in mind that Hong Kong and Macao are largely inconsequential in terms of immigration into the EC, and that the agreements with these entities did not result from any Community initiative or interest. Negotiations with Sri Lanka were relatively easy while the readmission of third country nationals is not an issue with this country. Negotiations with Russia and Ukraine, by contrast, were extremely difficult and took four to five years to complete.

With regard to the remaining countries, the results are not encouraging. The Council adopted directives for agreements with Morocco and Pakistan in September 2000, and negotiations were still ongoing at the time of writing. The Council furthermore adopted directives for agreements with Algeria, China, and Turkey in November 2002. Algeria is a particularly salient failure, considering that negotiations have yet to begin. Reaching agreement with China will still require long-term investment, and progress in the negotiations with Turkey remains elusive.

This relative lack of success is the political responsibility of the Commission. The Commission is charged with the negotiations, and has indeed been held accountable for the limited results by the Member States. The Member States and the Council, however, arguably share in this political responsibility. Besides a general shrewdness on the part of the third countries involved, one can point to two important explanations for the difficult negotiations. Firstly, the lack of flexibility in the content of the Community readmission agreements has greatly hampered the advancement of the negotiations, referring especially to the standard obligation to readmit third country nationals and stateless persons. Secondly, there is the lack of incentives, which the Commission has been authorised to apply as leverage in the negotiations, at least initially. The content of the agreements, and the amount and type of negotiating leverage, is controlled by the Council and the Member States, which therefore also bear responsibility for the limited results of the common readmission policy thus far.

Regardless of the reasons for the limited results, one must conclude that the presumed effect of concluding readmission agreements at the Community level, rather than the Member State level, has not materialised in practice. Considering the results thus far, Community competence in the area of readmission has not greatly facilitated the negotiation and conclusion of readmission agreements with third countries.

Referring to the discussion in section 4.3 above, this conclusion questions the compliance of the common readmission policy with the principle of subsidiarity. Based on assessment of the effects *a posteriori*, rather than the effects *a priori*, it is highly doubtful whether the objective of readmission of unauthorised immigrants to third countries is "better achieved"[193] at the Community level than at the Member State level.

### 7.3.2 *The strategy of the readmission countries*

Having the European Community (instead of an individual Member State) approach third countries for the conclusion of a readmission agreement has not generally extracted a greater degree of compliance. Faced with an invitation from the Commission to enter into a Community readmission agreement, the initial reaction of third countries has generally been apprehensive. It is superfluous to point out that to receive back migrants from a minimum of twenty-four States[194] is a daunting prospect. Furthermore, although drawn up in a reciprocal manner, Community readmission agreements do not present mutual, but rather opposing interests. They imply an advantage for the Community, which is at the disadvantage of the third country concerned. Except for the case of Albania, less than concrete perspectives of approximation to the EU, or indirect political, economic or financial benefits through the improvement of external relations, have not been sufficient to offset this apprehension.

After this initial reaction, however, third countries have arguably viewed the establishment of readmission relations with the Community as an opportunity for attaining further, more concrete benefits. Instead of rejecting the Commission's invitation, the implicated third countries have therefore made counter-demands. These have included technical and financial assistance to prepare for the readmission of migrants, but also additional compensating benefits, either in the field of migration or other fields. Rather than exerting more compliance, having the European Community at the other side of the negotiating table has led third countries to stand firm and ask for more.

In addition to specifying quid pro quo for the conclusion of a readmission agreement, some third countries have set conditions for agreeing to even negotiate. The cases of Algeria and Pakistan are especially illustrative. Establishing links with other EC agreements and policy areas in the external field is not the prerogative of the Commission. By requiring the 2001 EC-Algeria Euro-Med Agreement to enter into force before considering readmission negotiations, Algeria has firstly delayed the conclusion of a disadvantageous agreement that is not to its benefit. Secondly, it provided the Community with an incentive to complete procedures, necessary for the entry into force of the, for Algeria, advantageous Euro-Med Agreement. Pakistan followed a similar course of action. It received the request to enter into a readmission agreement with the EC during a period, where protracted political obstacles prevented the conclusion of the EC-Pakistan Cooperation Agreement. Conceding to the start readmission negotiations provided Pakistan with valuable leverage in this process.

Typical of the negotiation process overall is that most of the Commission's negotiating opponents appear to hold the initiative, occupy strong negotiating positions,

193 Article 5 TEC.

194 The maximum number of Member States implementing a Community readmission agreement with a third country is twenty-six in case of decisions by the UK and Ireland to "opt in". Denmark does not participate in Community readmission agreements.

and determine the pace and progress of negotiations. This is largely the result of the lack of negotiating leverage at the Commission's disposal, which we will discuss further below. Until the Community meets counter-demands or takes visible steps in that direction, third countries have commonly applied delaying tactics. Such tactics may range from not responding to an invitation to negotiate or continuous postponement of negotiating rounds, to filling formal negotiating sessions with time-consuming presentations of domestic immigration systems and readmission policies.

Interesting to note is that crosscutting interests between the respective readmission relations of third countries with the Community, as well as between third countries, are exercising an influence on the negotiating process. In subsection 5.1, we explained that the respective readmission negotiations interact with each other through the unilateral steering and coordination by the Commission in conclave with the Member States. Considering the importance of reaching an agreement which is at least comparable to that of other countries in the region, however, third countries establish links between their respective negotiations as well. Examples are Russia and Ukraine, and Algeria and Morocco. In light of the responsibility for transit migration in a region, third countries keep a close eye on each other and insist on the same textual compromises offered to their neighbours. This leads to a process, similar to that of the technique of the Commission and Member States, whereby favourable amendments are inserted into parallel negotiations with other countries. With such coordinating activity thus taking place at both sides of the negotiating table, there is a notable thrust towards harmonisation of the end-results of different negotiations, especially within the same region. This applies to the content of the agreements, as well as, likely, the compensating benefits afforded by the Commission.

Regarding the manner in which, respectively, Russia and Ukraine, and Algeria and Morocco, monitor and affect each other's negotiations with the Community, there is a significant difference. Ukraine and Russia are keeping an eye on each other in parallel negotiations, whilst Algeria is waiting to see the result of Morocco before starting its negotiations with the Community. The Commission expects that, once negotiations with Morocco are completed, initialling a readmission agreement with Algeria will follow relatively quickly. It moreover expects that other countries in the region will follow suit. Nevertheless, the situation regarding Algeria is not to the strategic advantage of the Community for the following reasons.

Considering their difficult course thus far, the EC-Morocco negotiations may not result in an agreement which the Commission and the Member States would necessarily want to see transposed to another country. One should also take into account that after taking the final text of the agreement with Morocco as the starting point of negotiations, Algeria is likely to look for further improvement of its position. In the meantime, the fact that the final text and "price tag" of the agreement with Morocco will be transposed to negotiations with Algeria ups the stakes of the EC-Morocco negotiations considerably. Every change to the Moroccan text and every offering of compensation must be carefully considered in this light, which complicates and slows down the EC-Morocco negotiations. Furthermore, one cannot exclude the possibility that further countries of the Maghreb- as well as the Mashreq region would pursue a similar strategy, once approached for the conclusion of a Community readmission agreement. In such a scenario, readmission negotiations would run along the North African coast accumulating in substance. Running alongside would be demands for compensation equal to, or trumping those posited by Morocco, explaining some of the apprehension of the Member States in granting immigration benefits to this country.

It is arguable that conducting simultaneous, rather than consecutive negotiations with countries in a region is generally more favourable for the Community. Parallel tracks prevent a situation whereby one country waits for the results achieved by another, looking for subsequent improvement. It moreover enables the Commission to generate a dynamic of competition between countries, and to exercise greater control in working towards harmonised readmission obligations.

There are further regional considerations relevant to the readmission negotiations with Morocco and Algeria. Traffic from Morocco into the EU is at present heavier, but there are already reports of smuggling activities shifting from Morocco to Algeria as a result of the increase in control of Spain's maritime borders.[195] The more this shift in migratory flows continues whilst a readmission agreement with Algeria remains absent, the more the effect of an agreement with Morocco would be cancelled out. Shifting migratory flows support the pursuit of a regional approach by the Community. It also means that starting the negotiations with Algeria is becoming an increasingly pressing matter.

It is however possible that concluding a readmission agreement with Algeria, in turn, would only be of temporary effect before a need for agreements with yet further countries would arise. Reports suggest that, as Tunisia is accepting a degree of readmission of third country nationals from EC Member States, migrants increasingly favour Libya as a point of entry into the EC.[196] This trend may be reinforced when Morocco and Algeria accept readmission obligations towards the Community and subsequently conclude agreements of their own with neighbouring countries. One expects that the recent intensification of emigration control by Libya will have a similar shifting effect.

The main transit flow from Sub-Saharan Africa into the EU may thus be expected to shift eastwards along the North African coast. It would be logical for the negotiation and conclusion of Community readmission agreements to follow in the same direction. In theory, the shifting of migration flows in response to control measures by the Community, unilaterally or in cooperation with third countries, will continue to create a need for additional readmission agreements until the cordon of "migration-responsible" States surrounding the EU is completed.

195 ICMPD 2004, p. 14.

196 CIVIPOL 2003, Council Doc. 11490/1/03, p. 19. This study of EU maritime border control also mentions that Libya lifted visa requirements for Sub-Saharan nationals, which is another factor explaining why Libya is attracting more migrants, *Ibid.*, p. 39. It is thus difficult to extract from this example the degree to which the acceptance of readmission obligations in relation to EC Member States or the Community could cause a shift in migration flows to neighbouring countries.

An important effect of the readmission negotiations at the EC level, finally, is that third countries are triggered to develop readmission policies of their own. We have noted a number of countries – *inter alia* Albania, Morocco, Russia, Ukraine, and Turkey – which consider concluding readmission agreements as a means to engage in regional burden sharing. Rather than negotiating a multilateral burden-sharing scheme, such as the Dublin Convention concluded by the EC Member States, the ambition of these countries is to implement a network of bilateral readmission agreements.

However, any arrangement (whether concerning a network of bilateral agreements or a multilateral agreement) involving the readmission of third country nationals between countries in the same region, is unlikely to lead to equitable burden sharing. Recalling the concentration of Dublin claims in Germany and other Member States on the EU's external border,[197] responsibility for undocumented transit migrants concentrates on countries through which these migrants enter the region.[198]

Under such an arrangement, countries at the external border of a region thus have a clear interest in expulsion to countries outside the region. This interest is shared by neighbouring countries in the region, considering possible attempts at re-entry into their territories. The Community's readmission countries hence aim to conclude agreements also with countries of transit outside their region, and with countries of origin. In turn, this may be expected to trigger similar dynamics in the next region, and so on and so forth.

The conclusion of Community readmission agreements thus clearly has a ripple-effect. It is arguable that each negotiation of a readmission agreement will always create a need for further agreements, when including an obligation to readmit third country nationals and/or stateless persons. This need arises on part of both negotiating parties. The requesting State will negotiate further agreements to anticipate a possible shift in migration flows. The requested State will negotiate further agreements to avoid incurring an immigration burden. In theory, this ripple-effect would not be exhausted until complete chains of readmission agreements leading from States of destination to States of origin would cover the globe, leaving no State excluded.

### *7.3.3 The Council's insistence on responsibility for transit migration*

Chapters 3 and 6 demonstrated that the emphasis of the EC's external immigration and asylum policies is on establishing responsibility for transit migration on the part of third countries. The conclusion of readmission agreements is considered central to the achievement of this objective. This explains the attitude of the Council, which has been unwilling to compromise on the uniform imposition by Community readmission agreements of an obligation to readmit third country nationals and stateless persons.

An example of the rigidity of the Council on this point is the case of Turkey. Concluding a readmission agreement with Turkey would have been greatly facilitated, had it been limited to Turkish nationals and permanent residents. This option was not considered, despite the categorical refusal of this country to negotiate a readmission

197 Noted in SEC(2000) 522, para. 35.

198 Noll 1998, p. 37.

agreement (until its accession perspectives arguably became dependent on it). A further example is the case of Sri Lanka, which illustrates that the Council insists on an obligation to readmit third country nationals, even with regard to countries which do not experience transit migration. The geography of Sri Lanka as an island on the Southern tip of India's coastline excludes it from the itineraries of migrants and migration facilitators. Logically, therefore, the Commission proposal for a Council negotiating directive for a Community readmission agreement with Sri Lanka recommended limitation to the readmission of own nationals. From the fact that the Commission negotiated a readmission agreement with Sri Lanka with the same personal scope as imposed on other readmission countries, one can deduce that the Council discarded this recommendation.

The Council arguably has several motives for insisting so heavily on the readmission of third country nationals and stateless persons. Uniform, rather than differentiated imposition of an obligation to readmit third country nationals and stateless persons provides a stronger negotiating position. It moreover precludes claims of unequal treatment. It is possible that the Council is seeking to pre-empt requests of equal treatment from readmission countries, which are relevant in terms of transit migration. The countries with which the Commission is negotiating keep informed of each other's negotiations. The risk of such requests is thus not negligible, which would compromise an important objective of EC external immigration and asylum policies. Furthermore, the negotiation of an obligation to readmit transit migrants with a country, which does not experience transit migration, is relatively easily attained. A commitment regarding the readmission of transit migrants can thus be established with little investment, but has a certain political value regardless of implementation in practice. Finally, a motive of the Council for insisting on the readmission of transit migrants may be to anticipate potential shifts in migration flows.

Faced with adversity in the readmission negotiations, the Commission has however pleaded for greater flexibility in this regard. In order to reach a higher success-rate in the negotiations, the Commission would favour introducing a "lite" variety of the standard draft text of Community readmission agreements. One of the suggestions of the July 2004 report on the priorities for the successful development of a common readmission policy was to allow for the negotiation of a readmission agreement, covering only the readmission of nationals. In the view of the Commission, appropriate cases for a readmission agreement "lite" would be countries of origin, which do not pose problems to the Community in terms of transit migration. One imagines that countries, experiencing transit migration of little interest to the Community (due to for instance limited size, or geographical distance from Community territory), could also be eligible. Good examples of countries with which negotiating only the readmission of nationals would be appropriate are ACP countries in Sub-Saharan Africa. Third countries, which would clearly not be considered for such a "lite" agreement, are EU neighbouring countries.

In the November 2004 GAER Council conclusions, adopted in response to the Commission's July 2004 report, the Council rejected the possibility of varying the personal scope of Community readmission agreements.[199] The Council confirmed the continued imposition of readmission obligations for third country nationals and stateless persons in a uniform manner:

Effective migration management is a major policy priority of the European Union. Community readmission agreements make an important contribution to an effective joint migration management and play a valuable role in the fight against illegal immigration. Against this background, the Council underlines once more the importance of concluding Community readmission agreements with third countries of origin and transit, which also include an obligation for these countries to readmit third-country nationals and stateless persons who have passed through their territories before illegally arriving in the EU.

The rejection of the Commission's suggestion to allow for a more flexible content of Community readmission agreements should be placed in perspective, however. The overall impact of a reduced personal scope of Community readmission agreements with countries of origin on the negotiation process would likely have been limited. Experience has shown that the negotiation of an obligation to readmit third country nationals and stateless persons with countries that do not experience transit migration is already less problematic. One may thus consider that the Council's rejection of the readmission agreement "lite" did not necessarily prevent a more successful common readmission policy. The success of the common readmission policy depends to a far greater degree on resolving obstacles in negotiations with countries such as Algeria, Morocco, Pakistan, Ukraine, and Turkey, which are not eligible for the suggested "lite" approach.

In order to achieve more progress in the readmission negotiations, the Council really has two options. The first option would be to discard the readmission of third country nationals and stateless persons as an absolute requirement. Arguably, most of the remaining readmission countries would be quite ready to conclude an agreement with the Community, pertaining only to the readmission of their nationals. The political will for this option, which would reduce the intensity of the pursuit of responsibility for transit migration in the external field, is however clearly absent within the Council. The second option, then, would be to meet the counter-demands of third countries, which are willing to accept responsibility for transit migration at a certain price. At present, the Council is indeed moving in this direction, which we will analyse in the following subsection.

### *7.3.4 The Commission's quest for negotiating leverage*

As detailed in subsection 5.2, the Commission has adopted a political and pragmatic approach to the negotiation of Community readmission agreements. It is conscious of the fact that granting benefits to one country may create a precedent, leading other countries to make similar requests. The Commission considers this an inevitable risk, while without the granting of benefits it would be impossible to fulfil the Council's negotiating directives. In order to reach agreement with third countries on readmission,

199 Council Doc. 13578/04.

the Commission needs the capacity to conduct negotiations effectively. Especially with DG JFS in the driver's seat,[200] a main preoccupation of the Commission in the development of the common readmission policy has thus been to gain the necessary negotiating "leverage", otherwise referred to as incentives, compensating measures or benefits, or quid pro quo.

The Council has authorised the Commission to provide third countries with financial assistance in receiving and processing readmitted migrants. Community readmission agreements, or the Council's negotiating directives, do not generally refer to this authorisation, or any other incentive for that matter.[201] A passage, authorising the Commission to offer such financial assistance, is however included in the minutes of the Council meeting, which adopted the negotiating directives for Morocco, Pakistan, Russia, and Sri Lanka. The Commission is obliged to relate to the Council any further requests by third countries, made in addition to financial assistance. Within the Council, the Member States then have to agree on authorising the Commission to negotiate such particular counter-demands.

The third countries in question have almost invariably made such additional demands. This was arguably to be expected. Financial and/or technical assistance in receiving back persons, which a third country would not have to deal with in the absence of the agreement, hardly constitutes quid pro quo. Furthermore, Community readmission agreements establish obligations beyond the scope of customary international law insofar as requiring the readmission of third country nationals. In addition, Community readmission agreements represent possible returns from a large number of States.

The possibility of offering technical and financial assistance aside, the Commission entered into the negotiations empty-handed. It has thus continuously been required to appeal to the Member States for more negotiating leverage. Generally, however, the Member States have been either unwilling or slow to empower the Commission further.

In addition to the Council's insistence on the readmission of transit migrants, we can thus identify the lack of sufficient negotiating leverage as central to the limited success in reaching agreements with third countries. Exemplary of the deficiency of this principal function of the common readmission policy is that the Commission has been incapable of avoiding the generally weak negotiating position it holds. The Commission has had no choice but to wait for next to certain counter-demands, and has perpetually fallen short in its response. It has in particular faced two obstacles to seiz-

200 *Supra*, subsection 5.2.

201 Concerning negotiating strategy, the Council's directives contain only one reference. The Council specifies that the granting of any financial assistance should not be included in the text of the agreement in order to avoid the creation of a link therewith by the other negotiating party. It is possible that this strategy also intends to avoid claims to equal treatment by other countries. The Commission has since adopted this strategy in general. The involvement of any and all compensatory benefits is mentioned only in joint declarations of the contracting parties, annexed to the readmission agreement.

ing the initiative, and controlling the negotiation process. It suffers from a shortage of negotiating means, and a lack of procedural flexibility to correct that shortage and provide a timely response to requests for compensation. The Commission has attempted to overcome these obstacles in several ways.

The Commission has been inventive in expanding its arsenal of negotiation means in the absence of Council action. Firstly, the Commission has attempted to give effect to the integration of migration issues into EU external relations. Politically endorsed by the European Council, this activity is carried out free from (direct) Member State influence. Without prejudice to the budgeting role of the EP, the Commission manages the programming and expenditure in the external field. This provides it with opportunities to establish links between spending in the external JHA field and the readmission negotiations, relatively autonomously. This resource is still underexploited, regarding which especially DG JFS is thus looking to expand. The fact that the integration of migration issues into external programming and budgeting is generally more advanced where managed by DG RELEX than by DG DEV (as mentioned in chapter 6) is relevant in this regard. At present, budgets, which support the external relations of the EU, are mainly a resource for providing technical and financial assistance, rather than for channelling development assistance to the benefit of the readmission negotiations.

Secondly, the Commission has proposed relevant legislation. The proposal for the Aeneas Regulation is a clear example of a Commission initiative to create more negotiating means. Thirdly, the Commission has supported other legislative or political initiatives, which could benefit the readmission agenda. The best example to date is the monitoring and evaluation mechanism, developed within the context of the Council. The Commission is an avid supporter of applying negative incentives to stimulate the conclusion of readmission agreements. It is thus likely to support any initiative that would further translate stated intentions in this regard into practice. Lastly, banking on the interest of the readmission countries in the position of their nationals abroad and the level of incoming remittances, the Commission has relied on related EC legislative or policy developments to exercise a beneficial effect on the readmission negotiations. The Commission has thus made sure to present EC legislation pertaining to the position of third country nationals and their families, and the development of a Community policy to facilitate migrants' remittances, in a favourable light during negotiations.

With regard to procedure, the Commission tables its requests to the Council for more negotiating means in different ways. The Commission has included appeals for linkage of the readmission negotiations with other policy fields in every related policy document.[202] With regard to specific counter-demands by individual third countries, the primary strategy of the Commission to attain concessions from the Member States has been to discuss such matters during informal meetings with Member State readmission experts.[203] We described this above in relation to the negotiations with Morocco.

202 See for example, COM(2002) 175 final; COM(2002) 564 final; COM(2002) 703 final; COM(2003) 323 final; and COM(2004) 412 final.

203 For a description of the general purpose and nature of these regular meetings, see *supra*, subsection 5.1.

The Commission hereby attempts to rally support at working level first, from where the matter is inserted into the Council apparatus, if requiring a decision at the political level. A second strategy is to appeal to the Member States directly at that level. An example is the meeting of the JHA Council on 6 November 2003. The JHA Commissioner reported on the state of play of each of the readmission negotiations, using the opportunity to communicate the Commission's precise needs to ensure completion thereof and apply pressure. Council working groups, such as the Migration/Expulsion Working Group and the HLWG, also provide the Commission with a platform, albeit lower on the political ladder.

In order to gain the upper hand in negotiations, and increase the chance of their successful completion, the Commission is in favour of adopting a so-called "package approach". This would involve the identification of suitable compensation, prior to contacting the third country in question with a request to conclude a Community readmission agreement. The Council would mandate the Commission to use certain incentives, together with the adoption of a directive for the negotiation of a readmission agreement. In a scenario where the Council would provide the Commission with ideal negotiating conditions, the type of incentive used for a particular third country would be flexible and tailor-made, and of a positive or negative nature. A combination of "carrots and sticks" would also be a possibility.

With this approach, the Commission would be able to present the draft text of a Community readmission agreement and the associated compensation simultaneously to a third country in the form of a "package deal". The Commission would make clear from the onset what a third country would stand to gain by concluding a readmission agreement with the Community, or lose by refraining to do so. Such an approach proved effective in relation to Albania, where linkage with the negotiation of a Stabilisation and Association Agreement was immediately established. In the alternative, the Commission would keep previously agreed package elements at the ready for tabling during negotiations if and when necessary. The Commission expects that adoption of this approach would avoid the passive position it currently holds, and enable a more pro-active stance towards ensuring the success of the common readmission policy.

The July 2004 report of the Commission on the priorities for the successful development of a common readmission policy report was yet a further attempt to secure greater and more flexible negotiating means from the Council. The report was politically laden. It provided the Commission with an opportunity to respond to criticism from the Member States concerning its negotiation record,[204] allowing it to place the lack of negotiating results in perspective. A favourable development for the Commission at the time was the relatively swift and favourable completion of negotiations with Albania in December 2003, which had already eased some of the Member States' criticism. Together with the subsequent report, presented in July 2004, the Commission managed to shift the debate away from the incompetence of which it had been implicitly accused. Since the November 2004 conclusions, the focus of the debate has

204 See *supra*, section 5.2, at n. 13; subsection 7.1.4, at n. 38-40.

arguably been on strengthening, rather than criticising the negotiating capacity of the Commission.

The report did not provoke the Council to respond in the manner and to the degree the Commission had hoped. Relevant in this regard is that instead of leaving space for discussion and a political decision at Council level, the preparation of the related November 2004 Council conclusions ran the full institutional gauntlet. The Member States hashed out the text, passing successively through the HLWG, the Migration/Expulsion Working Group, and the SCIFA,[205] before arriving at the GAER Council in near finalised form rigid with political compromises. Nevertheless, the November 2004 conclusions did upgrade the level of commitment of the Member States to the common readmission policy when compared with previous occasions.[206] Relevant general statements are the following:

> The Council is determined to make further use of this tool [of readmission agreements, NC] and to intensify all efforts to pursue such agreements by fully supporting the Commission throughout the negotiating process. [...] The Council welcomes the progress on Community readmission agreements made by the Commission so far and encourages it to actively pursue pending negotiations. The Council considers the conclusion of the pending negotiations as a priority for the Community. The Council recognises the need to evaluate and assess periodically the progress made and to draw the appropriate conclusions.[207]

Furthermore, the Council determined that Commission proposals for the conclusion of readmission agreements with further third countries "should be accompanied by an assessment of the appropriate strategy and necessary measures, which may include measures in all Community areas, to conclude a specific readmission agreement within a desirable timeframe".[208] This hints at a procedure akin to the above "package approach". With regard to backing up such a strategy in substantive terms, however, the conclusions are largely limited to the habitual abstract commitments, though at a broader level.[209] Noteworthy is the reference to "measures in all Community areas",

---

205 GAER Council conclusions on the priorities for the successful development of a common readmission policy, Council Doc. 13578/04, p. 1.

206 Referring in particular to the European Council meetings in Seville in June 2002 and Thessaloniki in June 2003, and more recently the European Council meeting in Brussels on 16 and 17 October 2003 (see the Presidency conclusions of these meetings). Relevant also in terms of previously stated commitment of the Council and Member States to increase support of the readmission negotiations is the Council's Return Action Programme, see especially Council Doc. 14673/02, para. 64.

207 GAER Council conclusions nos. 1 and 2, Council Doc. 13578/04.

208 GAER Council conclusions no. 4, Council Doc. 13578/04.

209 The Council did take one concrete decision, which is to link future negotiations of a readmission agreement with that of other Community- or mixed agreements. We will discuss this decision further below.

which may serve as negotiating leverage. This was a considerably broader commitment in comparison with "the use of all appropriate instruments of the EU's external relations", as previously referred to by the Council.[210]

A relevant development, finally, is that the The Hague Programme introduced an institutional innovation concerning the common readmission policy.[211] It called for "the prompt appointment by the Commission of a Special Representative for a common readmission policy" without elaborating on the purpose of this new office.[212] In December 2005, the Commission's Deputy Director-General for External Relations was appointed as the Special Representative for a common readmission policy. The Commission furthermore appointed, as Deputy-Special Representative for a common readmission policy, the director for Immigration, Asylum and Borders of DG JFS, reflecting the joint involvement of DG RELEX and DG JFS in the readmission negotiations. The Special Representative coordinates the development of the common readmission policy between different DGs, and is involved in the readmission negotiations on a political level. It is also likely that this figure, operating within the framework of the Commission, is committed to attaining more negotiating space from the Member States.

### *7.3.5 Between support and punishment – expansion of the Commission's negotiating arsenal*

Pressure from the Commission, and the negotiating strategies of the readmission countries, have led the Council to slowly expand the negotiating arsenal of the Commission. Especially the Council mandate to negotiate a visa facilitation agreement with Russia in July 2004 is significant in this regard, which arguably marks a shift in the general attitude of the Member States towards the common readmission policy. From the start of the readmission negotiations in April 2001, this attitude was defined by an unwillingness to invest beyond the provision of technical and financial assistance. It became clear that the political weight of the European Community would not carry the Commission through negotiations already at an early stage. The political will of the Member States to correct this overestimation and expand on their investment in the common readmission policy was limited. The Commission's calls for more negotiating means went unanswered for a considerable period, whether pertaining to concrete responses to the counter-demands of individual third countries, or general policy decisions enabling linkage between readmission and measures in other areas.

The Member States entered into their common endeavour to attain formal concessions from third countries on readmission with prudence as well as a degree of ambivalence. They were eager to explore the possibilities offered by the Community level. When it became clear, however, that third countries would not cooperate in exchange for mere political credit or vague prospects of approximation to the EU, the Member

210 See the Return Action Programme, Council Doc. 14673/02, para. 64; and Presidency Conclusions, Brussels European Council of 16 and 17 October 2003.

211 See Council Doc. 16054/04 for the text of the The Hague Programme.

212 Council Doc. 16054/04, p. 14. See also COM(2005) 184 final, p. 17.

States were frugal in providing the Commission with more negotiating leverage. In addition, the Member States did not wish to abandon their national readmission policies. They wanted to continue with the conclusion of agreements at the national level with as little interference from the Community as possible.[213] It is possible that, with the Commission achieving only limited negotiating results, the Member States considered their interests best served at the national level, engaged, as they are, in venue shopping. This, in turn, may have strengthened their hesitance to further invest at the Community level. The general impression is that the Member States were waiting and seeing what the Commission could achieve, whilst meanwhile continuing to fulfil readmission needs at the national level.

It should be borne in mind that throughout this initial period the requirements of the Council regarding the content of Community readmission agreements were high. Member States individually experience either significant difficulty in negotiating an obligation to readmit third country nationals and stateless persons, or for this reason choose not to negotiate such an obligation at all. The Commission is nevertheless required to include this obligation as a standard provision. In combination with limited negotiating means, the Council handed the Commission a difficult, if not unrealistic task. The development of the common readmission policy after the Treaty of Amsterdam is thus characterised by a most inefficient use of Community resources.

Nevertheless, the hesitance of the Member States to further empower the Commission is arguably justified. The conclusion of readmission agreements was a new Community competence, which the Member States would understandably strengthen only if and when necessary. Moreover, the desirability of granting certain benefits in exchange for readmission indeed requires careful consideration. We will elaborate on this latter point further below.

Although prudence in expanding investment in the common readmission policy still prevails, the political will of the Member States to provide quid pro quo for Community readmission agreements has clearly increased. Arguably, the Member States became slowly convinced of the limits of the negotiating capacity afforded to the Commission, and of the fact that more results would not be forthcoming unless this was expanded.

We can now distinguish concrete Member State support expanding the Commission's means in aid of the readmission negotiations in three areas. Member State support was already present for providing third countries with relevant technical and financial assistance, where we have seen the Commission's capacity deepen. The second is the field of visa policy. The visa facilitation negotiations with Russia marked the first widening of the Commission's negotiating means, as well as explicit recognition by the Council of an incentive-driven negotiation practice of Community readmission agreements. The third and most recent increase of Member State support is in the field of EU external relations, where the Council has sanctioned a negotiating means already applied de facto by the Commission. This refers to direct linkage between a readmission agreement and other Community- or mixed agreements. We will consider

213 *Infra*, subsection 7.3.6.

the latter expansions of the common readmission policy – into visa- and external relations policy – more closely.

Russia was the first to engage in negotiation of a visa facilitation agreement with the Commission in parallel with the readmission negotiations. The negotiation of readmission agreements with Bosnia and Herzegovina, Macedonia, Moldova, Montenegro, Serbia, and Ukraine was also combined with visa facilitation agreements.[214] A similar concession in relation to China is underway. Linking readmission to visa has clearly become the principal strategy for securing the establishment of readmission obligations on the part of third countries on the EU external border.

These developments are remarkable, while they revive the compensatory exchange between readmission and visa. In the history of European readmission agreements, this was once a common exchange, but stopped being part of the negotiation practice in the late nineties. Alongside the increasing importance of the issue of unauthorised immigration in domestic Western European politics, readmission agreements and visa requirements evolved into popular tools to control migration from countries of origin to countries of destination. When concluding readmission agreements with countries from where immigration is undesired, the lifting of visa requirements may be counterproductive, explaining why this quid pro quo exchange went out of fashion. In addition, the role of visa requirements as an instrument to safeguard internal security gained in importance throughout the nineties, increasing exponentially after the attacks by Al Qaeda in New York in September 2001. The Commission itself repeatedly stressed that the lifting of visa requirements, or facilitation thereof, can be considered only in a limited number of cases, and is therefore of little use as leverage in the readmission negotiations.[215]

However, the negotiation of Community readmission agreements has now reintroduced visa concessions as appropriate quid pro quo; it would seem, moreover, as a general policy measure. The attitude at the EC level regarding visa requirements has changed in reaction to third countries' demands in the readmission negotiations. In a September 2004 note on common visa policy, the Presidency stated:

> The role of visa policy in broad external relations with third countries is becoming more important. Recent development in relations with third countries like Russia [...] show that these third countries want more facilities in the area of free movement of persons before they are willing to agree on readmission agreements etc., whereas the EU takes an opposite approach. The EU must strike a balance between the fulfilment of certain wishes of third countries and the need of safeguarding the internal security of its territory.[216]

214 Commission work-programme 2006, p. 102, 128 (available on: www.europa.eu.int/comm); SPEECH/05/754.

215 See COM(2002) 175 final; COM(2002) 564 final; COM(2002) 703 final; and COM(2004) 412 final.

216 Council Doc. 12709/04.

In the same vein, the European Council, meeting in Brussels on 4 and 5 November 2004, invited the Council and Commission:

> to examine, with a view to developing a common approach, whether in the context of the EC readmission policy it would be opportune to facilitate, on a case by case basis, the issuance of short stay visas to third country nationals, where possible and on a basis of reciprocity, as part of a real partnership in external relations, including migration-related issues.[217]

The political priority that the readmission of migrants enjoys at the EC level has enabled third countries to open up the visa regime of the EC. Visa facilitation is a direct benefit resulting from the conclusion of Community readmission agreements. Moreover, visa free travel from several of the readmission countries is now an item of discussion on the EC's agenda, albeit as a strictly long-term perspective. Bosnia and Herzegovina, China, Macedonia, Moldova, Montenegro, Russia, Serbia and Ukraine are subject to visa requirements for reasons of migration control, internal security, and public order. The lifting, or even facilitation of these visa requirements would arguably not have been considered in the absence of a Community interest in readmitting migrants to these countries.

Regarding the expansion of the common readmission policy into the field of EU external relations, the November 2004 conclusions on the priorities for the successful development of a common readmission policy contained one concrete decision, which enhanced the bargaining power of the Community. The GEAR Council determined that "on a case-by-case basis, a direct link should be established between the negotiation of co-operation, association or equivalent agreements and the conclusion of readmission agreements with the same third countries".[218] Encouraged, possibly, by the result achieved with Albania, the GAER Council hereby adopted the Commission's continuous recommendations to make greater use of the Community's bargaining potential in the external field.

The Community concludes a variety of Community- and mixed agreements, which are of economic, developmental or other benefit to third countries. Examples are Association Agreements, (Partnership and) Cooperation Agreements, Stabilisation and Association Agreements, and Free Trade Agreements. A degree of quid pro quo often already accompanies such agreements through the insertion of readmission clauses. The November 2004 conclusions, however, permitted the Commission to extend the strategy it pursued with Albania.

Accordingly, rather than waiting for the entry into force of an agreement carrying a readmission clause, the Commission is able to establish a link with readmission

217 See the The Hague Programme, approved by the European Council in Brussels on 5 November 2004, Council Doc. 16054/04, p. 18.

218 GAER Council conclusions no. 5, Council Doc. 13578/04.

negotiations directly.[219] This increases the return on benefits granted by the Community to third countries through the conclusion of Community- and mixed agreements. It moreover prevents the need to provide further compensation when the Community decides to invoke a readmission clause, the bargaining chip of the Community- or mixed agreement being effectively "spent" once concluded.

It should be emphasised that, with the November 2004 conclusions, the Council sanctioned for the first time the use of a punitive measure in the context of the common readmission policy. In case a third country would refuse to negotiate a readmission agreement, negotiation or conclusion of a CA, AA, or equivalent agreement with the Community would not proceed, which may be considered a punitive measure.

One can conclude that the Council has expanded the Commission's negotiating arsenal. It should however be underlined that it has not relinquished any control over the negotiation process. It was apparent from the beginning that the Member States would closely monitor the Commission, prying into strongly Member State-controlled policy areas in search of negotiating leverage. Although possibilities to use incentives are expanding, the Member States continue to ensure that such happens on a case-by-case basis only, and after careful consideration within the Council.

Following the "package approach", decided upon by the November 2004 GAER Council, the Commission will specify and request appropriate negotiating means in future proposals for negotiating directives. This requires the Council to clarify the Commission's negotiating space – by allowing or denying the use of certain compensating measures – prior to, rather than during negotiations. From the perspective of conducting effective negotiations, this procedural innovation is an improvement. However, it does not reduce the control of the Member States over the application of incentives to the negotiation of Community readmission agreements.

Notwithstanding the expansion of the Commission's negotiating means, it remains questionable whether it will be sufficient to complete all of the ongoing negotiations. Looking at the range of counter-demands of the third countries involved, concessions in the field of labour immigration may still be required. Unlike visa, however, such concessions still appear to be a non-starter.

Section 7.2.1 noted the experience of Italy in exerting cooperation on readmission from third countries in exchange for immigration quota for low-skilled workers. This strategy appears to be very effective. An example is Nigeria. Both Ireland and Italy have a readmission agreement with this country. Ireland is not receiving adequate cooperation from the Nigerian authorities in implementing the agreement. Unlike Ireland, Italy combined its readmission agreement with Nigeria with an agreement on labour migration, and implementation of the readmission agreement is proceeding satisfactorily.[220] Looking to elevate such practice to the EC level, Italy tabled a proposal

219 Regarding the possible consequences of this change in strategy for the further incorporation of readmission clauses into Community- and mixed agreements, see *infra*, section 8.2.

220 This is firstly an example of the successful combining of external relations policy and objectives in the field of migration control. It also suggests that, in addition to incentives

for an EC immigration quota system at an informal Council meeting in September 2004, which the Commission welcomed as a useful bargaining tool in readmission negotiations. The European Council meeting on 16 and 17 October 2004 rejected the proposal, prominent opponents being France and Germany.[221] Resistance is thus still strong, although the negotiation of Community readmission agreements does appear to have brought the issue of labour immigration to the table again.

Labour immigration incentives would arguably provide the common readmission policy with a significant stimulus. There are several measures which the Council could consider introducing. The field of labour immigration is where the impact of symbolic or political gestures on the readmission negotiations is greatest. Section 7.2 pointed to the influence of public opinion on the motivation of third countries to conclude a readmission agreement with the Community. In this context, attaining concessions from the EC on immigration may have an important domestic political value for third countries. Low-commitment measures, such as mere dialogue regarding labour immigration issues, may already have a facilitating effect on readmission negotiations.

In order to secure completion of the outstanding negotiations, as well as the successful implementation of the agreements, however, the Council would arguably need to go further. It would need to consider establishing links with compensating measures, such as bilateral Member State agreements on the admission of seasonal workers, or, indeed, labour immigration quota. Further expanding on the Italian example, quota agreements for low-skilled workers have proven a very flexible means of leverage. Considered a positive incentive, once concluded, labour immigration agreements become a tool with a potentially negative character. Where cooperation on implementing the readmission agreement falls short, Italy is able to respond by reducing immigration quota (which are awarded on a yearly basis) until the desired level of cooperation is back up to par. Italy has moreover found that cooperation on labour immigration improves the readiness of its partner countries on a wider level to increase migration control, and take action against smuggling and trafficking activities.

When considering such beneficial effects, it may be in the interest of the Member States to overcome their reservations against addressing labour immigration issues at the EC level. The readmission negotiations with Morocco, and the expansion of the common readmission policy vis-à-vis the Southern Mediterranean region, may require such action. Considering the mounting pressure from the Commission as well as individual Member States to introduce relevant changes, one cannot exclude the possibility of movement within the Council also in this policy area.

---

for starting and completing negotiations, some cases may require an incentive also to ensure implementation of the agreement once in force, i.e. for the actual readmission of migrants pursuant to the agreement. In this context, it is instructive to point to our earlier analysis of the evidence requirements under Articles 8 and 9 of the standard draft Community readmission agreement. This analysis illustrates possibilities for "problem" States to withhold effective cooperation on the implementation of an agreement, unless sufficiently incentivised.

221 European Parliament, session document A5-0096/2004, p. 7.

Considering the negotiating means required for ensuring an effective common readmission policy, it is necessary to distinguish between regions. It is arguable that visa facilitation would sustain negotiations on the Eastern- and South Eastern borders of the EU. To the South, immigration quota might carry the Commission through negotiations with countries of the Maghreb and Mashreq regions. A break-through within the Council on this matter would thus bring the creation of a "cordon" of responsible States around the EU significantly closer. Expansion of the common readmission policy into regions which are further away, however, is likely to require negotiating leverage of a yet different kind. With regard to ACP countries, for example, the Community may well receive requests for intensified development assistance.[222] Furthermore, the Commission has on occasion received requests from third countries involving also closer economic cooperation, trade expansion, improved market access, and WTO compatible tariff preferences.[223]

A relevant question is how far the Commission would be willing to go in meeting such counter-demands of third countries, considering that the Commission relays such requests to the Council, and is the main thrust behind the increase in the use of incentives. Relevant is that the Commission services are internally divided on this issue. Section 5.2 already discussed the difference in approach between the DGs JFS and RELEX. Considering the above requests for compensation, one would also expect a degree of resistance from DGs DEV, AIDCO, ECHO, Internal Market, and Trade. In general, however, if the Council would ever create optimal negotiating conditions for the Commission, the latter is likely to use a relatively broad range of supportive and punitive measures as "package deals" together with Community readmission agreements.

There are arguably two main reasons why the Commission is an overall staunch supporter of incentive-driven readmission negotiations. One is the political and pragmatic view regarding the negotiation of this type of agreement, which is dominant within the Commission. The second is the fact that improving the rate of fulfilment of the Council's negotiating mandates has become an important political priority. Indeed, the Commission shows signs of path-dependent thinking, or tunnel vision, in this regard. In the pursuit of success in the readmission negotiations, there appears to be little room for re-evaluation of this process. In the face of heavy resistance from third countries, the Commission, rather than review the desirability of Community action in this field, focuses entirely on finding more negotiating leverage. Moreover, the Com-

222 Regarding the ACP, the Commission is of the opinion that the Cotonou Convention itself (which contains a political obligation for ACP countries to negotiate a readmission agreement if so requested in Article 13) already contains sufficient compensating benefits, and that additional incentives should thus not be considered, COM(2002) 703 final, p. 26; COM(2003) 323 final, p. 14. It is however doubtful that Sub-Saharan countries would negotiate and conclude readmission agreements with the Community without additional compensation. The leverage in this regard, which the Cotonou Convention represents, was arguably lost when the convention entered into force.

223 COM(2002) 703 final, p. 26; COM(2003) 323, p. 14.

mission does not sufficiently consider the consequences of granting certain types of benefits, or whether the Community's objectives in the area of readmission would justify these consequences.

The readmission negotiations are having an impact on wider EU policies. The lack of success in the negotiation of Community readmission agreements has clearly provided the Council with an impetus to take decisions in certain policy areas. The policy changes precipitated by the need for more negotiating leverage have internal as well as external implications, some of which may be considered favourable. Allowing greater flexibility in the admission of labour migrants, for example, is generally expected to reduce unauthorised immigration, as well as the number of protection applications. A similar effect may result from intensified economic- and trade relations, which may stimulate development and thereby lead to lower migration levels, although concessions of this kind in exchange for readmission remain a more remote, if not unlikely possibility. The linkage between readmission and other policy areas may however also have unfavourable consequences. These relate to the double standard we signalled earlier in relation to the influence of migration issues on international relations.[224]

One may question, for example, the provision of anti-terrorism and border surveillance equipment to Pakistan.[225] The risk of indirect sponsoring of the conflict in the Kashmir region appears difficult to exclude entirely here. One could also point to the aforementioned risk, associated with visa facilitation for Ukrainian service- and diplomatic passport holders.[226] Levels of corruption and the influence of criminal organisations in public administration and business are problems also in Russia, implying a similar risk there. The Council introduced visa requirements for Ukrainian and Russian nationals, *inter alia*, because it perceived risks in relation to internal security and public order. In exchange for wider perspectives on the readmission of unauthorised immigrants, the Council now appears willing to take risks it previously considered prohibitive. Furthermore, one wonders whether the Community would have truly impeded the continued approximation of Turkey to the EU,[227] and risked sacrificing an important strategic partner in its pursuit of readmission obligations. Finally, it is arguable that the use of punitive measures, as advanced by the common readmission policy, is harmful to the external relations of the EU as well as its economic and strategic position.[228]

In sum, there are questionable developments, attached to the expanding negotiation of Community readmission agreements. Considering that the Commission is not raising these questions, it is advisable that the Member States and the Council continue to exercise general prudence in enabling a more effective incentive-driven negotiation of readmission agreements.

224 *Supra*, subsection 7.1.5.

225 *Supra*, subsection 7.2.2.

226 *Supra*, subsection 7.2.6.

227 *Supra*, section 7.2.10.

228 *Supra*, section 6.3, at n. 128.

### 7.3.6 *The continued pursuit of Member State readmission policies*

Section 4.4 discussed how the Council and the Council's Legal Service (LS) in May 1999 formulated a number of rules, according to which Member States individually would be allowed to continue to enter into readmission agreements with third countries. Complemented with the position of the Commission, a set of five rules was deduced regarding which implicit consensus appeared to exist at the Community level.[229] These rules were as follows:

1. The Member States collectively may not conclude readmission agreements with third countries;
2. A Member State must notify the Council of its intention to negotiate a readmission agreement with a third country;
3. A Member State may negotiate or conclude a readmission agreement with a third country only insofar as the Council has not (yet) adopted a negotiating directive for a Community agreement concerning that country;
4. Regarding third countries for which the Council has adopted a negotiating directive for a Community readmission agreement, a Member State may exceptionally conclude an agreement containing more detailed arrangements, if required;
5. A Member State may not negotiate or conclude a readmission agreement in case this might be detrimental to the implementation of a Community agreement, or to readmission negotiations conducted at the EC level.

These rules recognise that the Community and the Member States share the competence to conclude readmission agreements with third countries. Setting limits and conditions, they allow the operation of national readmission policies to continue, contrary to the Commission's initial claim to exclusive competence in the area. The Member States, however, have overstepped these boundaries on a regular basis, disturbing the implicit balance which was established within the competence debate.

In particular, there have been repeated infractions of rules number two, three and five. Regarding rule number three, different Member States have on several occasions either initiated new bilateral negotiations, or failed to cease ongoing bilateral negotiations, after the adoption of a negotiating directive by the Council relating to the same third country. In contravention of rule number two, the Member States have generally not notified the Council of, or requested authorisation for intended bilateral negotiations. The Member States generally inform the Council formally of respective bilateral negotiation activities only in case explicit inventory thereof is undertaken. Furthermore, some Member States have developed bilateral relations with a readmission target country of the Community, not pertaining directly to readmission, but nonetheless impinging on the Commission's readmission negotiations, thereby arguably contravening rule number five.

The clearest challenge to the above rules has been by Member States, which have commenced or continued readmission negotiations with third countries, which are subject to a Council negotiating directive. There have been several instances where

229 *Supra*, section 4.4.

Member States have conducted negotiations with a country in parallel with the Commission. A prime example is the readmission agreement between the United Kingdom and Albania. The UK signed a fully-fledged bilateral readmission agreement with Albania on 14 October 2003, approximately three weeks before the third (and what would be final) round of formal negotiations between the Commission and that country.[230]

The UK could easily have avoided the chance of conflict with the Commission by not "opting in" to the Community readmission agreement with Albania. The UK however opted in at the occasion of the adoption of the Council negotiating directive for Albania in November 2002. In accordance with the Protocol on the position of the UK and Ireland, the UK also opted in to the Council decision on the signing in February 2005,[231] and the Council decision on the conclusion of the EC-Albania agreement in October 2005.[232] By explicitly retaining its participation in the Community agreement whilst at the same time entertaining bilateral readmission negotiations with the same country, the UK appears to have purposely placed itself on a collision course with the Commission. The UK has moreover acted contrary to the opinion of the Council LS and the political assessment of the May 1999 JHA Council, both having confirmed the content of rule number three.

Relevant is that the UK's actions did not compromise the Community's negotiating position in relation to Albania, nor alter or hinder in any apparent way the course or completion of the Commission's negotiations. The negotiation of the EC text was finalised at the third negotiating round on 5 November 2003 as planned, and initialling followed without delay on 18 December 2003. In retrospect, one could thus argue that the UK's actions were not "detrimental" to the exercise of the Council's negotiating directive concerning Albania and the related Community interest.[233] One could however also argue that the UK could not have foreseen this course of events and risked interference with the interests of the Community. The UK thereby acted contrary to rule number five in addition to rule number two, recalling that both these rules follow directly from the duty of sincere cooperation of Article 10 TEC. In any case, the course of action pursued by the UK was a blatant challenge of the division of competence in the area of readmission, agreed in 1999.

The UK is not the only Member State which has overstepped boundaries, impinging on the Community competence to conclude a readmission agreement with Albania. In the 2004 Stabilisation and Association Report on Albania, the Commission noted

230 British embassy Tirana 2003. For the text of UK-Albania readmission agreement plus protocol for its implementation of 14 October 2003, see Albania No. 1 (2004), Cm 6267 (available on: www.fco.gov.uk).

231 See Council Docs. 6513/05, and 5614/05.

232 Council Doc. 12361/05.

233 See rule number five, which states that "Member States may no longer conclude agreements if these might be detrimental to existing Community agreements" as formulated by the May 1999 JHA Council. In conjunction with rule number two, this book interprets this rule broadly to pertain to all effects detrimental to a Council directive for the negotiation of a Community readmission agreement.

that bilateral negotiations were still ongoing between Albania and Luxembourg, the Netherlands,[234] Slovenia, and Slovakia. With regard to these negotiations, the Commission pointed out that:

> In view of the initialling of the readmission agreement between the European Community and Albania on 18 December 2003, it is important to note that bilateral readmission negotiations between Albania and individual Member States or acceding Member States are *neither necessary nor legally permissible*, in accordance with Article 10 TEC. Consequently, the only bilateral negotiations between these States and Albania that can be conducted in the future are those on the Implementing Protocols, as provided for by Article 19 of the Community readmission agreement.[235] [Italics added, NC]

The Commission issued a warning to these Member States to adjust their behaviour in accordance with Community law. The Council's Legal Service has issued similar warnings. It has on several occasions during meetings within the Council context appealed to Member States to cease particular bilateral readmission negotiations, which, in its opinion, were in contravention of Community law.[236]

Notwithstanding a possible conflict with Community law, parallel invitations by Member States to enter into a readmission agreement send ambiguous signals to third countries, and can interfere with negotiations at the Community level. It raises questions concerning the internal division of power regarding immigration in the EC, and raises doubts concerning the degree to which the Community truly has a common readmission policy. It also reduces the credibility of the Commission as acting on behalf of the Community in the external field, which arguably weakens its negotiating position.[237] Furthermore, it provides third countries with an opportunity to play Commission and Member State off against each other.[238] Due to interference with the Commission's readmission negotiations, it is arguable that such Member State actions

234 Negotiations with Luxemburg and the Netherlands are presumably being conducted within a Benelux context. Belgium already has a readmission agreement with Albania, which was signed in 2001, SEC(2004) 374/2, p. 32.

235 SEC(2004) 374/2, p. 32.

236 Interview with the head of the Justice and Home Affairs unit of the Council's Legal Service, 17 November 2004.

237 A similar argument was made by the Commission in relation to WTO membership of the Member States next to membership of the Community. The Commission argued it should be the sole spokesman and negotiator in the WTO context. Otherwise, the Member States could voice views on which a lack of consensus existed within the Community, as a result of which, the Commission posited, "the Commission's unity of action *vis-à-vis* the rest of the world would be undermined and its negotiating power greatly weakened", Hyett 2000, p. 249-250.

238 Regarding this risk, see Nordic Joint Advisory Group on Refugee Policy 1999, Council Doc. 7707/99, p. 12, 15.

undermine the effective operation of the common readmission policy. This is relevant both in practical terms, as well as in terms of a possible violation of the duty of sincere cooperation.

One wonders what a Member State stands to gain by having two readmission agreements – one at the Community level, and one at the national level – with the same third country at its disposal. In the above citation, the Commission correctly points to the lack of necessity of a bilateral agreement in the presence of an agreement at Community level. Community agreements are fully-fledged agreements of a personal scope, often larger than attempted to negotiate by the Member States. They have thus far not been limited to "general statements", referred to as a possibility by the JHA Council in May 1999, in which case an additional bilateral agreement would have a clear added value. The text of the EC-Albania agreement and the text of the bilateral UK-Albania agreement, for example, contain only minor differences.[239] Both agreements arrange for the readmission of persons on largely the same terms, including third country nationals and stateless persons. The UK now essentially has the same instrument twice, bearing in mind that the Community agreement takes precedence.[240]

In general, the main advantages of bilateral readmission agreements at the national level are considered to be the ability to establish detailed relations specific to the contracting parties, and the speediness of negotiation.[241] The level of detail of the agreement would seem irrelevant with regard to the common readmission policy. Community readmission agreements are already very detailed, and allow for the conclusion of more specific bilateral implementing protocols if necessary. This leaves the speediness of negotiations for consideration. The motivation to start concluding readmission agreements at the Community level was, in a nutshell, to enable better negotiating results, faster. The Community level, however, does not allow for short-term responses, for example in case a Member State is faced with a sudden influx of migrants from a particular third country. Rather than wait for the Commission to submit a proposal for a new negotiating directive to the Council, and/or wait for the completion of ongoing negotiations at the Community level, the Member State is likely to want to take prompt action at the national level in such a case. Furthermore, the state of negotiations described in section 7.2 illustrates that the common readmission policy has thus far not fulfilled expectations regarding speedy negotiations. The element of speed may therefore explain why the Member States have insisted on retaining the possibility of concluding readmission agreements with third countries at the national level.

In addition, the Member States arguably have political motivations for retaining national readmission policies. Most of the Member States have adopted restrictive immigration policies. Since the Treaty of Amsterdam empowered the Community to conclude readmission agreements, immigration, aliens, and their integration into host

239 UK-Albania readmission of 14 October 2003, Albania No. 1 (2004), Cm 6267 (available on: www.fco.gov.uk).

240 See Article 20 of the readmission agreement between the Community and Albania, *OJ* L 124, 17 May 2005, p. 22.

241 Nordic Joint Advisory Group on Refugee Policy 1999, Council Doc. 7707/99, p. 13.

societies have become pivotal electoral issues in many of the EC Member States. Measures that demonstrate "toughness" regarding unauthorised immigration are popular in the current European political climate. Expulsion is therefore an issue of high political interest, to which end the conclusion of readmission agreements is considered an important means. From this perspective, the need to retain political visibility at the domestic level may be an additional explanation why the Member States have continued to negotiate and conclude readmission agreements individually.

Further potential conflicts with the Commission's readmission negotiations have resulted from Member State relations with Russia in the area of visa. Germany signed an agreement on visa facilitation with Russia on 10 December 2003.[242] As described above, the facilitation of EC visa requirements has been Russia's steady demand in exchange for a Community readmission agreement. Ad hoc discussion between the Commission and Russia on visa, in parallel with the readmission negotiations, started in October 2003. The subsequent signing of the bilateral agreement between Germany and Russia took place in the middle of the build-up of political support within the Council for the formal negotiation of visa facilitation with Russia.[243]

France and Italy were also engaged in visa talks with Russia in this period. Both signed bilateral visa facilitation agreements with Russia on 15 June 2004.[244] France informed the Member States and the Commission of the signing of its agreement with Russia during a meeting of the Council's Visa Working Party on 8 and 9 July 2004.[245] The adoption of the negotiating directive for EC visa facilitation, scheduled for 12 July, was also discussed at this meeting. In this context, the Commission noted "that after the final adoption of the negotiating directive[…], bilateral negotiations concerning visa facilitations no longer had neither legal nor political justification".[246]

Explaining its reasons for not requesting authorisation from the Commission, Germany has argued that its agreement with Russia on visa facilitation is not relevant to the European Community.[247] Germany insisted it made use of possibilities offered by Schengen rules. The Treaty of Amsterdam formally incorporated Schengen rules into Community law. Contrary to Germany's assertion, therefore, the application of Schengen visa rules would be by definition "relevant" to the EC, even though in practice Schengen may still operate as a separate intergovernmental body of rules.[248] However, Germany was presumably referring to certain forms of visa facilitation mentioned in

242 Council Doc. 5139/04.

243 The Commission submitted a proposal for a negotiating directive to this end in April 2004 (see Council Doc. 10601/04, p. 5), which was subsequently adopted by the Council in July 2004.

244 Council Doc. 11555/04, p. 8; Council Doc. 11035/04.

245 Council Doc. 11555/04.

246 Council 11555/04, p. 8.

247 Interfax 2003.

248 Guild 2005.

the Common Consular Instruction, the introduction of which is at the discretion of the Member States.

Regardless of the validity of Germany's argument, it is certain that each time Russia concludes a visa facilitation agreement with an individual Member State, its need for, and thus the value of a visa facilitation agreement with the EC is reduced. This is especially salient when those Member States are important partner countries of Russia, and main political players within the EC, such as Germany, France and Italy. The pursuit by these Member States of their respective individual interests in relations with Russia has risked weakening the position of the Commission in the readmission negotiations with this country.[249] This Member State action could thus also be considered "detrimental" to the exercise of the Council's negotiating directives, as prohibited by rule number five.

Despite several clear cases of violation of the above rules by the Member States, the Commission has not responded with an infringement procedure. This lack of response is remarkable, especially because the Commission has explicitly qualified the actions of some of the Member States as "not legally permissible".[250] As noted in section 4.4, bringing such a case before the Court would also serve the wider purpose of finally settling the competence debate, considering that the Member States have not acted in accordance with the political assessment of the Council in May 1999. The Court would presumably have to decide whether the conclusion of readmission agreements with third countries is an area of exclusive, or of shared competence. In the latter case, the Court may be expected to establish clear boundaries for the continued conclusion of readmission agreements at the national level. Notwithstanding the possibility that legal action is still forthcoming, there are several practical as well as political reasons that have arguably prevented the Commission from undertaking this action thus far.

Although initially eager to claim an exclusive Community competence to conclude readmission agreements, it is possible that the Commission has since changed its position. Exclusive competence would be undesirable for the Commission from a practical perspective.[251] The Member States' need for readmission agreements exceeds the Commission's negotiating capacity and resources. Even with a significant expansion thereof, it would remain unfeasible for the Commission to act as effectively the sole negotiator of readmission agreements with third countries in the EC.

Furthermore, from a political perspective, exclusive competence would not be advisable, either. Firstly, exclusive Community competence would lead to a significant expansion of the number of agreements under negotiation, further amplifying the Commission's accountability for limited or slow negotiation results. Unless the Member States would expand the Commission's negotiating power, necessary to back

249 See also Council Doc. 15995/03, where the Commission complains that such agreements may interfere with its readmission negotiations with Russia. For a similar argument, see Kuijper 2004, p. 619.

250 *Supra*, n. 231.

251 *Supra*, section 4.2, at n. 13-14.

up an exclusive negotiating role (which is unlikely), the Commission would set itself up for political failure. Bringing the matter before the ECJ, which might decide the Community's competence is exclusive, is therefore risky from this point of view.

Secondly, in order to achieve more progress in the readmission negotiations before finally expanding the common readmission policy, the Commission needs the assistance of the Member States. The Commission depends on the Member States for widening its negotiating arsenal within the Council, but has also requested their explicit support outside the Community context. It has asked the Member States for political and diplomatic flanking support for some of the ongoing readmission negotiations.[252] It is thus in the interest of the Commission to avoid conflict with the Member States, at least until it attains a stronger foothold in the negotiations.

From these perspectives, a political rather than legal course of action to dissuade the Member States from interfering with the Commission's readmission negotiations appears more viable for the time being. The political strategy that the Commission has pursued in this regard has essentially been to appeal to the Member States to "close ranks" and "sing the same tune".

As noted, the Commission has requested the Member States for political and diplomatic support for its readmission negotiations. This increases the pressure on third countries to start or complete negotiations, and sends a signal that the EU institutions and the Member States are unified in pursuing Community objectives in the area of readmission. A prerequisite in this regard is that the Member States cease and refrain from further bilateral negotiations, which is implicitly included in the Commission's request. Furthermore, the Commission has suggested adding Member State experts to its negotiating teams. The Commission does not require additional technical expertise as such. The joint representation of the Community by Commission and Member State officials would be a political gesture, which may strengthen the Community's negotiating position.[253] Arguably, the Commission is also hoping that it would become more difficult politically for those Member States to entertain bilateral readmission relations on the side. The Member States also would have an interest in having their staff join the negotiations. It would be a further opportunity to control the negotiation process at working level, and enable a close watch on the Commission, especially in the administering of incentives.

## 7.4 Conclusion

This chapter has discussed the selection of readmission countries, and the state of the readmission negotiations. It has also provided a set of general observations relating to the negotiation process.

It was noted that the selection of readmission countries, as well as the implementation of the common readmission policy in general, was generally impromptu after

252 See, for example, the report of a meeting of the HLWG in December 2004, reiterating a request from the Commission to increase pressure on Turkey to commence readmission negotiations, Council Doc. 6293/04, p. 6.

253 An argument supported by Hyett in the context of the WTO, Hyett 2000, p. 252.

the entry into force of the Treaty of Amsterdam. The Commission and Council have since introduced explicit strategic criteria by which to select countries, and develop the common readmission policy. It was furthermore noted that this strategy has certain perverse effects while based on a double standard. The Community is not taking political factors into account when selecting readmission countries, and is responding to demands for quid pro quo. As a result, it is developing relations with third countries with doubtful track-records in light of respect for human rights, democratic principles, and the rule of law, which would arguably not have been developed otherwise. Considering that such countries often produce refugees, the Community's strategy hypothetically has legal implications, which are discussed further below in chapter 9.

It was found that after more than six years of negotiating Community readmission agreements with third countries, the overall results have been limited. It was argued that the compliance of the common readmission policy with the principle of subsidiarity is therefore in question.

This chapter identified the main reason for the limited results as being the reluctance of third countries to conclude a readmission agreement with the Community, unless their demands for concrete quid pro quo are met. For this reason, the Council is gradually empowering the Commission to conduct more incentive-driven negotiations, using supportive, and, to a lesser degree, punitive incentives. The slowly expanding negotiation of Community readmission agreements is thus having a wider impact within different EU policy fields, which, it was argued, is a questionable development.

Finally, this chapter noted that the Member States have continued to conduct negotiations with some of the readmission countries at the national level, at times infringing upon the division of competence as implicitly agreed upon in 1999. The possibility of the Commission making such instances subject to an infringement procedure was explored, but it was concluded that legal action before the European Court of Justice seems unlikely for several practical and political reasons.

# Chapter 8 Readmission clauses

A core element of the common readmission policy is to incorporate readmission clauses into other Community or "mixed" agreements.[1] A readmission clause generally consists of two principal parts. The first is an obligation to readmit own nationals. The second is a political commitment to negotiate a fully-fledged readmission agreement, including an obligation to readmit third country nationals and stateless persons, if so requested by one of the contracting parties to the agreement. This chapter will first outline the development of readmission clauses at the EC level since 1995 before discussing the negotiation of readmission clauses, their practical meaning as instruments for the return and readmission of migrants, and their relevance as part of the common readmission policy. One specific element of the new migration management clause, regarding the international protection of refugees will also be considered.

## 8.1 From readmission clause to migration management clause

An interest in establishing cooperation with third countries on the readmission of immigrants without a claim to residence or presence has been present at the EC level since the early nineties, well before the Community gained competence in the area.[2] The aim of the first EC policy measures in this area was mainly to encourage third countries to conclude bilateral readmission agreements with the EC Member States. To this end, the Commission and Council decided to establish links between readmission agreements, and other agreements with third countries concluded by the Community and its Member States.[3]

1 Mixed agreements are concluded between the Community, its Member States and a third country. On the Community side, these agreements therefore require ratification by the respective Member States, and by the European Community itself (in the form of a Council decision).

2 Peers and Rogers 2006; *supra*, section 1.4.

3 COM(94) 23 final, para. 115.

After adopting Recommendations aimed at the harmonisation of bilateral readmission agreements between the Member States and third countries,[4] the Council took a first concrete step towards linking readmission to other external policy objectives in late 1995. The Council adopted a standard text for a readmission clause, intended for incorporation in Community agreements with third countries on a case-by-case basis.[5] In January 1996, the Council further adopted a standard text for a readmission clause, intended specifically for incorporation into *mixed* agreements on a case-by-case basis.[6] The text of these readmission clauses may be found in Annex 2 and Annex 3, respectively.

Considering that readmission was at the time strictly a matter of Member State competence, the 1995 standard clause regarding Community agreements was very limited in content. It consisted of a political declaration, which was incorporated into the final act of the agreement. This declaration reiterated that the Member States attach importance to cooperating with third countries on the readmission of nationals, and determined that the third country in question would "undertake to conclude readmission agreements with the Member States of the European Union which so request".[7]

The 1996 standard clause regarding mixed agreements was more elaborate. It inserted a preamble recital declaring prevention and control of illegal immigration as one of the primary objectives of the agreement, and three standardised provisions into the main body of the agreement. The first of these three provisions contained a reciprocal obligation to readmit nationals, illegally present on the territory of one of the Member States or the third country in question, and to do so "without further formalities". It also specified an obligation to issue identity documents, necessary for the purpose of readmission. The second provision contained a commitment on the part of the third country to conclude a bilateral readmission agreement, including an obligation to readmit third country nationals and stateless persons, at a Member State's request. The third provision was limited to stating that the Cooperation Council, as established under the mixed agreement, would examine possible further joint efforts concerning migration control.[8]

The advent of Community competence to conclude readmission agreements with third countries with the Treaty of Amsterdam required a revision of the standard readmission clause. The Council adopted a new standard text, applicable to both Community- and mixed agreements, in November 1999.[9] This text may be found in Annex 4.

4 Council Recommendation of 30 November 1994 concerning a specimen bilateral readmission agreement between a Member State and a third country (*OJ* C 274, 19 September 1996, p. 20); Council recommendation of 24 July 1995 on the guiding principles to be followed in drawing up protocols on the implementation of re-admission agreements (*OJ* C 274, 19 September 1996, p. 25).

5 Council Doc. 12509/95, 8 December 1995.

6 Council Doc. 4272/96, 22 January 1996.

7 Council Doc. 12509/95, "Draft statements by the Community and by State X".

8 Council Doc. 4272/96.

9 Council Doc. 13409/99.

This text largely replicated the 1996 standard clause regarding mixed agreements, with two important differences. Firstly, the political commitment of the third country to conclude a fully-fledged readmission agreement upon request now pertained primarily to an agreement at the Community level.[10] The third country remained committed to the conclusion of a bilateral agreement, if so requested by a Member State, but only pending the possible conclusion of a Community agreement.[11] This confirms the division of competence as implicitly agreed upon between the EC and the Member States after the Treaty of Amsterdam, and the resulting primacy of Community over Member State readmission agreements. The second difference is that the Council decided to include the standard clause in *all* future Community and mixed agreements, rather than assessing a need therefore on a case-by-case basis. This change in strategy was informed by the limited success in inserting the 1995 and 1996 standard clauses in agreements with third countries. Arguably, the Council expected that by treating third countries equally by invariably including a readmission clause, the Community's negotiation position would be strengthened.[12]

The most notable readmission clause as negotiated by the Community in this period is Article 13 of the Cotonou Convention. The negotiation of the Cotonou Convention, which concerns trade and development cooperation, between the Community and the African, Caribbean and Pacific countries (ACP) was completed in 2000, after which it entered into force on 1 April 2003. Considering the time-frame of negotiations, one would have expected the Cotonou Convention to include the 1999 standard readmission clause. Article 13, however, is in fact a prelude to the wider migration management clause, as launched by the Seville European Council in June 2002. The migration management clause includes a readmission clause, but places it within a broader framework of cooperation in the fields of migration and asylum.

The European Council meeting in Seville decided that all future cooperation, association or equivalent agreements with the European Union or the European Community should include a provision for cooperation on readmission as well as the "joint management of migration flows".[13] The General Affairs and External Relations (GAER) Council Conclusions of November 2002 subsequently determined the main elements of the content of this new clause, which is generally referred to as the migration management clause.[14] The Council explicitly did not adopt a standard text, which

10 Council Doc. 13409/99, Article B.

11 Council Doc. 13409/99, Article C.

12 Peers has noted a further reason for including clauses in all future Community and mixed agreements. The inclusion of a readmission clause involves an inevitable trade-off between justice and home affairs objectives on the one hand, and for example development, general external relations, or trade objectives on the other. This exchange has met with varying enthusiasm from policy makers in the latter fields, which led to frequent compromises on the inclusion of a readmission clause when this was still dependent on a case-by-case assessment, Peers 2004, p. 198.

13 Presidency Conclusions, Seville European Council of 21 and 22 June 2002, para. 33.

14 Council Doc. 13894/02, 14 November 2002, para. 8.

is a likely result of the limited success in inserting the standard readmission clause into agreements with third countries. The Member States arguably realised that while third countries rarely accept clauses without modification, developing a standard text within the context of the Council would be of limited relevance. As it does for the negotiation of Community readmission agreements, the Commission makes use of an informal and flexible standard text for the migration management clause, which is (partially) based on the above GAER Council conclusions.[15] Rather than attempting to impose a standard text, the clause is adapted – "tailor-made" – according to the third country in question before and during actual negotiations.

The first post-Seville migration management clauses were incorporated successfully into Political Dialogue and Cooperation agreements with a group of Central American countries,[16] and the Andean Community countries.[17] Post-Seville clauses have also been included in a Political Dialogue and Cooperation agreement with the Mercosur/Mercosul countries, a Free Trade Agreement with the countries of the Gulf Cooperation Council,[18] and an Association Agreement with Syria,[19] which are at different stages of negotiation. We have deduced the principal content of the migration management clause from the texts of the agreements with a group of Central American countries, and the Andean Community.[20] The text of the migration management clause in the agreement with the Andean Community can be found in Annex 5.

The first paragraph of the migration management clause commits the contracting parties to hold a dialogue on migration-related issues, such as illegal immigration, smuggling and trafficking, and on the development of regions from which migrants originate. Paragraph 2 establishes general parameters for related future cooperation. It does so rather loosely by making actual cooperation dependent on a so-called "specific

15 While the text of the migration management clause as actually included in agreements with third countries differs considerably from the GAER Council conclusions, we will not outline the latter.

16 Article 49 of the Political Dialogue and Cooperation Agreement between the European Community and its Member States and Costa Rica, El Salvador, Guatemala, Honduras, Nicaragua and Panama, signed on 15 December 2003. Full text available on: www.europa.eu.int/comm/external_relations.

17 Article 49 of the Political Dialogue and Cooperation Agreement between the European Community and its Member States and the Andean Community and its Member countries, initialled on 15 December 2003. Full text available on: www.europa.eu.int/comm/external_relations.

18 The negotiation of a new Free Trade Agreement between the European Community and its Member States and Bahrain, Kuwait, Oman, Qatar, Saudi Arabia and United Arab Emirates started in March 2002 (www.europa.eu.int/comm/trade, consulted on 15 April 2005). To the knowledge of the author this is the first time a clause concerning readmission is incorporated in an agreement in the field of trade.

19 Negotiations of a Euro-Med Association Agreement between the EU and Syria were finalised on 9 December 2003 (www.europa.eu.int/comm/external_relations, consulted on 15 April 2005).

20 *Supra*, n. 16 and 17.

needs assessment conducted in mutual consultation".[21] In particular, paragraph two specifies a number of areas on which cooperation will focus. These include the root causes of migration, visa policies, admission- and integration policies, and measures against racism and xenophobia. Also included is capacity building to the benefit of the international protection of refugees, on which we will elaborate below in section 8.3. On the enforcement side, cooperation will focus on border control measures such as training exercises and the provision of equipment, measures against illegal immigration, smuggling and trafficking, and measures concerning the return of illegal residents "under humane and dignified conditions".

Paragraph 3 contains a modified version of the readmission clause, by which the contracting parties agree to "readmit their illegal migrants". This commitment firstly translates into an obligation to readmit nationals, illegally resident in the territory of another contracting State, which has been slightly expanded in comparison with the 1999 clause. In addition to allowing readmission "without further formalities" and issuing appropriate documents, a requested State should now also extend "the administrative facilities necessary for such purposes". The second principal part of the readmission clause – the commitment to conclude a readmission agreement upon request including an obligation to readmit third country nationals and stateless persons – has also been altered. Contrary to the November 2002 GAER Council Conclusions upon which it is based,[22] the migration management clause does not express the same regard for the primacy of Community- over bilateral readmission agreements as the 1999 clause.[23] It determines that a third country in question will agree to conclude a readmission agreement upon a request from the Community or one its Member States, without distinction. This does not, as such, affect the division of competence in the field of readmission under EC law, or the resulting relation between Community- and bilateral Member State readmission agreements. Considering the still simmering competence debate, however, this amendment of the readmission clause is politically controversial.

## 8.2 The negotiation, practical meaning, and continued relevance of readmission clauses

The concept of linkage between internal and external policy objectives, or between different external policy objectives, has steadily gained in political currency at the EC level. The negotiation of Community- or mixed agreements now includes up to three "extra-curricular" provisions. These are a migration management clause, a human rights clause, and an anti-terrorism clause. The incorporation of human rights clauses began in the 1980s, enabling suspension of an agreement with a third country in case of serious violation of the principles of respect for human rights, democracy, and the

21 See Article 49(2) of the Political Dialogue and Cooperation Agreement between the European Community and its Member States and the Andean Community, *supra*, n. 17.

22 See, in particular, Council Doc. 13894/02, para. 8.

23 *Supra*, at n. 11.

rule of law.[24] The incorporation of anti-terrorism clauses started after the Al Qaeda attacks on US soil of 11 September 2001, establishing cooperation with third countries in combating terrorism and the financing thereof.[25]

Council mandates to incorporate such clauses have impacted upon the negotiation of Community and mixed agreements in several ways. On a technical level, firstly, this linking of policies has complicated and thus slowed down the work of Commission negotiators, and required a greater degree of coordination on the Community side. Third countries have generally not accepted proposed standard texts for clauses on migration or readmission without demanding modifications. The incorporation of these clauses has required heavy negotiation, contrary to initial expectations that the Community's assumed negotiating weight would enable a proverbial "take it or leave it" approach. In order to provide the expertise necessary for negotiating a readmission- or migration management clause, officials from DG Justice, Freedom and Security join the Commission team that negotiates agreements of a general nature, such as Association- or Cooperation agreements. Within the context of more specialised agreements, however, such as in the field of trade or agriculture, clauses are negotiated by officials who lack this expertise, relying on prior *ad hoc* briefings by colleagues from DG JFS.

Secondly, the incorporation of clauses involves an inevitable trade-off between justice and home affairs on the one hand, and development cooperation, general external relations, trade, agriculture, *etcetera*, on the other. This new case of 'conditionality', consisting of the inclusion of not directly related clauses in Community- or mixed agreements, has met with varying enthusiasm from EC policy makers in the latter policy fields[26] as well as criticism from outside sources. The extraction of concessions in this manner concerning, for example, the readmission of unauthorised residents is perceived as the archetypal example of the European Community exploiting its political and economic dominance to the detriment of lesser developed countries.[27] In practice, however, exploiting the "accumulated bargaining power of the Fifteen"[28] has had only limited success, and third countries have been able to turn negotiations to their advantage.

Peers has reviewed the content of readmission clauses inserted since 1995 in Association Agreements with Mediterranean third countries, Partnership- and Cooperation Agreements with ex-Soviet countries, Stabilisation and Association Agreements with Western Balkan countries, the Cotonou Convention concerning ACP countries,

---

24 Hurwitz 2002, p. 9.

25 Press release 6247/02 (Presse 30); Council Doc. 7750/02, cited in Council Doc. 13909/1/02, p. 21; see also Brouwer, Catz and Guild, p. 100.

26 We can note the limited success with which immigration policy objectives have thus far been received in the field of development cooperation, in particular, *supra*, subsection 6.2.1.

27 See, for example, Statewatch on the Cotonou Convention, *Lomé Convention used to impose repatriation on the world's poorest countries*, available on: www.statewatch.org; and Peers 2004, p. 216-217.

28 Noll 2000, p. 206.

and agreements with Asian and Latin American countries.[29] Readmission clauses, as resulting from these negotiations, vary in wording, substance and form. The Commission has on occasion failed to fulfil Council mandates to include a readmission clause, unable to secure an obligation to readmit nationals and/or a commitment to future conclusion of a readmission agreement. The more successful negotiation results range from a standard readmission clause with little or no modification in the main body of the text of the agreement, to general declarations concerning cooperation on combating illegal immigration in an annex, to a unilateral EC statement reiterating the importance of readmission cooperation.

The effect of the negotiating weight of the European Community on the incorporation of readmission clauses in Community- and mixed agreements has thus been disappointing from the viewpoint of the Member States. As happened with the negotiation of Community readmission agreements, discussed in the preceding chapter, the political importance of issues relating to immigration in the EC has strengthened the negotiation position of third countries. It is remarkable that third countries have not simply accepted readmission obligations as demanded by the EC, even when counterweighted by the substantial benefits contained in Association-, Cooperation or equivalent agreements. It should however be noted that the compromise solutions reached on readmission clauses not only demonstrate resilience of third countries in negotiations, but also flexibility on the part of the Community. The Commission and Council have apparently not been willing to exploit the available leverage to its fullest, and "play hardball" by threatening to stall important developmental, economic or otherwise cooperative relations for relatively minor concessions on readmission.

The most recent version of the EC readmission clause is also the most far-reaching with regard to the obligation to readmit nationals. It obliges the contracting parties to readmit nationals without further formalities, to issue appropriate documents for this purpose, and to extend the necessary administrative facilities.[30] However, without clear agreement on the means by which to demonstrate nationality to the satisfaction of the other contracting party, the implementation of this clause is as susceptible to practical and bureaucratic obstacles as the purported obligation to readmit own nationals under international law.[31]

One can therefore question the practical significance of readmission clauses as instruments for achieving the return and readmission of migrants. Like readmission

29 Peers 2004, p. 199-205.

30 See Article 49(3) of the political dialogue and cooperation agreements between the European Community and its Member States and the Andean Community, and Central American countries, respectively, *supra*, n. 16 and 17.

31 This finding applies even more to the 1995, 1996 and 1999 standard readmission clauses, which do not contain a reference to necessary administrative facilities, and is especially clear in relation to Article 13 of the Cotonou Convention. Article 13(5)(c)(i) thereof states that the obligations of ACP States to readmit their own nationals "apply only in respect of those persons who are considered as their nationals in accordance with their respective legal system".

agreements, readmission clauses provide an obligation to readmit own nationals, but without the added value of establishing a procedure and common rules on evidence for this purpose. Clauses thus confirm the purported rule of customary international law that States must readmit their own nationals, but do not give this rule practical meaning. The one relevant difference, and possible added value of a readmission clause, is an arguable increase in political pressure to comply with this obligation.

Furthermore, the follow-up to the second principal part of readmission clauses – the political commitment by third countries to conclude a fully-fledged readmission agreement upon request – has thus far been limited, as well as problematic. After the arduous negotiation of Article 13 of the Cotonou Convention,[32] for example, the Community is yet to act upon this clause despite pressure from North African transit countries as well as several Member States to conclude readmission agreements with Sub-Saharan countries.[33] We should note in this regard that the political commitment to conclude future readmission agreements under the Cotonou Convention is particularly minimal. Unlike other readmission clauses, Article 13(5)(c)(ii) of the Cotonou Convention does not commit to actual *conclusion* of an agreement. The commitment of ACP countries is restricted to initiating negotiations, if so requested by the Community or one of its Member States.

Moreover, where the Community *has* invoked a readmission clause as a basis for concluding a fully-fledged readmission agreement, results have been limited. Pursuant to the November 1999[34] and April 2002 selection criteria,[35] a number of the current negotiations of Community readmission agreements with third countries may be related to a readmission clause under a Community- or mixed agreement. Excepting Albania, however, prior political commitments to conclude a readmission agreement have had very little impact on subsequent negotiations. The ongoing negotiations with Algeria, Morocco, Pakistan, Russia, and Ukraine are a case in point, demonstrating that readmission clauses have not implied a faster or otherwise facilitated negotiation process for fully-fledged readmission agreements. In some exceptional cases, extracting prior concessions from third countries through a readmission clause has even worked to the strategic disadvantage of the Community. Algeria and Pakistan, for example, have been able to fend off requests by the Community to enter into a readmission agreement

32 Statewatch, *Lomé Convention used to impose repatriation on the world's poorest countries*, available on: www.statewatch.org.

33 Morocco has repeatedly requested the Community to conclude readmission agreements with countries of origin in Sub-Saharan Africa in order to relieve some of the migration pressure on its territory. Noteworthy, also, is the bid by Spain for follow-up at the EC level to Article 13 of the Cotonou Convention around the period of the European Council meeting in Seville. In addition, Ireland has pushed for a negotiating mandate for a Community readmission agreement with Nigeria, while experiencing an influx of immigrants from this country, and receiving insufficient cooperation under a bilateral readmission agreement.

34 Council Doc. 13888/99.

35 Council Doc. 7990/02, 16 April 2002.

by referring to, respectively, an Association Agreement and a Cooperation Agreement containing a readmission clause, which had not yet entered into force or been ratified.

Finally, in the preceding chapter we discussed a shift in the Community's negotiating strategy under the common readmission policy, which may render the incorporation of readmission clauses into Community- and mixed agreements obsolete.[36] In the experience of the Commission, readmission clauses have provided insufficient leverage in subsequent negotiations for a fully-fledged readmission agreement. Third countries have generally demanded additional compensation, considering that the negotiating leverage provided by the cooperation, association or equivalent agreement is effectively "spent" once the agreement is concluded. In order to make more effective use of the Community's resources in the external field, and prevent requests for additional *quid pro quo*, the GEAR Council in November 2004 changed tack.[37] The Council is now able to link the negotiation of cooperation, association or equivalent agreements to the immediate negotiation of a readmission agreement, rather than waiting for the first to enter into force before requesting the conclusion of the latter.

Assuming that the Council will make use of this new possibility, the continued relevance of the incorporation of clauses into Community- and mixed agreements as part of the common readmission policy will be highly limited. It is clear that the post-Seville migration management clause would not be affected insofar as establishing a wider framework of cooperation on migration and asylum policies. Considering that the general objective of migration cooperation is to limit the number of new arrivals, the migration management clause would as such retain an indirect relation to the common readmission policy. In terms of establishing specific cooperation on readmission, however, the clause would be largely superfluous. One could imagine only exceptional cases where including a readmission clause may continue to fulfil a strategic purpose in working towards a wider cooperation on readmission. A past example in this regard is China. As discussed in subsection 7.3.9, an obligation to readmit Chinese tourists was successfully included in the EC-China ADS agreement of February 2004. This agreement arguably paved the way for negotiation of a Community readmission agreement by broaching the, within external relations with China, particularly sensitive issue of illegal immigration and readmission of Chinese nationals.

## 8.3 The migration management clause and the extension of international refugee protection

This subsection will highlight one specific element of the new migration management clause, which is related to the stimulation of international refugee protection in third countries as part of the external policy of the EC, discussed earlier in subsection 3.2.5 and section 6.2. The migration management clause incorporated into the Political Dialogue and Cooperation Agreement of December 2003 with the Andean Community[38]

36 *Supra*, subsection 7.3.5, at n. 219.

37 Council Doc. 13578/04.

38 *Supra*, n. 17.

includes the international protection of refugees as an area of cooperation. In particular, it states that cooperation will focus on:

> the development and implementation of national legislation and practices with regard to international protection, with a view to satisfying the provisions of the Geneva Convention of 1951 on the status of refugees and of its Protocol of 1967 and other relevant international instruments, and to ensuring the respect of the principle of "*non refoulement*".[39]

The migration management clause as incorporated in the Political Dialogue and Cooperation Agreement of December 2003 with several Central American countries includes the same provision with near identical wording.[40] The migration management clause as incorporated into the draft Association Agreement with Syria,[41] however, is formulated differently on this point. Cooperation between the EC and Syria will focus on:

> the development and implementation of national legislation and practices with regard to persons in need of international protection, with a view to satisfying the provisions of applicable international instruments.

The difference in wording is explained by the fact that, unlike the above countries of the Andean Community and Central American countries, Syria is not party to the Geneva Refugee Convention or to other instruments relevant to the international protection of refugees. Syria was therefore unwilling to include any reference to the GC, the term "refugees", or "the principle of non-refoulement". The negotiators reached a compromise by referring to "persons in need of international protection", which is neutral in that it does not pertain to any particular treaty.

In subsection 5.3.9, a similar reluctance in relation to the negotiation of Community readmission agreements was highlighted. Community readmission agreements contain a so-called non-affection clause, which determines the agreement to be without prejudice to other international law obligations. Hong Kong and Macao, in particular, were unwilling to include a reference to international conventions relating to refugee protection to which they were not party. The non-affection clauses in the Community readmission agreements with Hong Kong and Macao therefore contain only a generic reference to obligations "arising from International Law", instead of the standard clause which mentions a number of relevant conventions specifically.[42] The Community readmission agreement with Sri Lanka, also not party to the GC, contains

39 Article 49(2)(b).

40 Article 49(2)(b) of the Political Dialogue and Cooperation Agreement between the European Community and its Member States and Costa Rica, El Salvador, Guatemala, Honduras, Nicaragua and Panama, signed on 15 December 2003, *supra*, n. 16.

41 *Supra*, n. 19.

42 See Article 16 of the Community readmission agreements with Hong Kong (*OJ* L 17. 24 January 2004, p. 30) and Macao (*OJ* L 143, 30 April 2004, p. 104), respectively.

a non-affection clause with similar general wording.[43] We furthermore noted that this reluctance to include references to, for example, the GC or the European Convention of Human Rights, does not have a legal basis. The non-affection clause in Community readmission agreements does not create international obligations for a contracting party; it only confirms obligations to which it is already bound by treaty. From this perspective, the position of Syria is more understandable, considering the wording of the migration management clause as included in the agreements with the Andean Community and Central American countries. To agree to capacity building "with a view to satisfying the provisions"[44] of the Geneva Refugee Convention and other relevant conventions, to which Syria is not party, would come a lot closer to accepting the obligations contained therein.

Although dependent on the outcome of negotiations with third countries, it is arguable that the migration management clause could cause a further spill-over of international protection norms from Europe into other regions where such norms are less developed.[45] After substantial amendment of the migration management clause, Syria finally agreed to capacity building in reference to "persons in need of international protection with a view to satisfying the provisions of applicable international instruments". This commitment is less specific in comparison with the agreements with the Andean Community and Latin American countries. Also, the degree to which international instruments, of which Syria is not a party-member, may be considered "applicable" is unclear. Nevertheless, Syria has hereby accepted a clear-cut reference to international protection norms by treaty. In this context, it will be highly relevant to compare the outcome of the migration management clause in the Free Trade Agreement under negotiation with the Gulf Cooperation Council.[46] None of the GCC countries – Bahrain, Kuwait, Oman, Qatar, Saudi Arabia, and United Arab Emirates – is party to the Geneva Refugee Convention. Together with Asia, the Middle East is one of the regions in the world where the rate of ratification of the GC is lowest.[47] The form in which the contracting parties to this FTA will agree to cooperate towards capacity building in the field of refugee protection will thus be important in determining the degree to which the migration management clause may be considered to contribute to the extension of international refugee protection norms to new countries.

43 See Article 16 of the Community readmission agreement with Sri Lanka, *OJ* L 124, 17 May 2005, p. 43. The text of the readmission agreement with Pakistan, the last of the target countries for Community readmission agreements which are not party to the GC, is not yet publicly available at the time of writing.

44 *Supra*, at n. 39 and 40.

45 This comes in addition to the financing of capacity building in the reception of refugees under the Community's external assistance programmes and New Neighbourhood policy, and the EC's political efforts at stimulating third countries to ratify the GC, see chapter 6 and 3, respectively.

46 *Supra*, n. 18.

47 Coleman 2003, p. 47-48.

## 8.4 Conclusion

This chapter has discussed a core element of the common readmission policy, additional to the conclusion of readmission agreements, which is the incorporation of readmission clauses into Community or mixed agreements. It has outlined the development in the content of readmission clauses, since their introduction in 1995. The standard readmission clause – consisting of a reiteration of the obligation to readmit own nationals as well as a political commitment to conclude an agreement in future, including also third country nationals and stateless persons – has remained largely the same. It is now imbedded, however, within the much wider migration management clause, which seeks to establish a broad framework of cooperation in the fields of migration and asylum.

This chapter has also discussed the negotiation process regarding readmission clauses, and found that it has similar dynamics to that of Community readmission agreements. Third countries have not simply accepted the standard text offered to them by the Commission, despite the often substantial benefits presented by a Community or mixed agreement. Incorporating readmission clauses has required real negotiations. These have had varying success, leading to significant differences between agreements in the wording, substance and form of the readmission clauses. From the perspective of the Community and the Member States, the purported negotiating weight of the Community has again had disappointing results.

It was furthermore argued that the practical significance of readmission clauses, as instruments for facilitating the return of unauthorised immigrants, is very limited. This concerns the obligation to readmit own nationals, as well as the commitment to conclude a fully-fledged readmission agreement upon a request by the Community. In addition, it was argued that readmission clauses will become increasingly obsolete, as the Council is now able to link the negotiation of a fully-fledged readmission agreement directly to negotiations for a Community or mixed agreement.

Finally, this chapter discussed a particular characteristic of the new migration management clause, which is that it seeks to establish cooperation on refugee protection with a view to satisfying international refugee law. It was argued that this is potentially significant, while some Community or mixed agreements are concluded with third countries which are not party to the Geneva Refugee Convention or other relevant international conventions. The migration management clause hereby arguably contributes to the extension of the international protection regime to new countries.

# Chapter 9 Community readmission agreements and the international protection of refugees

Readmission agreements intend to enable an orderly management of the return of immigrants. Their text generally refers only to immigrants without a title to residence or presence. In practice, however, the Member States have used readmission agreements also to facilitate the expulsion of protection seekers and refugees, regardless of the lack of reference to this group of persons in the text. Academics and members of civil society widely consider readmission agreements as raising issues of international refugee protection. This chapter examines these issues in relation to the common readmission policy.

Subsection 9.1 outlines concerns of international refugee protection raised by readmission agreements. These pertain in particular to the expulsion of protection seekers to third countries, which is therefore the focus of this chapter. Subsection 9.2 identifies a series of obligations of international law, constituting the international legal framework regarding the expulsion of protection seekers from EU Member States to third countries. Subsection 9.3, finally, determines whether Community readmission agreements are in accordance with these obligations. For reasons set out below, this includes a review of the legality of the common safe third country policy in light of those obligations.

## 9.1 Protection concerns raised by readmission agreements

As outlined in subsection 3.2.4, the use of readmission agreements for the expulsion of protection seekers intensified in the early nineties with the broad introduction of safe third country policies in the Member States. Surprisingly, perhaps, the office of the United Nations High Commissioner for Refugees (UNHCR) initially considered this a relatively favourable development.[1] It considered that readmission agreements would help prevent secondary refugee movements, provide a "removal end"[2] to asylum procedures, and discourage the misuse of asylum procedures by economic immigrants. The procedural requirement of prior consent by the requested State, as promoted by

1 See, for example, UNHCR 1994.

2 UNHCR 2001a.

readmission agreements, would furthermore reduce the possibility of refugees ending up "in orbit".[3]

Since the early nineties, the UNHCR has especially emphasised the fact that readmission agreements could potentially contribute towards securing a safe haven for refugees. It has firstly encouraged the adoption of multilateral readmission instruments similar to the Dublin Convention, which not only ensure readmission to territory but also guarantee consideration of a protection claim. In the same vein, UNHCR has advocated the conclusion of bilateral readmission agreements, which would take explicit account of the special needs of protection seekers, allocate responsibility for protection seekers on the basis of more than mere transit through a third country, and include certain refugee protection safeguards such as status determination in the requested State.[4]

A general concern raised in the literature is that, despite these longstanding recommendations, the text of readmission agreements still generally disregards their application to protection seekers and refugees in practice.[5] Community readmission agreements do not make special or separate provision for the readmission of protection seekers and refugees, either. The Member States may be expected to implement Community readmission agreements, aiding the expulsion of this group of persons, in the same manner as under their own bilateral agreements. The Member States will readmit protection seekers and refugees to third countries without distinction, meaning as unauthorised immigrants. They will be readmitted as "nationals" or "third country nationals" without a title to residence or presence, depending on whether readmission takes place to the country of origin or a third country.

The lack of reference to protection seekers and refugees in readmission agreements has led to protection concerns, especially given the fact that these agreements are often concluded without regard for the general safety of requested States for protection seekers and refugees. As a result, readmission agreements are regularly concluded with countries, for example, which produce refugees, which are not party to international conventions relevant to refugee protection, or which do not qualify as safe third countries for different reasons.[6] We noted earlier that the Community has concluded, or is negotiating, agreements with several such countries.[7]

More specific concerns raised in the literature, regarding readmission agreements, invariably relate to the expulsion of protection seekers to so-called safe third

3 *Supra*, subsection 5.3.5.5, at n. 52.

4 UNHCR 1968; UNHCR 1979; UNHCR 1994: UNHCR 2001c; and UNHCR 2001e.

5 UNHCR 1994; ECRE 1995, para. 23; Kumin 1995, p. 1, 5; Byrne and Shacknove 1996, p. 202; Noll 1997; Landgren 1999, p. 23, 28-29; Lavenex 1999, p. 23, 79, 82, 94, 98; Noll 2000, p. 203-204; Crosland and Morrison 2001, p. 36-38; van Selm 2001, p. 21, 33; Hurwitz 2002, p. 2; Legomsky 2003, p. 583.

6 Kumin 1995, p. 3-4; Noll 1997, p. 422, 439-440; Abell 1999, p. 99; Landgren 1999, p. 28; Legomsky 2003, p. 585-586; Human Rights Watch 2005, p. 12.

7 *Supra*, subsection 7.1.5.

countries.[8] Indeed, protection concerns raised by readmission agreements are usually the most distinct where their application builds upon the shaky foundations of the safe third country concept. If, after a substantive examination of a protection claim, a person has not been found to be a refugee, then expulsion to another country based on a readmission agreement will normally not raise an issue of international refugee protection. The risk of violation of international obligations is more pronounced, however, where States use readmission agreements to expel persons whose protection claims are not considered on their merits, because they can be returned to a third country. We recall that facilitating return to safe third countries is one of the objectives of the common readmission policy.[9]

The general relation between readmission agreements and safe third country policies is as follows. As we discussed in section 2.2, international law does not impose a legal obligation on states to (re)admit non-nationals to their territory, regarding which readmission agreements thus have an enabling function. In the same manner, readmission agreements facilitate the implementation of safe third country policies. The transfer of responsibility for protection seekers to third countries does not have an established legal basis in international law, either.[10] In order to secure, nevertheless, the cooperation of third countries on readmitting rejected protection seekers, the Member States and the Community may rely on readmission agreements, in particular on the obligation to readmit third country nationals as established by those agreements.

It should be remembered that a readmission agreement does not provide an absolute guarantee that a third country will accept a protection seeker back on its territory.[11] Nor is a readmission agreement an absolute necessity for successful expulsion. Expulsion may be exercised through a number of other, including less formal, means, depending on the level of cooperation received from a third country in question. Readmission agreements do generally improve chances of receiving the required cooperation from a third country, however. They therefore facilitate the implementation of Member State decisions, rejecting a protection seeker under a safe third country policy.

---

8 UNHCR 1994, p. 3; ECRE 1995, para. 19-25, 52-53; Kumin 1995, p. 3-6; Marx 1995, p. 386, 395-397, 403-406; Noll 1997, p. 422-423; Abell 1999, p. 66; Landgren 1999, p. 22-29; Lavenex 1999, p. 77-78, 94; Noll 2000, p. 209-210; Crosland and Morrison 2001, p. 36-38; van Selm 2001, p. 32-34, 58-59; Byrne, Noll and Vedsted-Hansen 2002, p. 383-391; Hurwitz 2002, p. 5-6; Bouteillet-Paquet 2003, p. 368; Legomsky 2003, p. 583-586, 630-633, 654-655; Human Rights Watch 2005b, p. 8-18, 72.

9 *Supra*, subsection 3.2.4.

10 Regarding Article 31(1) of the Geneva refugee Convention as the alleged legal basis of safe third country policies, see Zwaan 2003, p. 22-30; van Selm 2001, p. 47-50; Vedsted-Hansen 1999, p. 277-278; cited also above, subsection 2.2.2, n. 98. See furthermore the European Commission, SEC(2000) 522, para. 65. Hathaway sums up the general consensus regarding the legal basis of the safe third country concept in international law by noting that "while not anchored in the requirements of the Refugee Convention, [it] is also not necessarily in breach of it", Hathaway 2005, p. 323.

11 *Supra*, section 3.2.4, at n. 67; subsection 5.3.5.2.

Safe third country policies generally consist of a number of different safe third country "exceptions", each rejecting a protection seeker under different circumstances.[12] The term "exception" refers to the fact that a State, exceptionally, will not assume responsibility for a refugee in case a third country can do so. Initially, safe third country policies mainly provided for the transfer of responsibility for persons, who had been recognised as refugees, but for whom a safe-haven existed elsewhere. During the nineties, however, the emphasis shifted to transfer without status determination under the influence of Schengen[13] and other intergovernmental European[14] regulation.[15] Since this period, the Member States chiefly implement safe third country polices in order to minimise the number of persons within the asylum procedure.[16] The most relevant, and indeed also the most controversial, safe third country exceptions are therefore those, which exclude protection seekers from substantive asylum procedures, and proceed with expulsion without prior status determination.

The UNHCR has generally supported safe third country policies, and the concept of "protection elsewhere"[17] which underpins them. The starting point of the UNHCR's policies and recommendations is "that there must be at least one country in the world willing and able to provide protection and quality, durable asylum to each and every refugee".[18] The refugee agency considers that safe third country policies can contribute towards the distribution of the international refugee burden according to this principle, provided certain conditions are respected. In particular, the constant position of the UNHCR has been that expulsion of a protection seeker should only take place to a third country, which:

- readmits the protection seeker to its territory;
- protects the protection seeker against refoulement;
- grants the protection seeker the possibility to seek and enjoy asylum; and

12 Dutch asylum legislation, for example, includes five safe third country exceptions, leading to rejection and expulsion to a third country in case of applicability of the Dublin Convention, the existence of a readmission agreement with a third country, previous transit through a third country, previous stay in a third country, or status determination with a negative outcome, respectively, Zwaan 2003, p. 193-194.

13 In particular, the 1990 Schengen Convention.

14 In particular, the 1990 Dublin Convention; and the Resolution on a harmonised approach to questions concerning host third countries, adopted at the meeting of the Ministers responsible for immigration in London of 30 November to 1 December 1992, SN4823/92. The text of the latter resolution can be found in Guild and Niessen 1996, p. 161-164. Both these instruments originated from intergovernmental cooperation between the EC Member States within the *Ad Hoc* Group on Immigration, see Guild and Niessen 1996.

15 Zwaan 2003, p. 6, 55-56, 59, 62-63. Spijkerboer and Vermeulen 1999, p. 273-274.

16 Noll 2000, p. 200.

17 UNHCR 1994.

18 UNHCR 2001c.

- treats the protection seeker in accordance with accepted international standards.[19]

Protection against refoulement, the possibility to seek and enjoy asylum, and treatment in accordance with international standards, are conditions for safe return. They are criteria, which determine the safety of a third country for a protection seeker. The first requirement in this listing – an assurance of readmission to territory – is there to prevent situations of refugees "in orbit". The UNHCR has specified in this regard that readmission should be based on "a meaningful link or connection"[20] between a protection seeker and a third country. It should be borne in mind that this specification is not a protection safeguard. A link or connection between a protection seeker and a country is important for the sustainability of return, and for finding a durable solution of refugee protection. In this light, the UNHCR has explicitly advised against readmission based on mere transit. It has insisted on the presence of family- or cultural ties, or a title to permanent residence in a third country. The issue of whether readmission to a third country should be based on a link or connection, which is stronger than mere transit, should however be considered as separate from the conditions for safe return.

In practice, the Member States have implemented safe third country policies with differing regard for safety conditions. A large body of literature has accumulated since the early nineties, addressing the resulting friction between safe third country policies and international refugee protection.[21] The main concern is that safe third country policies take insufficient account of the risk of refoulement. Refoulement, in general terms, refers to the return of a refugee to a country from which s/he fled, and is prohibited by international law.[22] The specific risk involved with expulsion to a third country is one of so-called indirect, or chain refoulement, in which case a protection seeker is returned to the country from which s/he fled *via* a chain of expulsions involving one or more third countries.[23]

A particular problem in the implementation of safe third country policies is that the Member State objective of minimising the amount of persons in the asylum procedure has reduced the guarantee of safety in individual cases. A full and individualised

19 UNHCR, EXCOM Conclusion No. 85 (1998), para. (aa). See also UNHCR 2001f; and UNHCR 2001b.

20 UNHCR 2001b.

21 Selected publications in this area are: Goodwin-Gill 1992; Achermann and Gattiker 1995; ECRE 1995; Kumin 1995; Marx 1995; Byrne and Shacknove 1996; Fernhout 1999; Noll 1997; Abell 1999; Landgren 1999; Lavenex 1999; Vedsted-Hansen 1999; Noll 2001; Crosland and Morrison 2001; Van Selm 2001; Legomsky 2003; Zwaan 2003; Human Rights Watch 2005b.

22 We will define the principle of non-refoulement more precisely below, in subsection 9.2.1.2, at n. 33-35, and subsection 9.2.2.1.

23 ECRE 1995; Kumin 1995, p. 1, 5.; Byrne and Shacknove 1996, p. 202; Landgren 1999, p. 28-29; Lavenex 1999, p. 98; Noll 2000, p. 209; Crosland and Morrison 2001, p. 37-38; Van Selm 2001, p. 21; Legomsky 2003, p. 583-585.

examination of the safety of a third country for a protection seeker can be just as time- and resource-consuming as the substantive examination of a protection claim. For reasons of "procedural economy",[24] it is imperative that safe third country exceptions enable the Member States to reject protection seekers as a preliminary, and thus speedy, matter. The Member States have therefore resorted to general safety examinations, and to broad application of the principle of interstate trust.

General safety assessments of third countries allow the Member States to reject protection seekers without regard for the particulars of their individual case. An important factor in this regard is the principle of interstate trust. The principle of interstate trust is used to establish the safety of a third country in general, as well as in individual cases. If a third country is party to relevant international conventions, such as the GC or the ECHR, a Member State may appeal to the principle of interstate trust, thereby considering the conditions for safe return as fulfilled. Protection seekers are in this manner rejected, based on a reasonable presumption of safety, rather than an assessment of actual safety in their individual case.

Although potentially compromising the protection of individual refugees, the application of the principle of interstate trust in this context is generally accepted in State practice.[25] Interstate trust is the presumption that a State party's laws, policies, procedures, and resulting protection decisions, are in accordance with the minimum level of protection prescribed by a particular international convention. The degree to which such a presumption is justified depends significantly on the convention involved. Relevant in this regard are the textual clarity of the convention, and the resulting margin for differing interpretations and standards, the degree of discretion left to State parties in implementation, and the presence or absence of a supranational body with supervisory and/or judiciary powers. Where States appeal to interstate trust to satisfy the conditions for rejection on safe third country grounds, a possibility to rebut the presumption of safety is generally considered a protection imperative.[26] A protection seeker should at least be given the opportunity to present contra-indications of the safety of a third country, according to his or her particular situation.

Readmission agreements have been implicated in the protection concerns resulting from safe third country policies, while they facilitate the implementation of these policies. As such, readmission agreements are considered to create, or heighten, a risk of indirect refoulement. It should however be noted that the literature often fails to draw the necessary distinction between safe third country policies and readmission agreements.[27] With regard to protection issues raised by expulsion to third countries, there is a tendency to simply identify readmission agreements with safe third country policies.

24 Noll 2000, p. 200.

25 Zwaan 2003, p. 1; Spijkerboer and Vermeulen 2005, p. 92.

26 Vermeulen 1999, p. 182-184.

27 See, in particular, Achermann and Gattiker 1995; Marx 1995; Abell 1999; Landgren 1999; Lavenex 1999; Crosland and Morrison 2001; Van Selm 2001; Hurwitz 2002; Byrne, Noll and Vedsted-Hansen 2002, p. 383-391; Bouteillet-Paquet 2003; Legomsky 2003; Human Rights Watch 2005b.

This identification is inaccurate, and prevents a clear understanding of the impact of readmission agreements on refugee protection. Safe third country policies are unilateral measures under national law. Readmission agreements are treaties under general international law. Each has a different function in the expulsion of protection seekers to third countries, and each stands in a different relation to international obligations of refugee protection. We will return to these points in more detail later, in section 9.3.2.1.

Disregarding for a moment the general identification of protection issues resulting from readmission agreements with those raised by safe third country policies, specific concerns, which the literature constantly points to, regard the lack of refugee protection safeguards in the text of readmission agreements. In particular, commentators have objected to the lack of the following safeguards: an obligation to notify the requested State that a readmittee is a protection seeker, an explicit reference to the principle of non-refoulement, and an obligation to determine the status of readmitted protection seekers.[28] We recall that such safeguards are not included in Community readmission agreements, either.

Prior notification of the fact that a readmittee is a protection seeker, whose claim has not been rejected on substantive grounds, can be an important protection safeguard. It prevents the requested State from assuming that the person in question was rejected on substantive grounds, consequently finding the claim unfounded, and expelling him or her onwards without regard for the prohibition of refoulement.

Another arguable safeguard is an explicit reference to respect for the refoulement prohibitions under international law. Contemporary readmission agreements, including those of the Community, often contain an indirect reference in the form of a non-affection clause[29] – a provision determining the precedence of certain international conventions, such as the GC and ECHR, in case of conflict. Non-affection clauses have however been criticised as insufficient safeguards against refoulement.[30]

An obligation on the part of the requested State to determine the refugee status of readmitted protection seekers, who are rejected by the Member States on safe third country grounds, is certainly an important protection safeguard. It would prevent the possibility of continuous onward expulsion of a protection seeker between countries, without substantive examination of the protection claim anywhere, and the risk of eventual refoulement.

In sum, we have identified general concerns, and specific concerns relating directly to readmission agreements in the context of international refugee protection, which also regard Community readmission agreements. General concerns are the fact

28 UNHCR 1994, p. 3; ECRE 1995, para. 19-25, 52-53; Kumin 1995, p. 3-6; Marx 1995, p. 386, 395-397, 403-406; Noll 1997, p. 422; Abell 1999, p. 66; Landgren 1999, p. 22-29; Lavenex 1999, p. 77-78, 94; Noll 1997, p. 422-423; Noll 2000, p. 209-210; Crosland and Morrison 2001, p. 36-38; van Selm 2001, p. 32-34, 58-59; Hurwitz 2002, p. 5-6; Byrne, Noll and Vedsted-Hansen 2002, p. 383-391; Bouteillet-Paquet 2003, p. 368; Legomsky 2003, p. 583-586, 630-633, 654-655; Human Rights Watch 2005b, p. 8-18, 72.

29 *Supra*, subsection 5.3.9.

30 Lavenex 1999, p. 94; Hurwitz 2002, p. 5-6; Legomsky 2003, p. 583.

that protection seekers and refugees are readmitted as unauthorised immigrants, and the fact that readmission agreements are concluded with countries, without regard for their general safety for protection seekers and refugees. Specific concerns concentrate on the expulsion of protection seekers to third countries, and the lack of safeguards of refugee protection in readmission agreements, which facilitate such expulsion. We will revisit these concerns, and consider whether they indeed raise issues under international refugee law, in section 9.3. Before doing so, section 9.2 will first identify a series of international obligations relevant to the expulsion of protection seekers to third countries.

## 9.2 International protection obligations regarding expulsion to third countries

The previous section found that readmission agreements have raised concerns of refugee protection, specifically with regard to the expulsion of protection seekers to third countries. Further examination of these concerns in relation to the common readmission policy requires identification of the relevant international law. This section identifies a series of international obligations of refugee protection, which apply to the practice of expulsion of protection seekers to third countries. These are minimum standards of international law that restrict Member State sovereignty and discretion in this practice, roughly dividing into two categories – conditions for safe return and procedural requirements.

International law lays down conditions, according to which it must be determined whether a third country is safe for an individual protection seeker before allowing expulsion to that country. International law also imposes procedural requirements with which decisions to expel a protection seeker to a third country must comply.

This section draws a mixture of conditions for safe return and procedural requirements from several international conventions. The identification and analysis of conditions of safe return, in particular, is based on a general principle. The first subsection outlines this general principle, together with an explanation of the selection of treaty provisions for analysis.

### *9.2.1 General principle and demarcation of the analysis*

#### 9.2.1.1 General principle of analysis

The identification and analysis of international law obligations, laying down conditions for safe return to a third country, in this section is based on the following general principle:

The conditions by which to determine the safety of a third country are delimited by the international obligations, which a State holds towards protection seekers remaining on its territory.

Arguably, an expulsion to a third country cannot create obligations, which are more far-reaching than the international minimum obligations a State holds towards protection seekers, whom it would (hypothetically) not expel and allow to remain within its jurisdiction. In other words, under relevant international law, the conditions required to be present in a third country cannot be more favourable for protection seekers than the conditions required to be present in the country of destination.

According to this general principle, for example, food and shelter in a third country could only be a condition for safe return to that country, insofar as providing food and shelter is an international obligation of States regarding protection seekers who claim protection on their territory. If States are not obliged under international law to provide protection seekers, who claim protection and remain on their territory, with food and shelter, then this cannot be a condition, determining the safety of, and therewith the legality of expulsion to, a third country.

It should be emphasised that this general principle acts only as a ceiling for the identification of conditions for safe return under international law. It posits that international law is precluded from requiring safety conditions in a third country, which are *more* favourable for protection seekers than conditions in the country where they claimed protection. It does not mean to imply that conditions in a third country, which are *less* favourable for protection seekers, would necessarily always prohibit expulsion. Deriving any general rule to this effect from international law does not appear possible.[31] According to such a rule, the international obligations of a destination State would be normative for the level of protection in a third country required to allow expulsion there, regardless of the international obligations to which the third country subscribes. This would in effect constitute a right for protection seekers to choose, as their destination, States that adhere to the highest level of protection under international law. It is generally accepted that a right of choice of destination State for refugees does not exist.[32]

#### 9.2.1.2 Demarcation of the analysis

International obligations relevant to the expulsion of protection seekers to third countries generally follow from explicit or implicit prohibitions of refoulement. The term refoulement is derived from the word *refouler*, the literal meaning of which is to drive back, repel, or "reconduct".[33] Prohibitions of refoulement preclude the expulsion[34] of a person to a country where s/he would be exposed to a specifically defined risk. Refoulement prohibitions define the outer limits of international refugee protection, and are therefore the primary yardstick for testing the boundaries of asylum policy.

This chapter interprets the term refoulement broadly, covering not only relevant provisions of the Geneva Refugee Convention,[35] but also provisions of international

31 Contrary to occasional claims in the literature, which we will address below, in subsection 9.2.2.3.

32 On a right of choice, see *inter alia* Hathaway 1991, p. 46-47; Vedsted-Hansen 1999, p. 276-279, 284-287; Legomsky 2003, p. 613.

33 Robinson 1953, p. 162.

34 Interchangeably with the term expulsion, we will also use the terms transfer and removal, all of which seek to move a person from the jurisdiction of one State to that of another.

35 Convention Relating to the Status of Refugees, adopted by the United Nations Conference of Plenipotentiaries on the Status of Refugees and Stateless Persons on 28 July 1951

fundamental rights law with the potential of blocking the expulsion of a protection seeker. The objective is not to provide an exhaustive discussion of prohibitions of refoulement under international law. The analysis is limited to refoulement prohibitions with a particular relevance to the expulsion of protection seekers from EC Member States to third countries. Hence, we discuss provisions of the GC, and of the European Convention for the protection of human rights and fundamental freedoms.[36] This excludes a number of prohibitions of refoulement under international law, as clarified in the following outline.

The Cartagena Declaration on Refugees[37] and the OAU Convention[38] contain explicit prohibitions of refoulement, which fall outside the scope of this research while not concerning obligations of the EC Member States. Furthermore, the prohibition of torture or cruel, inhuman or degrading treatment or punishment in Article 7 of the International Covenant of civil and political rights (ICCPR) is not discussed.[39] The application of this implicit prohibition of refoulement depends on stricter criteria, and therefore heavier burden of proof, than required for blocking expulsion under the ECHR.[40] Article 3 of the Convention against torture and other cruel, inhuman or degrading treatment or punishment[41] (CAT) is disregarded for similar reasons. The value of this prohibition of refoulement for European expulsion practice has recently diminished in comparison with protection under the ECHR.[42]

---

(hereinafter referred to as the Geneva refugee Convention, or with the acronym GC). All references are to the Geneva refugee Convention as modified by the Protocol relating to the status of refugees of 31 January 1967.

36 European Convention for the Protection of Human Rights and Fundamental Freedoms, Council of Europe, 4 November 1950 (hereinafter European Convention, or ECHR).

37 Adopted at the *Coloquio Sobre la Proteccíon Internacional de los Refugiados en Amérićan Central, México y Panamá: Problemas Jurídicos y Humanitarios*, Cartagena, Colombia, 19-22 November 1984.

38 Organisation of African Unity Convention governing the specific aspects of refugee problems in Africa, adopted by the Assembly of Heads of State and Government on 10 September 1969.

39 International Covenant of Civil and Political Rights, adopted by the General Assembly of the United Nations on 19 December 1966 (hereinafter ICCPR).

40 Vermeulen 1999, p. 175-176; Zwaan 2003, p. 40, n. 155; Spijkerboer and Vermeulen 2005, p. 67-68.

41 Convention against Torture and Other Cruel, Inhuman or Degrading Treatment or Punishment, adopted by the General Assembly of the United Nations on 10 December 1984 (hereinafter Convention against Torture, or CAT).

42 Recent case law of the Committee Against Torture has approximated the, previously less strict, criteria for protection against expulsion under Article 3 CAT, to the criteria for protection used by the European Court of Human Rights under Article 3 ECHR (Vermeulen 1999, p. 189, 195; Spijkerboer and Vermeulen 2005, p. 87). The European Court under Article 3 ECHR now requires examination of the situation in the country of origin before expelling a protection seeker to a third country, previously a unique requirement of the Committee Against Torture (Zwaan 2003, p. 42-43, 49; Spijkerboer and Vermeulen 2005,

As will be explained further below, the prohibition of inhuman or degrading treatment or punishment in Article 3 ECHR can forbid expulsion of a protection seeker. Article 16 CAT also prohibits acts of cruel, inhuman or degrading treatment or punishment, but has to date not been accepted as an implicit prohibition of refoulement, and is therefore excluded. Considering that the drafters of the CAT in Article 3 decided to explicitly prohibit refoulement in case of torture, only, it is moreover questionable that the CAT would allow interpretation of Article 16 as such.[43]

Furthermore disregarded are a number of provisions of the European Convention of Human Rights. Article 2 ECHR is recognised as prohibiting the return of a person to a country where there is a risk of being subjected to the death penalty, or which would result in shortening a person's life expectancy. The provision is rarely applied while overlapping with Article 3 of the European Convention, which has a lower burden of proof.[44] Article 6 ECHR could potentially bar expulsion in case of a "flagrant denial" of a fair trial in the receiving country.[45] This provision is however of limited meaning to the protection of refugees,[46] and yet to be successfully invoked before the European Court of Human Rights as prohibiting expulsion.

Another deliberate omission is Article 8 ECHR. The right to respect for family life, as contained in this provision, has evolved into an important tool for challenging the removal of immigrants.[47] A refugee may indeed have family life in a destination country, or gain family life whilst undergoing an asylum procedure. If s/he can not enjoy

---

p. 95). Article 3 ECHR has a wider field of application than 3 CAT, which does not include inhuman or degrading treatment or punishment in its prohibitive scope, nor acts by non-State actors. A final reason for excluding consideration of Article 3 CAT is that the ECHR has a stronger enforcement mechanism. The legally binding nature of judgements of the European Court of Human Rights is clear, unlike those of the Committee Against Torture. Individual complaints procedures, moreover, indicate that the Committee Against Torture is increasingly less assertive in requiring protection standards, which supplement protection at the national level (Vermeulen 1999, p. 195-196; Spijkerboer and Vermeulen 2005, p. 87).

43 Steenbergen, Spijkerboer, Vermeulen en Fernhout 1999, p. 166-167.

44 Steendijk 2001, p. 185. Steenbergen, Spijkerboer, Vermeulen en Fernhout 1999, p. 174-175. Dugard and Wyngaert 1998, p. 196-197, 199.

45 Soering v. United Kingdom, 7 July 1989, Series A, 161, para. 113; Drozd and Janousek v. France and Spain, 240 26 June 1992, Eur.Ct.H.R., ser. A, para. 110.

46 Article 6 applies only to exceptional cases, namely to refugees who would be involved in a judicial procedure concerning "the determination of [...] civil rights and obligations or any criminal charge [...]", either in the destination State, or in a country to which expulsion has been ordered. Moreover, involvement in a criminal procedure in another country would imply use of the extradition process, thus not involving expulsion or the application of a readmission agreement.

47 Berrehab v. The Netherlands, judgement, 21 June 1988, Series A, 138. On Article 8 and expulsion, see *inter alia* Battjes 2006, p. 469-474. The right to respect for private life, also enshrined in Article 8, is arguably also acquiring the potential to prohibit expulsion, in particular where this would involve "sufficiently adverse affects on physical and moral

this family life elsewhere – in the country of origin, or, possibly, a third country – s/he may prevent expulsion by claiming protection under Article 8 ECHR. Claims to Article 8 ECHR, however, do not relate specifically to international refugee law, and are not of particular relevance to the expulsion of protection seekers to third countries.

Excluded, finally, are several provisions of the Charter of Fundamental Rights of the European Union.[48] Article 4 of the Charter (a literal copy of Article 3 ECHR) is an implicit prohibition of refoulement. This is further confirmed by Article 19(2), which reflects case law of the European Court of Human Rights, recognising Article 3 ECHR as an implicit prohibition of refoulement. Due to the reproductive character of these provisions, they will not be addressed separately.

The following subsections 9.2.2 and 9.2.3 thus pertain exclusively to the Geneva Refugee Convention and the European Convention of human rights. These conventions are discussed separately, according to the particular issues each raises in relation to the expulsion of protection seekers to third countries. There is a degree of overlap in these issues. Thus, both subsections discuss at least the prohibition of indirect refoulement, the right to status determination, the right to residence, other conditions for safe return additional to the prohibition of refoulement, and the extraterritorial applicability of the prohibition of refoulement.

### *9.2.2 The 1951 Convention relating to the status of refugees*

The relevant provisions of the Geneva refugee Convention are the refugee definition in Article 1(A)(2) and the principle of non-refoulement in Article 33(1).

The relevant part of Article 1(A)(2) GC reads:

> For the purposes of the present Convention, the term "refugee" shall apply to any person who [...] owing to well-founded fear of being persecuted for reasons of race, religion, nationality, membership of a particular social group or political opinion, is outside the country of his nationality and unable or, owing to such fear, is unwilling to avail himself of the protection of that country [...].

Article 33(1) GC reads:

> No Contracting State shall expel or return ("refouler") a refugee in any manner whatsoever to the frontiers of territories where his life or freedom would be threatened on

integrity" (Bensaid v. the United Kingdom, 6 February 2001, 33 EHRR 10, para. 46), but is yet to do so.

48 Charter of Fundamental Rights of the European Union, signed and proclaimed by the Presidents of the European Parliament, the Council and the Commission on 7 December 2000, *OJ* 2000/C 364/0118, 18 December 2000. The days of the Charter as a (formally) non-binding instrument appear numbered, although linked to the uncertain fate of the draft Treaty establishing the Constitution of the European Union. The provisions of the Charter have been incorporated as Part II of the Constitutional Treaty, which still awaits ratification by the Member States at the time of writing.

> account of his race, religion, nationality, membership of a particular social group or political opinion.

Based on these provisions, subsection 9.2.2.1 considers whether the Geneva Refugee Convention prohibits also *indirect* refoulement, such as might result from expulsion to a third country. Subsection 9.2.2.2 determines whether the GC contains a duty to undertake status determination, and a right to residence for refugees, as relevant to expulsion to third countries. Subsection 9.2.2.3 considers possible conditions for safe return to a third country, additional to the principle of non-refoulement, which might follow from the GC. Subsection 9.2.2.4, finally, determines the extraterritorial applicability of Article 33(1) GC.

#### 9.2.2.1 Indirect refoulement

Interpreting the principle of non-refoulement as covering also *indirect* refoulement is undisputed, which means we can be brief. The prohibition of refoulement of Article 33(1) GC is defined by a result, which is that a refugee would end up at the frontiers of any country – country of origin or third country – where he or she would be under threat to life or liberty because of race, religion, nationality, membership of a particular social group, or political opinion.[49] The manner in which this result comes about is irrelevant ("in any manner whatsoever"), as long as pertaining to a State action amounting to "expulsion", "return" or "refoulement".[50] Article 33(1) GC thus equally prohibits an expulsion to a third country, in which territory there is no threat to life or liberty, but which would send the refugee onwards to a country where there is. This reading follows from the ordinary meaning of the phrase "in any manner whatsoever", and is confirmed by the *travaux préparatoires*.[51]

If a State decides to expel a protection seeker to a third country instead of the country of origin, it is therefore in principle under duty to examine whether this could not result in refoulement. One way of complying with this duty would be to undertake status determination, implying a substantive examination of the protection claim in relation to the country of origin. Whether this could be considered an obligation under the GC is the subject of the next subsection. Another way of determining whether there is a risk of indirect refoulement would be to examine the "safety" of the protection seeker in the third country, in particular the protection s/he would receive there against refoulement. This is a procedural requirement, and the relevant minimum obligation following from Article 33(1) GC regarding expulsion to third countries.

This obligation is without prejudice to the fact that States, in practice, might forego a safety examination in an individual case, where concerning a third country that is party to the GC. The GC does not in general prevent its State parties from relying on the principle of interstate trust in this manner.

49 Zwaan 2003, p. 28.

50 *Supra*, at n. 33.

51 Zwaan 2003, p. 19-20; Spijkerboer and Vermeulen 2005, p. 92. See also Hathaway 2005, p. 322-323.

### 9.2.2.2 Status determination and right to residence

The Geneva Refugee Convention does not stipulate that States must determine the status of persons claiming international protection,[52] nor does it specify any procedures to this end. Whether the GC, nevertheless, would oblige State parties to determine the refugee status of persons claiming protection within their jurisdiction is still a somewhat contested issue in the literature. Current State practice, in any case, does not support such an obligation.

The personal scope of Article 33(1) includes persons recognised as refugees within the meaning of Article 1(A)(2) GC, but also protection seekers – those whose status has not (yet) been determined. It is widely accepted that the status of refugee is of a declaratory nature, and that recognition as a refugee has no constitutive effect.[53] A person is a refugee the moment s/he satisfies the criteria of Article 1(A), which occurs when crossing the border of a country of persecution into the jurisdiction of another State.[54] The duty to provide international protection pursuant to the GC arises when this person arrives at the border[55] of a State party of the GC. A protection seeker is covered by the terms of Article 33(1) *as if* a refugee[56] until a determination of his status would discredit this claim, enjoying what may be considered "presumptive"[57] or "*prima facie*"[58] refugee status.

Were this any different, the Geneva Refugee Convention would lose practical meaning. If formal recognition would be constitutive of the status of refugee, State parties would be able to circumvent the principle of non-refoulement (and the further application of the GC) by simply refusing to consider the merits of a protection claim. Protecting also claimants under Article 33(1) GC is the only way to ensure the effectiveness of this provision.[59]

---

52 A duty to undertake status determination is often considered the counterpart of a right to *seek* asylum, as included in Article 14 Universal Declaration of Human Rights (UDHR) (right to seek and enjoy asylum), Zwaan 2003, p. 15-16; Vedsted-Hansen 1999, p. 275. The UDHR is not a binding instrument. Aside that fact, it should be mentioned that Article 14 has been interpreted, arguably correctly, as limited to a right to *apply* for protection; not entailing a right to receive a decision on a protection claim in a country of one's choosing, Legomsky 2003, p. 613.

53 UNHCR Handbook, para. 28; Grahl-Madsen 1966, p. 340-341; Goodwin-Gill 1996, p. 32, 141; Vedsted-Hansen 1999, p. 275; Hathaway 2003, p. 2; Hathaway 2005, p. 11.

54 A person can also fulfil the criteria of Article 1(A) by declaring to be unable to return to the country of origin for fear of being persecuted, while already abroad (refugee *sur place*), Grahl-Madsen 1966, p. 157-158; Goodwin-Gill 1996, p. 141.

55 Regarding the application of the prohibition of refoulement at the border, see subsection 9.2.2.4.

56 Spijkerboer and Vermeulen 1999, p. 276, 284.

57 Vedsted-Hansen 1999, p. 275.

58 Grahl-Madsen 1972, p. 224.

59 Spijkerboer and Vermeulen 2005, p. 70; Battjes 2006, p. 460-461.

The fact that protection seekers fall within the ambit of Article 33(1) GC has invited commentators to deduce a State obligation to determine the status of protection seekers. The most common argument is that a State could not be sure that it is not committing refoulement by sending a protection seeker back, until determination of his or her status would discredit the protection claim, implying a duty to determine the status of protection seekers.[60] It has also been argued that compliance in good faith with this obligation would entail a further positive obligation of State parties to the GC, namely to provide procedures and facilities for the processing of protection claims.[61]

Such a broad interpretation of Article 33(1) GC in combination with the declaratory nature of refugee status is unwarranted.[62] The prohibition of refoulement of Article 33(1) GC requires a State to examine the merits of a protection claim *only* if it would wish to expel the claimant without being restricted by the GC. States have two further options that are both compatible with Article 33(1). One is to allow stay on their territory without status determination, either informally,[63] or by granting some form of residence title at their discretion. Another is to expel to an eligible third country, *i.e.* one that would not in turn commit refoulement. In other words, claiming refugee-hood in a country does not imply that such a claim must be decided or even examined on its merits there. Consequently, the GC cannot be considered to oblige States to have the administrative and technical capacity to implement refugee determination procedures. Status determination under the Geneva Refugee Convention is a discretionary choice, although it is a practical necessity if a State wishes to avoid the presence on its territory of all persons who claim protection and cannot be removed to a third country.

The *Travaux Préparatoires* confirm that the Geneva Refugee Convention does not imply a positive obligation to determine the status of refugees. The drafters intended to secure the highest possible amount of signatories in order to optimise the effectiveness of the Convention. This called for a restrictive attitude regarding the inclusion of binding State obligations. The emphasis of the GC came to rest on granting protection against refoulement. The drafters not only omitted a right to asylum, but also a duty to undertake status determination.[64]

In a similar vein, should a protection seeker secure access to a refugee determination procedure, and be recognised as a refugee within the definition of Article 1(A) GC, this does not automatically translate to *admission* as a refugee. The GC does not guarantee refugees an entitlement to residence, nor does it contain an obligation to assess whether a refugee would qualify for residence. These are thus questions of national

60 In this vein, Vedsted-Hansen 1999, p. 275-276. For a related argument, following from a broad understanding of "protection", see Meijers, cited in Spijkerboer and Vermeulen 1999, p. 274. See also Battjes 2006, p. 466-469.

61 Marx 1995, p. 401; Spijkerboer and Vermeulen 2005, p. 70.

62 Spijkerboer and Vermeulen 1999, p. 276, 283-284; Zwaan 2003, p. 14-22.

63 Grahl-Madsen has pointed to the advantages of the possibility of informal stay. A minimum of binding obligations is likely to stimulate the hospitality of States, increasing the chances of protection seekers receiving "asylum", Grahl-Madsen 1980, p. 55-56.

64 Zwaan 2003, p. 15-16.

law, left to the jurisdiction of the State parties. This often translates into a procedural distinction between recognition and admission, the latter being constitutive in nature and requiring an additional decision by the state.[65]

We can thus conclude that undertaking status determination, and granting a formal title of residence, are not obligations under the Geneva refugee Convention. With regard to the expulsion of protection seekers to third countries, this means, firstly, that expulsion may take place without prior substantive examination of the protection claim. Secondly, in conformity with the general principle presented in subsection 9.2.1.1, whether a third country will undertake status determination, or grant the protection seeker a right of residence, does not determine the legality of expulsion to that country. Thirdly, considering that the GC allows a destination State to expel a protection seeker to a third country, the possibility of onward expulsion to another third country – a "fourth" country – does not *prima facie* determine the legality of expulsion, either.

In other words, as long as States respect the prohibition of direct and indirect refoulement, the Geneva Refugee Convention does not prevent the continuous expulsion of a protection seeker from one country to another. From this perspective, the declaratory nature of refugee status is a mixed blessing. It safeguards international refugee protection, preventing State parties from circumventing the applicability of the GC. But it also allows State parties to disconnect the treatment of a protection seeker from the reasons of flight. Protection seekers may be subjected to a chain of expulsions, treated as if a refugee for the purposes of Article 33(1) GC by every State, but without consideration of the merits of the protection claim anywhere.[66] This may result in a situation of protracted uncertainty, where a protection seeker is unable to attain stable residence outside the country of origin.

#### 9.2.2.3 Additional standards drawn from the GC

The Executive Committee of the UNHCR, several commentators, and national judicial authorities suggest that the GC contains conditions for the expulsion of protection seekers to third countries, which go beyond mere adherence to the prohibition of (indirect) refoulement. The primary question addressed in this subsection is whether the minimum obligation under the GC to treat a protection seeker *as if* a refugee[67] implies any further obligations, in addition to the obligation not to *refoule*.

65 Spijkerboer en Vermeulen 1999, p. 212-214. For clarification, this does not imply that entitlement to the rights contained in the GC, in addition to non-refoulement, always depends on a (further) decision of national law. The GC affords certain rights to refugees independent of admission, although some of its provisions do presuppose a form of admission in order to be claimed effectively, Goodwin-Gill 1996, p. 307-311; Hathaway 2003, p. 3; Zwaan 2003, p. 14-15.

66 We will see below that in the context of the European Convention of Human Rights, a degree of consideration of the substance of the claim is required when expelling to a third country, *infra*, subsection 9.2.3.5.

67 *Supra*, subsection 9.2.2.2, at n. 56.

With a view to the general principle of analysis presented in subsection 9.2.1.1, we will test the additional standards for expulsion to third countries, as suggested by the above sources, against the international obligations held towards protection seekers, whom, hypothetically, a destination State would allow to remain within its jurisdiction. To this end, subsection 9.2.2.3.1 examines possible obligations following from provisions of the GC, other than Article 33(1) GC. Subsection 9.2.2.3.2 examines whether additional obligations towards protection seeker follow from Article 33(1) itself, implicitly.

*9.2.2.3.1 Additional GC standards*

We start with relevant expressions of the Executive Committee of the UNHCR (EXCOM). One of the tasks of the EXCOM is to adopt conclusions on international protection, which contain guidelines and recommendations for the protection of refugees. EXCOM conclusions are not binding on the State parties to the Geneva Refugee Convention, but may provide an authoritative interpretation thereof. Considering the rules of treaty interpretation, EXCOM Conclusions arguably form part of the context of the GC.[68]

EXCOM Conclusion No. 85 (1998) is relevant to the expulsion of protection seekers to third countries without consideration of the substance of their protection claim.[69] In this conclusion, the EXCOM stresses that the destination country should first establish that a third country would ensure effective protection against refoulement, provide a possibility to enjoy and seek asylum, and treat the asylum seeker in accordance with "accepted international standards".[70] The EXCOM has not specified what these "accepted international standards" may be, nor from which source they would derive. Similar expressions can be found in EXCOM Conclusion No. 58 ("basic human standards") regarding the specific question of expulsion of protection seekers to third countries where they had already found protection,[71] and EXCOM Conclusion No. 22 ("minimum basic human standards") on mass influx.[72]

68 As specified, most notably, in Article 31(2)(b) of the Vienna Convention on the law of treaties.

69 Executive Committee Conclusion No. 85 (XLIX) 1998, "Conclusion on international protection".

70 EXCOM Conclusion No. 85 (1998), para. (aa), see also *supra*, subsection 9.1, at n. 19.

71 Executive Committee Conclusion No. 58 (XL) 1989, "Problem of refugees and asylum-seekers who move in an irregular manner from a country in which they had already found protection".

72 Executive Committee Conclusion No. 22 (XXXII) 1981, "Protection of asylum-seekers in situations of large-scale influx". This Conclusion provides a long and detailed list of "minimum basic human standards", which Fernhout and Meijers posit as an indicator also of the "basic human standards" mentioned in Conclusion No. 58 (cited in Spijkerboer and Vermeulen 1999, p. 230). Conclusion No. 22 is thus understood to reflect the EXCOM's general understanding of references of this kind. This transposition is difficult to follow. It equates conditions, allowing expulsion to third countries by destination States, with

Several commentators have latched on to these EXCOM dicta and attempted to provide them with a legal underpinning. Legomsky takes a very broad approach to identifying requirements for the transfer of protection seekers to third countries, including standards of treatment derived from the GC.[73] Spijkerboer and Vermeulen also argue that the GC is a source of additional standards for expulsion to safe third countries, borrowing heavily from (other) fundamental rights law standards.[74]

Legomsky proposes introducing a so-called "complicity principle" of general application.[75] According to this principle, expulsion of a protection seeker is illegal if it takes place to a third country, which would violate any international norm of refugee protection to which the destination State is bound. The underlying argument is that destination States should retain full responsibility for persons claiming protection within their jurisdiction, preventing them from being able to violate norms, to which they are bound by international law, *via* a third country.

The word "complicity" has been used before to characterise the prohibition of indirect refoulement.[76] Legomsky's argument extends beyond the principle of non-refoulement. It widens the number of applicable norms, which must be respected in a third country in order to allow expulsion there, to include all relevant international obligations adhered to by a destination State. Indeed, this proposal would amount to the inverse of the general principle of analysis of this chapter. It would prohibit any lowering of protection standards resulting from expulsion to a third country, the level of protection as assumed by a destination State being normative.

We earlier disregarded such a proposition, while it would constitute a right for protection seekers to choose a destination State, contrary to the general understanding that international law does not provide such a right.[77] In addition, the legal underpinning of the purported complicity principle is flawed. Legomsky argues that Article 16 of the draft Articles on state responsibility[78] provides the legal basis for the complicity principle.[79] Article 16 is entitled "Aid or assistance in the commission of an internationally wrongful act", and reads:

> A State which aids or assists another State in the commission of an internationally wrongful act by the latter is internationally responsible for doing so if:

---

requirements incumbent on a country when faced with a mass influx of refugees, for which there is no apparent basis.

73 Legomsky 2003.

74 Spijkerboer and Vermeulen 1999, p. 231.

75 Legomsky 2003, p. 620-626, 639-645.

76 Spijkerboer and Vermeulen 1999, p. 189; and Steenbergen, Spijkerboer, Vermeulen and Fernhout 1999, p. 166.

77 *Supra*, subsection 9.2.1.1, at n. 31.

78 Draft articles on Responsibility of States for internationally wrongful acts, endorsed by UNGA Resolution 56/83, 12 December 2002.

79 Legomsky 2003, p. 620-626.

(a) That State does so with knowledge of the circumstances of the internationally wrongful act; and
(b) The act would be internationally wrongful if committed by that State.

The ordinary meaning of the verbs "to aid" or "to assist" already suggests that this provision requires an active participating role by one State in the commission of an internationally wrongful act by another. This interpretation is strengthened by the requirement that a State must aid or assist "with knowledge of the circumstances of the internationally wrongful act". In my view, this would generally exclude responsibility under Article 16 of States which expel a protection seeker to a third country, leading to subsequent violation of, for example, the principle of non-refoulement in Article 33(1) of the Geneva Refugee Convention. Article 16 requires bad faith, if not intent, on the part of an expelling State, which, one may reasonably assume, will normally not be present. The commentary of Article 16 unequivocally confirms that the ILC drafted this provision with States of (at least) bad faith in mind.[80]

Spijkerboer and Vermeulen hold that although the GC does not require third countries to comply with *all* the standards of treatment it contains before allowing the expulsion of a protection seeker, the GC does imply that conditions in the third country must reflect a minimum level of human rights guarantees. This minimum level is determined, firstly, by full respect for the principle of non-refoulement. Secondly, it is determined by respect for other rights following from the GC, but only to the extent that these would not be "flagrantly violated" in the third country.[81]

The criterion of a flagrant violation (or, rather, "flagrant denial"[82]) originates from the context of the European Convention of Human Rights. In order to prohibit expulsion, this criterion requires a higher level of severity for the threatening violation of European Convention rights in a third country, which are of less acute importance to the protection of physical and mental integrity.[83] More than a mere violation of

80 The ILC *inter alia* comments that Article 16 "deals with cases where one State provides aid or assistance to another State *with a view to* assisting in the commission of a wrongful act by the latter". On several counts it speaks of "*willing assistance*", and mentions furthermore that a State must have "*intended*, by the aid or assistance given, to facilitate the occurrence of the wrongful conduct". Finally, regarding the violation of human rights, specifically, the ILC states that "where the allegation is that the assistance of a State has facilitated human rights abuses by another State, the particular circumstances of each case must be carefully examined to determine whether the aiding State by its aid *was aware of and intended* to facilitate the commission of the internationally wrongful conduct". See the ILC Commentaries to the draft Articles on State responsibility, p. 155-159. [Italics, added, NC] Legomsky takes note of part of these comments by the ILC, but, using a convoluted and unsatisfactory interpretation, contends that Article 16 would not as a result require bad faith or intent on part of an expelling State, Legomsky 2003, p. 621-622.

81 The authors do not specify which other GC rights would be implicated.

82 *Supra*, subsection 9.2.1.2, at n. 45.

83 This construct has recently been confirmed by the UK House of Lords in R . Special Adjudicator ex parte Ullah ([2004] UKHL 26, cited in Phuong 2005, p. 3), but is yet to be

such rights, the violation must be "flagrant" in order to bar expulsion. Spijkerboer and Vermeulen consider this reasoning applicable also to other fundamental rights instruments. Transposed to the context of the GC, the authors reason that this higher level of severity is not reached if the protection seeker would be able to remain in a third country in "conditions which can not be considered abnormal according to local standards", a criterion stemming from Dutch case law.[84] Although only a relative criterion,[85] it clearly broadens obligations beyond the principle of non-refoulement.

Determining whether the GC would indeed contain certain conditions for the expulsion of protection seekers to third countries in addition to the principle of non-refoulement, requires using the general principle of analysis outlined above. In particular, it should be considered which international obligations a State holds towards a protection seeker, whose claim to refugee-hood is not examined, but who is allowed to stay in compliance with Article 33(1) GC. Subsection 9.2.2.2 concluded that the minimum level of protection required by the GC is a situation of informal stay without status determination. We will now consider whether protection seekers in such a situation are owed any further rights under the GC. Following the general principle of analysis, these rights also determine the legality of expulsion of protection seekers to a third country.

Regarding the provisions of the GC applicable to protection seekers whose status is not (yet) determined, there are three certainties. The declaratory nature of refugee status does not imply that all persons who claim to be a refugee are entitled to the full package of rights afforded by the GC.[86] Only persons recognised and admitted as a refugee can effectively claim all the rights contained in the GC.[87] Articles 31 and 33 GC apply to all persons who claim to be a refugee.[88] Beyond these certainties, deter-

---

sanctioned by the European Court of Human Rights.

84 Spijkerboer and Vermeulen 1999, p. 241-243, 285-287. It should be noted that this criterion finds some support in the text of the GC. Many of the GC's provisions afford rights to refugees on a relative basis, requiring treatment, for example, as "nationals", as "most favoured aliens", or as "aliens generally".

85 The situation of the expelled protection seeker in the third country is required to be *extraordinarily* unfavourable in comparison with local conditions there (unlike Legomsky's argument outlined above, which compares with conditions in the destination country from which expulsion takes place). According to a strict application of this criterion (ignoring for a moment other applicable norms governing expulsion), a risk of starvation would thus not prevent expulsion to a third country in a perpetual state of famine, a protection seeker suffering from a fatal illness may be expelled to a third country where medical treatment for such cases is not available, and so on and so forth. From the opposite perspective, the treatment required when expelling a protection seeker to, for example, a Western European country would be high, possibly implying the provision of shelter, social benefits, access to the labour market, and family reunification (Spijkerboer and Vermeulen 1999, p. 287).

86 This is contrary to earlier views of commentators such as Grahl-Madsen 1966, p. 340. See further Vedsted-Hansen 1999, p. 275-276; and, in general, Hathaway 2003.

87 Zwaan 2003, p. 14-15.

88 Grahl-Madsen 1972, p. 224; Goodwin-Gill 1996, p. 307; Spijkerboer and Vermeulen 1999, p. 275-276; Hathaway 2003, p. 4; Battjes 2006, p. 460-464.

mining which further provisions of the GC would apply to protection seekers is a complicated and imprecise interpretative endeavour. This is largely because the text of the GC does not evolve explicitly around access to procedures, recognition, and admission as a refugee. These critical decision-making instances in the international protection of refugees are, formally speaking, strictly matters of national law. There have been attempts in the literature to identify which provisions of the GC would fit with these various stages of domestic decision-making in asylum cases.

The provisions of the Geneva Refugee Convention refer to "refugees" without qualification, or to refugees "in" or "within", refugees "lawfully in", refugees "lawfully present in", refugees "lawfully staying in", or refugees with "habitual residence" in, the territory of a State party. Goodwin-Gill divides these qualifications into categories of rights which accrue according to whether a refugee enjoys "simple presence", "lawful presence", "lawful residence", or "habitual residence".[89] Although the author does not specify, protection seekers whose status has not (yet) been determined would arguably fall into the category of "simple presence". This would encompass a rather large number of provisions in the GC, referring to "refugees" without qualification, and refugees "in" or "within" the territory of a State party.

Hathaway, similarly, views the Geneva Refugee Convention as a system of "incremental entitlement",[90] where rights accrue according to the nature and duration of the attachment to the destination State. The lowest level of attachment and associated rights is attained as soon as a refugee comes within the jurisdiction of a destination State. Hathaway assigns to all such persons at least a number of "core rights" under the GC,[91] which amount to the same sizeable basket of GC provisions in Goodwin-Gill's category of "simple presence".[92]

Building upon Hathaway's system of incremental entitlement, Battjes reviews the provisions of the GC in detail, determining *inter alia* which rights belong to refugees independent of status determination. He finds that Articles 31 and 33 include protection seekers, and that Articles 1C, 5, 28, 32, and 34 pertain only to recognised refugees. The remaining provisions of the GC do not indicate clearly whether they would pertain to either protection seekers, recognised refugees, or both.[93] Battjes, however, argues that reading these provisions in conjunction with Article 1(A)(2), as well as the object and

89 Goodwin-Gill 1996, p. 307-311.

90 Hathaway 2003, p. 2; Hathaway 2005, p. 154 *et seq*.

91 Accordingly, Hathaway argues that refugees should "not be stripped of the rights which they have already acquired" in case of expulsion to a third country, positing these core rights as conditions determining the safety of a third country, Hathaway 2005, p. 329-333. This argument is similar to that of Legomsky, discussed above (*supra*, at n. 75-80),which we do not follow while constituting a right for protection seekers to choose a destination State, contrary to the general understanding that international law does not provide such a right.

92 Hathaway 2003, p. 2-4, 10. As applicable GC provisions, Hathaway mentions Articles 3, 4, 12, 13, 16(1), 20, 22, 25, 27, 29, 31 and 33(1). See also Hathaway 2005, p. 154 *et seq*.

93 Battjes 2006, 460-464, 469.

purpose of the GC,[94] implies that they pertain to persons claiming protection, regardless of recognition as a refugee.[95]

The above authors thus have a broad understanding of the declaratory nature of refugee status, and consider that treating a protection seeker *as if* a refugee goes much further than non-refoulement. Pending status determination, which we recall is not an obligation following from the GC,[96] protection seekers would have such rights as afforded under the GC to acquire property (Article 13), and engage in gainful employment (Articles 17-19), as well as rights to housing (Article 21), education (Article 22), public assistance, and social security (Articles 23-24).

Although in first instance strengthening the rights of individual refugees, one may question whether international refugee protection would ultimately benefit from such a broad reading of the GC. One could argue that a generous basket of provisional rights for protection seekers would stimulate destination States to undertake status determination. This implies an increase in procedural costs, however, which States would be reluctant to incur. Destination States would furthermore be concerned that guaranteed rights to employment, housing, social benefits, and so on, would have a significant "pull" effect. Awarding such rights to protection claimants is therefore more likely to redouble efforts to expel claimants to third countries, and establish cooperation with third countries to ensure interception *en route*. Additionally, increasing the cost of membership to the GC would arguably stimulate States with limited resources to withdraw from it, and strengthen calls to replace the GC altogether with a contemporary instrument more accommodating of State discretion.

Current State practice does not generally support a broad reading of the declaratory nature of refugee status, at least not to the degree suggested above. Moreover, guaranteeing protection seekers (costly) economic and social rights is arguably not in accordance with the intention of the drafters of the GC. The fact that the GC is not explicit on the rights it affords to claimants calls for consideration of the drafting history.[97] So do the potentially unreasonable consequences of the arguments of the above authors, which would impose far-reaching obligations on State parties of the GC.[98]

Rather than focusing on the object and purpose of the GC as derived from the very general and generous language of the Preamble, one should arguably stay closer to the *travaux préparatoires*, and the intention of the drafters. As noted earlier, the *travaux* indicate that the drafters chose to limit hard obligations under the GC to non-refoulement.[99] This choice was made in order to secure the highest possible number of signa-

94 Based on the Preamble of the GC, the object and purpose of the Convention may be considered to be "the protection of refugees and the widest possible assurance of their fundamental rights and freedoms", Goodwin-Gill 1996, p. 367. See further Battjes 2006, p. 459-460.

95 Battjes 2006, p. 448-469.

96 *Supra*, subsection 9.2.2.2.

97 Vienna Convention on the law of treaties, Article 32(a).

98 Vienna Convention on the law of treaties, Article 32(b).

99 *Supra*, subsection 9.2.2.2, at n. 64.

tories, and, arguably, to ensure and stimulate the willingness of States to host refugees. It is therefore arguable that the GC intends to provide immediate protection against the violation of fundamental rights in the country of origin; not to grant rights which enable the building of a new life elsewhere the moment a refugee enters the territory of another State, pending an examination of the validity of the protection claim.

In addition, even the generous language of the Preamble has its limits. Battjes holds that the Preamble favours an interpretation of the GC which secures *more* protection (a broad understanding of the declaratory nature of refugee status), as opposed to an interpretation which entails *less* protection (a narrow understanding of the declaratory nature of refugee status), of the fundamental rights of refugees.[100] Reason for this is that the object and purpose of the GC is generally understood to be reflected in the Preamble, where it states: "to assure refugees the *widest possible* exercise of [...] fundamental rights and freedoms" [Italics added, NC]. This is however not the same as aiming for the "*widest* assurance of fundamental rights and freedoms" for refugees, as this phrase appears to have been interpreted. The word "possible" allows reading an element of discretion into the hospitality expected of States under the GC. This would be especially relevant to the awarding of far-reaching rights to protection seekers such as employment, education, housing, and social security.

In the light of these two opposing arguments, those provisions of the GC which do not pertain clearly either to protection seekers or recognised refugees[101] should rather be assumed to be dependent on formal recognition of refugee status.

This leaves Article 31 GC for consideration, as the only provision in the GC clearly concerning protection seekers, in addition to Article 33 GC.[102] Article 31 prohibits penalising protection seekers for unauthorised entry or presence, as well as unnecessary free movement restrictions for such protection seekers.[103] Unlike Article 33, however, it seems that Article 31 cannot be (indirectly) violated by expulsion to a safe third country. Article 31 is limited to protection seekers coming "directly" from a country of persecution. It is generally accepted that "directly" should not be interpreted literally. A protection seeker, who travelled without undue delay through a third

100 Battjes 2006, p. 459-460.

101 *Supra*, at n. 93.

102 *Supra*, n. 59.

103 Article 31, titled "Refugees unlawfully in the country of refuge", reads:

1. The Contracting States shall not impose penalties, on account of their illegal entry or presence, on refugees who, coming directly from a territory where their life or freedom was threatened in the sense of article 1, enter or are present in their territory without authorization, provided they present themselves without delay to the authorities and show good cause for their illegal entry or presence.

2. The Contracting States shall not apply to the movements of such refugees restrictions other than those which are necessary and such restrictions shall only be applied until their status in the country is regularized or they obtain admission into another country. The Contracting States shall allow such refugees a reasonable period and all the necessary facilities to obtain admission into another country.

country where s/he could *not* find protection, also comes "directly" from a country of persecution in the meaning of Article 31.[104] Expulsion on safe third country grounds is based on the presumption that a protection seeker *could* have found protection in a third country through which s/he travelled. In case a protection seeker can be expelled under a safe third country exception, therefore, s/he did not arrive directly in the destination State, which is thus not bound by Article 31. It follows that Article 31 GC does not apply to the expulsion of protection seekers to third countries.

In sum, the question whether the Geneva Refugee Convention contains State obligations towards protection seekers, which go further than the prohibition of refoulement, is still subject to debate. Excepting Article 31 GC, which does not apply to expulsion to third countries, such additional obligations can therefore not be considered as established. Correspondingly, it is unclear whether the GC contains conditions for safe return to third countries, in addition to respect for the principle of non-refoulement. The GC is not a clear source of "accepted international standards ", or "basic human standards", as conditions for safe return to third countries, referred to by the EXCOM.

*9.2.2.3.2 Additional standards implicit in Article 33(1) GC*

The previous subsection found that it is uncertain whether standards for the expulsion of protection seekers to third countries follow from the Geneva refugee Convention, other than Article 33(1) GC. An alternative possibility would be to read additional standards into the principle of non-refoulement of Article 33(1) GC itself, exploring the extent to which the definition of (non-)refoulement may be stretched.

The UK Court of appeal took this course of interpretation in the joined cases of *Adan, Subaskaran and Aitseguer*.[105] These cases concerned transfers from the UK to Germany and France under the Dublin Convention. The issue in dispute was whether Germany and France qualified as safe third countries. Confronted with the argument that a certain form of residence under German law was below the Geneva Refugee Convention standard, the Court remarked the following:

> In our judgement the Secretary of State [...] is only concerned with the question whether there exists a real risk that the third country will refoule the putative refugee in breach of the [Geneva Refugee, NC] convention. The Secretary of State is not concerned to see that the claimant will or may enjoy the social rights to which we have referred if he is permitted to stay in the third country. We would not, however, exclude the possibility that such a claimant might in the third country be faced with so destitute an existence, if he were wholly excluded both from the right to work and from access to social provision, and possessed no other resources upon which he might call, that he would be driven to return to the country of feared persecution

104 Zwaan 2003, p. 22-29; Battjes 2006, p. 405.

105 R v Secretary of State for the Home Department, ex parte Adan; ex parte Subaskaran; ex part Aitseguer, [1999] 4 All ER 774.

> even though he had successfully claimed such rights of residence in the third country as are offered [...].[106]

Contrary to Spijkerboer and Vermeulen and the Dutch courts,[107] the UK Court of Appeal does not consider the GC a source of independent obligations for expulsion to third countries, additional to non-refoulement. Instead, the Court of Appeal adopts a broad understanding of refoulement, expanding the requirements inherent in a State's compliance with Article 33(1) GC. Otherwise, the argument is quite similar to that proffered by Spijkerboer and Vermeulen above. The level of severity of the denial by the third country of certain standards, required to prohibit expulsion (*in casu* by bringing the possibility of indirect infringement of Article 33(1) GC into focus), appears equal to that of a "flagrant denial".[108]

The basic supposition of the UK Court of Appeal that a lack of subsistence may lead a refugee to decide to return to a country of persecution, amounting to *de facto* refoulement by the destination country, has also featured in literature regarding an internal flight alternative (IFA).[109] Hathaway and Foster, in formulating conditions under which an area within the country of origin would qualify as an IFA, draw a parallel with expulsion to a third country of which a refugee bears the nationality,[110] and the applicability of the prohibition of (indirect) refoulement. They posit that:

> account would clearly need to be taken of the duty of non-refoulement. That is, an asylum State would be prohibited from denying refugee status on grounds of actual or *de facto* third (safe) state nationality if there were reason to believe that the conditions in the third State – while not themselves amounting to direct risk of being persecuted – would nonetheless force the applicant back to his country of origin, thereby indirectly exposing the individual to the risk of being persecuted.[111]

106 R v Secretary of State, ex parte Adan, Subaskaran and Aitseguer, p. 27. See also Hathaway 2005, p, 318-319, 464.

107 *Supra*, at n. 55.

108 To be "wholly excluded" from the right to work and access to social provision is arguably equal to a "flagrant denial" of those standards. Whether, in addition, a "destitute existence" (not being a relative criterion) would imply "abnormal conditions according to local standards", depends on the third country to which expulsion takes place.

109 Hathaway and Foster 2003. The premise for rejection of a protection claim due to the existence of an internal flight alternative is that a person may be exposed to persecutory risk in one part of the country of origin, but not in another. As such, the person would not fulfil the refugee definition of Article 1(A)(2) GC, while able to avail himself of the protection of the country of nationality.

110 Protection seekers who also have the nationality of another country, which is not a country of persecution, would not fulfil the definition of refugee of Article 1(A)(2), while they would be able to avail themselves of the protection of a country of nationality.

111 Hathaway and Foster 2003, p. 39. For the sake of clarity we point of out that, while this case pertains to expulsion to a country of nationality, this would make a difference to the

Because it clarifies the conditions under which a refugee may decide to return and face a risk of persecution, we will also quote Hathaway and Foster's conclusion regarding expulsion to an area constituting an IFA. The authors would arguably use the same reasoning, *mututis mutandis*, for expulsion of protection seekers to third countries:

> Where the intensity of the harms specific to the proposed site of internal protection (such as, for example, famine or sustained conflict) rises to a particularly high level, even if not amounting to a risk of persecution, an asylum-seeker may in practice feel compelled to abandon the proposed site of protection, *even if the only alternative* is return to a known risk of persecution for a Convention reason elsewhere in the country of origin.[112] [italics added, NC]

Aside the question of whether a bonafide refugee would choose persecution over economic, social (or religious) destitution,[113] there are two objections to deducing additional standards for the expulsion of protection seekers to third countries from Article 33(1) GC in this manner.

The first stems from the definition of the principle of non-refoulement. The applicability of Article 33(1) GC depends on State action. Article 33(1) is defined by the result of a refugee ending up in a country where his life or liberty is at risk. It is however only applicable to State *acts* of expulsion, return, or refoulement as the means by which that result is achieved.[114] It is questionable whether a destination State can be held accountable under Article 33(1) for the return of a protection seeker to a country where such a risk exists, but which is "voluntary" in the sense of not being implemented by a State. Such a return would arguably fall outside the terms of Article 33(1), whether occurring directly, or following expulsion to a third country.

The second objection is from the viewpoint of causality. Expulsion to a third country where conditions do not allow for basic subsistence may indeed force a protection seeker to decide not to remain there, but such does not necessarily imply return to the country of origin. The protection seeker would be free to go to any other third country that would grant admission to its territory and not commit refoulement. A causal link between expulsion to a third country with substandard living conditions,

---

terms of his or her readmission to that country under international law, or a readmission agreement. It is however irrelevant to the applicability of the principle of (direct or indirect) non-refoulement.

112 Hathaway and Foster 2003, p. 55. See also Hathaway 2005, p, 318-319, 464.

113 In the IFA context, Hathaway and Foster reject the assumption that a person would never return to a home region if he or she truly has a well-founded fear of being persecuted there. In support of this rejection, they quote the German Higher Administrative Court as stating: "[o]ne can, of course, see how it might logically be that strongly religious communities would feel compelled to risk persecution in order to return to a region of the country of origin in which they could practice their faith", Hathaway and Foster 2003, p. 40.

114 *Supra*, subsection 9.2.2.1.

and a protection seeker leaving to a country of origin, can be considered to exist only in exceptional cases.

The requirement of causality for a violation of Article 33(1) is only fulfilled if return to the country of origin would indeed be "the only alternative".[115] It effectively presupposes the expulsion of a protection seeker, who does not have the financial means to travel by air or sea, to a third country that is enclosed by the country of origin, or surrounded by countries, none of which would grant protection against refoulement. Under these circumstances, the first objection, regarding the text of Article 33(1) GC and the requirement of a State act implementing return to a country of persecution, would arguably be lifted, also.[116] The exceptional nature of these circumstances means that additional standards for the expulsion of protection seekers to third countries, as implicit in Article 33(1) GC, have little practical meaning.

A final obstacle to deriving additional standards from Article 33(1) GC itself follows from the general principle of analysis in this chapter. Accordingly, Article 33(1) GC can entail requirements for the expulsion of protection seekers to third countries only to the extent of the obligations it prescribes towards protection seekers that would remain within the jurisdiction of the destination State. The issue at hand is whether Article 33(1) GC might imply an obligation not to expel a protection seeker to a third country, where the denial of certain living standards would inevitably lead to return to the country of origin. This presupposes the existence of an obligation to provide a protection seeker, who is allowed informal stay on the territory of a destination State, with a basic level of subsistence.

The obstacle lies in the fact that, whereas non-expulsion to a third country offering substandard living conditions is a negative obligation akin to the wording of Article 33(1), providing a basic level of subsistence is a positive obligation. It entails an obligation to provide at least food and shelter, and perhaps rights to work and have access to social services. It is doubtful whether the wording, object and purpose of Article 33(1) stretch that far. Again, it would depend heavily on the circumstances, and be arguable only if the denial to provide basic subsistence would inevitably lead the protection seeker to return to a country of persecution. In other words, a general obligation to provide a protection seeker, whose status is not examined, with basic subsistence, does not follow from Article 33(1) GC. The conditions, which a destination State must ensure when allowing protection seekers informal stay on its territory in compliance with Article 33(1) GC, are thus highly limited. So are, therefore, the related additional standards for expulsion to third countries.

In sum, the Geneva Refugee Convention does not provide a conclusive basis for conditions of safe return to third countries, in addition to the principle of non-refoulement in Article 33(1). Arguably, it is not possible to derive such additional standards, either from other provisions of the GC or from Article 33(1) implicitly.

115 *Supra*, at n. 112.

116 If the decision of the protection seeker to return to the country of origin would be inevitable, such as in the circumstances described, one could argue that expulsion to a third country would amount to refoulement and thus fall within the terms of Article 33(1).

### 9.2.2.4 Extraterritorial applicability of Article 33(1) GC

The preceding subsections have established the international obligations arising from the Geneva Refugee Convention, pertaining to the expulsion of protection seekers to third countries, which centre on Article 33(1) GC. It is clear that these obligations apply to protection seekers, who are within the territory of a State party to the GC. The present subsection determines whether these obligations apply also to persons who claim protection at the border of a State party, and to protection seekers intercepted at sea. This requires establishing the extraterritorial applicability of Article 33(1) GC in relation to these groups of protection seekers. Not considered is the question of extraterritorial applicability of the principle of non-refoulement to protection seekers present in another State.[117] Whereas this question is potentially relevant to safe third country policy,[118] it is not relevant to expulsion to third countries, nor, therefore, to the application of readmission agreements for that purpose.

Considering that the GC is silent on the matter of its extraterritorial application, we must rely on interpretation of relevant individual provisions, *in casu* Article 33(1). The applicability of Article 33(1) GC at the border, to which we will devote most attention, is relatively uncontested, whereas its relation to interception at sea inspires more controversy. The issue at hand is whether non-refoulement can be interpreted to include non-rejection at the border and non-interception at sea. In clarification, rejecting such an interpretation implies that States would be able to pre-empt responsibility under the GC by not lifting the proverbial lever at the borderline, or by intercepting the protection seeker during an attempted border crossing by land or by sea. Accepting such an interpretation implies a right to entry to territory for protection seekers.

One could proffer different views as to whether an individual's right to entry would correspond with a positive, or a negative State obligation. If one views entry to territory as something that a State *grants*, then a qualification as a positive obligation would appear accurate. The opposite perspective, however, where entry to territory is something that a State *allows*, would point to a negative obligation. The difference in reasoning seems semantic, but is not without legal or practical consequence. Deriving a positive State obligation from a negatively formulated provision, such as Article 33 GC, stretches the limits of interpretation of treaty texts, regarding which certainly States, but also the judiciary, tend to be reluctant. This subsection adheres to the view that a right to entry corresponds with a negative State obligation, while closest to the wording of Article 33 GC, and while requiring a State to refrain from exercising border control that would hinder or obstruct entry, *i.e.* not to act.[119]

117 This excludes consideration of several issues, namely protection claims (or visa applications by protections seekers) filed at diplomatic representations, external processing centres, the role of carrier sanctions in enforcing visa requirements, and the role of immigration liaison officers.

118 Noll 2000, p. 387-388, 442-445.

119 Noll 2000, p. 443.

The application of the Geneva Refugee Convention to refugees at the border has been a subject of debate from its inception.[120] The consensus in the literature has come to rest on including non-rejection at the border within the scope of Article 33(1) GC, contrary to initial interpretations by Robinson[121] and Grahl-Madsen.[122] These seminal authors stressed the need for gaining entry, legally or illegally, into the territory of a State party to the GC for the principle of non-refoulement to apply.[123] Grahl-Madsen did emphasise that such does not always require passing a border checkpoint. The decisive factor is passing the frontier line.[124] Where a border crossing point is located within the territory of a State (as is often the case) a person who presents a protection claim to a border guard is protected by the principle of non-refoulement as an in-country matter. The same is arguably true regarding air- and seaports, which are generally located well within the territory of a State. The situation on which the issue of non-rejection centres is a border control point coinciding with, or interception at, the frontier line of a State party to the GC.

Before interpreting Article 33(1) GC in light of this situation, a preliminary question is whether this provision could apply, in principle, at the frontier between two bordering States, considering that a refugee is only a refugee *outside* his country of origin.[125] One could argue that, in the case of bordering States, a person at the frontier has not yet left the country of origin, and that the Geneva Refugee Convention would thus not apply.

It is clear that this argument does not hold in case a border consist of two opposite checkpoints divided by a strip of no man's land. Once passed the first checkpoint of the country of origin, the protection seeker will have left the country of origin, and the Geneva Refugee Convention would apply.[126] In case two countries share a single border crossing point on the frontier line, jurisdiction is decisive. The moment a person presents him- or herself at this border crossing point, s/he transfers from one jurisdiction to another. The State in which s/he is still physically present can no longer exercise jurisdiction over this person, without violating the sovereignty of the other State. This person may be considered to be outside the first State and thus subject to the Geneva Refugee

120 Reflecting the evolution of this debate, see Robinson 1953, p. 160-163; Grahl-Madsen 1972, p. 98-100, 223-225; Kälin 1982, p. 105-109; Stenberg 1989, p. 175-178, 200-201; Weis 1995, p. 325-343; Fitzpatrick 1996, p. 246-247; Goodwin-Gill 1996, p. 121-137; Noll 2000, p. 387-389, 423-431.

121 Robinson 1953, p. 162.

122 Grahl-Madsen 1972, p. 223-225.

123 An oft-quoted passage is the following: "If a refugee has succeeded in eluding the frontier guards, he is safe; if he has not, it is his hard luck", Robinson 1953, p. 162.

124 Grahl-Madsen 1972, p. 223.

125 *Supra*, subsection 9.2.2.2, n. 24.

126 The US Supreme Court might disagree, after finding in *Sale v. Haitian Centers Council* (Inc. 509 U.S. 155 (1993)) that the Geneva refugee Convention is not applicable on the high seas.

Convention, even though s/he has not yet physically entered the other State.[127] In case of interception at, or on the frontier line by the authorities of another State, a person would equally transfer to the jurisdiction of this State. Protection seekers at the border are thus always outside the country origin in accordance with Article 1(A)(2) GC.

Arguments in favour of a prohibition of rejecting protection seekers at the frontier rely firstly on interpretation of the ordinary meaning of Article 33(1) GC. This involves a broad interpretation of a treaty provision in disregard of ambiguous indications in the drafting history. On the one hand, the drafters decided to omit a provision on admission in the Geneva Refugee Convention,[128] and there are passages in the *travaux préparatoires* suggesting that certain States wanted to ensure that non-refoulement would not imply an entitlement to entry.[129] On the other hand, the *travaux préparatoires* equally contain passages in support of an inclusive reading of non-rejection.[130] It is however possible to bypass this debate, while interpretation of the text of Article 33(1) is sufficiently conclusive to avoid the need for recourse to its drafting history.[131]

The text of Article 33(1) GC offers several arguments in support of including rejection at the border within its prohibitive scope. The ordinary meaning of both the verbs to "expel" and to "return" presupposes a previous physical presence of a protection seeker within the territory.[132] The verb "*refouler*", added between brackets, how-

127 Kälin 1982, p. 105-106. Goodwin-Gill 1996, p. 123. Refusing entry would again hand the person over to the jurisdiction of the first State, Noll 2000, p. 389.

128 Grahl-Madsen 1972, p. 100. Goodwin-Gill speculates that the drafters felt such would come too close to a duty to grant asylum, Goodwin-Gill 1996, p. 122.

129 This refers to expressions by the Swiss and Dutch delegates at the Conference of Plenipotentiaries in 1951, drawing support from the Italian delegate (Robinson 1953, p. 163; Weis 1995, p. 328-329, 33(1)1). There has been a great deal of disagreement in the literature with regard to these passages. An important contribution to this debate by both Marx and Goodwin-Gill emphasised that the delegates in question were strictly concerned with ensuring that an obligation to allow entry would not exist in the particular case of a *mass influx*, but did not object to non-rejection in general (Marx 1995, p. 390; Goodwin-Gill 1996, p 121-122). In other words, this part of the drafting history concerns the specific issue of mass influx as an *exception* to the principle of non-refoulement (Coleman 2003, p. 44). Although referred to as mere "snippets of negotiating history" (Koh 1994, p. 17, 34), "confused passages" (Fitzpatrick 1996, p. 247) and "ambiguous comments" (Fitzpatrick 2000, p. 296), these passages were sufficient for the US Supreme Court in *Sale v. Haitian Centers Council* to find that such an exception exists (Inc. 509 U.S. 155 (1993)).

130 Spijkerboer and Vermeulen 1999, p. 184. In a similar vein, Noll 2000, p. 428. Stenberg claims that a majority of the drafters did not wish to exclude non-rejection entirely, Stenberg 1989, p. 200.

131 Kälin 1982, p. 108-109; Spijkerboer and Vermeulen 1999, p. 184; Noll 2000, p. 425-426.

132 Battjes, *the right to entry* (work in progress). Contrarily, Vermeulen considers "return" not to presuppose physical stay, thereby already indicating that Article 33(1) would also apply extraterritorially at the border, Vermeulen 1999, p. 178.

ever, clarifies and extends the meaning of "return" in this article.[133] As remarked earlier, the ordinary meaning of *refouler* is to drive back, repel, or reconduct,[134] which does not presuppose a presence in-country. At first sight, Article 33(1) would thus encompass rejection at the border, as well as the relocation of protection seekers at a distance from the border, for example at sea.[135] Furthermore, *refouler* has a technical legal meaning in francophone asylum law and practice (referred to in one source as "non-admittance at the frontier",[136] and in another as "police actions without formality which are applied to aliens which are in the country in an irregular manner or who are turned back at the frontier"[137]) pointing to an inclusive reading of, at least, rejection at the border.[138] Yet additional encouragement for the inclusion of non-rejection is derived from the phrase "in any manner whatsoever",[139] as well as the object and purpose of the GC in a teleological interpretation of Article 33(1).[140]

An important question is whether Article 33(1) GC would, on the basis of the above arguments, include a general prohibition of rejection at the border, applicable in all cases. A closer look at the wording of Article 33(1), and in particular the phrase "to the frontiers of territories", suggests that the prohibition of rejection at the border is a qualified obligation, applying only to certain protection seekers depending on the circumstances. Surely, only once a rejection at the border equals an act of direct or indirect refoulement, does Article 33(1) GC apply. A general prohibition of rejection assumes that a rejected protection seeker at the frontier of a destination country would automatically finish up at the frontier of a territory, where s/he claims to be at risk of persecution. This is clearly inaccurate. Automatic return to a country of persecution is possible, but only if a protection seeker is refused entry at the border with a country of persecution, or with a third country which would not protect against refoulement.

The applicability of Article 33(1) at the border thus depends on the circumstances. In principle, the prohibition of rejection is limited to protection seekers at the frontier of State parties of the GC, which border the country of persecution or a third country which is not safe. In practice, however, every protection claim at the frontier would require *investigation* of whether the neighbouring country is not a country of persecution or an unsafe third country, before rejection could take place. Refusing a protection seeker entry at the border can therefore never be automatic, implying a *de facto* general obligation of rejection at the frontier. In other words, it makes no difference whether a

133 See Noll for a discussion of the drafters' intention behind this "terminological 'couplet'", Noll 2000, p. 388-389.

134 *Supra*, at n.33.

135 Battjes, *the right to entry* (work in progress); Spijkerboer and Vermeulen 1999, p. 184.

136 Taken from the *Travaux Préparatoires*, Spijkerboer and Vermeulen 1999, p. 184. See also Noll 2000, p. 388, 428.

137 Stenberg 1989, p. 200. For an opposing opinion, see Robinson 1953, p. 162.

138 See *infra*, at n. 151, regarding interception at sea.

139 Noll 2000, p. 428.

140 Goodwin-Gill 1996, p. 367. See also Kälin 1982, p. 107.

protection seeker claims at the border, or within the territory of a State party to the GC. The State obligations following from Article 33(1) GC are equal in both cases.

The applicability of Article 33(1) GC at the border is widely confirmed in State practice. Considering the EU,[141] the Member States have validated the principle of non-refoulement at the border in a series of non-binding as well as binding instruments. Noteworthy is Council Resolution of 20 June 1995 on minimum guarantees for asylum procedures of the European Union.[142] Its relevant provisions read:

> 5. The authorities responsible for border controls and local authorities must receive clear instructions so the [asylum] applications can be forwarded without delay to the competent authority.
>
> [...]
>
> 9. Any asylum-seeker must be able to lodge an [asylum] application at the frontier. The application may then be examined to establish, prior to the decision on admission, whether it is manifestly unfounded [...].

The Council Directive on minimum standards on procedures in Member States for granting and withdrawing refugee status, adopted on 1 December 2005,[143] also confirms the applicability of Article 33(1) GC at the border. Its Article 3(1) reads:

> This Directive shall apply to all applications for asylum made in the territory, including at the border, or in the transit zones of the Member States [...].

Furthermore, Article 2(b) of the procedures Directive defines an "application for asylum" as "an application made by a third country national or stateless person which can be understood as a request for international protection from a Member State under the Geneva Convention". The Explanatory Memorandum of the original Commission proposal for the Directive on minimum procedures adds that "[a]ny request by a person for protection at the border or on the territory of the Member States shall be understood to fall within the terms of the Geneva Convention".[144] In addition, Article 2(k) determines that for the purposes of the Directive the phrase ""[r]emain in the Member State" means to remain in the territory, including at the border or in transit zones of the Member State in which the application for asylum has been made or is being examined". Border claims are thus considered and treated as in-country claims.

---

141 For relevant material within the Council of Europe framework, see Recommendation No. R (84) 1 regarding the *Protection of persons satisfying the criteria in the Geneva Convention but who are not formally recognised as refugees*, adopted by the Committee of Ministers of the Council of Europe on 25 January 1984, and Recommendation No. R (98) 15 of the Committee of Ministers to Member States *on the training of officials who first come into contact with protection seekers, in particular at border points,* of 15 December 1998.

142 *OJ* C 274, 19 September 1996.

143 *OJ* L 326, 13 December 2005, p. 13.

144 COM(2000) 578 final, p. 7.

A further instrument, relevant to State practice in the EU, is the Dublin Convention,[145] later replaced by the Dublin Regulation. Article 3(1) DC read:

> Member States undertake to examine the application of any alien who applies at the border or in their territory to any one of them for asylum.

It has been argued that the obligation to examine asylum applications at the border in Article 3(1) DC meant that rejection at the border would not only violate the Dublin Convention, but also imply an act of refoulement under Article 33(1) GC.[146] The Dublin Convention was concluded between the Member States of the European Union. All State parties to the Dublin Convention were also party to the Geneva Refugee Convention, which was thus part of the context of Article 3(1) DC.[147] The Member States of the EU hereby accepted the applicability of Article 33(1) GC at the border.[148]

The Dublin Convention was replaced by EC secondary legislation – the so-called Dublin Regulation – on 18 February 2003.[149] Article 3(1) of the Dublin Regulation[150] is a near literal copy of Article 3(1) DC. The Vienna rules of treaty interpretation do not apply to secondary EC legislation. Considering that the Dublin Regulation is the explicit successor of the Dublin Convention, however, Article 3(1) of the Dublin Regulation may arguably be considered to have the same meaning.

Regarding the interception of protection seekers at sea, we remarked earlier that interpretation of the ordinary meaning of the text of Article 33(1) GC – in particular, the verb "*refouler*" – would allow application of the principle of non-refoulement to this particular State action.[151] Following the above findings, Article 33(1) GC is arguably applicable to the interception of protection seekers at sea, and their redirection to the country of embarkation or another country, depending on whether there is a risk

145 The Dublin Convention entered into force 19 August 1997. It replaced chapter 7 of the Schengen Convention which regulated the division of responsibility for protection claims between Member States.

146 Steenbergen, Spijkerboer, Vermeulen en Fernhout 1999, p. 178-179; Noll 2000, p. 432.

147 Article 31(3) Vienna Convention on the Law of Treaties.

148 Noll 2000, p. 432.

149 Article 24(1) of Council Regulation of 18 February 2003 establishing the criteria and mechanisms for determining the Member State responsible for examining an asylum application lodged in one of the Member States by a third-country national, *OJ* L 50, p. 1, 25 February 2003 (hereinafter the Dublin Regulation). The Dublin Regulation does not fully replace the Dublin Convention. The Preamble of the Dublin Regulation (recital 19) recognises the continued application of the Dublin Convention to the transfer of protection seekers between Denmark and the other Member States, considering that Denmark does not participate in the Dublin Regulation, adopted under Title IV TEC.

150 Article 3(1) of the Dublin Regulation: "Member States shall examine the application of any third country national who applies at the border or in their territory to any one of them for asylum."

151 *Supra*, at n. 106.

of persecution or indirect refoulement. Investigation of that risk would be required in order to determine whether return is permitted, or entry to territory must be allowed.

Battjes, however, notes two opposing arguments. Firstly, it is arguable that the technical legal meaning of *refouler* in fact presupposes physical contact with the border, and would thus not include actions before the border.[152] In theory, this would mean that the protection seeker would have to reach the territorial sea line of a State party for Article 33(1) GC to apply. State practice, however, indicates that the protection seeker would most likely be required to have reached the coast or internal waters.[153] Secondly, State practice does not support application of Article 33(1) GC to interception at sea, pointing to the interception of Haitian boat refugees over a protracted period by the US during the early nineties, which did not provoke protest from other States.[154]

In sum, the international obligations regarding expulsion to third countries following from Article 33(1) GC apply to protection seekers within the territory of a State party, as well as those at the border. The applicability of the principle of non-refoulement of Article 33(1) GC to protection seekers intercepted at sea is not conclusive.

### *9.2.3 The European Convention for the protection of human rights and fundamental freedoms*

The provisions of the European Convention for the protection of human rights and fundamental freedoms relevant to the discussion in this subsection are Articles 1, 3, and 13:

Article 1 of the European Convention – titled "obligation to respect human rights" – reads:

> The High Contracting Parties shall secure to everyone within their jurisdiction the rights and freedoms defined in Section I of this Convention.

Article 3 – titled "prohibition of torture" – reads:

> No one shall be subjected to torture or to inhuman or degrading treatment or punishment.

Article 13 of the European Convention – titled "right to an effective remedy" – reads:

> Everyone whose rights and freedoms as set forth in this Convention are violated shall have an effective remedy before a national authority notwithstanding that the violation has been committed by persons acting in an official capacity.

152 Battjes, *the right to entry* (work in progress); Noll 2000, p. 387; Spijkerboer and Vermeulen 2005, p. 62.

153 Goodwin-Gill notes that in State practice entry to territory is considered to occur upon reaching the coastline or internal waters, Goodwin-Gill 1996, p. 163, cited in Battjes, *the right to entry* (work in progress).

154 Battjes, *the right to entry* (work in progress).

In the following, subsection 9.2.3.1 first establishes that Article 3 ECHR is an implicit prohibition of refoulement. Subsection 9.2.3.2 then determines whether Article 3 ECHR also includes a prohibition of *indirect* refoulement. This is followed by subsection 9.2.3.3, which discusses the prohibition of inhuman or degrading treatment or punishment (IDTP), and explores the limits of interpretation of that concept. Subsection 9.2.3.4 subsequently addresses the issue of status determination of protection seekers, and the procedural requirement of an effective remedy under the ECHR. Subsection 9.2.3.5, finally, determines the extraterritorial applicability of Article 3 ECHR.

#### 9.2.3.1 Article 3 ECHR as an implicit prohibition of refoulement

The potential of Article 3 of the European Convention to prevent the involuntary removal of a person from one State to another was first recognised by the European Commission of Human Rights[155] in a series of extradition[156] and expulsion[157] cases. In the latter cases, the Commission held that expulsion of an alien, which would result in exposure to treatment contrary to Article 3 ECHR upon return, could constitute a violation of that provision. Confirmation by the European Court of Human Rights that Article 3 indeed implied a refoulement prohibition followed with the landmark 1989 *Soering* case in the context of extradition,[158] extended soon thereafter to the context of asylum with *Cruz Varas*.[159]

Jens Soering is a German national who murdered the parents of his girlfriend in the State of Virginia in the US. After fleeing to the United Kingdom, he was arrested and imprisoned, pending a final decision on his extradition as requested by the US under a bilateral agreement. In Virginia, he would face trial and the possibility of the death penalty. Before the European Court of Human Rights Soering invoked Article 3, arguing that the "death row phenomenon" would subject him to treatment contrary to the prohibition of inhuman or degrading treatment or punishment (IDTP).

The Government of the United Kingdom forwarded several significant objections against the possibility of an extraditing State incurring responsibility for acts committed after extradition by a recipient State. The UK argued, *inter alia*, that Article 3 ECHR could not impose responsibility on a State party for acts committed outside its territory, and that it would be beyond the language of Article 3 to hold that the UK would "subject" a person to any treatment he might receive after extradition at the hands of another State. The UK also pointed to the fact that responsibility under Article

155 Following the remodelling of the structure of the European Court of Human Rights after the entry into force of the 11th Protocol to the ECHR on 1 November 1998, the European Commission of Human Rights ceased to exist as of 31 October 1999. Its function had been to establish the facts of a case and sift out inadmissible cases, referring those that merited further investigation to the Court. This task is now performed by a "Committee" of the Court itself, Lawson and Schermers 1999, p. xxxi-x1.

156 See Weissbrodt and Hörtreiter 1999, p. 28.

157 See Zwaan 2003, p. 44.

158 Soering v. United Kingdom, 7 July 1989, Series A, 161.

159 Cruz Varas v. Sweden, 20 March 1991, Series A, 201.

3 in extradition cases would interfere with other treaty obligations (notably, extradition treaties), and entail adjudication in the internal affairs of another State. This would not only conflict with norms of international judicial process, it would also require the UK to undertake difficult examinations of "alien systems of law and conditions in foreign States".[160] *If* such a responsibility would exist, the UK Government contended, then surely it would arise only in case the illicit treatment abroad would be "certain, imminent and serious".[161]

In response, the Court stressed the special character of the European Convention as an instrument of collective enforcement of fundamental rights. It went on to refer to previous judgements, explaining that interpretation and application of Convention provisions must result in "practical and effective" safeguards, if the object and purpose of the Convention ("the protection of individual human beings") is to be realised.[162] With regard to Article 3 in particular, the Court recalled that its prohibition is absolute, enshrines a fundamental value of democratic societies, and reflects an internationally accepted norm with reference to the ICCPR and CAT.[163] These considerations led the Court to overrule the UK Government's objections. The Court rejected the UK's position as unable to "absolve the Contracting Parties from responsibility under Article 3 for all and any foreseen consequences of extradition suffered outside their jurisdiction".[164] Furthermore, the Court introduced the "real risk" criterion for assessing the likelihood of treatment contrary to Article 3 in the recipient State, thereby rejecting the UK's plea for the much stricter standard, mentioned above.[165]

The Court still needed to address the fact that the European Convention does not in any way refer to extradition, in the knowledge that other instruments such as the Geneva refugee Convention and the CAT do contain specific references. The Court found that an absence of explicit reference did not exclude the possibility that responsibility under Article 3 for extradition cases could be inherent in the general terms of Article 3. The extradition of a person, leading to torture or to inhuman or degrading treatment or punishment, namely, "would plainly be contrary to the spirit and intendment" of Article 3.[166] Consequently, the Court decided that an extraditing State party incurs liability under Article 3 "by reason of its having taken action which has as a direct consequence the exposure of an individual to proscribed ill-treatment".[167] One should firstly remark that this basis for responsibility under Article 3 is independent of whether the receiving State is party to the European Convention of Human Rights. The potential maltreatment need not necessarily be a violation as such within the jurisdic-

160 Soering v. United Kingdom, para. 83.
161 Soering v. United Kingdom, para. 84.
162 Soering v. United Kingdom, para. 87.
163 Soering v. United Kingdom, para. 88.
164 Soering v. United Kingdom, para. 86.
165 Soering v. United Kingdom, para. 88, 91.
166 Soering v. United Kingdom, para. 86 and 88.
167 Soering v. United Kingdom, para. 91.

tion of the receiving State itself. What is relevant is whether the maltreatment would have been illegal under the terms of Article 3 ECHR, had it, hypothetically, occurred within the jurisdiction of the extraditing State. Secondly, the Court requires a causal link between the decision to extradite and the exposure to maltreatment.

With regard to the extension of this case law to the context of asylum with the 1991 *Cruz Varas* case, we can be brief. This case concerned the expulsion of a Chilean protection seeker by Sweden to Chile. The Court starts the examination of the case in light of Article 3 of the European Convention by referring to *Soering*. The Court repeats the principal consideration that extradition of a fugitive may give rise to an issue under Article 3 and therefore engage responsibility under the European Convention.[168] It then states: "Although the present case concerns expulsion as opposed to a decision to extradite, the Court considers that the above principle also applies to expulsion decisions and a fortiori to cases of actual expulsion".[169]

Thus, a definition of the implicit prohibition of refoulement of Article 3 is that a protection seeker may not be removed to a country where substantial grounds have been shown for believing that he or she would face a real risk of being subjected to torture or inhuman or degrading treatment or punishment.[170]

In *Soering*, the Court made sure to remind that the European Convention is not an instrument, which governs the actions of States not party to it, or requires State parties to impose its standards on other States.[171] However, "the establishment of [...] responsibility inevitably involves an assessment of conditions in the requesting country against the standards of Article 3".[172] The Court illustrated this finding by undertaking a detailed investigation of the Virginia justice- and penal system in relation to the death penalty. What became clear from the proceedings of this case is that the Court does not shy away from requiring one State to scrutinise conditions in another, whether a State party to the European Convention, or not. It thereby arguably deputised State parties to the ECHR in what is essentially the Court's prerogative.

It is clear that treaties provide requirements for the behaviour of State signatories, and the European Convention of Human Rights or Geneva Refugee Convention is no exception to this rule. These instruments, however, can also contain requirements for the safety of – conditions in – countries when it comes to the expulsion of protection seekers. Although such requirements still only govern the behaviour of State parties, they do force States to look at other States' compliance with a fundamental rights instrument, and if need be, outside the inner circle of signatories.

Arguably, this has a potential spill-over effect through encouraging State parties to exercise pressure on non-parties to adopt certain standards. This would, on a political level, extend the implications of certain international fundamental rights

168 Cruz Varas v. Sweden, para. 69.

169 *Ibid.*, para. 70.

170 Soering v. United Kingdom, para. 91, and Cruz Varas v. Sweden, paras. 69 and 70.

171 Soering v. United Kingdom, para. 86.

172 Soering v. United Kingdom, para. 91.

instruments beyond the realm of creating obligations for its parties. The main point of relevance for this chapter, however, is simply that fundamental rights instruments, in the exercise of the removal of certain persons to other countries, can require States to scrutinise others.

#### 9.2.3.2 Indirect refoulement

In the wake of a longstanding consensus in the literature[173] and several decisions by the European Commission of Human Rights,[174] the European Court of Human Rights finally determined that Article 3 of the European Convention also forbids indirect refoulement in the *T.I.* case in 2000.[175] *T.I.* was a Sri Lankan national who challenged his transfer under the Dublin Convention from the United Kingdom to Germany. With regard to the responsibility of the UK for a potential expulsion to Sri Lanka by Germany, the Court stated:

> It is accepted by all parties that the applicant is not, as such, threatened with any treatment contrary to Article 3 in Germany. His removal to Germany is however one link in a possible chain of events which might result in his return to Sri Lanka where it is alleged he would face the real risk of such treatment. The Court finds that the indirect removal in this case to an intermediary country, which is also a Contracting State, does not affect the responsibility of the United Kingdom to ensure that the applicant is not, as a result of its decision to expel, exposed to treatment contrary to Article 3 of the Convention.[176]

The Court concluded that the UK would be responsible under Article 3 ECHR for such an indirect removal.[177] In other words, the responsibility of a State party to the European Convention of Human Rights, which expels a protection seeker to a third State, is engaged if that third State might send the person onwards to a country from which a risk of torture or IDTP emanates.

This implies that a State, intent on expulsion to a third country, must consider whether the protection seeker would face a real risk of onward removal to another country in breach of Article 3 ECHR.[178] We will discuss this duty to investigate in light of the principle of interstate trust below in subsection 9.2.3.4.

---

173 Spijkerboer and Vermeulen 1999, p. 203, n. 138.

174 It should be noted, however, that the Commission wavered between confirming and denying the applicability of Article 3 to indirect returns, Zwaan 2003, p. 46-48.

175 T.I. v. United Kingdom, 7 March 2000, Application No. 43844/98.

176 T.I. v. United Kingdom, p. 14.

177 T.I. v. United Kingdom, p. 14.

178 T.I. v. United Kingdom, p. 17.

### 9.2.3.3 Inhuman or degrading treatment or punishment

The substantive reach of the prohibition of refoulement, implicit in Article 3 ECHR, is difficult to determine. This is due, firstly, to the fact that the European Court of Human Rights takes a teleological, and therefore expansive approach to the interpretation of Article 3, as seen in *Soering* as well as in other cases. We will discuss this aspect, insofar as relevant to expulsion to safe third countries, below in subsection 9.2.3.4. A second cause of uncertainty as to the limits of Article 3 ECHR is its broad terms: the notions of inhuman or degrading treatment or punishment (IDTP) are not defined. This invites inclusion of a potentially wide range of acts or omissions.

The Court has emphasised the distinction in Article 3 between torture on the one hand, and inhuman or degrading treatment or punishment on the other. Torture is a form of inhuman treatment or punishment, but the drafters of the European Convention chose to classify it separately due to its distinguishing characteristic as causing especially "serious and cruel suffering".[179] In terms of the severity of treatment, the degree increases from "degrading", to "inhuman", to "torture". In order to qualify as any of these forms of treatment or punishment, it must reach a "minimum level of severity".[180] Exactly when a certain treatment or punishment would cross the threshold for being, at the very least, "degrading" cannot be established generally. It depends on the circumstances of the case. In *Soering*, the Court confirms previous case law, determining that:

> ill-treatment, including punishment, must attain a minimum level of severity if it is to fall within the scope of Article 3 [...]. The assessment of this minimum is, in the nature of things, relative; it depends on all the circumstances of the case, such as the nature and context of the treatment or punishment, the manner and method of its execution, its duration, its physical or mental effects and, in some instances, the sex, age and state of health of the victim.[181]

What is certain, however, is that a "real risk" of exposure to *any* of the forms of maltreatment covered by Article 3 ECHR in another country would be sufficient to prohibit expulsion.[182] Regarding the distinction between "inhuman" and "degrading" treatment or punishment, the Court in *Soering* stated the following:

> Treatment has been held by the Court to be both "inhuman" because it was premeditated, was applied for hours at a stretch and "caused, if not actual bodily injury, at least intense physical and mental suffering", and also "degrading" because it was

179 Selmouni v. France, 28 July 1999, Reports 1999-V, para. 96.

180 Ireland v. United Kingdom, 18 January 1978, Series A, 25, para. 162; Soering v. United Kingdom, para. 100; Selmouni v. France, para. 100.

181 Soering v. United Kingdom, para. 100.

182 Soering v. United Kingdom, para. 88. For a listing of examples from European Commission- and European Court of Human Rights case law, see Spijkerboer and Vermeulen 1999, p. 190-191.

> "such as to arouse in [its] victims feelings of fear, anguish and inferiority capable of humiliating and debasing them and possibly breaking their physical or moral resistance" [...]. In order for a punishment or treatment associated with it to be "inhuman" or "degrading", the suffering or humiliation involved must in any event go beyond that inevitable element of suffering or humiliation connected with a given form of legitimate punishment [...]. In this connection, account is to be taken not only of the physical pain experienced but also, where there is a considerable delay before execution of the punishment, of the sentenced person's mental anguish of anticipating the violence he is to have inflicted on him.[183]

Based on these and other indications in the Court's case law, the following subsections will explore two specific questions that are of special relevance in the context of readmission policies. These are whether the availability of basic means of subsistence in a third country is a condition for expulsion to that country, in view of the prohibition of IDTP in Article 3 of the European Convention, and whether subjecting a protection seeker to a potential chain of expulsions between third countries may be contrary to the prohibition of IDTP.

*9.2.3.3.1 Lack of basic means of subsistence*

The absolute character of Article 3 ECHR implies that the prohibition of refoulement it contains may pertain to acts or omissions in another country, not only by State actors but also by non-State actors.[184] There is some question as to whether this prohibition may also relate to the general situation or general conditions in a country of origin or a third country, unrelated to action or inaction by any actor. In particular, the question has arisen in the literature whether the concept of inhuman "treatment"[185] would stretch to include an inhuman "situation" or inhuman "conditions".[186]

The 1989 *Soering* case has been interpreted as supporting such a broad interpretation of Article 3,[187] which is questionable. In *Soering*, the Court indeed based its finding of inhuman "treatment" largely on an assessment of the general "situation" which would await Soering on "deathrow"; incarcerated pending execution pursuant to a death penalty.[188] Conditions in connection with a certain form of incarceration are,

183 Soering v. United Kingdom, para. 100.

184 Ahmed v. Austria, 17 December 1996, *Reports*-VI, para. 46; H.L.R. v. France, 29 April 1997, *Reports* 1997-III, para. 40; T.I. v. United Kingdom, p. 14.

185 The Concise Oxford English dictionary defines "treatment" as "the process or manner of treating someone or something in a certain way". The relevant meaning of the verb to "treat" is to "behave towards or deal with in a certain way" (Concise Oxford English dictionary, tenth edition, Oxford University Press. Oxford, 2002). A certain "treatment", to its ordinary meaning, thus always presupposes the action or inaction of another party.

186 Simon 1999; Vermeulen 1999, p. 170; Spijkerboer and Vermeulen 1999, p. 193.

187 Simon 1999.

188 Simon 1999, p. 1437-1438, 1440.

however, clearly created and imposed by another party, *in casu* the State, thus qualifying as "treatment" and perhaps even as "punishment".

Some judgments seem to indicate that the European Court of Human Rights is willing to bring exposure to certain general situations within the scope of Article 3 ECHR. In the 1997 case of *D.* v. the United Kingdom,[189] the Court determined that it would be contrary to Article 3 to expel D., who suffered from AIDS in a terminal stage, to St. Kitts where medical treatment for this disease was not available.[190] In doing so, the Court rejected the argument of the UK that D. did not have a valid claim under Article 3 since he would not be exposed to any form of *treatment* contrary to Article 3 in St Kitts.[191] After elaborating on the applicant's situation in the UK, where he was receiving medical treatment allowing at least a limited quality of life, and the situation in which would find himself in St. Kitts,[192] the Court considered that:

> In view of these exceptional circumstances and bearing in mind the critical stage now reached in the applicant's fatal illness, the implementation of the decision to remove him to St Kitts would amount to inhuman treatment by the respondent State in violation of Article 3 [...]. [...] Although it cannot be said that the conditions which would confront him in the receiving country are themselves a breach of the standards of Article 3 [...], his removal would expose him to a real risk of dying under most distressing circumstances and would thus amount to inhuman treatment.[193]

The Court furthermore found that, under the "very exceptional circumstances of this case and given the compelling humanitarian considerations at stake", the UK was held to continue to provide D. with essential medical care.[194] From Article 3 ECHR, the Court thus deduces a (highly qualified) positive obligation to provide essential medical care, which is normally available in a destination State, to protection seekers within its jurisdiction.

---

189 D. v. the United Kingdom, judgment, 2 May 1997, *Reports* 1997-III.

190 Vermeulen 1999, p. 170; Spijkerboer and Vermeulen 1999, p. 193.

191 "The Government requested the Court to find that the applicant had no valid claim under Article 3 (art. 3) in the circumstances of the case since he would not be exposed in the receiving country to any form of treatment which breached the standards of Article 3 (art. 3). His hardship and reduced life expectancy would stem from his terminal and incurable illness coupled with the deficiencies in the health and social-welfare system of a poor, developing country. He would find himself in the same situation as other AIDS victims in St Kitts", D. v. the United Kingdom, para. 42.

192 In particular, the Court considered that "[t]he abrupt withdrawal of these facilities will entail the most dramatic consequences for him. It is not disputed that his removal will hasten his death. There is a serious danger that the conditions of adversity which await him in St Kitts will further reduce his already limited life expectancy and subject him to acute mental and physical suffering", D. v. the United Kingdom, para. 52.

193 D. v. the United Kingdom, para. 53.

194 D. v. the United Kingdom, para. 53.

Regarding the expulsion of protection seekers to third countries, this means that the requirements following from *D.* v UK are in accordance with the general principle of analysis, outlined above in subsection 9.2.1.1. Under exceptional circumstances, Article 3 ECHR prevents expulsion to a third country where essential medical care[195] is either absent, or would be denied. Under those circumstances, there exists arguably an entitlement to medical care within the jurisdiction of the destination State.

The emphasis of the Court on the exceptional nature of the case of *D.* leaves little room for application of Article 3 in similar cases.[196] One arguable analogy would be the expulsion of a protection seeker to a country in a state of famine. The applicability of Article 3 ECHR to less exceptional circumstances with more practical meaning, however, is difficult to establish. A case of especial relevance to this research is expulsion to third countries where reception conditions for protection seekers are insufficient. A lack of reception facilities and/or capacity to process protection seekers might qualify as a "treatment", which, if attaining a "minimum level of severity", would bring it within the scope of Article 3. Alternatively, in case reception conditions could not be considered in accordance with the ordinary meaning of "treatment", the position of the protection seeker in the third country would need to be exceptionally destitute so as to render the act of expulsion to that country contrary to Article 3.

A situation in which a protection seeker would not have a right to work and have no access to social services (essential medical care excluded) in the third country would arguably not qualify as inhuman or degrading treatment, nor would it likely give rise to exceptionally destitute circumstances.[197] An incapacity or refusal to process or consider the merits of a protection claim would not raise such issues, either. Expulsion of a protection seeker to a country, which is not in a state of famine, but where s/he would not have access to food and shelter, would come closer to falling within the scope of Article 3. Following the general principle of analysis of this chapter, however, this would imply that destination States are obliged under Article 3 to provide protection seekers within their jurisdiction with basic means of subsistence, which is doubtful.

Positing access to basic means of subsistence in a third country as a requirement for the legality of expulsion implies the existence of a positive obligation for the destination State to provide basic means of subsistence to protection seekers within its jurisdiction. The European Court of Human Rights has repeatedly emphasised that the

195 Subsequent case law has further clarified just how exceptional medical circumstances, and thus how essential the medical care, are required to be before raising an issue under Article 3, see Vermeulen 1999, p. 191; Spijkerboer and Vermeulen 2005, p. 75.

196 As illustrated by the case of *Bensaïd*, in which the Court did not consider that Article 3 prevented expulsion to Algeria of the applicant, a schizophrenic suffering from a psychotic illness, despite less favourable medical conditions in Algeria, and a likely regression in his condition after removal, Bensaïd v. the United Kingdom, judgement, 6 February 2001, 33 EHRR 10.

197 For a contrary opinion, see the UK Court of Appeal in *Adan, Subaskaran and Aitseguer*, quoted *supra*, subsection 9.2.2.3.2, at n. 106.

European Convention does not contain a "right to political asylum".[198] This is understood to mean that the European Convention can protect against removal, but that it does not entitle to residence, or regulate the conditions of stay in a host country. While protection seekers may arguably claim the fundamental rights and freedoms contained in the European Convention, as may "everyone" within the jurisdiction of a State party,[199] the European Court has not invited the deduction of positive State obligations regarding conditions of stay. Providing protection seekers with basic subsistence should thus be considered a discretionary decision of State parties to the European Convention. By the same token, the availability of basic subsistence in a third country could arguably not determine the legality of expulsion to that country under Article 3 of the European Convention.

*9.2.3.3.2 Chain expulsion*

9.2.3.3.2.1 Chain expulsion as a new form of protection seekers "in orbit"

In sections 1.2 and 5.3.5.5, we referred to cases of migrants "in orbit" – the shuttling of migrants back and forth between States refusing to take responsibility – and the mitigating effect that readmission agreements may have on this phenomenon. If properly implemented, the readmission procedure established by these agreements guarantees that persons will not be removed to the requested State without the consent of the latter. In fact, one of the purposes of a readmission agreement is to regulate the practice of expulsion/readmission by preventing improper attempts by States to pass the burden of an unwanted immigrant on to another. This prevents friction in the relations between States resulting from such practices, but may also be in the interest of the migrant as the possibility of ending up "in orbit" is reduced.

Similarly, one of the objectives of the Dublin Convention was to address situations of protection seekers "in orbit" between EC Member States. The principle of the Dublin Convention to ensure responsibility of a single Member State for a protection seeker intended to put an end to such situations.[200] Article 3(5) of the Dublin Convention, however, explicitly retained the possibility to expel to a third country. This allowed the exclusion of protection seekers from substantive procedures and expulsion based on safe third country exceptions.[201] This raised the concern that new "in orbit"

198 Vilvarajah v. United Kingdom, 30 October 1991, Series A, 215, para. 102; Vermeulen 1999, p. 190-191; Spijkerboer and Vermeulen 1999, p. 188-189; Harvey 2000, p. 384; Zwaan 2003, p. 45.

199 Article 1 ECHR.

200 For potential cases of continued orbit within the EC under the Dublin regime, see Byrne and Shacknove 1996, p. 208.

201 Article 3(5) pertained to expulsion to third countries, but only *after* transfer to the responsible Member State under the Dublin Convention. However, the 1992 London Resolution on a harmonised approach to questions concerning host third countries specified that expulsion to a safe third country should also be considered *before* application of the DC. On this provision of the resolution on host third countries, see Achermann and Gattiker 1995, p. 22-23; and Byrne, Noll and Vedsted-Hansen 2002, p. 22. This construct, whereby both the

situations, instead of between the Member States, would occur between Member States and third countries, merely shifting the problem. Several commentators expected that protection seekers would attempt re-entry into the EC after being expelled to a third country, followed again by expulsion, and so on.[202]

In addition to a shuttling back and forth between a Member State and a third country, yet another new "in orbit" situation that may be set in motion by expulsion to a third country is that of continuous *onward* expulsion.[203] Such a chain of expulsions could result from the consecutive application of safe third country exceptions by different countries, which may be facilitated by the application of readmission agreements.

We saw above that the Geneva refugee Convention does not prevent chain expulsion from occurring.[204] As long as no breach occurs of the prohibition of direct and indirect refoulement, the GC permits continuous expulsion to another country. In subsection 9.2.3.4 below we will consider whether there are procedural requirements which follow from the European Convention, preventing continuous onward removal without substantive examination of the protection claim anywhere. Here, we will consider whether a chain of expulsions of a protection seeker from a destination State along a string of third countries may constitute a violation of Article 3 ECHR.

9.2.3.3.2.2 The European Commission of Human Rights

From the mid-seventies until the mid-eighties, the European Commission of Human Rights decided on a series of cases of migrants "in orbit", brought mostly against the Netherlands[205] and Belgium.[206] In this line of case law, the Commission held:

---

Member State in which the protection seeker is present before transfer, and the responsible Member State after transfer, may expel to a safe third country, has been incorporated into Article 3(3) of the Dublin Regulation (*OJ* L 50, 25 November 2003, p. 1).

202 Achermann and Gattiker 1995, p. 22, 37; Byrne and Shacknove 1996, p. 207-208; Byrne, Noll and Vedsted-Hansen 2002, p. 96-99.

203 Under the Dublin regime, such chain expulsion would include a maximum of one other Member State before continuing to a third country outside the European Community.

204 *Supra*, subsection 9.2.2.2.

205 The cases brought against the Netherlands, cited below, pertained to the so-called "Roosendaal method" used by the Dutch authorities. Illegal immigrants, found in the Netherlands and believed to have entered from Belgium, would be "expelled", placed unescorted on a train in Roosendaal on the Southern border with a one-way ticket to France. Benelux law, namely, determined that immigrants without residence entitlement must be expelled across the external border of the Benelux area after the abolishment of internal border controls. The immigrant, however, would often disembark at one of the several stops at train stations in Belgium, and illegally re-enter the Netherlands, only to be expelled in the same manner, *etcetera*. In one case such as this, expulsion was carried out 20 to 25 times over a period of roughly ten years, European Commisson of Human Rights, Appl. No. 10798/84, X v. the Netherlands, 5 March 1986, *RV* 1986, 94.

206 European Commisson of Human Rights, Appl. No. 7752/76, X v. Belgium, 15 December 1977 (struck off the list of cases); Appl. No. 8100/77, X v. the Federal Republic of Germany, 6 October 1978 (inadmissible); Appl. No. 7612/76, Giama v. Belgium, 17 July 1980

> The repeated expulsion of an individual whose identity it was impossible to establish to a country where his admission is not guaranteed, may raise an issue under Article 3 of the Convention, which forbids inhuman or degrading treatment.[207]

As in *D.* v. the UK, discussed above, the European Commission of Human Rights held that the implementation of a decision to expel, *in casu* a series thereof, could under certain circumstances constitute inhuman or degrading treatment contrary to Article 3 ECHR. In *X* v. the Netherlands of 5 March 1986, the Commission further determined that in order for such a complaint to be successful, the "in orbit" situation should not be of the applicant's own making by continuous voluntary illegal re-entry into the State from which s/he was removed.[208]

The same case suggests that, where referring to "admission", the Commission understood a State taking responsibility for a migrant in a more durable sense than merely allowing entry to territory.[209] Such an understanding would be justified. An inability to secure entry to the territory of a country may create an "in orbit" situation, but only a sustainable presence can effectively prevent it. Securing entry alone (which is what a readmission agreement does) is ineffective if the requested State subsequently declares the immigrant present without authorisation, and issues an order to leave the country, or expel him or her. A relevant characteristic of the "in orbit" cases before the Commission, finally, is that the applicants were arrested and placed in detention several times, pending expulsion, due to their unauthorised presence or in connection with minor criminal offences.

In a 1987 case, the appeals court in The Hague decided that one more attempt at expulsion after "countless" failures to expel to a country where admission was not guaranteed would violate Article 3 of the European Convention, and was thus prohibited.[210] In other words, accumulating previous counts of expulsion rendered any additional decision to expel illegal, constituting the proverbial drop which made the bucket spill. Post 1989 and *Soering*, this reasoning is arguably outdated. To prevent expulsion it would arguably be necessary to demonstrate a "real risk"[211] of a migrant ending up in "in orbit".

---

(friendly settlement); Appl. No. 10400/83, X v. the Netherlands, 14 May 1984, (manifestly unfounded); Appl. No. 10798/84, X v. the Netherlands, 5 March 1986, (manifestly unfounded).

207 Giama v. Belgium, 17 July 1980; X v. the Netherlands, 14 May 1984; X v. the Netherlands, 5 March 1986.

208 X v. the Netherlands, 5 March 1986, p. 278.

209 "Such an issue [under Article 3, NC] may arise, *a fortiori*, if an alien is over a long period of time deported repeatedly from one country to another without any country taking measures to *regularise his situation*" [Italics added, NC], X v. the Netherlands, 5 March 1986, p. 278.

210 The Hague appeals court, 29 October 1987, *RV* 1987, 94, p. 343.

211 Soering v. the United Kingdom, para. 88.

Summing up, the circumstances required for the situation of a migrant "in orbit" to reach the "minimum level of severity" constituting inhuman or degrading treatment under Article 3 ECHR are: a) repeated expulsion, by b) different States, to c) a third country where sustainable presence is not guaranteed, of d) an immigrant whose identity cannot be established. A relevant factor, which, although not strictly required may arguably contribute to the severity of the inhuman or degrading treatment, is whether the immigrant would be placed in detention pending expulsion. An expulsion, exposing a protection seeker to a real risk of such a situation constituting inhuman or degrading treatment, is arguably contrary to Article 3 ECHR.

Circumstances a) and b) excludes from the scope of Article 3 ECHR protection seekers who are "in orbit" back and forth between an EC Member State and a third country. As noted above, this form of being "in orbit" entails a series of involuntary removals followed by a voluntary movement of the protection seeker back into the EC.[212] Following the reasoning of the European Commission of Human Rights, this situation would be of the protection seeker's own making, and could therefore not raise an issue under Article 3 ECHR.[213]

This leaves for consideration the possibility of chain expulsion, set in motion by the expulsion of a protection seeker by a Member State pursuant to a safe third country exception. This could be a transfer under the multilateral safe third country- and readmission scheme established by the Dublin Regulation, or an expulsion to a safe third country outside the EC as facilitated by a bilateral readmission agreement.

It is firstly important to establish that the Dublin Regulation, or bilateral readmission agreements, do not safeguard against chain expulsion. Relevant to circumstance c) above, these instruments only guarantee readmission to the territory of a requested State. They do not guarantee residence, sustainable presence, or even consideration of the merits of the protection claim, after transfer of the readmittee. Rather to the contrary, the Dublin Regulation encourages onward removal after transfer,[214] as does the negotiation practice of readmission agreements at the Member State- and the Community level.[215]

Still, the circumstances under which the European Commission of Human Rights considered "in orbit" situations contrary to Article 3 ECHR are difficult to square with the characteristics of chain expulsion of protection seekers. The fact that chain expulsion is expulsion by successive different countries, rather than a shuttling back and forth between the same countries, does not exclude the European Commission's findings from applying. Protection seekers, also, may be undocumented, and claim an identity and nationality that is impossible or difficult to confirm. The unknown or unconfirmed identity of the expellee would not have the same importance, however. Central to the cases before the European Commission was whether it was permis-

212 *Supra*, subsection 9.2.3.3.2.1, at n. 202.

213 *Supra*, at n. 208.

214 See Article 3(3) of the Dublin Regulation, and *supra*, n. 201.

215 See *supra*, subsection 3.2.3.

sible to expel a person, for whom no responsible State can be identified under international law, to a third country. Central to the case of an undocumented protection seeker rejected on safe third country grounds is that expulsion is prohibited, regardless of whether a responsible State is identifiable.

Furthermore, cases of chain expulsion lack the same high frequency of expulsion, so salient a circumstance of the cases brought before the European Commission.[216] Although potentially endless in theory, reported cases of consecutive onward removal of protection seekers do not generally exceed a chain of three third countries.[217] Uncertain, moreover, is the factor of detention, which depends highly on the domestic policies of the third countries implicated in a potential chain of removals. The detention of protection seekers upon readmission to a third country cannot be excluded,[218] but it is not a necessary consequence or characteristic of chain expulsion.

The above case law of the European Commission of Human Rights alone thus provides insufficient footing for bringing chain expulsion of protection seekers within the remit of Article 3 of the European Convention. We therefore consider additional characteristics of the chain expulsion of protection seekers.

9.2.3.3.2.3 Chain expulsion in light of Soering v. the United Kingdom

Special consideration is arguably required of the fact that the persons, potentially being subjected to chain expulsion, are presumed to be in need of international protection.[219] The risk of torture or IDTP, claimed to emanate from a certain country, must therefore be considered real, unless and until disproved. Due to safe third country policies in conjunction with readmission agreements, which establish responsibility for transit migration, chain expulsion necessarily reverses the travel route of protection seekers back in the direction of that risk country, which draws closer at each count of expulsion. This is arguably legally relevant, in particular with regard to the level of severity required to raise an issue under Article 3 ECHR.

A relevant passage in the *Soering* case is the applicant's argument that several aspects of incarceration on death row would *cumulatively* constitute such serious treatment that his extradition, resulting in exposure thereto, would be contrary to Article 3 ECHR. As relevant aspects, the applicant *inter alia* cited "the delays in the appeal and review procedures following a death sentence, during which time he would be

216 See *supra*, n. 205.

217 Kumin 1995, p. 1, citing a case history documented in ECRE 1995.

218 Regarding detention of protection seekers in central and Eastern European countries, see Byrne, Noll and Vedsted-Hansen 2002, p. 354, 370. Regarding immigrant detention practices in certain CEECs, implicating also protection seekers and including detention pending expulsion, see FFM 1997; and FFM 2000.

219 Refugee status is of a declaratory nature. Spijkerboer and Vermeulen argue that protection under fundamental rights instruments other than the Geneva refugee Convention relies on the same concept. Spijkerboer and Vermeulen 2005, p. 70, 203-204.

subject to increasing tension and psychological trauma", and "the constant spectre of the execution itself".[220]

The Court seemed to agree with Soering that the *perspective* or *anticipation* of a certain dreaded event is important to the minimum level of severity bringing treatment within the scope of Article 3 ECHR. In its general considerations, the Court remarked: "account is to be taken not only of the physical pain experienced but also, where there is a considerable delay before execution of the punishment, of the sentenced person's mental anguish of anticipating the violence he is to have inflicted on him".[221] Related to the death row phenomenon in particular, the Court emphasised that "the condemned prisoner has to endure for many years the conditions on death row and the anguish and mounting tension of living in the ever-present shadow of death".[222] In this vein, the conclusion of the Court regarding the alleged breach of Article 3 stressed the following:

> For any prisoner condemned to death, some element of delay between imposition and execution of the sentence and the experience of severe stress in conditions necessary for strict incarceration are inevitable. [...] However, in the Court's view, having regard to the very long period of time spent on death row in such extreme conditions, with the ever present and mounting anguish of awaiting execution of the death penalty, and to the personal circumstances of the applicant, especially his age and mental state at the time of the offence, the applicant's extradition to the United States would expose him to a real risk of treatment going beyond the threshold set by Article 3 [...].[223]

The chain expulsion of persons, seeking protection under Article 3 ECHR, involves drawing ever closer to the risk of torture or IDTP from which they fled. Each count of expulsion to another third country is arguably accompanied by insecurity regarding the level of protection offered by that country. Although safe third country policy is premised upon expulsion taking place only to countries that would offer protection against refoulement, a considerable margin of fallibility exists in practice. This is due, *inter alia*, to the soundness of protection systems deteriorating the further East or South one travels, application of the principle of interstate trust despite differing interpretation of relevant treaties between State parties, reliance on general, instead of individual safety determinations, and expulsion to countries which are not party to relevant treaties. Objectively, one can state that the further a chain of expulsions carries, the more the guarantee of non-refoulement diminishes. Subjectively, even if eventual expulsion to the country of origin does not take place, this increases the level of mental stress and anguish experienced by a protection seeker, dreading exposure to torture or IDTP. In

220 Soering v. United Kingdom, para. 105.
221 Soering v. United Kingdom, para. 100.
222 Soering v. United Kingdom, para. 106.
223 Soering v. United Kingdom, para. 111.

other words, one can argue that chain expulsion of a protection seeker is accompanied by an "ever present and mounting anguish of anticipating" or by "living in the ever-present shadow" of torture or IDTP, which the protection seeker "is to have inflicted on him".

Further elements of importance in the case of Soering were the personal circumstances of the applicant, and the duration of the treatment. These were contributing factors in the Court's finding that the "death row phenomenon" constituted IDTP.[224] In this regard, one can point out that the mental health, and in some cases also physical health of victims of torture or IDTP can be poor. The mental condition of a person anticipating such maltreatment, without having experienced it in the past, may also be affected. The duration of a period of chain expulsion would depend on the circumstances, but it is possible that a protection seeker would remain "in orbit" for a lengthy period of time.

Under the above circumstances, it is arguable that a real risk of chain expulsion of a protection seeker could raise an issue under Article 3 ECHR. The repeated onward expulsion by States of a potential victim of torture or inhuman or degrading treatment or punishment to a third country, where sustainable presence is not guaranteed, may constitute inhuman or degrading treatment. Whether the identity and nationality of the protection seeker is confirmed is arguably not relevant in this regard. A factor, contributing to the overall severity of the inhuman or degrading treatment, would be potential detention, as well as, arguably, reception in substandard conditions, pending further expulsion. An expulsion by a Member State, exposing a protection seeker to a real risk of chain expulsion constituting inhuman or degrading treatment, would be contrary to Article 3 ECHR. This implies an obligation not to expel, thereby guaranteeing sustainable presence and preventing an "in orbit" situation from occurring.[225]

The practical relevance of the argument in this subsection depends highly on the conditions attached to demonstrating a real risk of chain expulsion. The burden of proof would most likely be on the protection seeker. S/he may be required at least to demonstrate the conclusion of readmission agreements between third countries along his or her travel route, and the presence of safe third country exceptions within the domestic policy or legislation of these countries. Furthermore, of relevance in this regard is the extent to which an expelling State may be required to investigate third countries down a potential chain of expulsions, which is discussed further below in subsection 9.2.3.4.3.

224 See *supra*, at n. 223.

225 It is not necessary to test this international obligation against the general principle of analysis of this chapter. The argument in this subsection does not pertain to a criterion determining the safety of a third country, as such. This means it does not imply the existence of a corresponding obligation held towards a protection seeker, who would remain within the jurisdiction of a destination State.

#### 9.2.3.4 Status determination

This subsection considers whether the European Convention of Human Rights contains an obligation to determine the status of protection seekers. It firstly analyses general requirements for the examination of claims to protection against expulsion under Article 3 ECHR. Secondly, it relates these requirements to expulsion to a third country in case of a risk of onward expulsion to the country of origin, and, thirdly, in case of a risk of onward expulsion to another third country – a "fourth" country.

##### *9.2.3.4.1 General requirements for the examination of protection claims*

In expulsion cases, the European Court of Human Rights has constantly found that its own examination of the existence of a risk of maltreatment in breach of Article 3 ECHR "must necessarily be a rigorous one in view of the absolute character of this provision and the fact that it enshrines one of the fundamental values of the democratic societies making up the Council of Europe".[226] The Court has extended this requirement of *rigorous examination* to legal remedies at the national level against the rejection of a protection claim, as well as the examination of the claim by the State.[227]

The requirements for the examination of protection claims against expulsion under Article 3 ECHR in (judiciary or administrative) appeal are determined by Article 13 ECHR. This provision requires an "effective remedy" against violations of European Convention rights. According to constant case law, an effective remedy is one which is "available and sufficient to afford redress in respect of the breaches alleged",[228] and allows the competent authority "both to deal with the substance of the relevant Convention complaint and to grant appropriate relief".[229]

In *Jabari* v. Turkey, the Court formulated additional requirements for remedies against a risk of treatment contrary to Article 3 ECHR in expulsion cases. Jabari was an Iranian national who failed to request asylum in Turkey within five days after her entry into Turkish territory, and was therefore rejected without substantive consideration of her protection claim by the Turkish administration as well as the judiciary. She held that expulsion to Iran would expose her to treatment contrary to Article 3. The Court found that she had been denied an effective remedy, specifying that:

> given the irreversible nature of the harm that might occur if the risk of torture or ill-treatment alleged materialised and the importance which [the Court, NC] attaches to Article 3, the notion of an effective remedy under Article 13 requires independent and

226 Vilvarajah v. the United Kingdom, para. 108.

227 The role of the Court in the protection of fundamental rights under the European Convention is subsidiary to that of the State parties and national judiciary authorities. It follows that the examination of a case as carried out by the Court is a minimum standard, and an instruction to the national judiciary, as well as, indirectly, the national administration, Spijkerboer and Vermeulen 2005, p. 291-293.

228 Akdivar and Others v. Turkey, 16 September 1996, para. 66.

229 Soering v. the United Kingdom, para. 120.

> rigorous scrutiny of a claim that there exist substantial grounds for fearing a real risk of treatment contrary to Article 3 [...].[230]

An effective remedy against an Article 3 complaint in an expulsion case requires "rigorous", as well as "independent" scrutiny. Rigorous scrutiny implies consideration of the merits of the complaint, *i.e.* the alleged risk of torture or IDTP. In the context of this case, independent scrutiny arguably implies that, where a State in first instance rejects a protection claim on purely procedural grounds (*in casu* for not respecting the five-day rule) this does not limit the administrative or legal review of that decision accordingly. It does not exclude consideration of the merits of the claim in appeal.

The Court furthermore delineated the leeway of the State to reject an Article 3 claim in expulsion cases on procedural grounds. Concerning the obligations of the State, the Court found that:

> having regard to the fact that Article 3 enshrines one of the most fundamental values of a democratic society and prohibits in absolute terms torture or inhuman or degrading treatment or punishment, a rigorous scrutiny must necessarily be conducted of an individual's claim that his or her deportation to a [...] country will expose that individual to treatment prohibited by Article 3.[231]

The State's decision regarding a protection claim must also be based on a rigorous examination. The especial value and nature of Article 3 implies a duty to examine the merits of a protection claim prior to expulsion. This clearly places limits on procedural obstacles under national law, which would prevent such an examination from taking place.

The Court continued by suggesting that failing to undertake a substantive examination would under certain circumstances – in this case, "the automatic and mechanical application of such a short time-limit for submitting an asylum application"[232] as the five-day rule – be "*at variance* with the protection of the fundamental value embodied in Article 3".[233] This particular formulation of the Court has raised questions.

The Court did not state that the five-day rule of Turkish law was *in violation* of Article 3. Instead, it considered it was *at variance* with the fundamental value of democratic societies that Article 3 represents. Spijkerboer and Vermeulen argue this implies that disregard of the substance of a protection claim, in particular as resulting from national procedural rules, would merely *contribute* towards finding that a State's decision to expel is in violation of Article 3.[234] This argument is unclear, however, and does not necessarily follow from the Court's choice of words.

230 Jabari v. Turkey, Judgement, Appl. No. 40035/98, 11 July 2000, para. 50.

231 Jabari v. Turkey, para. 39.

232 Jabari v. Turkey, para. 40 [Italics added, NC].

233 Jabari v. Turkey, para. 40.

234 Spijkerboer and Vermeulen 2005, p. 311.

In *Soering*, the Court's approach to reading inherent obligations into the short and general text of Article 3 was very similar. In *Soering*, the Court did not find the extradition of the applicant in violation of Article 3 *sec*, either. The Court's reasoning in *Soering* started by establishing that Article 3 enshrines a fundamental value of the democratic societies of the Council of Europe. Within that context, the Court found that extradition, resulting in exposure to illicit maltreatment in another country, would "hardly be compatible" with the underlying values of the Convention as a whole.[235] Furthermore, it would in particular be "contrary to the spirit and intendment" of Article 3, which was sufficient to find the UK's decision to extradite in violation of Article 3.[236] To be "at variance with" is a synonym of "incompatible with" and "contrary to". There is thus no apparent reason why expulsion in disregard of the merits of a claim to a real risk of torture or IDTP, thereby failing to abide by the inherent duty of rigorous examination, would not be able to constitute a violation of Article 3 by itself.

In sum, this first part of the analysis makes clear that the Court tends to insist on substantive examination of an Article 3 claim in expulsion cases, and displays a certain intolerance of procedural obstacles preventing the administration and/or the judiciary from doing so.[237] The Court's requirement of rigorous examination of protection claims under Article 3 ECHR confirms that this provision entails a positive obligation to assess the consequences of an intended expulsion, *i.e.* to status determination.[238]

It should be emphasised that this obligation arises *only* in case a State wishes to expel a protection seeker without being restricted by the ECHR.[239] State parties to the European Convention remain able to grant residence at their discretion, or allow informal stay, without undertaking status determination. The European Convention can therefore not be considered to contain a general obligation to determine the status of all persons claiming protection under Article 3.

In this respect, this subsection demonstrates that, as under the Geneva refugee Convention, the status of protection seekers under the European Convention is of a

235 These being a "common heritage of political traditions, ideals, freedom and the rule of law" as mentioned in the Preamble, Soering v. the United Kingdom, para. 88.

236 Soering v. the United Kingdom, para. 88.

237 Further testimony in this regard is the Court's case law regarding Article 35 ECHR and the exhaustion of national remedies. Where protection seekers have failed to meet procedural requirements under national law and therefore did not exhaust national remedies (risking expulsion without substantive review of their case at the national level, and by the European Court of Human Rights) the Court has determined that a degree of flexibility is in order. The leading case in this regard is Bahaddar v. the Netherlands, Judgement, 19 February 1998, para. 45. For a review of this line of case law, see Spijkerboer and Vermeulen 2005, p. 291-296, 307-312.

238 This positive obligation is arguably inherent in all prohibitions of refoulement, Battjes 2006.

239 We earlier used this argument in relation to the Geneva refugee Convention, *supra*, subsection 9.2.2.2, at n. 62, 63.

declaratory nature, at least where concerning expulsion to the country of origin.[240] Protecting claimants under Article 3 ECHR against expulsion to the country of origin, pending substantive examination of their case, ensures the effectiveness of this provision.[241] We will now examine this requirement in case of expulsion to a third country.

*9.2.3.4.2 Expulsion to a third country*

This subsection considers whether a State is obliged to undertake status determination under Article 3 ECHR in case it decides to expel, not to the country where the claimant fears a risk of torture or IDTP, but to a third country. It determines if, and if so to what degree, a State party to the European Convention can avoid the duty to undertake status determination by expelling to a third country. It furthermore considers whether status determination *by the third country* may be considered a requirement determining the safety of that country, and thus the legality of expelling a protection seeker to that country.

9.2.3.4.2.1 Status determination before expulsion

The case of *T.I.* v. the United Kingdom[242] is central to this subject-matter. T.I. claimed protection from non-State persecution in Germany. The German authorities rejected his claim and ordered his deportation to Sri Lanka, while German law did not recognise actions or omissions by non-State agents as grounds for protection under the Geneva refugee Convention or the European Convention. T.I. travelled onwards to seek protection in the UK, which did accept non-State persecution. The UK however rejected the claim without consideration of the merits, identifying Germany as the responsible Member State under the Dublin Convention. At issue before the European Court of Human Rights was the compatibility of the UK's decision to expel to Germany with Article 3 ECHR.

After finding that the UK cannot avoid responsibility under Article 3 ECHR for a protection seeker by expelling to a third country,[243] the Court elaborated on the relation between responsibility under the European Convention and the application of the Dublin Convention, determining that:

> Nor can the United Kingdom rely automatically in that context on the arrangements made in the Dublin Convention concerning the attribution of responsibility between European countries for deciding asylum claims. Where States establish international organisations, or *mutatis mutandis* international agreements, to pursue co-operation in certain fields of activities, there may be implications for the protection of fundamental rights. It would be incompatible with the purpose and object of the Convention if Contracting States were thereby absolved from their responsibility under the

240 *Supra*, subsection 9.2.2.2, at n. 59.

241 Spijkerboer and Vermeulen 2005, p. 70; Battjes 2006, p. 460-461.

242 T.I. v. United Kingdom, 7 March 2000, Application No. 43844/98.

243 *Supra*, subsection 9.2.3.2, at n. 176.

> Convention in relation to the field of activity covered by such attribution [...]. The Court notes [...] that, while the Dublin Convention may pursue laudable objectives, its effectiveness may be undermined in practice by the differing approaches adopted by Contracting States to the scope of protection offered.[244]

The Court again showed its intolerance towards procedural rules, which prevent consideration of Article 3 ECHR claims on their merits. It found that Article 3 does not allow *automatic* application of the Dublin Convention, that is, without consideration of possible implications for the fundamental rights of the affected individual. This finding would arguably apply also to unilateral safe third country policies, and the expulsion of protection seekers to countries outside the Dublin area.

A problem, central to both the Dublin Convention and safe third country policies, is that these instruments are based on the underlying assumption of equal, or at least harmonised, protection standards between countries. In *T.I.*, the Court recognised that this assumption may be detrimental to international protection, and that it warrants examination. The extent and detail of this examination, however, appears to depend still on interstate trust, and the presence of contra-indication of a third country's safety for an individual protection seeker.

The contra-indication at issue was a different appreciation under German law of persecution, or torture or IDTP, at the hands of non-State actors. Not only was there a difference in standard in this regard between the UK and Germany, German law also appeared inconsistent with the Court's case law in this regard. The Court has determined that actions or omissions by non-State actors may raise an issue under Article 3 ECHR, considering its absolute nature.[245]

In this context, the Court reiterated that an Article 3 claim requires a "rigorous scrutiny".[246] In order to determine whether the UK had complied with its international obligations, this duty *in casu* translated into a marginal examination of the applicant's situation in Sri Lanka, followed by a very elaborate and detailed examination of his situation in Germany.

The Court firstly reviewed the alleged risk of ill-treatment in the country of origin Sri Lanka, even though the UK or Germany did not submit observations or comments concerning the merits of the applicant's protection claim. Concluding this examination, the Court noted:

> that it has not heard substantial arguments from either the United Kingdom or German Governments as to the merits of the asylum claim. Nevertheless it considers that the materials presented by the applicant at this stage *give rise to concerns* as to

244 T.I. v. the United Kingdom, p. 14.

245 *Supra*, subsection 9.2.3.3.1, at n. 184.

246 T.I. v. the United Kingdom, p. 13-14. The T.I. case was decided four months prior to *Jabari* v. Turkey, in which case the Court elaborates further on this duty to rigorous examination, as discussed above.

> the risks faced by the applicant, should he be returned to Sri Lanka [...].[247] [Italics added, NC]

This passage has been interpreted as implying an obligation to consider the merits of a protection claim – to the degree of whether the situation in the country of origin "gives rise to concern" – before expulsion to a third country.[248] The Court does not clearly indicate that it considers this examination compulsory. However, as found above, the Court's examination of a protection claim may be considered instructive for the examination required of the national judiciary as well as administration.[249] Of relevance, furthermore, is that the UK decided to expel T.I. to Germany without status determination, and did not refer to the merits of the protection claim during the proceedings before the Court. The Court's explicit consideration of the merits ("nevertheless") illustrates the importance it attributes to a substantive examination. It is thus arguable that the Court hereby imposed such a requirement.

It is necessary to specify the content of this requirement. Determining whether the applicant's situation in the country, where s/he fears torture or IDTP, "gives rise to concern" clearly entails a more marginal examination than required by the "real risk" criterion. The Court thus did not impose a full examination of the merits, but a status determination "lite". *T.I.* v. the UK would thus indicate that States partly escape the duty to undertake status determination under Article 3 ECHR by expelling a protection seeker to a third country. In this case, the duty of *rigorous* examination would be replaced by a duty of *marginal* examination of the applicant's situation in the country of origin.

However, it is doubtful whether this examination is a protection imperative. It should arguably be considered a practical consideration. In *T.I.*, the Court arguably wished to determine first whether the applicant's protection claim was not manifestly unfounded. This ensured that undertaking a detailed examination of the possibility of indirect refoulement *via* Germany was not superfluous. A preliminary examination of the merits of a claim, based on a lighter criterion, enables sifting out protection seekers whose claims are evidently without merit, and who may therefore be expelled without restrictions. Undertaking such an examination is arguably at the discretion of State parties to the ECHR.[250]

247 T.I. v. United Kingdom, p. 15.

248 Zwaan 2003, p. 49-50.

249 See *supra*, subsection 9.2.3.4.1, n. 227.

250 See also *supra*, section 9.1, at n. 24. Opting to undertake such a preliminary examination could be more economical from a procedural point of view. Determining the safety of third countries for protection seekers can be very resource- and time-consuming, depending on how detailed that safety determination is required to be. The requirements of the Court regarding the determination of the safety of Germany in *T.I.* v. the United Kingdom, for example, were quite far-reaching.

#### 9.2.3.4.2.2 Status determination as a safety condition

This leaves the question of whether the European Convention requires status determination in the third country as a condition determining its safety, and thus a prerequisite for expulsion to that country. *T.I.* v. the United Kingdom is again relevant, but does not provide a conclusive answer to this question.

After finding that T.I.'s situation in Sri Lanka gave "rise to concern", the Court turned its attention to the German protection system, which it subjected to a rigorous examination. Prompted by an "apparent gap"[251] in the German protection system regarding non-State persecution, the Court considered in detail the different categories of protection under German law, as well as the available legal remedies. In particular, the Court searched for "effective procedural safeguards of any kind protecting the applicant from being removed from Germany to Sri Lanka".[252] In the reasoning of the Court, this would determine whether the UK had acted in accordance with Article 3 by deciding to expel to Germany.

As noted above, the view of the German administrative and judicial authorities regarding the relevance of non-State acts is inconsistent with the view of the Court. Despite this inconsistency, the Court found that German law contained an effective procedural safeguard, which sufficiently provided for cases such as T.I.'s. The apparent protection gap was considered filled, because Germany offered a form of protection against expulsion for persons who are in substantial danger to life, personal integrity or liberty.

Several further circumstances contributed to the Court's finding that Germany was "safe" for T.I. to return. Germany assured the Court that he would not be in danger of "immediate or summary removal" [253] to Sri Lanka, while his case would be subject to an examination before onward expulsion, arguably qualifying as "rigorous". The German government namely guaranteed that T.I. would be able to file a new claim, which would be subject to *status determination.* In addition, an outstanding order to deport T.I. to Sri Lanka had expired, requiring a new deportation order, which would be subject to a legal remedy.[254] Under these circumstances, the Court concluded that a "real risk" of removal by Germany to Sri Lanka in breach of Article 3 ECHR was absent, implying that the UK's decision to expel was legal, and T.I.'s complaint manifestly unfounded.[255]

This suggests that the Court might have ruled differently, had status determination in Germany not been guaranteed. It is clear that the Court required at least some form of *procedural interruption* in the third country of the "possible chain of events"[256] leading to expulsion to the country of origin. The Court insisted on certain safety condi-

251 T.I. v. the United Kingdom, p. 16.

252 T.I. v. the United Kingdom, p. 15.

253 T.I. v. the United Kingdom, p. 15.

254 T.I. v. the United Kingdom, p. 15.

255 T.I. v. the United Kingdom, p. 17.

256 T.I. v. the United Kingdom, p. 14.

tions in Germany preventing, at least, "immediate or summary removal" to the country of origin. This arguably refers to an administrative decision on expulsion in the third country, as well as a remedy against a negative decision in accordance with Article 13 ECHR. Whether the Court would go so far as require status determination in the third country, however, is uncertain.

It appears arguable that in case of a risk of onward expulsion to the country of origin, like in *T.I.* v. the UK, the Court would posit status determination in the third country as a safety condition. The Court generally insists on rigorous examination before expulsion to the country of origin. One therefore expects that the Court would seek a guarantee of examination of the merits of the protection claim in the third country, before onward expulsion. This would also be in accordance with the general principle of analysis of this chapter, outlined in subsection 9.2.1.1. The criterion determining the safety of the third country – status determination – corresponds with the obligation incumbent on a destination State, which expels a protection seeker directly to the country of origin.

It should however be emphasised that the principle of interstate trust mitigates any hard requirements regarding the safety examination of third countries, which may be derived from *T.I.* v. the UK. Some authors have interpreted *T.I.* as prohibiting State practice, which foregoes an individualised safety determination of a third country by appealing to the principle of interstate trust.[257] As pointed out above, however, the Court's detailed examination of the German protection system was prompted by a clear contra-indication that Germany would protect T.I. against refoulement.[258] It has been argued rightly that this case therefore sanctions States' reliance on the principle of interstate trust with regard to expulsion to third countries, which are party to the European Convention.[259]

Accordingly, the expelling State may trust that a fellow State party would adhere to its obligations under the European Convention, and not remove to the country of origin in violation of Article 3 ECHR, unless the protection seeker is able to provide indication of the contrary. In case the protection seeker is able to do so, a "rigorous" individual safety determination must arguably be undertaken, as demonstrated by the Court. Safety criteria would include the possibility of receiving protection under the third country's asylum legislation. They would also include the availability of procedures, which prevent immediate onward removal and ensure protection if warranted, probably including status determination.

It is yet unclear how the Court would decide in a case of expulsion to a third country, which is *not* party to the European Convention. There is, however, indication that the Court might require a concrete guarantee of non-refoulement from such a third country.[260]

257 Zwaan 2003, p. 51.

258 *Supra*, at n. 251.

259 Spijkerboer and Vermeulen 2005, p. 94.

260 Amuur v. France, Judgement, 25 June 1996 ; Spijkerboer and Vermeulen 2005, p. 94.

*9.2.3.4.3 Onward expulsion to a "fourth" country*

This final subsection considers which procedural requirements apply in case a protection seeker risks onward expulsion by the third country, in turn, to another third country – a "fourth" country. What would have been the investigative obligations of the UK under Article 3 ECHR in case T.I., after transfer from the UK to Germany, would have faced expulsion to another third country pursuant to a safe third country exception? In *T.I.*, the Court stated that indirect removal to an intermediary country does not affect the responsibility of the destination country to ensure that a protection seeker is not exposed to illicit maltreatment as a result.[261] The destination country retains responsibility, which is in principle independent of the length of a potential chain. Would Article 3 therefore imply an obligation to examine the safety of all third countries in a potential chain, notwithstanding application of the principle of interstate trust?

Arguably, the positive obligation of a destination State to examine the consequences of a decision to expel does not extend beyond the first third country in a potential chain of fourth, fifth, sixth countries. In *T.I.*, after finding that the possibility of protection in Germany was not *prima facie* excluded, and that procedures were in place for preventing immediate onward removal as well as for consideration of T.I.'s claim, the Court was not willing to entertain the possible outcome of those procedures:

> While it may be that on any re-examination of the applicant's case the German authorities might still reject it, this is largely a matter of *speculation and conjecture*. There is furthermore no basis on which the Court could assume in this case that Germany would fail to fulfil its obligations under Article 3 of the Convention to provide the applicant with protection against removal to Sri Lanka if he put forward substantial grounds that he faces a risk of torture and ill-treatment in that country. To the extent therefore that there is the possibility of such a removal, it has not been shown in the circumstances of this case to be sufficiently concrete or determinate.[262] [Italics added, NC]

With the potential for protection and the basic tools to ensure it present, the Court's trust that Germany would adhere to its obligations under the European Convention not to refoule was restored. Despite recognition of the fact that T.I. would most likely not be allowed to submit new evidence of the torture he had undergone in Sri Lanka,[263] possible rejection by Germany in violation of Article 3 ECHR was considered too much "speculation and conjecture", and not "sufficiently concrete or determinate". Under these circumstances, in other words, the UK was able to rely on the principle of interstate trust and expel to Germany.

One expects that in case of similar indications that Germany would not refoule *indirectly*, the Court would not have required the UK to entertain a possible outcome of

261 *Supra*, subsection 9.2.3.2, at n. 176.

262 T.I. v. the United Kingdom, p. 16.

263 T.I. v. the United Kingdom, p. 15.

expulsion to another third country in violation of Article 3 ECHR, either. One can thus arguably deduce that the Court would limit the duty of an expelling State to examine a potential chain of expulsions to the protection system of the third country to which it expels a protection seeker.

Continuing on the basis of this finding, it is necessary to specify the duty to examine the protection system of a third country in case of a risk of onward removal to a "fourth" country. In *T.I.*, the Court examined procedural safeguards against removal to the country of origin, including status determination. In case of onward expulsion to a fourth country, one expects that the subject of examination, instead, would need to be the safe third country policy of the third country in question.

The extent of this examination would depend on the principle of interstate trust. In the absence of contra-indications, the destination State may trust a third country, party to the European Convention, to exercise its safe third country policy in accordance with its obligations under the Convention. It may then expel a protection seeker without further examination. In the presence of contra-indications, however, the destination State would arguably be required to verify whether the third country would, in turn, undertake a safety determination of the fourth country in accordance with the Court's examination in *T.I.* v. the UK. It must verify whether the third country will undertake a "rigorous" safety determination of the fourth country, as outlined above.[264] In case of indication that the third country would undertake this examination, trust in its protection system and safety would be restored, and expulsion would be permissible. In case of indication that the third country would not undertake this examination, expulsion by the destination State to this country would be prohibited under Article 3 ECHR.

These findings affect the argument made in subsection 9.2.3.3.2 regarding chain expulsion. Based on *T.I.*, the European Court of Human Rights would arguably not require an expelling State to investigate beyond the first third country in a potential chain. Accordingly, it is possible that the Court would also reject evidence of the possibility of onward expulsion beyond that country as "speculation and conjecture".[265] This would render it difficult for a protection seeker to demonstrate a real risk of chain expulsion, amounting to inhuman or degrading treatment or punishment.

#### *9.2.3.4.4 Interim conclusion*

The above findings regarding a duty to undertake status determination under Article 3 ECHR may be summarised as follows.

States must examine the merits of a protection claim under Article 3 ECHR "rigorously" before implementing expulsion to the country of origin, the country where the protection seeker is allegedly at risk of torture or IDTP. An effective remedy must be available against possible rejection, entailing again consideration of the merits.

In case of expulsion to a third country, States may not automatically apply the Dublin Convention or, arguably, unilateral safe third country exceptions, but must consider the implications for the fundamental rights of the individual involved. Individu-

264 *Supra*, subsection 9.2.3.4.2.2.

265 *Supra*, at n. 262.

alised and detailed examination of the safety of the third country in question, however, depends on the applicability of the principle of interstate trust. In the absence of contra-indications of the safety of a third country, party to the European Convention, expulsion may take place without further examination by the destination State. In the case of contra-indications, the destination State must:

a) if the applicant is at risk of expulsion by the third country to the country of origin, examine whether the protection system of the third country provides the possibility of protection, as well as effective procedural safeguards to ensure protection, including an effective remedy against rejection, and probably status determination;
b) if the applicant is at risk of expulsion by the third country to a fourth country, examine whether the third country will, in turn, undertake a safety examination of the fourth country in accordance with the above under a).

Requirements a) and b) are both in accordance with the general principle of analysis of this chapter. The criteria under a) and b), determining the safety of the third country and thus the legality of expulsion to that country, correspond with the obligations incumbent on a destination State, which would expel to the country of origin, or a third country, respectively.

#### 9.2.3.5 Extraterritorial application of Article 3 ECHR

This subsection discusses extraterritorial application of Article 3 ECHR. It considers whether protection seekers at the border and protection seekers intercepted at sea enjoy protection under Article 3 ECHR.[266]

Outside the context of refugee protection, the European Commission of Human Rights found early on that the European Convention affected the sovereign right of State parties to control the entry of aliens.[267] In a 1959 case, the applicant argued that the refusal of an entry permit preventing a personal appearance in court proceedings was contrary to Article 6 of the European Convention. The argument of the Swedish government that "the right to enter a foreign country is not one of the rights guaranteed by the Convention",[268] prompted the Commission to comment that:

> Under general international law a State has the right, in virtue of its sovereignty, to control the entry and exit of foreigners into and out of its territory. It is true that a right or freedom to enter the territory of States, Members of the Council of Europe, is not, as such, included among the rights and freedoms guaranteed in Section I of the Convention. However, a State which signs and ratifies the European Convention

266 Regarding the exclusion from the analysis of the extraterritorial application of Article 3 ECHR to persons claiming protection in another State, see *supra*, subsection 9.2.2.4, at. n. 117-118.

267 *X v. Government of Sweden*, 30 June 1959, Application No. 434/58, 28 ILR 242 (1959); cited in Grahl-Madsen 1972, p. 276.

268 X v. Sweden, 28 ILR 246.

> on Human Rights and Fundamental Freedoms must be understood as agreeing to restrict the free exercise of its rights under general international law, including its right to control the entry and exit of foreigners, to the extent and within the limits of the obligations which it has accepted under that Convention.[269]

In other words, the Commission found that the European Convention regulates the entry of aliens *if and insofar as necessary* for the enjoyment of European Convention rights and freedoms. This particular underpinning and broad reading of extraterritorial applicability of the European Convention has not found its way into the case law of the European Court of Human Rights. The Court is moreover yet to express on a right of entry for protection seekers under the European Convention. Such a right may nevertheless be derived from relevant case law concerning the meaning of the phrase "within their jurisdiction" in Article 1 ECHR.

Noll has deduced the applicability of Article 3 of the European Convention to protection seekers at the border from the geographical scope of Article 3 as delineated by Article 1 of the European Convention.[270] This would imply a right of entry to territory, still under the assumption that the resulting State obligation to allow entry is of a negative nature.[271] Article 1 obliges State parties to secure to everyone within their jurisdiction the rights and freedoms defined in Section I of the European Convention. Noll's argument rests on the meaning of the phrase "within their jurisdiction" as determined in a 1983 case before the European Commission of Human Rights.[272] The Commission found that with this choice of words the drafters had stressed, in conformity with the object of Article 1 and the purpose of the European Convention as a whole, that the reach of the rights and freedoms of the European Convention is not limited to the national territories of the State parties. Rather:

> [...] the High Contracting Parties are bound to secure the said rights and freedoms to all persons under their actual authority and responsibility, not only when the authority is exercised within their own territory but also when it is exercised abroad. As Stated by the Commission in Applications Nos. 6780/74 and 6950/75, the authorised agents of the State, including diplomatic or consular agents and armed forces, not only remain under its jurisdiction when abroad but bring any other persons or property "within the jurisdiction" of that State, to the extent that they exercise authority over such persons or property. Insofar as, by their acts or omissions, they affect such persons or property, the responsibility of the State is engaged. [273]

269 X v. Sweden, 28 ILR 250.

270 See Noll 2000, p. 441-445.

271 *Supra*, subsection 9.2.2.4, at n. 119.

272 W v. Ireland, Dec. Adm. Com. Ap. 9360/81, 28 February 1983, D&R 32.

273 W v. Ireland, para. 14, D&R 32, p. 214-215.

Noll hence argues that a protection seeker who requests entry at the border of a State party to the European Convention of Human Rights is under the authority, and thereby within the jurisdiction of that State. An act or omission by a State with regard to entry affects that protection seeker, which engages the responsibility of that State under the European Convention. More specifically, it would trigger Article 3 ECHR and the implicit prohibition of refoulement therein if denying entry has "as a direct consequence the exposure of an individual to proscribed ill-treatment".[274]

Battjes builds further on this subject-matter, taking into account subsequent case law of the European Court of Human Rights concerning Article 1 ECHR, and the question of when a person is "within the jurisdiction" of a State party.[275] He concludes that the Court has implicitly accepted the exercise of authority by agents of a State as definitive of bringing a person within the jurisdiction of that State, whilst taking into account that extraterritorial jurisdiction is limited by the sovereignty of other States. Protection seekers who request border guards to allow entry to territory are thus within the jurisdiction of the relevant State, as are protection seekers intercepted at sea. Exercising authority over a protection seeker at the border or at sea, moreover, does not affect the sovereign rights of other States, and is therefore not problematic from that perspective.[276]

Furthermore, the practice of the Member States confirms the application of the prohibition of refoulement implicit in Article 3 to protection claims at the border.[277] In the present context of the European Convention, there is no negative State practice regarding the interception of protection seekers at sea.[278]

Reiterating our earlier analysis,[279] *mutatis mutandis*, the obligation to allow entry following from Article 3 ECHR is a qualified one. It does not apply to all persons at the border claiming protection under Article 3 from *any* country. It is limited to protection seekers at the border with a neighbouring country from which a real risk of exposure to torture or IDTP emanates, directly or indirectly. The applicability of Article 3 to interception of protection seekers at sea entailing redirection to the country of embarkation or another country equally depends on whether such a direct or indirect risk would exist there. Only in these cases could the exposure of an individual to maltreatment

274 Soering v. UK, para. 91.

275 *Bankovic et al v. Belgium and 16 other States*, 12 December 2001, Appl. no. 52207/00; *Öcalan v. Turkey*, 12 March 2003, Appl. no. 46221/99.

276 Battjes, *the right to entry* (work in progress).

277 The argument expounded above regarding Article 3(1) of the Dublin Regulation, implying the application of Article 33(1) GC at the border, applies *mutatis mutandis* to Article 3 ECHR. See further, Battjes, *the right to entry* (work in progress).

278 The lack of protest by (EC Member) States against the interception of Haitians on the high seas by the US is relevant exclusively to the context of the Geneva Refugee Convention, the US not being party to the ECHR.

279 *Supra*, subsection 9.2.2.4, after n. 140.

as prohibited by Article 3 ECHR be "a direct consequence" of a denial of entry, as is required by the Court.[280]

In practice, however, every protection claim at the frontier would thus require *investigation* of whether a real risk of exposure to torture or IDTP exists. Under Article 3 ECHR, refusing a protection seeker entry at the border or at sea can therefore never be automatic, implying a *de facto* general obligation of rejection at the frontier. It makes no difference whether a protection seeker claims at the border, at sea, or within the territory of a State party to the European Convention.[281]

### *9.2.4 Interim conclusion*

This section has identified a series of international obligations in the Geneva refugee Convention and the European Convention of Human Rights, relevant to the expulsion of protection seekers to third countries. As the basis for this analysis, the following general principle was used:

> The conditions by which to determine the safety of a third country are delimited by the international obligations, which a State holds towards protection seekers remaining on its territory.

According to this general principle, it was concluded that expulsion to a third country is allowed as long as the prohibition of (indirect) refoulement is respected. This implies a duty to investigate the protection of an individual protection seeker against refoulement in the third country concerned; a duty that is delimited by the principle of interstate trust. In the context of the ECHR in particular, this duty was defined in detail, distinguishing between a risk of onward removal to the country of origin, and onward removal to another third country. It was furthermore concluded that the obligations following from the prohibition of refoulement apply to persons claiming the protection of a European Union Member State at the border in the same manner as to persons claiming protection *in-country*. In the context of the ECHR, moreover, the principle of non-refoulement applies to persons claiming protection at sea.

It was argued that status determination in a Member State before expulsion to a third country is not required, as long as the principle of non-refoulement is respected. Under certain circumstances, status determination in a third country could be a condition for the safety of that country for a protection seeker, thus forming part of the investigation required of a Member State before expulsion. It was furthermore argued that the GC and ECHR are unlikely sources for further safety standards in third countries, additional to protection against refoulement, such as access to employment, education, housing, social security, or basic means of subsistence.

Furthermore, it was found that, under certain circumstances, a real risk of chain expulsion of a protection seeker could raise an issue under Article 3 ECHR. The repeated onward expulsion by States of a potential victim of torture or inhuman or

280 Battjes, *the right to entry* (work in progress); Soering v. UK, para. 91 (*supra*, at n. 274).

281 Battjes, *the right to entry* (work in progress).

degrading treatment or punishment to a third country, where sustainable presence is not guaranteed, may arguably constitute inhuman or degrading treatment. It was however concluded that the practical relevance of this finding is likely to be limited, while the European Court of Human Rights does not seem inclined to require safety investigation beyond the first country in a potential chain of expulsions.

Finally, it was pointed out that, by requiring States to scrutinise other States in light of certain fundamental rights standards before expulsion of a protection seeker, the GC and ECHR have a potential spill-over effect. State parties are arguably encouraged to exercise pressure on non-parties to adopt these standards. On a political level, the GC and ECHR hereby have possible implications outside the inner circle of signatories.

## 9.3 Compatibility of Community readmission agreements with international refugee protection obligations

Readmission agreements do not provide a legal basis for the rejection of protection seekers,[282] nor for their expulsion. Readmission agreements may facilitate expulsion after a Member State decides to reject a protection claim. In other words, the application of a readmission agreement to facilitate the expulsion of a protection seeker is never a solitary act; it must always be preceded by a decision under national law to reject and expel that protection seeker.

It is therefore not possible to review the relationship between the application of readmission agreements to expel protection seekers to third countries, and obligations of international refugee protection, in an isolated manner. It is necessary to incorporate the general relation between readmission agreements and safe third country policies into this analysis. Arguably, the legality of a decision to reject and expel a protection seeker under a safe third country exception is a factor, determining the legality of a consequent application of a readmission agreement.

In addition to a common readmission policy, the Community is developing what could be considered a common safe third country policy. Safe third country decisions of the Member States are partially determined by the Directive on minimum standards on procedures in Member States for granting and withdrawing of refugee status (hereinafter the procedures Directive), which was adopted by the Council on 1 December 2005.[283]

In order to determine whether Community readmission agreements are compatible with the international refugee protection obligations, identified in section 9.2, subsection 9.3.1 reviews the legality of the procedures Directive in light of these obligations. Subsection 9.3.2 then establishes whether the concerns relating to readmission agreements in the context of international refugee protection, identified in section 9.1, raise any separate issues under international refugee law.

Considering that sections 9.1 and 9.2 focused entirely on the readmission of protection seekers to third countries, the following review does not include consideration

282 Fernhout 1999, p. 89.

283 *OJ* L 326, 13 December 2005, p. 13.

of readmission *clauses*. The incorporation of readmission clauses into other Community- and mixed agreements is part of the common readmission policy. Such clauses, however, commit only to the readmission of nationals, and are thus unrelated to the issues under review here.

### *9.3.1 The common safe third country policy*

This subsection reviews the legality of the safe third country exceptions included in the procedures Directive. It does so in three steps. It first analyses the content of these safe third country exceptions in subsection 9.3.1.1. Subsection 9.3.1.2 then determines the relationship in general between the procedures Directive, which establishes minimum standards in the asylum field, and international obligations of refugee protection. Based on this general relation, subsection 9.3.1.3, reviews the procedures directive in light of relevant obligations of international refugee law, as identified in section 9.2.

#### 9.3.1.1 Safe third country exceptions under the procedures Directive

This subsection analyses the content of the developing common safe third country policy.[284] Two pieces of secondary legislation determine this common policy. The first is the Dublin Regulation, which is excluded from consideration. This instrument does not directly regulate the rejection of protection seekers, leading to expulsion to a non-EU Member State with possible application of a Community readmission agreement.[285] The second is the procedures Directive,[286] which is examined in detail.

The procedures Directive is the result of long and arduous negotiations in the Council. Since the original proposal by the Commission on 20 September 2000, the directive has shed its skin several times.[287] As a result of the repeated political compromises necessary to have the text adopted, there is doubt as to the value of the procedures directive as a harmonising instrument.

The desire of the Member States to retain their respective domestic policies has moulded the directive into an *à-la-carte* instrument, or "a catalogue of national practices",[288] listing discretionary options instead of prescribing uniform procedure. A number of important aspects of asylum procedures, moreover, have been cut out. Unable to agree on a minimum standard for a common approach, for example, the directive no longer regulates the suspensive effect of remedies on expulsion.[289] Although a major obstacle during the negotiations, the provisions pertaining to safe third country policy were not removed. The procedures directive provides for the rejection of protec-

284 For an earlier review of the current safe third country exceptions under the procedures Directive, see Spijkerboer and Vermeulen 2005, p. 167, 183-186.

285 The Dublin Regulation merely *allows* Member States this possibility in Article 3(3), see *supra*, subsection 9.2.3.3.2.1, n. 171.

286 *Supra*, at n. 283.

287 COM(2000) 578 final, 20 September 2000; COM(2002) 326 final, 3 July 2002; Council Doc. 15198/03, 4 December 2003; Council Doc. 14203/04, 9 November 2004.

288 European parliament, session document PE 357.562v02-00, p. 53.

289 Draft procedures Directive, Council Doc. 14203/04, Article 38(3)(a).

tion seekers on the basis of several safe third country exceptions. In comparison with the original Commission proposal,[290] however, these provisions have less harmonising effect, and provide a lower level of fundamental rights protection.

The procedures Directive contains five safe third country exceptions. The first is Article 25(1), which confirms that a Member State is not required to determine the status of a protection seeker for whom another Member State is responsible under the Dublin Regulation. The second is Article 25(2)(a), which allows Member State to declare as inadmissible – meaning exclusion from substantive procedures – the protection claims of persons who have been granted refugee status in another Member State. The third is Article 25(2)(b) in conjunction with Article 26, and pertains to so-called "first countries of asylum". It allows Member States to declare as inadmissible the protection claims of persons, who enjoy protection in a third country as a refugee, or an otherwise sufficient form of protection.

The fourth and fifth safe third country exceptions, respectively, pertain to "safe third countries" – Article 25(2)(c) in conjunction with Article 27 – and to "European safe third countries" – Article 36. These exceptions are the most controversial, requiring elaboration.[291]

#### *9.3.1.1.1 "Safe third countries"*

Article 25(2)(c) in conjunction with Article 27 – titled "The safe third country concept" – allows a Member State to declare as inadmissible the protection claims of persons for whom a safe third country (which is not a Member State) can be identified.

##### 9.3.1.1.1.1 Safety criteria

Third countries may be considered safe according to four cumulative criteria listed in Article 27(1):

> (a) life and liberty are not threatened on account of race, religion, nationality, membership of a particular social group or political opinion; and
> (b) the principle of non-refoulement in accordance with the Geneva Convention is respected; and
> (c) the prohibition on removal in breach of the right to freedom from torture and cruel, inhuman or degrading treatment as laid down in international law is respected; and
> (d) the possibility exists to request refugee status and, if found to be a refugee, to receive protection in accordance with the Geneva Convention.[292]

290 COM(2000) 578 final.

291 The EP has strongly rejected these two safe third country exceptions, proposing substantial amendments to Article 27, and deletion of Article 35A, European parliament 2005. See European parliament, session document PE 357.562v02-00, amendments 69, 74-81, and 104.

292 Article 27(1) of the procedures Directive.

These safety criteria reiterate the refoulement prohibitions of Article 33 of the Geneva Refugee Convention and Article 3 of the European Convention of Human Rights,[293] and require the presence of a protection system. This system should offer the possibility for requesting protection, and, in case of recognition as a refugee, the potential for receiving protection in accordance with the GC. Ratification of these two conventions, however, is not necessarily required. This means that expulsion to third countries which are not party to the GC and ECHR is not excluded, provided these countries would *de facto* adhere to the listed obligations.

Article 27(2)(a) of the procedures Directive contains a further condition, which is that the protection seeker must have a "connection" with the third country "on the basis of which which it would be reasonable for that person to go to that country".[294] It was argued in section 9.1 that a connection between the protection seeker and a third country is not strictly a criterion determining the safe of that country, and as such not a protection imperative.[295] A connection between the protection seeker and a third country does determine the suitability of that country as a host State. This condition therefore pertains primarily to the finding of a durable solution of refugee protection after expulsion, and to the sustainability of return.

The procedures Directive does not specify what kind of connection is required, other than that it must form a "reasonable" basis for return. The Directive thereby fails to decide the central question of whether protection seekers may be expelled to safe third countries through which they merely travelled. It leaves this question to the national law of the Member States, whilst not excluding the possibility of expulsion due to transit through a third country. At the European level, the Member States have generally shown to prioritise wider expulsion possibilities over sustainability of return and reduction of the risk of re-entry attempts, or other secondary movements. The Member States would thus arguably be inclined to interpret mere transit through a safe third country as a "reasonable connection" in the sense of Article 27(2)(a) of the Directive. They would thereby align the rejection of protection seekers with the conditions, necessary for their subsequent readmission to third countries under Community- or bilateral readmission agreements.

#### 9.3.1.1.1.2 Procedural safeguards

The application of the safe third country exception of Article 25(2)(c) of the procedures Directive in conjunction with Article 27 is subject to a number of procedural requirements. Firstly, the competent authorities of a Member State must be "satisfied" that the safety criteria of Article 27(1) are fulfilled.[296] To "satisfy" is a subjective criterion, and lighter than, for example, a requirement to "establish" or "demonstrate" the safety of a country. Furthermore, in order for the Member State authorities to arrive at this

293 The criteria also reflect Article 3 CAT and Article 7 ICCPR, which are however outside the scope of the present research, as explained above in subsection 9.2.1.2.

294 Article 27(2)(a) of the procedures directive.

295 *Supra*, section 9.1, at n. 20.

296 Article 27(1) of the procedures Directive.

conclusion, national legislation is not necessarily required to provide for individualised examination,[297] except where a protection seeker would make use of the possibility to challenge a safety determination considering the particulars of his or her case.[298]

This means that the Directive would permit administrative decisions in first instance based solely on a general safety determination, "satisfying" the authorities that a particular third country is safe in an individual case.[299] Member States are able to continue to make use of national lists of third countries deemed safe, as long as incorporating the above four safety criteria.[300] We should moreover note that, even in case national legislation *would* guarantee individualised safety determination in first instance (a choice which is open to the Member States), Article 27 would not prevent an appeal to the principle of interstate trust from foregoing such an examination. Interstate trust is also a means by which the competent authorities could "satisfy" themselves that a particular third country is safe in an individual case.

We noted that the Directive does not require the national law of the Member States to guarantee an individualised safety examination, except when the protection seeker challenges a negative decision.[301] Remarkable is that this possibility to rebut the safety of a third country has been explicitly limited to grounds, stating that the applicant would be subjected to torture, cruel, inhuman or degrading treatment or punishment as a result of expulsion.[302] The safety determination of a third country is thus only partly refutable, limited to one of the four safety criteria listed in Article 27(1).[303]

297 Article 27(2)(b). According to this provision, Member States are held to adopt legislative "rules on the methodology by which the competent authorities satisfy themselves that the safe third country concept may be applied to a particular country or to a particular applicant". It continues, however, by determining that "such methodology shall include case by case consideration of the safety of the country for a particular applicant *and/or* national designation of countries considered to be generally safe". [Italics added, NC] Individualised safety examination is thus not guaranteed.

298 Article 27(2)(c). According to this provision, Member States are held to adopt legislative "rules, in accordance with international law, allowing an individual examination of whether the third country concerned is safe for a particular applicant which, as a minimum, shall permit the applicant to challenge the application of the safe third country concept on the grounds that he/she would be subjected to torture, cruel, inhuman or degrading treatment or punishment".

299 Article 27(2)(b), *supra*, n. 297.

300 The Member States abandoned their original intention to draw up a common list of safe third countries. The Member States are required to inform the Council of the third countries deemed safe in accordance with Article 27 of the Directive (See Article 27(5)). The Council will, however, adopt a list of "super" safe third countries pursuant to Article 36(2)(d) and 36(3).

301 Article 27(2)(b) and Article 27(2)(c), *supra*, n. 297 and 298.

302 Article 27(2)(b), *supra*, n. 298; Spijkerboer and Vermeulen 2005, p. 185.

303 The Directive extends this limitation to Article 39 of the Directive, which secures "the right to an effective remedy" regarding a decision of inadmissibility under Article 25(2)(c). Article 39(3)(c) allows Member States to adapt the concept of an "effective remedy" (within

A second procedural safeguard is contained in Article 27(3)(b). This provision obliges the Member States to provide the protection seeker with a document informing the authorities of the third country in question, in the language of that country, that his or her protection claim has not been examined on its merits.

A final remark regarding this safe third country exception is that readmission to the territory of the third country in question is not explicitly required.[304] Recital 25 of the Preamble, however, states that the practical effect of rejection on safe third country grounds under the directive presumes readmission. Article 27(4), moreover, guarantees access to an asylum procedure in a Member State in case the third country would refuse readmission to its territory. The procedures Directive hereby arguably safeguards against protection seekers ending up "in orbit" between Member States and third countries.

*9.3.1.1.2 "European safe third countries"*

The final safe third country exception contained in the procedures Directive is Article 36, titled "The European safe third countries concept". This provision allows the Member States to exclude from substantive asylum procedures protection seekers, who entered, or attempted to enter a Member State "illegally" from the territory of "European safe third countries", also known as "super safe third countries".[305]

The presumption of safety of these countries is stronger, and thus more difficult to rebut for the protection seeker. Expulsion to these countries is subject to a smaller number of procedural safeguards. A further difference with the "safe third country concept" of Article 27 is that the Council will identify third countries which are safe in the sense of Article 36, and draw up a common list.[306]

Except for its title, Article 36 does not explicitly refer to the geographical limitation of safe countries under this provision as being "European". Recital 24 of the Preamble, as well as a draft version of the Directive, however suggests that this provision was drafted primarily with third countries on the external border of the European Union in mind.[307] This is in line with the general "cordon" or "buffer zone" politics, pursued by the EU in the field of external immigration and asylum policy. In addition,

the meaning of the procedures Directive) to the limited grounds for challenging a safety determination under Article 27(2)(c).

304 Spijkerboer and Vermeulen 2005, p. 185.

305 European parliament, session document PE 357.562v02-00, p. 53.

306 Article 36(2)(c); and Article 36(3).

307 See draft procedures directive, Council Doc. 15198/03, Article 28A on "neighbouring safe third countries". Recital 24 of the Preamble (draft procedures directive Council Doc. 14203/04), refers to "certain European third countries, which observe particularly high human rights and refugee protection standards". After enlargement, most of the remaining "European countries" which have not become EU Member States, border on the EU, or will do so after the accession of Bulgaria and Rumania. In comparison with the earlier draft of the Directive, Neighbouring North African- and other Mediterranean countries are no longer explicitly included in the "super safe" category. The fact that only the title of Article

there is arguably a strong political incentive to designate bordering third countries as ("super") safe, considering the European Neighbourhood Policy.

With this provision of the procedures Directive, history appears to repeat itself. In the early nineties, the Member States declared the countries of Central and Eastern Europe "safe" whilst their protection systems were still largely insufficient. The Member States and the EC financed capacity building in the area of asylum during subsequent years, bringing practice up to par with this premature safety assumption.[308] Post-2004 and enlargement, the EU appears to be pursuing a similar course of action with regard to the new neighbouring countries. These include countries such as Albania, Belarus, Moldova and Ukraine where protection systems are, at best, in their infancy. In subsection 3.2.5 and section 6.2, we touched upon the EU funding going towards capacity building in refugee reception. This arguably indicates that the new neighbouring countries are not yet ready to receive, process, and protect protection seekers and refugees in accordance with international standards.

With these general considerations in mind, this subsection considers the safety criteria and procedural safeguards which the procedures Directive proposes, concerning expulsion to European "super" safe third countries.

##### 9.3.1.1.2.1 Safety criteria

Article 36(2) lists four criteria which allow the Member States to consider countries as "super" safe. A third country can only be considered safe for the purpose of Article 36 in case:

> (a) it has ratified and observes the provisions of the Geneva Convention without any geographical limitations; and
> (b) it has in place an asylum procedure prescribed by law; and
> (c) it has ratified the European Convention for the Protection of Human Rights and Fundamental Freedoms and it observes its provisions, including the standards relating to effective remedies.
> (d) it has been so designated by the Council [...].[309]

Criterion (d) is a purely procedural requirement. Criteria (a), (b) and (c) determine the safety of a country. Noteworthy of these last criteria, firstly, is that Article 36 is limited to third countries, which are at least party to the Geneva Refugee Convention and the European Convention of Human Rights. In addition to ratification, consideration of actual observance of these conventions in practice is also required. This is arguably an important correction of the presumption of safety regarding State parties to these conventions, and the application of the principle of interstate trust.

---

36 contains a geographical limitation, and not its wording, however, leaves a potential for discrepancies in the implementation of this provision by the Member States.

308 Kumin 1995, p. 3-4; Lavenex 1999, p. 85-90; *supra*, subsection 3.2.5, at n. 75-78.

309 Article 36(2).

Secondly, when comparing the safety criteria of Article 36(2) with those of Article 27(1), the first are more demanding.[310] The GC and ECHR are referred to in their entirety, instead of merely the refoulement prohibitions contained therein. Similarly, "an asylum procedure prescribed by law" is broader than the possibility to request refugee status and receive protection in accordance with the GC, as required by Article 27(1)(d). On the one hand, this increases the amount of applicable norms on the basis of which a third country must be scrutinised to determine its safety. On the other hand, once a third country has been designated as safe (in general) pursuant to these criteria, the presumption of safety, and validity of interstate trust, is more difficult to rebut. The margin of error in this regard, resulting in a decision in first instance to expel an individual to a third country which would not be safe, will depend on the strictness with which the Commission, Council and European Parliament will scrutinise the actual observance of these conventions by third countries in practice.[311]

9.3.1.1.2.2 Procedural safeguards

After general examination based on the criteria of Article 36, third countries may qualify as "*super*" safe. This translates into less procedural safeguards, pertaining to the rejection of protection seekers under this provision. Article 36 contains the same requirement to provide the protection seeker with a document informing the third country that s/he was not rejected on substantive grounds,[312] and the same guarantee of access to an asylum procedure should a third country refuse readmission to its territory.[313] However, whereas Article 27 may apply to general *or* individual examination of the safety of a third country,[314] Article 36 pertains exclusively to general safety designations. This does not prevent a Member State from undertaking an individual examination in first instance, but such an examination would not be based on the procedures Directive, at least not directly.[315] Article 36 furthermore does not determine that the protection seeker should have the possibility to challenge a safety determination. This possibility is, however, guaranteed by Article 39, which explicitly ensures the right to an effective remedy before a court or tribunal against a decision by a Member State to exclude a protection seeker from substantive procedures under Article 36.[316]

Finally, a general condition for the application of the safe third country exception of Article 36 is that a Member State must have "established, on the basis of the facts, that the applicant for asylum is seeking to enter or has entered illegally into its terri-

310 Spijkerboer and Vermeulen 2005, p. 186.

311 Article 36(2)(d) in conjunction with (3). The list of "super" safe third countries will be adopted (or amended) by the Council based on a Commission proposal and after consultation of the EP.

312 Article 36(5).

313 Article 36(6).

314 Article 27(2)(b), *supra*, n. 297.

315 See Article 36(4), *infra*, at n. 341.

316 Article 39(1)(a)(iii).

tory from a safe third country".[317] The procedures Directive does not specify the means by which the Member State should establish an unauthorised entry or attempt thereto, other than that it must be "on the basis of the facts". In practice, alignment may be expected with the means of evidence for an unauthorised EU external border crossing as specified in the Dublin Regulation,[318] and/or with the means of evidence specified in Community readmission agreements with third countries.[319]

#### 9.3.1.2 The general relation between the procedures Directive and international protection obligations

A prerequisite for determining the compatibility of the safe third country exceptions, outlined above, with international obligations of refugee protection is to determine the relationship in general between EC secondary legislation, which establishes minimum standards in the asylum field, and international law, relating to the same subject-matter.

This relationship is complex, and is determined by both European- and general international law. We will start by the latter. It is unclear how to resolve a possible conflict between EU secondary legislation and international law. The Vienna standard of the law of treaties is not readily applicable, as instruments of secondary legislation are not treaties of international law. They are a hybrid form of international agreement between states. Finding their legal basis in a treaty – TEU or TEC – secondary legislation is binding upon States but is formulated only in part by states, including also an input from supranational institutions.

Furthermore, it should be borne in mind that any claim regarding an alleged *breach* by EC secondary legislation of refugee- or fundamental rights conventions is problematic. A breach, or violation, implies an agreement to which the EU or EC is a party, or an obligation of international law which is otherwise binding on the EU or EC. Regarding the first, the European Union or the European Community is not party to conventions which are relevant to the international protection of refugees, nor are its institutions.[320] Regarding international obligations binding the EU or EC otherwise, this would arguably depend on the international norm involved.

International law scholarship does not agree that fundamental rights conventions, as a genus, are of a higher order.[321] Considering individual norms relevant to refugee protection, there have been occasional claims to a *jus cogens* status of the principle of *non-refoulement* as reflected in Article 33 GC. The 1984 Cartagena Declaration on Ref-

317 Article 36(1).

318 See Article 10(1) of the Dublin Regulation.

319 See *supra*, subection 5.3.5.2.

320 Notwithstanding the possibility that the Constitutional Treaty would be ratified and the EU would act upon the commitment in Article 7 thereof, which currently reads: "to seek accession to the European Convention for the protection of human rights and fundamental freedoms".

321 Mus 1996.

ugees[322] and statements by UNCHR's Executive Committee[323] are standard references in this regard. This is however not established law.[324] A stronger claim exists regarding the peremptory nature of the prohibition of torture, contained *inter alia* in Article 3 ECHR. Notably, the European Court of Human Rights has explicitly accepted that the prohibition of torture has achieved the status of a peremptory norm in international law.[325] This finding arguably extends to the prohibition of refoulement, implicit in the prohibition of torture.[326] A peremptory norm does not allow derogation and cannot be set aside by treaty, agreement, or rules of customary law.[327] A conflicting treaty, agreement or custom is void. Whether this consequence would also apply to supranational EC secondary legislation, conflicting with the prohibition of refoulement as inherent in the prohibition of torture, is debatable.

The possibility of EC secondary legislation actually being in *breach* of international law is in any case restricted to norms of a higher order. In the absence of a peremptory norm of international law, EC secondary legislation could be considered in *conflict* with international law, or, to use another term, "not in accordance" or "incompatible" therewith. A solution of such a conflict under international law would be difficult, while the Vienna rules governing conflict between treaties presupposes a subject which is party to two conflicting treaties, and hence can not apply. The EC is not party

322 The Cartagena Declaration on Refugees was the result of a 1984 colloquium of Southern American states, which stated *inter alia* that non-refoulement "in the present state of international law should be acknowledged and observed as a rule of *ius cogens*".

323 See EXCOM Conclusion Nos. 25 (1982) and 79 (1996). Especially No. 25 is noteworthy, which finds that "non-refoulement [is] progressively acquiring the chracter of a peremptory rule of international law".

324 An example of literature finding in favour of a *jus cogens* norm is Allain 2001. This attempt to demonstrate the jus cogens nature of non-refoulement is essentially a teleological argument. The existence of a peremptory norm of *non-refoulement* would indeed be of beneficial effect to the international protection of refugees, but is unlikely. See Coleman 2003, which argues that large-scale violations call the status of non-refoulement as customary international law into doubt. This would arguably apply, *mutatis mutandis*, to a *jus cogens* status. In addition, one could posit that too few countries in the Middle East and Asia have ratified the GC in order for the principle of non-refoulement to qualify as a universal (rather than regional) international customary norm (Coleman 2003, p. 47-49), or *jus cogens*. See furthermore Hannikainen 1988, p. 261-262.

325 Al-Adsani v. the United Kingdom, Judgement, 21 November 2001, para. 61. The Court has based this conclusion on expressions by authorities such as the International Criminal Tribunal for the Former Yugoslavia, and the UK House of Lords.

326 Considering the content of Article 3 ECHR and the related refoulement prohibition, it should be noted that the peremptory norm would not extend to the prohibition of inhuman or degrading treatment or punishment.

327 Article 38(1)(b) of the statute of the International Court of Justice; Article 53 Vienna Convention on the Law of Treaties; Brownlie 1990, p. 513 ; Meron 1986, p. 3 ; Villiger 1985, p. 34-36.

to relevant international conventions, and secondary legislation can not be construed as a treaty to which the EC itself would be party.

The solution of such a conflict *in casu* is offered by European law. The Member States have declared by treaty that the Community and Union, respectively, will comply with the Geneva Refugee Convention and the European Convention of Human Rights regardless of the absence of party-membership. Article 63(1) TEC determines that the Community will adopt certain of its measures on asylum "in accordance with" the Geneva Refugee Convention.[328] Article 6(2) TEU determines that the Union shall "respect" fundamental rights as contained in the European Convention of Human Rights. If Community and Union would fail to do so they would thus violate European law. If a conflict would arise between a provision of EC or EU secondary legislation and a provision of one of these conventions, the latter would prevail as a matter of EU law.

The question then arises as to when secondary legislation could be considered to be not "in accordance with" the GC, not to "respect" the European Convention, or in breach of the specific peremptory norm prohibiting torture. We would suggest that a rule of thumb in this regard is that in order to avoid conflict with international obligations, the EU should refrain from formulating secondary legislation which obliges its Member States to contravene obligations contained in international conventions to which the Member States are party, or peremptory norms of international law. This rule is arguably supported by Article 10 TEC, which establishes the duty of sincere cooperation. Article 10 obliges Member States to facilitate the achievement of the Community's tasks and abstain from measures which would jeopardise the attainment of the objectives of the TEC. The European Court of Justice has determined that Article 10 is of a reciprocal nature, and holds a corresponding duty for the Community institutions.[329] Accordingly, the Community institutions should refrain from jeopardising the fulfilment of the Member States' other international obligations.

It is therefore crucial that secondary legislation is formulated in such a way as to leave Member States a sufficient degree of manoeuvre to allow compliance with their other international obligations. At the minimum, the EU must ensure that, in case a rule contained in secondary legislation would contradict another international obligation of a Member State, that Member State would be able to honour the latter obligation without thereby incurring liability for a violation of European law. This can be ensured by formulating rules in a discretionary way, or by ensuring the presence of exceptions to mandatory rules allowing a sufficient degree of discretion to avoid conflict.[330] If

328 The part of Article 63(1), relevant to this analysis, reads: The Council [...] shall [...] adopt [...] measures on asylum, in accordance with the Geneva [refugee] Convention [...], within the following areas: [...] (d) minimum standards on procedures in Member States for granting or withdrawing refugee status.

329 For a commentary on the relevant ECJ case-law, see De Witte 2000, p. 86-88.

330 A good example of a discretionary exception to an otherwise mandatory rule is Article 3(2) of the Dublin Regulation, and its predecessor, Article 3(4) the 1990 Dublin Convention. This so called "sovereignty clause" allows a Member State to examine an asylum

secondary legislation is thus formulated, any conflict that arises is arguably the result of a discretionary choice by a Member State, thus involving a direct conflict between national law and international obligations, leaving European law out of the equation.

The instrument of EC secondary law presently under scrutiny is a directive, which is not directly applicable but requires Member States to implement its content in their respective national legal orders. All Member States are party to the refugee- and fundamental rights treaties which constitute the regime of international refugee protection (GC, ECHR, CAT and ICCPR). The international obligations contained in these conventions bind the Member States, which are safeguarded at the national level, also in the implementation and application of EC directives. This does not *ipso facto* absolve the Community of any responsibility for the soundness of its legislation in light of international fundamental rights standards. It does mean that the Community may legislate under the assumption that its Member States would honour their international obligations, to the effect of not being required to repeat and reiterate these obligations. Its legal obligation is limited to not interfering negatively in this process.

Furthermore, the procedures Directive explicitly formulates only minimum standards. A minimum standard by definition implies discretion. It leaves Member States free to comply with their other international obligations. A Member State may retain and continue to adopt national law which would offer a higher level of protection than that presented by the directive, without thereby acting in violation of European law.

This would imply that the procedures Directive, and any other directive prescribing minimum standards, would by its very nature comply with the above rule of thumb, and thus be compatible with international law regardless of its content.[331] It is arguable that a conflict or incompatibility could not arise, even if a prescribed minimum standard would be below the standard required by the Geneva Refugee Convention or the European Convention: the EC itself is not a party to those Conventions, and the member states retain the discretion to comply with them. However, legislating minimum asylum procedures which are expressly below the international standard prescribed by the GC and ECHR could not be considered an implementation in good faith of, respectively, Article 63(1)(d) TEC and Article 6(2) TEU. Additionally, a secondary norm of EU law which does not oblige the Member States to contravene other international obligations, but indirectly encourages or invites them to do so, would arguably not be in accordance with the principle of sincere cooperation in Article 10 TEC, either. It follows from European law that minimum standards for asylum procedures established by EC legislation must at least reflect the international minimum standard following from the GC and ECHR.

application even if not responsible and held to transfer to another Member State under the terms of the Dublin Regulation. This allows leeway *inter alia* to avoid conflict with other international obligations in case necessary.

331 For an argument to this extent, see Battjes 2006, p. 555-557.

### 9.3.1.3 Compatibility of the common safe third country policy with international protection obligations

In addition to the fact that the procedures Directive establishes only minimum standards, its discretionary character is highly pronounced. As noted, negotiations within the Council have resulted in an *à la carte* directive which is flexible to implement. In addition, we will see below that the rules, or rather, suggestions that the procedures Directive contains, have generally been tucked close to restrictively interpreted international obligations. In its current form, the directive may therefore be expected to have one of two possible effects. The first is that the limited harmonising effect of the directive would leave the current procedural differences between Member States' policies intact, rendering the directive relatively inconsequential. The second is that where Member States *would* decide to amend their national policies according to the directive, it is likely to exercise a downward effect on protection standards.

The safe third country exceptions detailed above in subsection 9.3.1.1 are especially prone to diverging implementation in the Member States. Article 27(2) of the procedures Directive, for example, explicitly determines that "application of the safe third country concept shall be subject to rules laid down in national legislation", formulating minimum rules for important procedural safeguards only in very general terms. For example, whether administrative decisions on protection claims require an individualised safety determination of a third country, or whether a general safety determination would suffice, has been left to the jurisdiction of the Member States. The procedural details of challenges by protection seekers to negative decisions have also been left open.[332]

The primacy which the directive accords to regulation at the Member State level also pertains to fundamental rights protection. Council minutes regarding the draft procedures Directive of November 2004 included a statement, specifically with regard to Article 27 of the Directive, which reads:

> In adopting this Directive the Council recognises, having regard to the differing legal and constitutional traditions, that the rights of individuals are safeguarded in Member States according to their varying administrative, judicial and legal systems.[333]

It is clear that the safeguarding of individual rights in the Member States, even though indeed subject to differing legal and constitutional traditions and administrative and judicial systems, are partially determined by common standards of international law. The Member States are all party to the Geneva Refugee Convention and the European Convention of Human Rights. The relevant provisions of these conventions, and the resulting requirements as identified above in subsection 9.2, are thus safeguarded at the national level, a fact which the Council apparently relied upon in drafting the procedures Directive. Subsection 9.3.1.2, however, established that there are limits to the degree to which the Council is able to do so. Even though a directive establishing

332 Article 27(2)(b) and (c), *supra*, n. 297, 298.

333 Council Doc. 14203/04, 9 November 2004, Annex II.

minimum standards by definition allows the necessary discretion to provide protection in accordance with international conventions to which all Member States are party, the EU remains responsible for legislating in good faith pursuant to Article 63(1) TEC and Article 6(2) TEU, and in accordance with Article 10 TEC. We must therefore consider whether the safe third country exceptions contained in the procedures Directive reflect at least the minimum requirements prescribed by the GC and ECHR, and do not suggest anything which falls short of that standard.

Without requiring further examination, it can be stated as a preliminary matter that the procedures Directive recognises the applicability of the refoulement prohibitions at the border.[334] Of especial relevance to expulsion to safe third countries is that the Directive also generally respects the prohibition of *indirect* refoulement.[335] In need of further examination, however, is the question whether the procedures Directive also respects the specific requirements that follow implicitly from the prohibition of indirect refoulement. To this end, subsection 9.3.1.3.1 discusses the procedural safeguards attached to rejection on the basis of the safe third country exceptions of Articles 27 and 36 of the Directive. Subsection 9.3.1.3.2 reviews the criteria determining the safety of third countries under these provisions.

*9.3.1.3.1 Procedural safeguards*

The Member States may reject a protection seeker in case a safe third country can be identified, and expel the protection seeker accordingly, without undertaking status determination. This is in accordance with Article 33 GC, Article 3 ECHR as well as Article 13 ECHR, which, as established above, permit expulsion to a third country without status determination.[336] The relevant minimum protection imperative is to treat a protection seeker *as if* a refugee under the GC, or *as if* the alleged risk of torture or IDTP is real under the ECHR, when expelling to a third country.

In this regard, the European Court of Human Rights has made clear that a Member State may choose to assess, firstly, whether the applicant's situation in the country of origin would "give rise to concern".[337] It was argued that this marginal examination of the merits was not a protection imperative, but a discretionary and practical consideration of procedural economy.[338] Accordingly, the safe third country exception of Article 25(2)(c) in conjunction with Article 27 of the procedures Directive does not expressly provide for, nor prevent such an examination. Article 36 appears to leave explicit room for a more marginal merits examination, stating that the Member States may decide to undertake "no, or no full" examination of a protection claim.

334 See *supra*, subsection 9.2.2.4, at n. 143, 144.

335 See the safety criteria of Articles 27 and 36 of the procedures Directive, *supra*, at n. 12 and 27.

336 *Supra*, subsections 9.2.2.2 and 9.2.3.4.

337 *Supra*, subsection 9.2.3.4.2.1, at n. 247.

338 *Supra*, 9.2.3.4.2.1, at n. 250.

In the absence of a duty to undertake status determination in case of expulsion to a third country, an important procedural safeguard is an individualised examination of the safety of that country. The procedures Directive does not impose this safeguard. Article 27 refers to individual examination, but suggests that the Member States may reject protection seekers based on a general safety designation under national law, only. With regard to "European safe third countries", Article 36 does not refer to individual examination at all, and bases the rejection of protection seekers on a general safety designation by the Council.

The positive obligation to examine a claim under Article 3 ECHR before expulsion does not rule out general safety determinations, but is more sophisticated. In case the third country is a fellow party to the European Convention, the Member State may trust that it will adhere to its international obligations. As such, it may designate the country safe in general without further examination. However, in case a protection seeker is able to provide a contra-indication of the safety of that country, the Member State is held to undertake a "rigorous" (meaning *inter alia* individual) examination of the protection system of that third country. Furthermore, in case the third country would *not* be a fellow party to the European Convention, it is arguable that a detailed individual examination would always be required.[339] Providing for the possibility of individual safety determination is thus not a fully discretionary choice under the international obligations of the Member States.

Article 27 of the procedures Directive does not expressly provide for examination along these requirements. Article 27(2)(b)[340] determines that the Member States must adopt legislative rules which include "case by case consideration of the safety of the country for a particular applicant *and/or* national designation of countries considered to be generally safe" [Italics added, NC]. This wording ("*and/or*") suggests that the Member States may refrain from laying down legislative rules concerning individualised examination altogether. Article 3 ECHR, however, arguably obliges the Member States to provide by law for the possibility of individualised examination of the safety of a third country, which is required in specific cases as described above.

It was argued in subsection 9.3.1.2 that the EC is not necessarily required to reiterate the international obligations of the Member States. EC legislation is required to refrain from obliging the Member States to contravene their other international obligations, and from inviting or encouraging them to do so. Article 27(2)(b) does not prevent the Member States from providing for individual examination in their national legislation, and to apply this provision when required by Article 3 ECHR; it only fails to guarantee it. Furthermore, it would go too far to find that Article 27(2)(b) invites or encourages the Member States to refrain from individualised examination in all cases. Its wording is merely a little ambiguous. Article 27(2)(b), arguably, does not conflict

339 Regarding the safe third country exceptions under scrutiny here, expulsion to a third country which is not party to the European Convention could only involve Article 27 of the procedures Directive. The safety criteria for third countries under Article 36 require ratification of the European Convention.

340 *Supra*, n. 297.

with Article 3 ECHR. Nevertheless, deleting the word "or" from this provision would align it more accurately with the requirements of Article 3 ECHR, whilst still allowing the Member States to forego individual examination whenever warranted by interstate trust.

Article 36 of the procedures Directive does not expressly provide for individual examination in any manner. This lack of express procedural requirements, concerning the rejection of protection seekers pursuant to this safe third country exception, is however compensated by a general safeguard contained in Article 36(4).[341] This provision determines that the Member States must adopt national law concerning the "modalities" for implementing Article 36. Such a modality could entail individual safety determination where required by the international obligations of the Member State. Moreover, Article 36(4) requires the Member States to provide for exceptions for humanitarian reasons or for reasons of public international law. Such an exception, arguably, could be to undertake an individualised- instead of a general safety determination, when required by Article 3 ECHR.

A further procedural safeguard, essential to international refugee protection, is the possibility to challenge a decision concerning the safety of a third country. Article 13 ECHR requires, and sets certain standards for such a remedy. Article 27 expressly provides for the possibility of challenging decisions under this safe third country exception.[342] It thereby guarantees an individual examination at least in appeal. It was noted, however, that the grounds for challenging the safety of a country pertain only to one of the four safety criteria listed in Article 27(1).[343] Examination in appeal of the situation of the individual in the third country would thus only consider a possible (direct or indirect) risk of torture and cruel, inhuman or degrading treatment or punishment. Possible persecution or a risk of refoulement in the third country in the sense of the Geneva Refugee Convention, and the possibility to request asylum and receive protection according to the GC, does not form part of the examination.[344]

This limitation is arguably in accordance with the minimum obligation following from international law. The European Convention requires an effective remedy against a complaint involving Article 3 ECHR. A denial thereof would not only violate Article 13, but also, arguably, the inherent obligation to rigorous examination contained in Article 3, itself. The Geneva Refugee Convention, on the other hand, does not contain procedural requirements. The GC leaves the manner in which the competent authorities of State parties would "satisfy"[345] themselves that an expulsion would not create a

341 Article 36(4) reads: "Member States concerned shall lay down in national law the modalities for implementing the provisions of paragraph 1 and the consequences of decisions pursuant to those provisions in accordance with the principle of non-refoulement under the Geneva Convention including providing for exceptions from the application of this Article for humanitarian or political reasons or for reasons of public international law".

342 Article 27(2)(c) of the procedures Directive.

343 *Supra*, 9.3.1.1.1.2, at n. 302-303.

344 See the safety criteria of Article 27(1).

345 Article 27(1) of the procedures Directive.

risk of refoulement to the jurisdiction of the State parties. Failing to guarantee consideration of Article 33 GC in appeal is therefore not incompatible with the GC.[346]

A possible risk of refoulement, moreover, resulting from a lack of consideration of Article 33 GC in appeal, is mitigated by the fact that protection under Article 3 ECHR is generally considered broader than under Article 33 GC. A real risk of torture or IDTP would in practice encompass most, if not all cases of a well-founded fear of persecution.[347] Nevertheless, even though in line with international obligations, Article 27 remains internally inconsistent. It has been rightly pointed out that if providing four criteria upon which to determine the safety of a third country, a challenge of that decision should offer the possibility to rebut, and guarantee scrutiny, of those same criteria.[348]

Considering Article 36 of the procedures Directive, we noted that this safe third country exception does not expressly provide for the possibility to challenge a safety designation, but that Article 39 fills this apparent gap.[349] Article 39 guarantees an effective remedy against decisions under Article 36, excluding protection seekers from substantive procedures. An effective remedy, *in casu*, is one which allows the possibility to rebut the designation of a third country as "super" safe in an individual case.[350] The fact that Article 36 does not expressly provide for such a remedy is not incompatible with the European Convention, because the Member States retain the opportunity to implement national legislation in accordance with Article 13 ECHR.

Finally, Articles 27 and 36 both contain an important procedural safeguard, requiring the Member States to provide a protection seeker with a document, which informs the authorities of a third country that s/he was not rejected on substantive grounds.[351] This satisfies a constant concern of commentators, UNHCR and NGOs that third countries might assume that a protection seeker was rejected on substantive grounds, consequently find the claim unfounded, and expel onwards as an "illegal" immigrant entailing a risk of refoulement.[352] This provision of the procedures Directive moreover takes privacy considerations into account, which may arise when providing a third country with this particular information.[353] By holding the document the protection seeker controls the information. Whether to present it to the authorities of the third country would be his or her choice.

346 This argument also applies to Article 38(3)(c) of the Directive, which allows the Member States to limit the guarantee of an effective remedy in accordance with Article 27(2)(c), *supra*, subsection 9.3.1.1.1.2, n. 303.

347 Vermeulen 1999, p. 171; Spijkerboer and Vermeulen 1999, p. 191; Spijkerboer and Vermeulen 2005, p. 88-91.

348 Spijkerboer and Vermeulen 2005, p. 185.

349 *Supra*, subsection 9.3.1.1.2.2 n. 316.

350 Spijkerboer and Vermeulen 2005, p. 185.

351 Article 27(3)(b) and 36(5)(b).

352 *Supra*, section 9.1, at n. 28.

353 On privacy concerns when providing a third country with information concerning a protection seeker, See Legomsky 2003, p. 633.

*9.3.1.3.2 Safety criteria*

The safety criteria under Articles 27 and 36 of the procedures Directive require in general that a third country would comply with the refoulement prohibitions of Article 33 GC and Article 3 ECHR. Article 36 in this regard also requires party membership to these conventions, which is not necessary for application of Article 27. Article 27 furthermore demands at least the possibility to request refugee status, and to receive protection in line with the GC if found to qualify as a refugee. Article 36 requires the presence of an asylum procedure prescribed by law. It should be emphasised that neither provision hereby requires a guarantee that the third country would undertake status determination. The possibility to request protection, or the presence of an asylum procedure, does not prevent rejection without status determination in the third country, for example on safe third country grounds.

It was argued above that a guarantee of status determination in the third country is not necessarily required for expulsion to that country. The minimum requirement under Article 3 ECHR is that there must be some form of "procedural interruption" in the third country, preventing summary or immediate onward removal.[354] This may entail status determination, but only under certain circumstances.

Status determination in the third country is not required if there is no risk of onward removal, for example where a third country would offer *de facto* protection against refoulement by allowing informal stay. Status determination is not required, either, if the third country would in turn expel to another third country. Instead, Article 3 ECHR then requires a guarantee that the third country will undertake a safety examination of that "fourth" country. Status determination in the third country is arguably required only in case there is a risk that the third country would expel onwards to the country of origin.[355]

The procedures Directive does not reflect this degree of detail, regarding the international obligations of the Member States under Article 3 ECHR. A further omission is that the procedures Directive does not require that an effective remedy against possible rejection of the protection claim in the third country is guaranteed. Such specific requirements, however, following from Article 3 and Article 13 ECHR, may be considered subsumed in the general safety criteria of Articles 27 and 36, specifically indents (c) thereof.[356]

---

354 *Supra*, subsection 9.2.3.4.2.2, at n. 256. It should be noted that the procedures Directive does not require a guarantee of any procedural interruption in the third country as such. Article 27(2)(d) does not demand that the opportunity to file a request for refugee status is guaranteed in an individual case. This provision may be interpreted as requiring only that this possibility would "exist" within the system (*supra*, at n. 292). Similarly, Article 36 requires an asylum procedure to be "in place" in the third country, but does not require access to that procedure (*supra*, at n. 309).

355 This is without prejudice to the fact that an actual duty to examine whether certain conditions in the third country are in place would depend on the principle of interstate trust and the presence of contra-indications, as outlined above, see subsection 9.2.3.4.4.

356 *Supra*, at n. 292 and 309.

In sum, the safe third country exceptions contained in the procedures Directive on several counts do not reiterate the international obligations of the Member States, omitting references to specific requirements. On all counts reviewed, however, the procedures Directive leaves sufficient space for the Member States to adhere to their international obligations when implementing the provisions involved. The procedures Directive, furthermore, does not invite or encourage the Member States to deviate from these obligations, or to lower standards below the internationally determined minimum.

The common safe third country policy as contained in the procedures Directive is therefore in line with international law, although it clearly explores the limits of restrictive interpretation of the international obligations of the Member States. As such, the common safe third country policy may not be expected to have a positive impact on refugee protection in the (enlarged) European Union. Those Member States, which already operate at the minimum level of protection permissible under international law, will be able to continue to do so. For other Member States, the procedures Directive provides an incentive to lower their standards regarding safe third country policy.

### *9.3.2 Community readmission agreements*

Section 9.1 noted that, with regard to refugee protection concerns, there is a tendency to identify readmission agreements with safe third country policies. It was argued that this identification is inaccurate, while readmission agreements and safe third country policies each fulfil a different function in the expulsion of protection seekers to third countries, and stand in a different relation to international obligations of refugee protection.

In the introduction to section 9.3, it was noted that readmission agreements do not provide a legal basis for the rejection, or expulsion, of protection seekers.[357] It was therefore argued that the legality of applying a readmission agreement to facilitate expulsion of a protection seeker to a third country is determined by a preceding safe third country decision. This already clarifies the impact which readmission agreements, and therewith the common readmission policy, have on refugee protection. In order to fully understand this impact, however, it is necessary to furthermore consider the relationship between obligations in readmission agreements, as treaties under general international law, and obligations of refugee protection in other treaties.

Subsection 9.3.2.1 analyses this relationship with regard to Community readmission agreements. Based on that analysis, the remaining subsections then address whether the refugee protection concerns identified in section 9.1, as pertaining to Community readmission agreements, raise any issues under international refugee law. In particular, subsection 9.3.2.2 discusses the fact that Community readmission agreements treat protection seekers as unauthorised immigrants. Subsection 9.3.2.3 looks specifically at the fact that Community readmission agreements are concluded with third countries which can not be considered "safe" for protection seekers to return to.

357 *Supra*, at n. 282.

Subsection 9.3.2.4, finally, discusses the absence of certain refugee protection safeguards in Community readmission agreements.

#### 9.3.2.1 The relation between Community readmission agreements and international protection obligations

The obligations of international refugee protection incumbent on the Member States apply to the expulsion of protection seekers, and therefore to any expulsion facilitated by a readmission agreement. The international regime administrated by the Geneva Refugee Convention and the European Convention of Human Rights is triggered the moment a person expresses a claim to protection. Until that claim is disproved, the Member States must grant the person in question protection against any expulsion in contravention to these conventions.[358] Persons claiming protection at the border must be treated in the same manner as persons claiming protection in-country.[359] The *method* of expulsion – with or without application of a readmission agreement, by formal or informal application of a readmission agreement, or summary removal after interception during a border crossing – does not affect the applicability of these obligations of international refugee law. Equally irrelevant is whether expulsion is facilitated by a readmission agreement at the Member State level, a Community readmission agreement, or a bilateral implementing protocol[360] pursuant to a Community readmission agreement.

The application of readmission agreements is not problematic from the viewpoint of general international law.[361] A readmission agreement establishes obligations to readmit a person to territory, which it by definition imposes on a requested – receiving – State. Conventions relevant to international refugee protection by definition impose obligations, *in casu* prohibitions of refoulement, on a requesting – expelling – State. As a consequence, the application of a readmission agreement cannot entail a conflict of treaties in the context of international refugee protection, unlike, for example, the application of an extradition treaty.[362] Requesting States will not encounter a situation of having to choose between two, potentially equal, and conflicting treaty obligations. International obligations of refugee protection could not be challenged in this manner by application of a readmission agreement.

As noted, readmission agreements in general, and Community readmission agreements in particular, do not provide a legal basis for the rejection of protection seekers.[363] These agreements do not provide a legal basis for expulsion, either. The transfer of a protection seeker under a readmission agreement with a third country must always be

358 *Supra*, subsections 9.2.2.2 and 9.2.3.4.1.

359 *Supra*, subsections 9.2.2.4 and 9.2.3.5.

360 *Supra*, subsection 5.3.11.

361 Contrary to occasional suggestions in the literature, see for example Landgren 1999.

362 On conflicts between extradition obligations and fundamental rights obligations, see Mus 1996; Dugard and Van den Wyngaert 1998.

363 Fernhout 1999, p. 89.

preceded by a decision of national law to reject and expel that protection seeker. Such decisions of national law are subject to the international obligations of the Member States, which are thus safeguarded at every application of a (bilateral or Community) readmission agreement.[364] We concluded in subsection 9.3.1 that the common safe third country policy as regulated by the procedures Directive does not adversely affect the compliance of the Member States with their other international obligations. These obligations are thus equally safeguarded in the application of a Community readmission agreement to expel a protection seeker, who has been rejected by a Member State pursuant to the procedures Directive.

Furthermore, all Community readmission agreements contain a non-affection clause. This clause determines that international obligations of refugee protection of the contracting parties will not be affected by application of the agreement. As a conflict clause, this provision is immaterial, because the application of a readmission agreement is not able to give rise to a treaty conflict with, for example, the GC or ECHR.[365] As a fundamental rights safeguard, furthermore, a non-affection clause is not strictly required. The non-affection clause is not constitutive of obligations of refugee protection on part of the contracting parties, but declaratory.[366] It confirms the applicability of international obligations to the degree that contracting parties are already bound. The clause could perhaps be considered as an additional (and thus not imperative) safeguard, preventing a contracting State from applying a Community readmission agreement, after deciding to reject and expel a protection seeker in violation of international law.

These considerations already enable the drawing of an important conclusion regarding refugee protection concerns that may exist in relation to the common readmission policy, in particular Community readmission agreements. When applying Community readmission agreements for the expulsion of protection seekers, it appears that the Member States are bound by the same range of international obligations as

364 This includes national policies, such as in The Netherlands, where the presence of a readmission agreement with a third country may provide a sufficient basis for the application of a safe third country exception. Under Dutch legislation, the existence of a readmission agreement forms part of the criteria determining a third country's safety, leading to a decision to reject and expel under national law. In this case, the agreement itself still does not form the legal basis for that decision (For a different view in this regard, see Zwaan 2003, p. 77, 173-178). The application of a safe third country exception such as this one, as usual, needs to comply with a Member State's international obligations. The readmission agreement, *in casu*, is taken as a basis for application of the principle of interstate trust. Considering that readmission agreements are not instruments of refugee protection, do not refer to protection seekers or refugees (excepting the so-called non-affection clause in, for example, the Community's agreements), nor provide for a monitoring or enforcement mechanism independent of the contracting parties, this basis has little validity. The claim to interstate trust would thus be relatively weak, and the safety presumption easier to rebut for the protection seeker.

365 *Supra*, at n. 361.

366 *Supra*, subsection 5.3.9.

when not using a readmission agreement. Therefore, an increase in the absolute number of expulsions, as hypothetically resulting from a readmission agreement, would not necessarily entail a relative increase in cases of refoulement. Arguably, the facilitation of expulsion by Community readmission agreements does not involve greater risks to international refugee protection.

#### 9.3.2.2 Readmission of protection seekers as unauthorised immigrants

The green paper on Community return policy defines an "illegal resident" as:

> Any person who does not, or no longer, fulfil [sic.] the conditions for entry to, presence in, or residence on the territories of the Member States of the European Union.[367]

Certain categories of persons, who fall within this definition, may be subject to readmission under a Community readmission agreement with a third country. Community readmission agreements provide for the readmission of nationals and former nationals of third countries,[368] third country nationals[369] and stateless persons,[370] "who do not, or no longer fulfil the conditions in force for entry to, presence in, or residence on, the territory of [a] requesting Member State".[371]

Two relevant categories of persons, which were discussed above in chapter 2,[372] are not included in the text of Community readmission agreements: persons who are formally recognised as refugees by a third country, and protection seekers. One may nevertheless expect the Member States to apply Community readmission agreements also to these persons.

Proof of recognition as a refugee by a third country, for example a travel document within the meaning of Article 28 of the Geneva Refugee Convention, may give rise to readmission as a third country national. A Member State would most likely consider that the third country issued a "residence authorisation", which creates a readmission obligation under the terms of a Community readmission agreement.[373] A Member State could also request readmission based on previous residence or stay in the third country in question, which is a further possibility offered by Community readmission agreements.[374]

367 COM(2002) 175 final, annex.

368 *Supra*, subsection 5.3.3.

369 In the sense of not being a national of any of the contracting parties to a readmission agreement, see *supra*, chapter 2, n. 4.

370 *Supra*, subsection 5.3.4.

371 See Articles 2 and 3 of the Community readmission agreement with Albania.

372 *Supra*, subsection 2.2.2 and section 2.4.

373 See for example Article 1(f) in conjunction with Article 3(1)(a) of the Community readmission agreement with Albania.

374 See for example Article 3(1)(b) of the Community readmission agreement with Albania.

By not including an explicit reference to the readmission of protection seekers, the Community follows a long-standing drafting tradition of European readmission agreements. As noted, the absence of reference to protection seekers in the text of these agreements has been an equally long-standing source of concern and criticism on the part of commentators and NGOs, given that, in practice, the EC Member States have used these agreements for expelling protection seekers.[375] This practice is likely to continue under the readmission agreements concluded by the Community.

Rejected protection seekers may be readmitted under the terms agreed between the contracting parties for the readmission of nationals, or those of third country nationals. In case a protection seeker is rejected on substantive grounds – found not to qualify as a refugee – a Member State may request readmission as an own national to the country of origin, or as a third country national to any third country. In case a protection seeker is not rejected on substantive grounds, but on account of a previous stay in, or transit through a safe third country, a Member State may request readmission as a third country national to that country.

The Commission contends that a rejected protection seeker falls within the above definition of an "illegal resident",[376] and therefore under the terms of Community readmission agreements.[377] The Council's Legal Service is of a similar opinion,[378] as is the Council itself.[379] From a policy perspective, protection seekers are thus transferred from the asylum context to the context of the fight against unauthorised immigration at the moment of their rejection. This however also suggests a transfer from a context of internationally guarded rights to a context, where these rights do not apply, at least terminologically speaking. To be sure, the change in labelling from protection seeker to illegal resident takes place regardless of whether rejection occurred on substantive or non-substantive grounds. The following first discusses whether the label of "illegal resident" is as such in conformity with international law, and subsequently whether it has any consequences for the rights of protection seekers.

Protection seekers who secure entry into another country without the requisite documents for that purpose are certainly unauthorised entrants, but are arguably not resident or present without authorisation once having requested international protection. At that point, the Geneva Refugee Convention and European Convention of Human Rights apply. A person who is consequently protected against expulsion, constituting direct or indirect refoulement, could not be considered resident or present without authorisation. The fact that the refoulement prohibitions are applicable also at the border, where they may require a State to allow entry to territory, further indicates that protection seekers enjoy some form of presence which is not without authorisa-

375 *Supra*, section 9.1, n. 5.

376 *Supra*, n. 367.

377 COM(2002) 175 final, p. 7; COM(2002) 564 final, p. 7. See also Schieffer 2003, p. 349.

378 Council Doc. 6658/99.

379 Negotiating directives for Community readmission agreements specify that the personal scope of the agreements "include persons whose asylum application has been rejected", Council Doc. 11180/00, 8 September 2000.

tion. If the State would subsequently undertake status determination and decide that the person is not a refugee in the sense of the GC, it is clear that s/he would from that moment (again) be present without authorisation. The situation is less clear in case rejection takes place on non-substantive grounds, in particular when based on a safe third country exception.

In the absence of status determination and rejection on substantive grounds, the claimant does not cease to be a protection seeker. S/he remains a "presumptive" or "*prima facie*" refugee under international law,[380] and would as such not be present or resident without authorisation. Under the domestic law of the Member State in question, however, the protection seeker would have no further claim to (physical) presence, and to all intended purposes become an unauthorised resident *vis-à-vis* the territory of that Member State.[381] In fact, given that the Dublin Regulation would prevent a protection seeker to travel to another Member State and also claim protection there, and the mutual recognition of expulsion decisions,[382] this person would effectively become an "illegal resident" throughout the territory of the EC. While this terminology is arguably not in line with international law, international law at the same time does not oppose it, as long as the prohibitions of refoulement are respected.

Community readmission agreements appear to be in line with the refoulement prohibitions of the GC and ECHR. These international obligations of the Member States apply to any application of a Community readmission agreement to facilitate the expulsion of a protection seeker.[383] Consequently, the transfer of a protection seeker from the field of refugee protection to the field of the fight against unauthorised immigration, at the point of his or her rejection, remains purely terminological. It has no legal effect regarding obligations under the GC or ECHR.

Considering protection seekers, who are rejected on safe third country grounds, as "illegal residents" for the purpose of their readmission to a third country under a Community readmission agreement is therefore arguably permissible. In addition, European law offers a relevant practical safeguard, which is the document that a Member

380 *Supra*, subsection 9.2.2.2, n. 57, 58.

381 It should be noted that there are differences in this regard between the Member States. In some Member States, such as the Netherlands, rejected protection seekers are declared to be illegally present aliens. The Dutch authorities consequently eject these persons from reception facilities with an order to leave the country. Unless removal is enforced, such persons frequently ignore this order and remain, unregistered by the authorities, becoming unauthorised residents in the real sense of the word. To avoid such situations, protection seekers rejected in Germany receive a *Duldung*, allowing legal presence for a certain period (Zwaan 2003, p. 118, 240-241). The equation at the Community level of rejected protection seekers with unauthorised residents is thus not valid in Germany. During the period of validity of a *Duldung*, a protection seeker rejected in Germany would therefore arguably fall outside the scope of a Community readmission agreement.

382 Council Directive 2001/40/EC of 28 May 2001 on the mutual recognition of decisions on the expulsion of third country nationals, *OJ* L 149, 2.6.2001, 34.

383 *Supra*, subsection 9.3.2.1.

State must provide under Article 27 and Article 36 of the procedures Directive.[384] This document mitigates the risk that a third country would erroneously treat a protection seeker, readmitted after rejection on safe third country grounds, as an "illegal immigrant" and ignore the refoulement prohibitions.

#### 9.3.2.3 The conclusion of Community readmission agreements with unsafe countries

The lack of reference to protection seekers in readmission agreements has led to protection concerns, especially because these agreements are often concluded without regard for the general safety of requested States. Subsection 7.1.5 posed the question of whether the conclusion of Community readmission agreements with unsafe third countries (resulting from double standards in international relations when involving migration-related interests) may have legal implications in relation to refugee protection.[385]

Arguably, the Community is free to conclude agreements in the field of migration with any third country, as long as the text of that agreement does not contravene international obligations of refugee protection. Contravention of another convention, relevant to refugee protection, would entail a treaty conflict, the solution of which would be problematic considering the equal status of treaties under general international law. In case the conflicting international norm has a peremptory nature (such as, possibly, the prohibition of refoulement as derived from the prohibition of torture[386]) the solution is not problematic. The conflicting provision in the Community agreement, or the agreement as a whole, would be void. Community readmission agreements, however, contain no such conflicting text. These agreements do not oblige to expulsion, nor do they oblige to submitting a readmission request or to transferring a person, which are entirely discretionary decisions.[387]

The *conclusion* of Community readmission agreements with unsafe third countries therefore does not in general raise an issue under international refugee law. Expulsion to unsafe countries, and the *application* of readmission agreements for that purpose, may of course raise an issue under international refugee law in an individual case. It was however established above that expulsion by a Member State of a protection seeker to a third country with application of a Community readmission agreement is and remains subject to international refugee protection obligations. Accordingly, where a country such as for example China, Pakistan, Russia, or Ukraine would be unsafe for

384 *Supra*, subsection 9.3.1.3.1, at n. 351.

385 *Supra*, section 7.1.5, at n. 51.

386 *Supra*, subsection 9.3.1.2, at n. 325-326.

387 The non-affection clause in Community readmission agreements confirms this, by determining that the agreement does not affect return under other formal or informal arrangements, *supra*, subsection 5.3.9. Pursuant to this provision, Member States are free to choose which *method* of expulsion to apply in an individual case. In general, Member States clearly may also refrain from application of a readmission agreement, even though technically possible.

an individual, a Member State must refrain from expulsion, and thus from the application of any Community readmission agreement with these countries. In other words, the less safe a country is with which a readmission agreement is concluded, the less applicable that agreement will be to the readmission of protection seekers.

In sum, the mere existence of a readmission agreement with an unsafe third country does not involve a greater risk of refoulement, and can thus not be considered to raise an issue of refugee protection.

#### 9.3.2.4 Incorporation of protection safeguards into Community readmission agreements

In subsection 9.1, we noted that appeals by commentators, NGOs and the UNHCR to take greater account of refugee protection in the text of readmission agreements generally pertain to three specific safeguards. These are a prior notification of the requested State that a readmittee is a protection seeker, an explicit reference to the principle of non-refoulement, and an obligation to undertake status determination of readmittees who are protection seekers.

In view of the preceding subsections, the possibility of the absence of these safeguards in readmission agreements raising an issue of international refugee protection is largely academic. Arguably, the fundamental rights of protection seekers, readmitted under Community readmission agreements, are already safeguarded at a preceding decision under national law to reject and expel a protection seeker. Readmission agreements, at the national or the Community level, do not enable the Member States to avoid or circumvent their international obligations. From this perspective, incorporating refugee protection safeguards in readmission agreements is not a protection imperative. However, commentators, NGOs and the UNHCR have on occasion claimed that such safeguards should be incorporated as a matter of international refugee law. This is a perspective which merits some further consideration.

In general, the validity of such claims is questionable. Readmission agreements and international conventions related to refugee protection, such as the GC or the ECHR, are treaties of equal status within the hierarchy of norms under general international law. There is no general obligation to reiterate relevant obligations under one treaty within another treaty touching on the same subject-matter. Where contracting States do decide on explicit reiteration, this generally serves the purpose of establishing a conflict clause. In the present case, however, there is no need for such a clause, while there is no risk of conflict between readmission agreements and conventions related to refugee protection.

Moreover, in case a difference in hierarchy between a readmission agreement and a refugee protection norm *would* exist (for example, where the latter has acquired a peremptory status) it is questionable whether explicit reiteration would be required. A peremptory norm binds all States in all their treaty- and other dealings with other States. Reiteration thereof in a readmission agreement would arguably be superfluous. Generally, it is therefore unlikely that the incorporation of explicit refugee protection safeguards into a readmission agreement could be considered an obligation of international law. The following discusses each of the three safeguards mentioned above separately.

*9.3.2.4.1 Prior notification*

The first safeguard commonly suggested in the literature is to include a provision obliging the contracting parties to notify the requested State in case the person, whose readmission is requested, is a protection seeker who has been rejected on non-substantive grounds. Although not an explicit international obligation of the Member States, such a provision would be a practical safeguard against a possible risk of refoulement. It was noted above that this notification is already guaranteed by the procedures Directive, and moreover in a manner which takes the privacy interests of the protection seeker into account.[388] We will thus not further consider the possibility of additional inclusion of such a safeguard in Community readmission agreements.

*9.3.2.4.2 Explicit reference to non-refoulement*

Subsection 9.1 identified a further claim commonly made in the literature, which is that an explicit reference to the principle of non-refoulement should be included in the text of readmission agreements. Such a reference is largely irrelevant with regard to Community readmission agreements, considering the non-affection clause which these agreements contain. This standard clause determines that Community readmission agreements do not affect other international obligations, *inter alia* in relation to refugee protection. This provision is a catch-all clause, referring to other international obligations of the contracting parties in general. In addition, it may include specific reference to the Geneva Refugee Convention and/or the European Convention of Human Rights, depending on the outcome of negotiations with a particular third country.[389] The principle of non-refoulement is thus already referred to in the text of Community readmission agreements, albeit implicitly.

It was pointed out above that the non-affection clause does not establish or create any obligations to which the contracting parties are not already bound.[390] This implies that adding a provision, referring specifically to the principle of non-refoulement, may be relevant regarding third countries which are not a party to the GC or ECHR.[391] Considering the fact that all Member States already adhere by treaty to the principle of non-refoulement, such a provision would only be constitutive of that obligation on the part of the third country. As such, it would have a certain relevance, but only with regard to readmission from the third country *to* a Member State. In other words, such a provision would have little or no practical meaning, while the Member States are not generally expected to receive readmission requests under Community readmission agreements from third countries. Additionally, a refugee protection safeguard which consists of

388 *Supra*, subsection 9.3.1.3.1 at n. 351-353.

389 *Supra*, subsection 5.3.9.

390 *Ibid.*

391 Regarding the readmission countries targeted by the Community, Pakistan and Sri Lanka are examples of such countries.

reiterating the prohibition of refoulement within a bilateral relation between States, in a readmission agreement or otherwise, is of questionable value. It has been rightfully pointed out that adherence to, and enforcement of such an obligation is uncertain.[392]

In sum, inserting an explicit reference to the principle of non-refoulement in the text of Community readmission agreements would be inconsequential from the viewpoint of international refugee protection.

*9.3.2.4.3 Status determination by the requested State*

A final safeguard, which some of the literature claims should be included in the text of readmission agreements, is a duty to undertake status determination of readmitted protection seekers on the part of the requested State. Should incorporation of such a safeguard indeed be found to be required by international refugee law, the practical consequences would be significant.

A guarantee of status determination would be arguably beneficial to refugee protection in individual cases. Provided that status determination in a third country would be in conformity with the GC and ECHR, it would eliminate the risk of chain expulsion, and of indirect refoulement. Readmission agreements which oblige third countries to undertake status determination would formalise the assumption of "protection elsewhere", which underpins safe third country policies.[393] The justification with which protection seekers are rejected, namely that *another* State is responsible for status determination and protection if merited, would be given concrete substance. Imposing an obligation to undertake status determination on third countries, however, may also entail risks to refugee protection. It would transfer a refugee burden onto countries which are less equipped to deal with immigration. This could eventually prove detrimental to international refugee protection.[394]

A duty to undertake status determination would formalise and fix the shifting of the refugee burden of the Member States onto third countries, concentrating *in casu* on the new neighbouring countries.[395] A definite concentration of protection seekers and refugees in parts of Central and Eastern Europe, the Western Balkans, and the Southern- and Eastern Mediterranean would be cause for concern. Unable to cope with large numbers of protection seekers and refugees, the fledgling protection systems of these countries might overload. As a result, countries might start refusing to adhere to their international obligations, leading to a breakdown of the regime of international refugee protection at the borders of the EU.[396] This would undo the efforts at the Member State- and EC level to establish responsibility for transit migration and build protection

392 Zwaan 2003, p. 176.

393 *Supra*, subsection 9.1, n. 17.

394 Spijkerboer and Vermeulen 1999, p. 393, footnote 31.

395 Assuming arrival by land, and considering the current emphasis on the development of EC cooperation with the "cordon" of third countries surrounding the EC, responsibility for protection seekers would arguably concentrate on the new neighbouring countries.

396 Spijkerboer and Vermeulen noted this possibility in relation to countries in Central and Eastern Europe in 1999, Spijkerboer and Vermeulen 1999, p. 393, footnote 31.

capacity in these regions. The number of protection seekers "in orbit", and attempts at entry and re-entry into the EU, would likely increase. These concerns are based on speculation, but the potential consequences of denying third countries the possibility of onward removal without status determination should be carefully considered.

Incorporating a duty to undertake status determination into readmission agreements would furthermore have a significant impact on the *negotiation* of this type of agreement. At the Community level, it would further reduce the success rate in the already faltering readmission negotiations. It is possible that Community readmission agreements would become virtually non-negotiable, except with third countries with a short-term accession perspective. The only manner in which the Community would be able to avoid the common readmission policy from failing, would be by providing an even greater degree of *quid pro quo* than currently demanded by third countries.

It is highly doubtful, however, that international law would require readmission agreements to establish a duty to determine the status of readmitted protection seekers. An obligation to incorporate such a provision in readmission agreements sits uneasy with the sovereignty of States to administer the entry and exit of aliens. Considering that readmission agreements formulate reciprocal obligations, such a provision would establish a mutual limitation of sovereignty for the contracting parties to implement, in particular, their respective safe third country policies. In practice, this limitation would apply only to the third countries with which the Member States and the Community conclude readmission agreements. Whereas the EC Member States would be able to apply safe third country exceptions, third countries would be denied this possibility by treaty.

The above analysis of status determination in third countries, as a possible criterion determining their safety under Article 3 of the European Convention,[397] confirms that such a limitation of sovereignty does not have a basis in general international law. In case of a potential onward removal to the country of origin, status determination in a third country determines the legality of expulsion to that country under Article 3 ECHR. Such is however not the case should possible onward removal take place to a fourth country. A guarantee of status determination in the third country is then not a condition determining the legality of expulsion to that country. Any conclusion to the contrary would imply a discrepancy between the sovereign rights of a Member State and a third country in their respective application of safe third country exceptions. A third country could commit to status determination of readmitted protection seekers voluntarily, for example by signing a treaty, but a *general* obligation to this effect is not supported by general international law.

As argued, there are circumstances in which status determination in the third country is a condition for expulsion to that country, namely in case of a risk of onward removal to the country of origin. Notwithstanding the applicability of interstate trust, a Member State is then under duty to investigate whether the third country will undertake status determination, and can arguably only expel the protection seeker if status determination is assured. This does not imply, however, that readmission agreements

397 *Supra*, subsection 9.2.3.4.2.2.

should necessarily impose an obligation to undertake status determination under these circumstances. The manner in which a Member State would seek assurance of status determination is discretionary. In addition, as equal treaties under general international law, readmission agreements are not required to reiterate obligations under the ECHR, *in casu* an obligation to assure status determination in a third country under certain circumstances. In the case of Community readmission agreements, moreover, this obligation may be considered subsumed within the non-affection clause.

In sum, including an obligation to undertake status determination of readmitted protection seekers in the text of readmission agreements can not be considered required by international refugee law.

## 9.4 Conclusion

This chapter has identified the main protection concerns which exist generally regarding the use of readmission agreements for the expulsion of rejected protection seekers, and which apply also to Community readmission agreements. General concerns are the fact that protection seekers and refugees are readmitted simply as unauthorised immigrants, and the fact that readmission agreements are concluded with countries, without regard for their general safety for protection seekers and refugees. Specific concerns concentrate largely on the expulsion of protection seekers to third countries, and the lack of safeguards of refugee protection in readmission agreements, which facilitate such expulsion.

Considering the latter specific concerns, this chapter identified a series of obligations in the Geneva Refugee Convention and the European Convention of Human Rights, relevant to the expulsion of protection seekers from EU Member States to third countries. As the basis for this analysis, the following general principle was used:

> The conditions by which to determine the safety of a third country are delimited by the international obligations, which a State holds towards protection seekers remaining on its territory.

A summary of the outcome of this analysis, constituting the international legal framework relevant to the expulsion of protection seekers from EU Member States to third countries, can be found in section 9.2.4.

It was subsequently determined whether Community readmission agreements are compatible with this international legal framework. Considering that readmission agreements do not provide a legal basis for rejecting protection seekers, their application to facilitate expulsion to a third country must always be preceded by a decision of national law, rejecting a protection seeker on safe third country grounds. It was argued that the legality of a decision to reject and expel a protection seeker under a safe third country exception is therefore a factor, determining the legality of a consequent application of a readmission agreement.

Firstly, therefore, the common safe third country policy, as contained in the Directive on minimum standards on procedures in Member States for granting and withdrawing of refugee status, was reviewed in light of the above framework. This review was based on the argument that although minimum standards of secondary EC law cannot conflict with the international law obligations of the Member States as a matter of international law; as a matter of *European* law, minimum standards for asylum procedures in EC legislation must at least reflect the international minimum standard following from the GC and ECHR.

Based on this argument, a detailed review of the safe third country exceptions of the procedures Directive did not reveal any incompatibility with obligations under the GC or ECHR. The procedures Directive leaves sufficient space for the Member States to adhere to their international obligations when implementing the provisions involved. By that token, these obligations are equally safeguarded in the application of a Community readmission agreement to expel a protection seeker to a third country, who has been rejected by a Member State pursuant to the procedures Directive.

It was finally considered whether Community readmission agreements raise any issues under international refugee law, independently of their relation with the common safe third country policy. It was pointed out that the international obligations of refugee protection of the Member States apply to every expulsion of a protection seeker, regardless of whether expulsion is implemented using a readmission agreement, or another method. Furthermore, readmission agreements cannot give rise to a treaty conflict with instruments of international refugee law. Readmission agreements, including those of the Community, only create obligations on the part of the requested (receiving) State, whereas protection obligations are incumbent only upon the requesting (expelling) State.

It was concluded that, when applying Community readmission agreements for the expulsion of protection seekers, the Member States are bound by their international obligations, same as otherwise. Arguably, therefore, the facilitation of expulsion by a Community readmission agreement does not involve a heightened risk of refoulement.

It was also found that considering rejected protection seekers as unauthorised immigrants for the purpose of applying a readmission agreement does not in itself raise an issue under international refugee law. Furthermore, the mere *conclusion* of a Community readmission agreement with an unsafe third country was not found in general to raise an issue under international refugee law, either. Given that international protection safeguards apply normally in the implementation of Community readmission agreements, agreements are less applicable to the readmission of protection seekers, the less safe the contracting third country is.

Finally, this chapter concluded that there is no basis in international refugee law for mandatory incorporation of certain additional protection safeguards into Community readmission agreements. Going by the literature, the procedural safeguards discussed were a prior notification that a protection seeker was rejected on non-substantive grounds, an explicit reference to the principle of non-refoulement, and a duty to undertake status determination on the part of the requested State.

# II Conclusions

This book set out to establish whether Community readmission agreements are compatible with international obligations of refugee protection. It also set out to establish how, and the degree of success with which the European Community persuades third countries to accept readmission agreements and readmission clauses. To this end, it has examined a wide range of issues concerning the common readmission policy.

Chapters 1 and 2 considered the historical context and the general international law context of the common readmission policy. Chapter 3 explored the motivation of the Member States for opting for a common readmission policy, as well as the objectives which the Community arguably pursues with this policy. Chapter 4 analysed the legal basis for the conclusion of Community readmission agreements with third countries, as well as the debate surrounding the nature of the Community's competence in this area. Chapter 5 analysed the technical content of Community readmission agreements, and several procedural and institutional factors which are relevant to this content.

Chapter 6 explained some of the external policy measures with which the EC tries to persuade third countries to accept Community readmission agreements. This discussion was completed by chapter 7, identifying several additional measures which have been developed in response to third countries' counter-demands, made during the readmission negotiations. This chapter furthermore provided a detailed overview and evaluation of the progress of those negotiations. Chapter 8 concluded the examination of the different elements of the common readmission policy with a concise analysis of the incorporation of readmission clauses into other Community or mixed agreements.

Chapter 9, finally, closely examined the application of Community readmission agreements in the context of international refugee law. In several steps, including a review of the common safe third country policy, it determined whether Community readmission agreements are compatible with protection obligations of the Member States under the Geneva Refugee Convention and the European Convention of Human Rights.

This book has made clear that readmission is concerned with returning unauthorised immigrants, but also with policy "export". The common readmission policy is a vehicle for the establishment of wider cooperation with third countries regarding migration and asylum. As such, readmission agreements could be considered the external face of EC immigration and asylum policies. This book has described the dynamics of this process, and weighted it, both from a policy perspective, and the perspective of international (refugee) law.

I will outline the main conclusions of this book under the following three headings. Section II.i compares the supposed effects of readmission agreements with some of the findings of this book, and makes suggestions for further research on this issue. Section II.ii considers the limited success of the common readmission policy, and reflects upon its further development. Section II.iii discusses the relationship between Community readmission agreements and international refugee protection.

### II.i The supposed effects of readmission agreements

Readmission agreements may be expected to limit but not eliminate return problems, and do not necessarily lead third countries to increase migration control on their territories. These are arguments following from chapters 2, 3 and 5, which are contrary to general expectations of the effects of readmission agreements.

Regarding the readmission of own nationals, which is required by international customary law, Chapter 2 identified the main obstacles in practice as being the lack of documents carried by migrants, coupled with the lack of cooperation received from requested States. The main obstacles facing the readmission of third country nationals is the lack of an obligation to readmit third country nationals under general international law, and the difficulty of proving transit through a requested State. In an effort to overcome these obstacles, States which need to expel aliens conclude readmission agreements. These not only spell out readmission obligations, but also list agreed means of evidence and establish procedures to underpin these obligations.[1]

Upon examining the provisions regarding evidence, however, chapter 5 concluded that Community readmission agreements cannot guarantee return, while leaving opportunity for both migrants and requested third countries to frustrate expulsion. Especially where migrants have disposed of documents and other paper-based evidence and are unwilling to return, "problem" States will be able to continue withholding effective cooperation on readmission. In the implementation of Community readmission agreements, the goodwill of third countries therefore remains an important factor.[2]

This implies that, regarding the implementation of the common readmission policy, much will continue to depend on the quality of general relations of the Community and the Member States with third countries. This, in turn, will depend in cases on specific incentives for cooperation. Some third countries may require a steady supply of benefits to ensure not only conclusion, but also implementation of a readmission agreement. It is therefore arguable that good bilateral relations, and the benefits granted in exchange for readmission agreements, are as important a guarantee of facilitated return of unauthorised immigrants as the technical content of those agreements, if not more important.

1 See, in particular, *supra*, subsections 2.1.2.1 and 2.2.1.

2 *Supra*, subsection, 5.3.5.2.

Because Community readmission agreements cannot guarantee return in all cases, it is uncertain whether concluding such an agreement will lead to a significant increase in the return of unauthorised immigrants, as is generally expected. The limited ability of readmission agreements to overcome practical (or, indeed, political) obstacles to return begs the question of what their practical value is. Limited research into the return practice of the Netherlands, discussed in chapter 3, shows that the amount of formal applications of readmission agreements is surprisingly low. This is partially due to the fact that the procedures established by readmission agreements (generally considered one of the great added values of such agreements) are experienced as arduous and time-consuming to implement in practice.[3]

However, certain of the agreements at the disposal of the Netherlands have shown to facilitate the establishment of *informal* readmission procedures, which are of great value in practice. The number of returns implemented through these informal procedures, relating to border apprehension but also charter flights, is difficult to quantify, but far greater than the number of formal applications of readmission agreements. These informal practices function well, partly because the formal procedure offered by a readmission agreement is available as a fall-back option in case cooperation would falter. For the other part, these informal practices are driven by good interstate relations or relations between border authorities (such as between the Netherlands and Germany), or by certain incentives (such as in the case of Bulgaria and Rumania).[4]

Clearly, more elaborate research is needed to arrive at any definite conclusions regarding the practical effects of readmission agreements, in particular the frequency and manner of their application. The application of readmission agreements by Member States on the external border of the EU, for example, is bound to be more significant. More comprehensive quantitative and qualitative research is necessary to fully comprehend the practical value of readmission agreements, and, therewith, the reasons of the European Community to pursue these agreements.

In particular, there is a need for more statistical data regarding the number of returns implemented by the Member States using a readmission agreement.[5] More qualitative data, regarding implementation problems, and the functioning of formal readmission procedures, are also required. Related to the latter, is the relationship between formal and informal readmission procedures and practices. Mapping the informal application of readmission agreements by the Member States, especially in border regions, is a prerequisite for understanding the practical impact of these agreements. The degree to which readmission agreements can act as a catalyst for informal returns is difficult to measure, but clearly an element which should be considered. It should be remembered

3 *Supra*, subsection 3.2.1.

4 *Ibid.*

5 The statistical data compiled for Byrne, Noll and Vedsted-Hansen's 2002 publication is the most elaborate I have seen to date, regarding readmission as well as the supposed effect of readmission agreements on migration control: see Byrne, Noll and Vedsted-Hansen 2002.

that Community readmission agreements explicitly allow informal "arrangements" of the Member States with relevant third countries.[6]

Given the limited number of Community readmission agreements in force, research would have to focus on the practices and experiences of a representative number of Member States. This could then serve as an indicator or predictor of the practical value of the Community agreements currently under negotiation.

In addition, this book indicates that more research into the supposedly stimulating effect of readmission agreements on migration control would also be valuable. It is generally expected that concluding a readmission agreement will lead third countries to increase migration and border control, because of concerns about the readmission of transit migrants. Readmission agreements are considered to add to existing fears of a "closed sack"[7] effect on the part of third countries bordering the EU. Migrants on their way to the EU enter these third countries relatively easily whilst exiting into an EU Member State is more difficult, considering EU external border control. A certain amount of migrants are left stranded on the territories of these third countries, on top of which a further amount might be readmitted under Community agreements. Hence, it is generally reasoned that readmission agreements stimulate third countries to increase control of their borders, as well as intercept transit migrants in-country.

Chapter 3 questioned the existence of any direct correlation between readmission agreements and the introduction of control measures in third countries.[8] The incentive for *border* control is arguable. However, given that readmission is and remains uncertain, third countries are unlikely to step up interception in-country and assume immediate responsibility for transit migrants in this manner. In addition, I argued that third countries may have ulterior motives, and are subject to strong ulterior influences, which lead them to strengthen control measures. It would therefore remain difficult in practice to corroborate the effects of readmission agreements in this regard, even in the face of qualitative and quantitative data indicating intensified control.

This finding is without prejudice to the fact that readmission negotiations are an opportunity to offer third countries assistance in the improvement of migration control, reception conditions, and the negotiation of agreements of their own. Community readmission agreements, as well as readmission clauses, may therefore be considered a vehicle for the establishment of wider cooperation between the EC and third countries concerning migration and asylum. It is important to realise that, regardless of their practical effects, readmission agreements and clauses therefore have a certain value for the EU.

Finally, research along the lines described above is becoming increasingly important, considering that not only the number of readmission agreements, but also the *compensation* awarded to third countries in exchange for these agreements, is steadily expanding. In order to enable public scrutiny of the legitimacy of this negotiating prac-

6 *Supra*, subsection 5.3.9.

7 See Byrne, Noll and Vedsted-Hansen 2002.

8 *Supra*, subsection 3.2.2.

tice, it is necessary to have a clear idea of the actual value of readmission agreements in returning migrants and stimulating migration control. Only then would it be possible to judge whether these agreements are worth bartering substantial benefits with third countries.

### II.ii The limited success of the common readmission policy

The common readmission policy is relatively unsuccessful yet has a questionable impact on other EU policy fields, including EU external relations. That is one of the main conclusions of this book, and the short answer to the question, formulated in the introduction; *how does the European Community attempt to persuade third countries to accept readmission agreements and readmission clauses, and is this strategy successful?*

Chapter 3 demonstrated that the main motivation of the Member States to choose to adopt a *common* readmission policy was to be able to use the negotiating weight of the Community. It was expected that reaching readmission agreements with third countries would become overall faster and easier. Smaller countries would comply with demands, eager to establish closer relations with the EU. In addition, the Community would be a better match for the larger countries, and difficult negotiating partners, such as Russia and China, than any single Member State. An arguably more significant reason for having a common readmission policy – namely to address the risk of circumvention of national readmission policies given the absence of internal border controls in the EU – did *not* inform this choice of the Member States. It is therefore primarily in the light of negotiation results that the success of the common readmission policy needs to be evaluated, and these are limited.[9]

It is possible that some of the smaller Member States will consider the common readmission policy beneficial, despite the limited success of the negotiations. Dwarf States such as Cyprus, Luxemburg or Malta, for example, are likely to have difficulty in reaching agreements on readmission with third countries. Especially for Malta, faced by a significant influx of unauthorised immigrants since it joined EU, the EC's competence in the area of readmission has significance. For the rest of the Member States, however, the added value of the common readmission policy is doubtful.

Contrary to expectations, negotiations at the EC level with important countries have been slow and arduous. Considering that the Member States sacrificed at least part of their freedom to conclude readmission agreements with third countries individually, one can understand that misgivings arose after the transfer of competence to the EC level.[10] In addition, a loss of confidence in the EC to achieve results likely accounts for the fact that certain Member States have pushed the boundaries of their own remaining competence in this area.[11]

9 *Supra*, subsection 7.3.1.

10 *Supra*, sections 4.2, 4.4 and 5.2.

11 *Supra*, subsection 7.3.6.

More fundamentally, the limited results in the negotiations arguably question whether a continuation of the common readmission policy is in accordance with the principle of subsidiarity. The relevant Community objective *in casu* is the "repatriation" of unauthorised immigrants to third countries.[12] Considering that the Member States are responsible for actual implementation, this objective should be interpreted narrowly as the conclusion of formal agreements on readmission with third countries. Based on an assessment of the effects of the common readmission policy *a posteriori*, rather than the effects *a priori*, it is highly doubtful whether this objective is "better achieved"[13] at the Community level than at the Member State level.[14]

As described in chapter 7, there are several interrelated explanations for the limited negotiating results. Firstly, the Council insists on the readmission of third country nationals,[15] which is not required by general international law, and which third countries are generally unwilling to accept. Secondly, third countries have been tough negotiators, and, excepting Albania, have been able to determine the pace of negotiations. Third countries exploit the negotiation process with their own agenda, seeking to benefit from entering into a Community readmission agreement.

Quite contrary to expectations that the Community level would provide a dominant vantage-point, third countries have generally held a strong negotiating position. This is due in particular to the standard inclusion of obligations to readmit third country nationals and stateless persons in Community readmission agreements. Limiting some of the agreements to the readmission of own nationals would simplify and advance the negotiations considerably. Furthermore, the fact that the contracting party is the European Community, and not an individual Member State, has also strengthened the negotiating position of third countries. Community readmission agreements regulate the readmission of unauthorised immigrants from at least twenty-four Member States.[16] Rather than be intimidated by this daunting prospect, or by the political and economic power of the Community, however, third countries have simply asked for more in return. Concluding readmission agreements at the Community level has elevated the price of these agreements, understandably, to benefits also at the Community level.

With regard to the negotiation of readmission *clauses*, similar observations were made in chapter 8. The variations in content and text of these clauses suggest that real negotiations took place. This is remarkable, considering that substantial *quid pro quo* is so obviously present in the Community or mixed agreements which carry such clauses.

12 *Supra*, section 4.1 and 4.2.

13 Article 5 TEC.

14 *Supra*, section 4.3, and subsection 7.3.1.

15 The term third country national is used here within the meaning of Community readmission agreements; a person who has the nationality of neither the requesting- nor the requested State. *In casu*, while all Community readmission agreements are concluded with third countries, this person will also always be a third country national within the more general meaning of not being a national of an EU Member State.

16 *Supra*, subsection 7.3.2, n. 194.

On the basis of the findings of chapters 6 to 8, it is possible to conclude that the common readmission policy is, on balance, beneficial to the third countries which fall under it. This conclusion takes issue with the prevailing view that third countries are the weaker party, and disadvantaged by having readmission agreements imposed on them by the EU. Readmitting unauthorised immigrants is undeniably disadvantageous to third countries. However, agreeing to negotiate agreements with the Community enables these countries to extract benefits. For this reason, third countries do not outright refuse to negotiate but make counter-demands, furthermore bearing in mind that an agreement does not guarantee readmission in all cases. In addition, the Community does not pursue a convincing punitive strategy in the negotiations. One may therefore assume that third countries consider concluding a readmission agreement with the Community as being overall in their interest.

The third explanation for the lack of progress in the negotiations is that the Council did not from the outset provide the Commission with sufficient negotiating leverage. As noted, the fact that third countries claim benefits at the Community level is understandable. However, granting such benefits is a complicated process, while touching upon policy areas where the Community has limited or no competence (such as labour immigration), or policy areas where the Commission is not authorised to barter (such as trade or development cooperation). The fact that the Commission is the negotiator, but not the decision-maker when it comes to most compensating benefits has further slowed negotiations down. Many of the Commission's resources have gone towards convincing the Council and the Member States to free up more negotiating leverage, unable to offer third countries a package deal at the start of negotiations, and unable to respond to third countries' subsequent requests in a timely manner.

Conscious of the need for more leverage, the Council is slowly but surely expanding the negotiating arsenal of the Commission. The Council has not only agreed to instruments, which expand the capability of the Community to offer relevant technical and financial assistance, it has also responded to concrete demands of compensation by third countries. The opening up of the EU's visa policy is the most notable example here. Russia's staunch refusal to negotiate readmission without parallel negotiations on visa facilitation has precipitated the use of visa facilitation as *the* incentive for securing agreements with countries to the East and South East of the EU. Ukraine, Moldova, and countries of the Western Balkans, can now look forward to the same preferential treatment in this regard as Russia.[17]

In this book, I have advocated on several counts the need for prudence in granting *quid pro quo* to secure readmission agreements. I argued in chapter 2 that the increasing use of incentives undermines the unconditionality as well as the customary status of the international obligation to readmit own nationals.[18] Furthermore, I pointed out in chapter 7 that the incentive-based negotiation practice so fervently pursued by the European Commission has implications for other EU policy fields, internal and exter-

17 *Supra*, subsection 7.3.5.

18 *Supra*, subsection 2.1.2.3.

nal. Some of these implications may be considered favourable, but others are highly questionable.[19]

Further expansion of the use of incentives would surely improve the success of the common readmission policy. Overall, however, careful consideration of the implications of such a strategy is necessary. The Commission shows signs of path-dependent thinking in developing the common readmission policy. It has a pragmatic approach and political interests, which do not allow for critical reflection regarding the possible wider implications of granting benefits in exchange for Community readmission agreements. It is thus primarily up to the Council and the Member States to continue exercising strict control over the negotiating process, and be prudent in authorising the Commission to use new incentives in support of the common readmission policy.

To be sure, this regards positive, as well as negative incentives. As noted, the Community does not yet pursue a convincing strategy of negative incentives to persuade third countries to sign readmission agreements. It is arguable that authorising the use of punitive action would enable the Commission to seize the initiative in negotiations, and extract concessions from third countries at no direct cost. The case of Albania clearly illustrates the benefits of such a strategy. Concrete action, beyond the *threat* of punishment, however, may ultimately damage the interests of the EU.[20]

In general, the development of the common readmission policy is arguably the clearest illustration of the current importance of the issue of migration within international relations. Responsibility for migrants is increasingly the subject of barter between States. In the negotiation of readmission at the Community level, in particular, there are three parties principally affected: the European Community, the third country, and the individual migrant. The European Community, it is assumed,[21] benefits from concluding readmission agreements and readmission clauses. The third country, I have argued, too benefits from the common readmission policy. The fact that the Community and third country both stand to gain, begs the question of whether the individual migrant stands to lose; in particular, whether this negotiation process compromises refugee rights.

### II.iii Community readmission agreements and international refugee protection

Community readmission agreements appear to be compatible with international protection obligations under the Geneva Refugee Convention and the European Convention of Human Rights in relation to expulsion to third countries, although the possibility of diverging practice needs to be taken into account. That is another main conclusion of this book in answer to the question, formulated in the introduction: *are Community readmission agreements compatible with relevant international obligations of refugee protection?*

19 *Supra*, subsection 7.3.5.

20 *Supra*, section 6.3 and subsection 7.3.5.

21 *Supra*, section II.i.

Readmission agreements continue to proliferate, having a bearing also on the expulsion of protection seekers. Insofar as pertaining to the readmission agreements concluded at the Community level, at least, this development does not appear to create tension with the international refugee protection obligations incumbent on the EU Member States. This conclusion is contrary to the prevailing view in the literature that readmission agreements are detrimental to refugee protection. I have taken issue with the view that readmission agreements heighten the risk of refoulement, especially in cases of expulsion to safe third countries.

There are two main reasons for this conclusion. Firstly, the common safe third country policy, as determined by the procedures directive, appears to be in line with the international protection obligations of the Member States, albeit a restrictive interpretation thereof. This means that applications of Community readmission agreements to expel protection seekers, who are rejected under that policy, cannot *ipso facto* be compromised in light of international law.

Secondly, using readmission agreements to implement expulsion does not affect the applicability of the Member States' international obligations of refugee protection. A Member State remains bound to these obligations, regardless of the method of expulsion it chooses, including a formal readmission procedure in agreement with a third country. This means *inter alia* that the facilitation of expulsion provided by a readmission agreement does not heighten the risk of refoulement. A rise in the absolute number of expulsions, which may result from a readmission agreement, does not necessarily entail a relative increase in cases of refoulement. Furthermore, concluding a readmission agreement with an unsafe country does not in of itself imply a risk to refugee protection. It simply means that such an agreement is not applicable in practice to the expulsion of protection seekers.

I recognise that a comprehensive understanding of the impact of readmission agreements on international refugee protection would once again require more quantitative and qualitative research, especially in relation to informal border practices. I have argued that readmission agreements do not heighten the risk of refoulement, while the same legal safeguards apply. This is relevant to the formal application of a readmission agreement after a decision of national law rejecting a protection seeker. The compliance in practice with international obligations during the *informal* application of readmission agreements could be a cause for concern. There is indication that international protection obligations are not strictly adhered to in such situations, for example, by new Member States on the enlarged external border of the EU.[22]

To be sure, the Member States are bound to their international protection obligations, also in the operation of informal procedures. If it is found, however, that readmission agreements are generally conducive to informal border practices that are harmful to international refugee protection, then there could be grounds for reconsidering the compatibility of readmission agreements with international protection obligations.

22 Human Rights Watch 2005b.

# Annex 1 Community readmission agreement with Albania

*Agreement between the European Community and the Republic of Albania on the readmission of persons residing without authorisation, OJ* L 124, 17 May 2005, p. 22.

**Agreement**

between the European Community and the Republic of Albania on the readmission of persons residing without authorisation

THE HIGH CONTRACTING PARTIES,

THE EUROPEAN COMMUNITY, hereinafter referred to as "the Community", and

THE REPUBLIC OF ALBANIA, hereinafter referred to as "Albania",

DETERMINED to strengthen their cooperation in order to combat illegal immigration more effectively,

DESIRING to establish, by means of this Agreement and on the basis of reciprocity, rapid and effective procedures for the identification and safe and orderly return of persons who do not, or no longer, fulfil the conditions for entry to, presence in, or residence on the territories of Albania or one of the Member States of the European Union, and to facilitate the transit of such persons in a spirit of cooperation,

EMPHASISING that this Agreement shall be without prejudice to the rights, obligations and responsibilities of the Community, the Member States of the European Union and Albania arising from International Law and, in particular, from the European Convention of 4 November 1950 for the Protection of Human Rights, the Convention of 28 July 1951 and the Protocol of 31 January 1967 on the Status of Refugees, and international instruments on extradition,

HAVE AGREED AS FOLLOWS:

**Article 1**

Definitions

For the purpose of this Agreement:

(a) "Member State" shall mean any Member State of the European Union, with the exception of the Kingdom of Denmark;

(b) "National of a Member State" shall mean any person who holds the nationality, as defined for Community purposes, of a Member State;

(c) "National of Albania" shall mean any person who holds the nationality of Albania;

(d) "Third-country national" shall mean any person who holds a nationality other than that of Albania or one of the Member States;

(e) "Stateless person" shall mean any person who does not hold a nationality;

(f) "Residence authorisation" shall mean a permit of any type issued by Albania or one of the Member States entitling a person to reside on its territory. This shall not include temporary permissions to remain on its territory in connection with the processing of an asylum application or an application for a residence authorisation;

(g) "Visa" shall mean an authorisation issued or a decision taken by Albania or one of the Member States which is required with a view to entry into, or transit through, its territory. This shall not include an airport transit visa.

SECTION I

READMISSION OBLIGATIONS BY ALBANIA

**Article 2**

Readmission of own nationals

1. Albania shall readmit, upon application by a Member State and without further formalities other than those provided for in this Agreement, all persons who do not, or who no longer, fulfil the conditions in force for entry into, presence in, or residence on, the territory of the requesting Member State provided that it is proved, or may be validly assumed on the basis of prima facie evidence furnished, that they are nationals of Albania.

The same shall apply to persons who have been deprived of, or who have renounced, the nationality of Albania since entering the territory of a Member State, unless such persons have at least been promised naturalisation by that Member State.

2. Albania shall, as necessary and without delay, issue the person whose readmission has been accepted with the travel document required for his or her return with a period of validity of at least six months. If, for legal or factual reasons, the person concerned cannot be transferred within the period of validity of the travel document that was initially issued, Albania shall, within 14 calendar days, extend the validity of the travel document or, where necessary, issue a new travel document with the same period of validity. If Albania has not, within 14 calendar days, issued the travel document,

extended its validity or, where necessary, renewed it, it shall be deemed to accept the use of the EU standard travel document for expulsion purposes [1].

**Article 3**

Readmission of third-country nationals and stateless persons

1. Albania shall readmit, upon application by a Member State and without further formalities other than those provided for in this Agreement, all third-country nationals or stateless persons who do not, or who no longer, fulfil the conditions in force for entry into, presence in, or residence on, the territory of the requesting Member State provided that it is proved, or may be validly assumed on the basis of prima facie evidence furnished, that such persons

(a) hold or at the time of entry held a valid visa or residence authorisation issued by Albania; or

(b) entered the territory of the Member States after having stayed on, or transited through, the territory of Albania.

2. The readmission obligation in paragraph 1 shall not apply if

(a) the third country national or stateless person has only been in airside transit via an international airport of Albania; or

(b) the requesting Member State has issued to the third-country national or stateless person a visa or residence authorisation before or after entering its territory unless

- that person is in possession of a visa or residence permit, issued by Albania, which has a longer period of validity, or
- the visa or residence authorisation issued by the requesting Member State has been obtained by using forged or falsified documents.

3. Albania shall, as necessary and without delay, issue the person whose readmission has been accepted with the travel document required for his or her return with a period of validity of at least six months. If, for legal or factual reasons, the person concerned cannot be transferred within the period of validity of the travel document that was initially issued, Albania shall, within 14 calendar days, extend the validity of the travel document or, where necessary, issue a new travel document with the same period of validity. If Albania has not, within 14 calendar days, issued the travel document, extended its validity or, where necessary, renewed it, it shall be deemed to accept the use of the EU standard travel document for expulsion purposes.

SECTION II
READMISSION OBLIGATIONS BY THE COMMUNITY

**Article 4**

Readmission of own nationals

1. A Member State shall readmit, upon application by Albania and without further formalities other than those provided for in this Agreement, all persons who do not, or who no longer, fulfil the conditions in force for entry into, presence in, or residence on, the territory of Albania provided that it is proved, or may be validly assumed on the basis of prima facie evidence furnished, that they are nationals of that Member State.

The same shall apply to persons who have been deprived of, or who have renounced, the nationality of a Member State since entering the territory of Albania unless such persons have at least been promised naturalisation by Albania.
2. A Member State shall, as necessary and without delay, issue the person whose readmission has been accepted with the travel document required for his or her return with a period of validity of at least six months. If, for legal or factual reasons, the person concerned cannot be transferred within the period of validity of the travel document that was initially issued, the Member State concerned shall, within 14 calendar days, extend the validity of the travel document or, where necessary, issue a new travel document with the same period of validity. If the Member State concerned has not, within 14 calendar days, issued the travel document, extended its validity or, where necessary, renewed it, it shall be deemed to accept the use of the Albanian certificate for expulsion purposes [2].

**Article 5**

Readmission of third-country nationals and stateless persons
1. A Member State shall readmit, upon application by Albania and without further formalities other than those provided for in this Agreement, all third-country nationals or stateless persons who do not, or who no longer, fulfil the conditions in force for entry into, presence in, or residence on, the territory of Albania provided that it is proved, or may be validly assumed on the basis of prima facie evidence furnished, that such persons
(a) hold or at the time of entry held a valid visa or residence authorisation issued by the requested Member State; or
(b) entered the territory of Albania after having stayed on, or transited through, the territory of the requested Member State.
2. The readmission obligation in paragraph 1 shall not apply if
(a) the third-country national or stateless person has only been in airside transit via an international airport of the requested Member State; or
(b) Albania has issued to the third-country national or stateless person a visa or residence authorisation before or after entering its territory unless
- that person is in possession of a visa or residence permit, issued by the requested Member State, which has a longer period of validity, or
- the visa or residence authorisation issued by Albania has been obtained by using forged or falsified documents.
3. The readmission obligation in paragraph 1 is for the Member State that issued a visa or residence authorisation. If two or more Member States issued a visa or residence authorisation, the readmission obligation in paragraph 1 is for the Member State that issued the document with a longer period of validity or, if one or several of them have already expired, the document that is still valid. If all of the documents have already expired, the readmission obligation in paragraph 1 is for the Member State that issued the document with the most recent expiry date. If no such documents can be presented, the readmission obligation in paragraph 1 is for the Member State of last exit.

4. A Member State shall, as necessary and without delay, issue the person whose readmission has been accepted with the travel document required for his or her return with a period of validity of at least six months. If, for legal or factual reasons, the person concerned cannot be transferred within the period of validity of the travel document that was initially issued, the Member State concerned shall, within 14 calendar days, extend the validity of the travel document or, where necessary, issue a new travel document with the same period of validity. If the Member State concerned has not within 14 calendar days issued the travel document, extended its validity or, where necessary, renewed it, it shall be deemed to accept the use of the Albanian certificate for expulsion purposes.

SECTION III
READMISSION PROCEDURE

**Article 6**

Principle

1. Subject to paragraph 2, any transfer of a person to be readmitted on the basis of one of the obligations contained in Articles 2 to 5 shall require the submission of a readmission application to the competent authority of the requested State.
2. The readmission application may be replaced by a written communication to the competent authority of the requested State within a reasonable time period prior to the return of the person concerned provided that the person to be readmitted is in possession of a valid travel document and, where applicable, a valid visa or residence authorisation of the requested State.

**Article 7**

Readmission application

1. To the extent possible, the readmission application shall contain the following information:
(a) the particulars of the person to be readmitted (e.g. given names, surnames, date of birth, and — where possible — place of birth, father's name, mother's name, and the last place of residence);
(b) indication of the means with which proof or prima facie evidence of nationality, transit, the conditions for the readmission of third-country nationals and stateless persons and unlawful entry and residence will be provided.
2. To the extent possible, the readmission application shall also contain the following information:
(a) a statement indicating that the person to be transferred may need help or care, provided that the person concerned has explicitly consented to the statement;
(b) any other protection or security measure which may be necessary in the individual transfer case.
3. A common form to be used for readmission applications is attached as Annex 5 to this Agreement.

**Article 8**

Means of evidence regarding nationality

1. Proof of nationality pursuant to Articles 2(1) and 4(1) can be particularly furnished through any of the documents listed in Annex 1 to this Agreement, even if their period of validity has expired. If such documents are presented, the Member States and Albania shall mutually recognise the nationality without further investigation being required. Proof of nationality cannot be furnished through false documents.

2. Prima facie evidence of nationality pursuant to Articles 2(1) and 4(1) can be particularly furnished through any of the documents listed in Annex 2 to this Agreement, even if their period of validity has expired. If such documents are presented, the Member States and Albania shall deem the nationality to be established, unless they can prove otherwise. Prima facie evidence of nationality cannot be furnished through false documents.

3. If none of the documents listed in Annexes 1 or 2 can be presented, the competent diplomatic and consular representations of Albania or the Member State concerned shall, upon request, make arrangements to interview the person to be readmitted without undue delay in order to establish his or her nationality.

**Article 9**

Means of evidence regarding third-country nationals and stateless persons

1. Proof of the conditions for the readmission of third-country nationals and stateless persons laid down in Articles 3(1) and 5(1) shall be particularly furnished through any of the means of evidence listed in Annex 3 to this Agreement; it cannot be furnished through false documents. Any such proof shall be mutually recognised by the Member States and Albania without any further investigation being required.

2. Prima facie evidence of the conditions for the readmission of third-country nationals and stateless persons laid down in Articles 3(1) and 5(1) shall be particularly furnished through any of the means of evidence listed in Annex 4 to this Agreement; it cannot be furnished through false documents. Where such prima facie evidence is presented, the Member States and Albania shall deem the conditions to be established, unless they can prove otherwise.

3. The unlawfulness of entry, presence or residence shall be established by means of the travel documents of the person concerned in which the necessary visa or other residence authorisation for the territory of the requesting State are missing. A statement by the requesting state that the person concerned has been found not having the necessary travel documents, visa or residence authorisation shall likewise provide prima facie evidence of the unlawful entry, presence or residence.

**Article 10**

Time limits

1. The application for readmission must be submitted to the competent authority of the requested State within a maximum of one year after the requesting State's competent authority has gained knowledge that a third-country national or a stateless person does not, or does no longer, fulfil the conditions in force for entry, presence or residence.

Where there are legal or factual obstacles to the application being submitted in time, the time limit shall, upon request by the requesting State, be extended but only until the obstacles have ceased to exist.
2. A readmission application must be replied to without undue delay, and in any event within a maximum of 14 calendar days; reasons shall be given for refusal of a readmission request. This time limit begins to run with the date of receipt of the readmission request. If there was no reply within this time limit, the transfer shall be deemed to have been agreed to.
3. After agreement has been given or, where appropriate, after expiry of the 14 calendar day time limit, the person concerned shall be transferred without undue delay and, at the most, within three months. Upon application by the requesting State, this time limit may be extended by the time taken to deal with legal or practical obstacles.

**Article 11**

Transfer modalities and modes of transportation
1. Before returning a person, the competent authorities of Albania and the Member State concerned shall make arrangements in writing in advance regarding the transfer date, the point of entry, possible escorts and other information relevant to the transfer.
2. No means of transportation, whether by air, land or sea, shall be prohibited. Return by air shall not be restricted to the use of the national carriers of Albania or the Member States and may take place by using scheduled or charter flights. In the event of escorted returns, such escorts shall not be restricted to authorised persons of the requesting State, provided that they are authorised persons from Albania or any Member State.

**Article 12**

Readmission in error
Albania shall take back without delay any person readmitted by a Member State, and a Member State shall take back without delay any person readmitted by Albania, if it is established, within a period of three months after the transfer of the person concerned, that the requirements laid down in Articles 2 to 5 of this Agreement were not met. In such cases, the competent authorities of Albania and the Member State concerned shall also exchange all available information relating to the actual identity, nationality or transit route of the person to be taken back.

SECTION IV
TRANSIT OPERATIONS

**Article 13**

Principles
1. The Member States and Albania should restrict the transit of third-country nationals or stateless persons to cases where such persons cannot be returned to the State of destination directly.
2. Albania shall allow the transit of third-country nationals or stateless persons if a Member State so requests, and a Member State shall authorise the transit of third-coun-

try nationals or stateless persons if Albania so requests, if the onward journey in possible other States of transit and the readmission by the State of destination is assured.
3. Transit can be refused by Albania or a Member State
(a) if the third-country national or the stateless person runs the real risk of being subjected to torture or to inhuman or degrading treatment or punishment or the death penalty or of persecution because of his or her race, religion, nationality, membership of a particular social group or political conviction in the State of destination or another State of transit; or
(b) if the third-country national or the stateless person is subject to criminal prosecution or sanctions in the requested State or in another State of transit; or
(c) on grounds of public health, domestic security, public order or other national interests of the requested State.
4. Albania or a Member State may revoke any authorisation issued if circumstances referred to in paragraph 3 subsequently arise or come to light which stand in the way of the transit operation, or if the onward journey in possible States of transit or the readmission by the State of destination is no longer assured. In this case, the requesting State shall take back the third-country national or the stateless person, as necessary and without delay.

**Article 14**

Transit procedure
1. An application for transit operations shall be submitted to the competent authority of the requested State in writing and shall contain the following information:
(a) type of transit (by air, land or sea), possible other States of transit and intended final destination;
(b) the particulars of the person concerned (e.g. given name, surname, maiden name, other names used/by which known or aliases, date of birth, sex and — where possible — place of birth, nationality, language, type and number of travel document);
(c) envisaged point of entry, time of transfer and possible use of escorts;
(d) a declaration that in the view of the requesting State the conditions pursuant to Article 13(2) are met, and that no reasons for a refusal pursuant to Article 13(3) are known of.
A common form to be used for transit applications is attached as Annex 6 to this Agreement.
2. The requested State shall, within five calendar days and in writing, inform the requesting State of the admission, confirming the point of entry and the envisaged time of admission, or inform it of the admission refusal and of the reasons for such refusal.
3. If the transit operation takes place by air, the person to be readmitted and possible escorts shall be exempted from having to obtain an airport transit visa.
4. The competent authorities of the requested State shall, subject to mutual consultations, assist in the transit operations, in particular through the surveillance of the persons in question and the provision of suitable amenities for that purpose.

SECTION V
COSTS

**Article 15**

Transport and transit costs

Without prejudice to the right of the competent authorities to recover the costs associated with the readmission from the person to be readmitted or third parties, all transport costs incurred in connection with readmission and transit operations pursuant to this Agreement as far as the border of the State of final destination shall be borne by the requesting State.

SECTION VI
DATA PROTECTION AND NON-AFFECTION CLAUSE

**Article 16**

Data Protection

The communication of personal data shall only take place if such communication is necessary for the implementation of this Agreement by the competent authorities of Albania or a Member State as the case may be. The processing and treatment of personal data in a particular case shall be subject to the domestic laws of Albania and, where the controller is a competent authority of a Member State, to the provisions of Directive 95/46/EC [3] and of the national legislation of that Member State adopted pursuant to this Directive. Additionally the following principles shall apply:

(a) personal data must be processed fairly and lawfully;

(b) personal data must be collected for the specified, explicit and legitimate purpose of implementing this Agreement and not further processed by the communicating authority nor by the receiving authority in a way incompatible with that purpose;

(c) personal data must be adequate, relevant and not excessive in relation to the purpose for which they are collected and/or further processed; in particular, personal data communicated may concern only the following:

- the particulars of the person to be transferred (e.g. given names, surnames, any previous names, other names used/by which known or aliases, sex, civil status, date and place of birth, current and any previous nationality),
- passport, identity card or driving licence (number, period of validity, date of issue, issuing authority, place of issue),
- stop-overs and itineraries,
- other information needed to identify the person to be transferred or to examine the readmission requirements pursuant to this Agreement;

(d) personal data must be accurate and, where necessary, kept up to date;

(e) personal data must be kept in a form which permits identification of data subjects for no longer than is necessary for the purpose for which the data were collected or for which they are further processed;

(f) both the communicating authority and the receiving authority shall take every reasonable step to ensure as appropriate the rectification, erasure or blocking of personal

data where the processing does not comply with the provisions of this Article, in particular because those data are not adequate, relevant, accurate, or they are excessive in relation to the purpose of processing. This includes the notification of any rectification, erasure or blocking to the other Party;
(g) upon request, the receiving authority shall inform the communicating authority of the use of the communicated data and of the results obtained therefrom;
(h) personal data may only be communicated to the competent authorities. Further communication to other bodies requires the prior consent of the communicating authority;
(i) the communicating and the receiving authorities are under an obligation to make a written record of the communication and receipt of personal data.

**Article 17**
Non-affection clause
1. This Agreement shall be without prejudice to the rights, obligations and responsibilities of the Community, the Member States and Albania arising from International Law and, in particular, from the European Convention of 4 November 1950 for the Protection of Human Rights, the Convention of 28 July 1951 and the Protocol of 31 January 1967 on the Status of Refugees, and international instruments on extradition.
2. Nothing in this Agreement shall prevent the return of a person under other formal or informal arrangements.

SECTION VII
IMPLEMENTATION AND APPLICATION

**Article 18**
Joint readmission committee
1. The Contracting Parties shall provide each other with mutual assistance in the application and interpretation of this Agreement. To this end, they shall set up a joint readmission committee (hereinafter referred to as the committee) which will, in particular, have the task
(a) to monitor the application of this Agreement;
(b) to decide on implementing arrangements necessary for the uniform application of this Agreement;
(c) to have regular exchanges of information on the implementing Protocols drawn up by individual Member States and Albania pursuant to Article 19;
(d) to decide on amendments to the annexes to this Agreement;
(e) to recommend amendments to this Agreement.
2. The decisions of the committee shall be binding on the Contracting Parties.
3. The committee shall be composed of representatives of the Community and Albania; the Community shall be represented by the Commission, assisted by experts from Member States.
4. The committee shall meet where necessary at the request of one of the Contracting Parties.
5. The committee shall establish its rules of procedure.

**Article 19**

Implementing Protocols

1. Albania and a Member State may draw up implementing Protocols which shall cover rules on

(a) designation of the competent authorities, border crossing points and exchange of contact points;

(b) conditions for escorted returns, including the transit of third-country nationals and stateless persons under escort;

(c) means and documents additional to those listed in the Annexes 1 to 4 to this Agreement.

2. The implementing Protocols referred to in paragraph 1 shall enter into force only after the readmission committee, referred to in Article 18, has been notified.

3. Albania agrees to apply any provision of an implementing Protocol drawn up with one Member State also in its relations with any other Member State upon request of the latter.

**Article 20**

Relation to bilateral readmission agreements or arrangements of Member States

The provisions of this Agreement shall take precedence over the provisions of any bilateral agreement or arrangement on the readmission of persons residing without authorisation which have been or may, under Article 19, be concluded between individual Member States and Albania.

SECTION VIII

FINAL PROVISIONS

**Article 21**

Territorial application

1. Subject to paragraph 2, this Agreement shall apply to the territory in which the Treaty establishing the European Community is applicable and to the territory of Albania.

2. This Agreement shall not apply to the territory of the Kingdom of Denmark.

**Article 22**

Entry into force, duration and termination

1. This Agreement shall be ratified or approved by the Contracting Parties in accordance with their respective procedures.

2. Subject to paragraph 3, this Agreement shall enter into force on the first day of the second month following the date on which the Contracting Parties notify each other that the procedures referred to in the first paragraph have been completed.

3. Articles 3 and 5 of this Agreement shall enter into force two years after the date referred to in paragraph 2.

4. This Agreement is concluded for an unlimited period.

5. Each Contracting Party may denounce this Agreement by officially notifying the other Contracting Party. This Agreement shall cease to apply six months after the date of such notification.

**Article 23**

***Annexes***

Annexes 1 to 6 shall form an integral part of this Agreement.
Done at Luxembourg on the fourtheenth day of April in the year two thousand and five in duplicate in the Czech, Danish, Dutch, English, Estonian, Finnish, French, German, Greek, Hungarian, Italian, Latvian, Lithuanian, Maltese, Polish, Portuguese, Slovak, Slovenian, Spanish, Swedish and Albanian languages, each of these texts being equally authentic.

Por la Comunidad Europea
Za Evropské společenství
For Det Europæiske Fællesskab
Für die Europäische Gemeinschaft
Euroopa Ühenduse nimel
Για την Ευρωπαϊκή Κοινότητα
For the European Community
Pour la Communauté européenne
Per la Comunità europea
Eiropas Kopienas vārdā
Europos bendrijos vardu
az Európai Közösség részéről
Għall-Komunità Ewropea
Voor de Europese Gemeenschap
W imieniu Wspólnoty Europejskiej
Pela Comunidade Europeia
Za Európske spoločenstvo
za Evropsko skupnost
Euroopan yhteisön puolesta
På Europeiska gemenskapens vägnar
Për Komunitetin Evropian

Por la República de Albania
Za Albánskou republiku
På Republikken Albaniens vegne
Für die Republik Albanien
Albaania Vabariigi nimel
Για τη Δημοκρατία της Αλβανίας
For the Republic of Albania
Pour la République d'Albanie

Per la Repubblica di Albania
Albānijas Republikas vārdā -
Albanijos Respublikos vardu
az Albán Köztársaság részéről
Għar-Repubblika ta' l-Albanija
Voor de Republiek Albanië
W imieniu Republiki Albanii
Për Republikën e Shqipërisë
För Republiken Albanien
Albanian tasavallan puolesta
Za Republiko Albanijo
Za Albánsku republiku
Pela República da Albânia

[1] Council Recommendation of 30 November 1994 concerning the adoption of a standard travel document for the expulsion of third-country nationals (OJ C 274, 19.9.1996, p. 18).
[2] Endorsed by Instruction No 553 of 19 November 2003 of the acting Minister of Foreign Affairs on the issuing of laissez-passer by the Albanian representations for returns to Albania.
[3] Directive 95/46/EC of the European Parliament and of the Council of 24 October 1995 on the protection of individuals with regard to the processing of personal data and on the free movement of such data (OJ L 281, 23.11.1995, p. 31). Directive as amended by Regulation (EC) No 1882/2003 (OJ L 284, 31.10.2003, p. 1).

-----------------------------------------------

ANNEX 1

Common list of documents the presentation of which is considered as proof of nationality

(Articles 2(1), 3(1), 4(1) and 5(1))

- Passports of any kind (national passports, diplomatic passports, service passports, collective passports and surrogate passports including children's passports),
- identity cards of any kind (including temporary and provisional ones),
- service books and military identity cards,
- seamen's registration books and skippers' service cards,
- citizenship certificates and other official documents that mention or indicate citizenship.

-----------------------------------------------

ANNEX 2

Common list of documents the presentation of which is considered as prima facie evidence of nationality

(Articles 2(1), 3(1), 4(1) and 5(1))

- Photocopies of any of the documents listed in Annex 1 to this Agreement,
- driving licences or photocopies thereof,
- birth certificates or photocopies thereof,
- company identity cards or photocopies thereof,
- statements by witnesses,
- statements made by the person concerned and language spoken by him or her, including by means of an official test result,
- any other document which may help to establish the nationality of the person concerned.

-----------------------------------------------

ANNEX 3

Common list of documents which are considered as proof of the conditions for the readmission of third-country nationals and stateless persons

(Articles 3(1) and 5(1))

- Entry/departure stamps or similar endorsement in the travel document of the person concerned or other evidence of entry/departure (e.g. photographic),
- documents, certificates and bills of any kind (e.g. hotel bills, appointments for medical or hospital treatment, entry cards for public/private institutions, car rental agreements, credit card receipts etc.) which clearly show that the person concerned stayed on the territory of the requested State,
- tickets and/or passenger lists of air, train, coach or boat passages which show the presence and the itinerary of the person concerned on the territory of the requested State,
- information showing that the person concerned has used the services of a courier or travel agency,
- official statements made, in particular, by border authority staff and other witnesses who can testify to the person concerned crossing the border,
- official statement by the person concerned in judicial or administrative proceedings.

-----------------------------------------------

ANNEX 4

Common list of documents which are considered as prima facie evidence of the conditions for the readmission of third-country nationals and stateless persons

(Articles 3(1) and 5(1))

- Description of place and circumstances under which the person concerned has been intercepted after entering the territory of the requesting State, issued by the relevant authorities of that State,

- information related to the identity and/or stay of a person which has been provided by an international organisation,
- statement by the person concerned,
- reports/confirmation of information by family members, travelling companions, etc.

-----------------------------------------------

ANNEX 5

(Emblem of Albania)

Photograph

.........................................................................................................................
(Place and date)

.........................................................................................................................
(Designation of requesting authority)

Reference:

.........................................................................................................................

To

.........................................................................................................................
.........................................................................................................................
.........................................................................................................................
(Designation of receiving authority)

**READMISSION APPLICATION**
pursuant to Article 7 of the Agreement of 14 April 2005 between the European Community and the Republic of Albania
on the readmission of persons residing without authorisation

A. **Personal Details**
1. Full name (underline surname):

.........................................................................................................................
2. Maiden name:

.........................................................................................................................
3. Date and place of birth:

.........................................................................................................................
4. Father's name, mother's name:

.........................................................................................................................
5. Sex and physical description (height, colour of eyes, distinguishing marks etc.):

.........................................................................................................................
6. Also known as (earlier names, other names used/by which known or aliases):

.........................................................................................................................

7. Nationality and language:

..............................................................................................................................

8. Civil status: □ married □ single □ divorced □ widowed

married: name of spouse: ..............................................................................................

Names and age of children (if any):

..............................................................................................................................

..............................................................................................................................

..............................................................................................................................

9. Last address in the requesting State:

..............................................................................................................................

B. **Special circumstances relating to the transferee**

1. State of health

(E.g. possible reference to special medical care; Latin name of contagious disease):

..............................................................................................................................

2. Indication of particularly dangerous person

(E.g. suspected of serious offence; aggressive behaviour):

..............................................................................................................................

C. **Means of Evidence Attached**

1.............................................................................................................................

(type of document) (serial number, date and place of issue)

..............................................................................................................................

(issuing authority) (expiry date)

2.............................................................................................................................

(type of document) (serial number, date and place of issue)

..............................................................................................................................

(issuing authority) (expiry date)

3.............................................................................................................................

(type of document) (serial number, date and place of issue)

..............................................................................................................................

(issuing authority) (expiry date)

4.............................................................................................................................

(type of document) (serial number, date and place of issue)

..............................................................................................................................

(issuing authority) (expiry date)

D. **Observations**

..............................................................................................................................

..............................................................................................................................

..............................................................................................................................

(Signature of the requesting authority) (Seal/stamp)

-----------------------------------------------

ANNEX 6

Emblem of Albania

Photograph

..........................................................................................................................

(Place and date)

..........................................................................................................................

(Designation of requesting authority)

Reference:

..........................................................................................................................

To

..........................................................................................................................

..........................................................................................................................

(Designation of receiving authority)

**TRANSIT APPLICATION**

pursuant to Article 14 of the Agreement of 14 April 2005 between the European Community and the Republic of Albania
on the readmission of persons residing without authorisation

A. **Personal details**

1. Full name (underline surname):

..........................................................................................................................

2. Maiden name:

..........................................................................................................................

3. Date and place of birth:

..........................................................................................................................

4. Sex and physical description (height, colour of eyes, distinguishing marks etc.):

..........................................................................................................................

5. Also known as (earlier names, nicknames or pseudonyms):

..........................................................................................................................

6. Nationality and language:

..........................................................................................................................

7. Type and number of travel document:

..........................................................................................................................

B. **Transit Operation**

1. Type of transit

□ by air □ by sea □ by land

2. State of final destination

..........................................................................................................................

3. Possible other States of transit

.......................................................................................................................................

4. Proposed border crossing point, date, time of transfer and possible escorts

.......................................................................................................................................

.......................................................................................................................................

.......................................................................................................................................

5. Admission guaranteed in any other transit State and in the State of fi nal destination (Article 13 paragraph 2)

□ yes □ no

6. **Knowledge of any reason for a refusal of transit**
(Article 13 paragraph 3)

□ yes □ no

C. **Observations**

.......................................................................................................................................

.......................................................................................................................................

.......................................................................................................................................

.......................................................................................................................................

(Signature of the requesting authority) (Seal/stamp)

-------------------------------------------------

JOINT DECLARATION ON THE RELATION TO THE FUTURE STABILISATION AND ASSOCIATION AGREEMENT

The Parties take note that, on 31 January 2003, negotiations were launched on the conclusion of a Stabilisation and Association Agreement (SAA) between Albania, of the one part, and the Community and its Member States, of the other part, which will also include provisions on the prevention and control of illegal immigration and readmission. The Parties therefore agree that this Agreement will be fully taken into account in the relevant provisions of the SAA.

-------------------------------------------------

JOINT DECLARATION ON ARTICLE 3

The Parties take note that the readmission obligation vis-à-vis third-country nationals and stateless persons holding a valid visa issued by Albania (Article 3(1)(a) of this Agreement) shall only apply if the visa has been used for entering the territory of Albania.

-------------------------------------------------

JOINT DECLARATION ON ARTICLE 18

The meeting of the Joint Readmission Committee shall be held, wherever possible, in parallel with the relevant Subcommittee set up under the future Stabilisation and Association Agreement.

It shall keep that Subcommittee informed of its work.

The rules of procedure of the Joint Readmission Committee shall be compatible with the rules of procedure of that Subcommittee.

-----------------------------------------------

JOINT DECLARATION CONCERNING DENMARK

The Contracting Parties take note that this Agreement does not apply to the territory of the Kingdom of Denmark, nor to nationals of the Kingdom of Denmark. In such circumstances it is appropriate that Albania and Denmark conclude a readmission agreement in the same terms as this Agreement.

-----------------------------------------------

JOINT DECLARATION CONCERNING ICELAND AND NORWAY

The Contracting Parties take note of the close relationship between the European Community and Iceland and Norway, particularly by virtue of the Agreement of 18 May 1999 concerning the association of these countries with the implementation, application and development of the Schengen acquis. In such circumstances it is appropriate that Albania conclude a readmission agreement with Iceland and Norway in the same terms as this Agreement.

-----------------------------------------------

# Annex 2 1995 standard readmission clause

*Draft conclusions approved by the Council and the Representatives of the Governments of the Member States meeting within the Council*, Council Doc. 12509/95, 8 December 1995.

The Council and the Representatives of the Governments of the Member States, meeting within the Council, agree that entry of the following draft statements in the negotiating mandate for a Community agreement will be considered on a case by case basis when directives for the negotiation of future such agreements are adopted:

1.Draft statements by the Community and by State X
(These statements would be made when the agreements were signed and would form part of the final act)

"The European Community recalls the importance attached by its Member States to effective cooperation with third countries to facilitate the readmission of nationals of the latter who are present illegally in the territory of a Member State."

"State X undertakes to conclude readmission agreements with the Member States of the European Union which so request."

2.Draft statement by the Representatives of the Governments of the Member States, meeting within the Council, for the Council minutes

At the time of the Decision concluding the Community agreement in question, to be adopted by the Council solely on the basis of the relevant provisions of the Treaty, the Representatives of the Governments of the Member States, meeting within the Council, duly prepared, will examine whether the third country with which that Community agreement has been signed subject to conclusion has complied with its commitment to conclude bilateral readmission agreements with the Member States of the European Union which have so requested.

# Annex 3 1996 standard readmission clause

*Council conclusions on clauses to be inserted in future mixed agreements*, Council Doc. 4272/96, 22 January 1996.

THE COUNCIL AND THE REPRESENTATIVES OF THE MEMBER STATES, MEETING WITHIN THE COUNCIL,

AGREE that with regard to future mixed agreements the insertion of the following clauses shall be considered on a case-by-case basis when adopting the guidelines for their negotiation:

(a)Recital in the Preamble
Recognizing that cooperation for the prevention and control of illegal immigration constitutes one of the primary objectives of this Agreement.

(b)Articles of the Agreement
The relevant articles may be, where appropriate, preceded by a Title "N" called "Readmission. Cooperation for the prevention and control of illegal immigration."

ARTICLE X
The Member States of the European Union and State X agree to cooperate in order to prevent and control illegal immigration. To this end:

– State X agrees to readmit any of its nationals illegally present on the territory of a Member State, upon request by the latter and without further formalities;

–and each Member State agrees to readmit any of its nationals, as defined for Community purposes, illegally present on the territory of State X, upon request by the latter and without further formalities.

The Member States and State X will also provide their nationals with appropriate identity documents for such purposes.

ARTICLE Y
State X agrees to conclude bilateral agreements with Member States which so request, regulating specific obligations for readmission including an obligation for the readmission of nationals of other countries and stateless persons who have arrived on the territory of any such Member State from State X or who have arrived on the territory of State X from any such Member State.

ARTICLE Z
The Cooperation Council shall examine what other joint efforts can be made to prevent and control illegal immigration.

# Annex 4 1999 standard readmission clause

*Consequences of the Treaty of Amsterdam on readmission clauses in Community agreements and in agreements between the European Community, its Member States and third countries - Adoption of a Council decision*, Council Doc. 13409/99, 25 November 1999.

The Council of the European Union has decided that the standard clauses set out below should be included in all future Community agreements and in agreements between the European Community, its Member States and third countries

Article A
The European Community and State X agree to cooperate in order to prevent and control illegal immigration. To this end:

- State X agrees to readmit any of its nationals illegally present on the territory of a Member State of the European Union, upon request by the latter and without further formalities;

- and each Member State of the European Union agrees to readmit any of its nationals, as defined for Community purposes, illegally present on the territory of State X, upon request by the latter and without further formalities.

The Member States of the European Union and State X will also provide their nationals with appropriate identity documents for such purposes.

Article B
The Parties agree to conclude upon request an agreement between State X and the European Community regulating the specific obligations for State X and the Member States of the European Community for readmission, including an obligation for the readmission of nationals of other countries and stateless persons.

Article C
Pending the conclusion of the agreement with the Community referred to in Article B, State X agrees to conclude, upon request of a Member State, bilateral agreements with individual Member States of the European Community regulating the specific obligations for readmission between State X and the Member State concerned, including an obligation for the readmission of nationals of other countries and stateless persons.

Article D
The Cooperation Council shall examine what other joint efforts can be made to prevent and control illegal immigration.

---

# Annex 5 Migration management clause

*Political Dialogue and Cooperation Agreement between the European Community and its Member States and the Andean Community and its Member countries (Bolivia, Colombia, Ecuador, Peru and Venezuela)*, 15 December 2003, CE/AND/en (available on: www.europa.eu.int/comm/external_relations), Article 49.

ARTICLE 49
Cooperation on migration

1. The Parties reaffirm the importance that they attach to a joint management of migration flows between their territories. With a view to strengthening cooperation between them, they shall establish a comprehensive dialogue on all migration-related issues, including illegal migration, smuggling and trafficking in human beings, as well as the inclusion of migration concerns in the national strategies for economic and social development of the areas from which migrants originate, also taking into consideration the historic and cultural linkages existing between both regions.

2. Cooperation shall be based on a specific needs assessment conducted in mutual consultation between the Parties and be implemented in accordance with the relevant Community and national legislation in force. It will focus in particular on:

(a) the root causes of migration;

(b) the development and implementation of national legislation and practices with regard to international protection, with a view to satisfying the provisions of the Geneva Convention of 1951 on the status of refugees and of its Protocol of 1967 and other relevant international instruments, and to ensuring the respect of the principle of "*non-refoulement*";

(c) the admission rules and rights and status of persons admitted, fair treatment and integration of legal residents into society, education and training of legal migrants and measures against racism and xenophobia;

(d) the establishment of an effective and preventive policy against illegal immigration, smuggling of migrants and trafficking in human beings, including the issue of how to combat networks of smugglers and traffickers and how to protect the victims of such trafficking;

(e) the return, under humane and dignified conditions, of persons residing illegally, and the readmission of such persons, in accordance with paragraph 3;

(f) the area of visas, on issues identified as being of mutual interest, such as visas granted to persons travelling for commercial, academic or cultural purposes;

(g) the subject of border controls, on issues related to organisation, training, best practices and other operational measures on the ground and, where relevant, the provision of equipment.

3. Within the framework of the cooperation to prevent and control illegal immigration, the Parties also agree to readmit their illegal migrants. To this end:

- each Andean Country shall, upon request and without further formalities, readmit any of its nationals illegally present on the territory of a Member State of the European Union, provide their nationals with appropriate identity documents and extend to them the administrative facilities necessary for such purpose; and

- each Member State of the European Union shall, upon request and without further formalities, readmit any of its nationals illegally present on the territory of an Andean Country, provide their nationals with appropriate identity documents and extend to them the administrative facilities necessary for such purpose.

The Parties agree to conclude, upon request and as soon as possible, an agreement regulating the specific obligations for Member States of the European Union and the Andean countries on readmission. This agreement will also address the readmission of nationals of other countries and stateless persons.
For this purpose, the term "Parties" shall mean the European Community, any of its Member States and any Andean Country.

# Bibliography


### Books and Articles

Abell 1999

Abell, N. A., 'The Compatability of Readmission Agreements with the 1951 Convention relating to the Status of Refugees, *International Journal of Refugee Law*, Vol.11 No. 1, 1999, p. 60-83.

Achermann and Gattiker 1995

Achermann, A., Gattiker, M., 'Safe Third Countries: European Developments', International Journal of Refugee Law, Vol. 7 No. 1, 1995, p. 19-38.

AFP 2003

AFP (Agence France Presse), "Drop in illegal immigration from southeast Europe to EU", 30 October 2003.

AP 2004

*AP* (Associated Press), "UN: Russians top list of refugees seeking safety in wealthy countries", 24 February 2004.

Allain 2001

Allain, J., "The *jus cogens* nature of *non-refoulement*", 13 *International Journal of Refugee Law* (2001), p. 533-558.

Battjes 2006

Battjes, H., *European asylum law and its relation to international law*, Leiden, Martinus Nijhoff, 2006.

Bouteillet-Paquet 1997

Bouteillet-Paquet, 'European Harmonisation in the Field of Readmission Agreements' (1997) 1 *Intl J of Human Rights* 31, p. 31-43.

Bouteillet-Paquet 2003

Bouteillet-Paquet, D., "Passing the buck: A critical analysis of the readmission policy implemented by the European Union and its Member States", *European Journal of Migration and Law*, No. 3, 2003, p. 359-377.

BBC News 2002

*BBC* (British Broadcasting Company), "New Tamil wave in Southern Italy", 8 January 2002 (available on: www.news.bbc.co.uk).

British embassy Tirana 2003

British embassy Tirana, Press release, *Britain and Albania sign readmission agreement*, 14 October 2003.

Brouwer, Catz and Guild 2003

E. Brouwer, P. Catz and E. Guild, *Immigration, Asylum and Terrorism: A changing dynamic in European law*, Serie Recht & Samenleving nr. 19, Centre for Migration Law, Nijmegen, 2003.

Brownlie 1990

Brownlie, I., *Principles of Public International Law*, fourth edition, Oxford, Clarendon Press, 1990.

Van Buuren and van der Schans 19999

Buuren, J. van, Schans, W. van der, "Het Verdrag van Genève in de terminale fase: Het Oostenrijkse strategiedocument", *Dossier Europa: Het Europees asielbeleid in 2000*, Uitgeverij De Papieren Tijger, 1999 (available on: www.xs4all.nl).

Byrne and Shacknove 1996

Byrne, R., Shacknove, A., 'The Safe Third Country Notion in European Asylum Law', *Harvard Human Rights Journal*, Vol. 9, Spring 1996, p. 185-228.

Byrne, Noll and Vedsted-Hansen 2002

Byrne, R., Noll, G., Vedsted-Hansen, J., *New Asylum Countries? Migration Control and Refugee Protection in an Enlarged European Union*, The Hague, Kluwer Law International, 2002.

Byrne, Noll and Vedsted-Hansen 2004

Byrne, R., Noll, G., Vedsted-Hansen, J., "Understanding refugee law in an enlarged European Union", *ejil* (2004), Vol. 15 No. 2, p. 355-379.

Callovi 1992

G. Callovi, "Regulation of immigration in 1993: Pieces of the European Community jig-saw puzzle", *International Migration Review*, Volume XXVI, Number 2, Summer 1992, p. 358 ff.

Central Directorate of Immigration and Border Policy 2004

Central Directorate of Immigration and Border Policy, Ministry of the Interior, Italy, Delicato, V., *National legislation and good practices in the fight against illegal immigration – The Italian Model*, CARDS Programme, Rome, 1 October 2004.

Cholewinski 2001

Cholewinski, R., 'The EU *Acquis* on Irregular Migration: Reinforcing Security at the Expense of Rights', *European Journal of Migration and Law*, vol. 2 Nos. 3 and 4, 2000, p. 361-405.

Coleman 2003

Coleman, N., '*Non-Refoulement* revised: Renewed Review of the Status of the Principle of *Non-Refoulement* as Customary International Law', *European Journal of Migration and Law*, No. 1, 2003, p. 23-68.

Craig and De Búrca 1998

Craig, P., De Búrca , G., *EU law - text, cases and materials, Second Edition*, Oxford, University Press, 1998.

Crosland and Morrison 2001

Crosland, B., Morrison, J., *The trafficking and smuggling of refugees: the end game in European asylum policy?*, UNHCR Working Paper No. 39, April 2001.

Cullen 2001

Cullen, P., "Editorial", *European Journal of Migration and Law*, No. 2, 2001, p. 135-140.

Davy 2004

Davy, U., "Einwanderung und Integrationspfade", *ZAR* 7/2004, p. 231 ff.

The Dawn 2003

*The Dawn*, "EU asked to ratify new pact soon", 7 November 2003 (available on: www.dawn.com).

Denoël 1993

Denoël, X., "Les accords de réadmission du Benelux à Schengen et au-delà", *Revue trimestrielle de droit européen*, No. 4, octobre-décembre 1993, p. 636-653.

Dugard and Wyngaert 1998

Dugard, J., Wyngaert C. van den, "Reconciling extradition with human rights", 92 *AJIL* 185 (1998), p. 187-212.

ECRE 1995

ECRE (European Council on Refugees and Exiles), *Safe Third Countries: Myths and Realities*, London, 1995.

Europolitque 2003

*Europolitique*, "Baisse du nombre des demandeurs d'asile en Europe", 5 December 2003.

Van Eysinga 1916

Eysinga, W.J.M. van, *Ontwikkeling en inhoud der Nederlandsche tractaten sedert 1813*, 'S-Gravenhage, Martinus Nijhoff, 1916.

FFM 1997

FFM (Forschungsgesellschaft Flucht und Migration), "Germany – Poland – Ukraine: The domino effect", *FFM booklet No. 5: Ukraine*, September 1997, (available on: www.ffm-berlin.de).

FFM 2000

FFM (Forschungsgesellschaft Flucht und Migration), *FFM contribution to the conference against immigration detention*, Oxford, 15-17 September 2000 (available on: on: www.ffm-berlin.de).

FECL 1998a

FECL ("Fortress Europe?" – Circular Letter), *EU Strategy Paper on asylum and immigration: Show of "political muscle"?*, 56, December 1998 (available on: www.fecl.org).

FECL 1998b

FECL ("Fortress Europe?" – Circular Letter), *"Zero Tolerance" policy on immigration is the real security threat"*, 56, December 1998 (available on: www.fecl.org).

Fernhout 1999

Fernhout, R., "Terug- en overname overeenkomsten: Mogelijkheden en onmogelijkheden, in: Winter, H.B., Kamminga, A., Herwijer (eds.), *Een grens gesteld. Een eerste evaluatie van het Nederlandse terugkeerbeleid*, Deventer, Kluwer, 1999.

Fitzpatrick 1996

Fitzpatrick, J., 'Revitalizing the 1951 Refugee Convention', *Harvard Human Rights Journal*, Vol. 9, Spring 1996, p. 229-253.

Fitzpatrick 2000

Fitzpatrick, J., 'Temporary protection of refugees: elements of a formalised regime', *The American Journal of International Law*, Vol. 94, 2000, p. 279-306.

Frankfurter Algemeine Zeitung 2003

*Frankfurter Algemeine Zeitung*, "Die Runde der Fünf, Die großen EU-Mitglieder koordinieren ihre innere Sicherheit",22 October 2003.

Frankfurter Algemeine Zeitung 2004

*Frankfurter Algemeine Zeitung*, "Absprachen der großen Fünf", 18 February 2004.

Goodwin-Gill 1978

Goodwin-Gill, G. S., *International law and the movement of persons between states*, Oxford, Oxford University Press, 1978.

Goodwin-Gill 1992

Goodwin-Gill, G. S., 'Safe Country? Says Who?', *International Journal of Refugee Law*, Oxford University Press, Vol. 4 No. 2, 1992.

Goodwin-Gill 1996

Goodwin-Gill, G.S., *The Refugee in International Law*, second edition, Oxford, Clarendon Press, 1996.

Government of Sri Lanka 2004

Government of Sri Lanka, Press release, *Sri Lanka signs readmission agreement with EC*, 7 June 2004 (available on the website of the Government of Sri Lanka: www.priu.gov.lk).

Grahl-Madsen 1996

*The Status of Refugees in international law, Volume I, Refugee Character*, Leiden, A.W. Sijthoff, 1966.

Grahl-Madsen 1972

Grahl-Madsen, A., *The Status of Refugees in international law, Volume II, Asylum, entry and sojourn*, Leiden, A.W. Sijthoff, 1972.

Grahl-Madsen 1980

Grahl-Madsen, A., *Territorial asylum*, New York, Oceania Publications, 1980.

Guild 2005

Guild, E., "Danger: Borders under construction: Assessing the first five years of border policy in an area of freedom, security and justice", conference paper, *An immigration policy for Europe?*, Florence, 13-15 March 2005.

Guild and Niessen 1996

J. Niessen, "The European Union's migration and asylum policies", in: E. Guild (ed.), *The developing immigration and asylum policies of the European Union: adopted conventions, resolutions, recommendations, decisions and conclusions*, The Hague, Kluwer Law International, 1996.

Hailbronner 1997

Hailbronner, K., "Readmission agreements and the obligation on states under public international law to readmit their own and foreign nationals", *Zeitschrift für ausländisches öffentliches Recht und Völkerrecht*, Band 57 (1997), p. 1-49.

Hannikainen 1988

Hannikainen, L., *Peremptory norms (jus cogens) in international law, Historical Development, Criteria, Present Status*, Helsinki, Lakimiesliiton Kustannus, Finnish Lawyers' Publishing Company, 1988.

Harvey 2000

Harvey, C., "Dissident voices: Refugees, human rights, and asylum in Europe", *Social & Legal Studies* Vol. 9(3), p. 367-396.

Hathaway 1991

Hathaway, J.C., *The law of refugee status*, Toronto, Butterworths, 1991.

Hathaway 2003

Hathaway, J.C., "What's in a label?", *European Journal of Migration and Law*, No. 1, 2003, p. 1-21.

Hathaway 2005

Hathaway, J.C., *The rights of refugees under international law*, Cambridge, Cambridge University Press, 2005.

Hathaway and Foster 2003

Hathaway, J.C., Foster, M., "International protection/relocation/flight alternative as an aspect of refugee status determination", in: Feller, E., Türk, V., Nicholson, F., *Refugee protection in international law: UNHCR's Global Consultations on international protection*, Cambridge, Cambridge University Press, 2003.

Hörtreiter and Weissbrodt 1999

Hörtreiter, I., and, Weissbrodt, D., "The Principle of Non-refoulement: Article 3 of the Convention Against Torture and Other Cruel, Inhuman or Degrading Treatment or Punishment in Comparison with the Non-refoulement Provisions of Other International Human Rights Treaties" (1999) 5 *Buffalo Human Rights Law Review* 1, p. 1-73.

Human Rights Watch 2005a

Human Rights Watch, *Deportations to Morocco Put Migrants at Risk, Violence against Migrants in Ceuta and Melilla Requires Independent Investigation*, Human Rights News, 13 October 2005 (available on: www.hrw.org).

Human Rights Watch 2005b

Human Rights Watch, *Ukraine: On the margins, Rights violations against migrants and asylum seekers at the New Eastern Border of the European Union*, November 2005, Vol. 17, No. 8(D).

Hurwitz 2002

Hurwitz, A., "The Externalization of EU Policies on Migration and Asylum: Readmission Agreements and Comprehensive Approaches", paper, *WIDER Conference on Poverty, International Migration and Asylum*, Helsinki, Finland, 27-28 September, 2002.

Hyett 2000

Hyett, S., "The duty of sincere cooperation: A flexible concept", in: Dashwood, A., Hillion, C. (eds.), *The general law of E.C. external relations*, London, Sweet & Maxwell, 2000.

Institute of European Affairs 2004

Institute of European Affairs, *Speech by Ermelinda Meksi, Albanian Minister of European Integration*, 19 January 2004.

ICMPD 2004

ICMPD (International Centre for Migration Policy Development), *Dialogue on Mediterranean transit migration, Working Material*, Meeting in Vienna, 5-6 February 2004.

ILA Statement of principles of customary international law 2000

International Law Association, *Statement of Principles Applicable to the Formation of General Customary International Law*, London Conference, Committee on Formation of Customary (General) International Law, London, 2000 (www.ila-hq.org).

Interfax 2003

*Interfax* (Interfax Information Service), "Germany will not seek EU's okay to ease visa regulations with Russia", 10 November 2003 (available on: www.interfax.com).

Itar-Tass 2004

*Itar-Tass* (Russian News Agency), "Russia interested in readmission elements with Eastern countries", 29 January 2004 (available on: www.itar-tass.com).

Kälin 1982

Kälin, W., *Das Prinzip des Non-Refoulement*, Bern, Verlag Peter Lang AG, 1982.

Kirişci 2004

Kirişci, K., Global Commission on International Migration (GCIM), "Reconciling refugee protection with efforts to combat irregular migration: the case of Turkey and the European Union", *Global migration perspectives*, No. 11, October 2004 (available on: www.gcim.org).

Koh 1994

Koh, H. H., 'The Haitian Centers Council Case: Reflections on *Refoulement* and Haitian Centers Council', 35 *Harvard International Law Journal* 30 (1994), p. 1-47.

Krabbe 1912

Krabbe, J., *Toelating en uitzetting van vreemdelingen*, Leiden, Eduard Ijdo., 1912.

Kumin 1995

Kumin, J., *Asylum in Europe: Sharing or Shifting the Burden?*, UNHCR World Refugee Survey, 1995.

Kruse 2004

Kruse, I., *The EU's policy on readmission of illegal migrants*, paper, 2004 Graduate Retreat, 14-15 May 2004, University of California, San Diego (available on: www.socsciz2.ucsd.edu).

Kuijper 2004

Kuijper, P.J., "The evolution of the Third Pillar from Maastricht to the European Constitution: institutional aspects", *common market law review* 41, 2004, p. 609-626.

Lammers 1984

Lammers, J.G., *Pollution of international watercourses*, The Hague, Martinus Nijhofff Publishers, 1984.

Landgren 1999

Landgren, K., *Deflecting international protection by treaty: bilateral and multilateral accords on extradition, readmission and the inadmissibility of asylum requests*, UNHCR Working Paper No. 10, June 1999.

Lassen and Hughes 1997

Lassen, N., Hughes, J., Danish Refugee Council, *"Safe third country" policies in European countries*, 1997 (available on: www.flygtning.dk).

Lavenex 1999

Lavenex, S., *Safe Third Countries: Extending the EU Asylum and Immigration Policies to Central and Eastern Europe*, Budapest, Central European University Press, 1999.

Lavenex 2001

Lavenex, S., *The Europeanisation of refugee policies*, Ashgate Publishing Limited, Hampshire, 2001.

Lawand 1996

Lawand, K., "The right to return of Palestinians in international law", *International Journal of Refugee Law*, Vol. 8 No. 4, 1996, p. 533-568.

Lawson and Schermers 1999

Lawson, R.A., Schermers, H.G., *Leading Cases of the European Court of Human Rights*, Nijmegen, Ars Aequi Libri, 1999.

Legomsky 2003

Legomsky, S.H., "Secondary refugee movements and the return of asylum seekers to third countries: The meaning of effective protection", *International journal of refugee law*, Vol. 15, No. 4, 2003, p. 567-677.

Lehnguth 1997

Lehnguth, G., "Die Verträge der Bundesrepublik Deutschland zur Rückübernahme ausreisepflichtiger Ausländer", *ZAR* 4/1997, p. 161-170.

Ludford 2004

Ludford, S., *Liberal Democrats back EU partnership with Pakistan*, 22 April 2004 (www.sarahludfordmep.co.uk).

Marx 1995

Marx, R., 'Non-Refoulement, Access to Procedures, and Responsibility for Determining Refugee Claims', *International Journal of Refugee Law*,, Vol. 7 No. 3, 1995, p. 383-406.

Malanczuk 1997

Malanczuk, P., *Akehurst's modern introduction to international law*, seventh revised edition, London, Routledge, 1997.

Meijers 1979

Meijers, H., *Fasen van Volkenrechtsvorming, en het nut van internationaal gewoonterecht*, Alphen aan den Rijn, H.D. Tjeenk Willink, 1979.

Meron 1986

Meron, T., "On hierarchy of international human rights", 80 *AJIL* (1986), p. 1-23.

Migration News Sheet 1999

*Migration News Sheet*, 'With the Amsterdam Treaty now in force, Member States may not collectively conclude re-admission agreements with third countries', No. 195/99-06, June 1999.

Mission of the Russian Federation to the European Communities 2003

*Russian MFA Consular Service Department Director V. V. Kotenev's Interview with the Finnish Television Company MTV-3 on the Problems of Switching to a Visa-Free Regime Between Russia and the European Union*, September 25, 2003, Press release No. 19/03 (available on: www.russiaeu.org).

Mus 1996

Mus, J. B., *Conflicts of Treaties in Dutch Courts*, Zwolle, Tjeenk Willink, 1996.

Noll 1997

Noll, G., 'The Non-Admission and Return of Protection Seekers in Germany', *International Journal of Refugee Law*, Vol. 9 No. 3, 1997, p. 415-452.

Noll 1998

Noll, G., "Readmission and the protection of refugees: Bilateral arrangements and NGO surveillance", Hakola, K., (ed.) *Migration and refugee policy on the Eastern border of the European Union*, Jyväskylä, University of Jyväskylä, 1998.

Noll 2000

Noll, G., *Negotiating Asylum: The EU Acquis, Extraterritorial Protection and the Common Market of Deflection*, The Hague, Martinus Nijhoff Publishers, 2000.

Noll 2001

Noll, G. "Formalism v. Empiricism: Some reflections on the Dublin Convention of the occasion of recent European case law", *Nordic Journal of international law*, 70, 2001, p. 161-182.

Noll and Vedsted-Hansen 2002

Noll, G., Vedsted-Hansen, J., Temporary protection and burden-sharing: Conditionalising access suspending refugee rights?", in: Guild, E., Harlow, C. (eds.), *Implementing Amsterdam: Immigration and Asylum Rights in EC Law*, Oxford, Hart Publishing, 2001.

NRC Handelsblad 2004a

*NRC Handelsblad*, "Italië wil soepeler embargo tegen Libië", 18 September 2004.

NRC Handelsblad 2004b

*NRC Handelsblad*, "EU gaat embargo opheffen", 18 September 2004.

NRC Handelsblad 2004c

*NRC Handelsblad*, "Lampedusa, draaischijf in mensensmokkel, 23 September 2004.

Oppenheim 1992

Jennings, R., Watts, A., *Oppenheim's International Law*, 9th edition, Harlow, Longman, 1992.

Oxfam GB 2000

Oxfam Great Britain, Olsen, N., *Albania, the background, the issues, the people, An Oxfam Country Profile*, Oxford, Oxfam GB, 2000.

Peers 2004

Peers, S., "Irregular migration and EU external relations", in: Bogusz B., Cholewinski R., Cygan A., and Szyszczak E. (eds.), *Irregular Immigration and Human Rights: Theoretical, European and international perspectives*, Leiden, Koninklijke Brill NV, 2004.

Peers and Rogers 2006

Peers, S., "EC readmission agreements", in: Peers, S., Rogers, N., (eds.), *EU immigration and asylum law: text and commentary*, Leiden, Martinus Nijhoff Publishers, 2006.

Phuong 2005

Phuong, C., "Returns and readmission agreements", conference paper, *How much freedom, security and justice? Developments in EU immigration and asylum law*, ILPA, London, 13-14 May 2005.

Pravda 2002

*Pravda News Agency*, "Russia-EU to launch readmission talks, January 23", 30 December 2002, (available on: www.english.pravda.ru).

Pravda 2003

*Pravda News Agency*, "Russia, Lithuania work out readmission draft agreement", 8 April 2003, (available on: www.english.pravda.ru).

RFERL 2004

*RFERL (Radio Free Europe Radio Liberty)*, "Ukraine, "pragmatic" EU dodges request for membership prospects", 13 February 2004 (available on: www.rferl.org).

La Repubblica 2004

*La Repubblica*, "Libia, anche la Ue revoca l'embargo", 23 September 2004.

Reuters 2003

*Reuters*, "Albania agree deal to return illegal migrants", 6 November 2003.

Robinson 1953

Robinson, N., *Convention Relating to the Status of Refugees: its history, contents and interpretation*, New York, Institute of Jewish Affairs, 1953.

Van Selm 2001

Selm, J. van, *Access to Procedures, 'Safe Third Countries', 'Safe Countries of Origin' and 'Time Limits'*, UNHCR Background Paper, 2001.

Schachter 1991

Schachter, O., *International law in theory and practice*, Dordrecht, Martinus Nijhofff Publishers, 1991.

Schieffer 1997

Schieffer, M., "The readmission of third-country nationals within bilateral and multilateral frameworks", in: Boer, M. den (ed.), *The implementation of Schengen, first the widening, now the deepening*, Maastricht, European Institute of Public Administration, 1997.

Schieffer 2003

Schieffer, M., "Community readmission agreements with third countries – objectives, substance and current state of negotiations", *European Journal of Migration and Law*, No. 3, 2003, p. 343-357.

Simon 1999

Simon, H. J., "Onmenselijke behandeling en asiel", *NJB* 37, 25 October 1990, p. 1437-1446.

Spijkerboer 2000

Spijkerboer., T.P., 'Europees Migratierecht na Dover', *De Balie*, 13 december 2000.

Spijkerboer 2005

Spijkerboer, T.P., "Ze stikken, verdrinken en verbranden en wij halen achteloos de schouders op", *NRC Handelsblad*, 5 november 2005.

Spijkerboer and Vermeulen 1999

Spijkerboer, T.P, Vermeulen, B.P., *Vluchtelingenrecht*, serie migratierecht III, Utrecht, NCB, 1999.

Spijkerboer and Vermeulen 2005

Spijkerboer, T.P, Vermeulen, B.P., *Vluchtelingenrecht*, Nijmegen, Ars Aequi Libri, 2005.

Statewatch 2000a

*Lomé Convention used to impose repatriation on the world's poorest countries*, Statewatch bulletin, 7 June 2000 (available on: www.statewatch.org/news).

Statewatch 2000b

Statewatch, *Monitoring the state and civil liberties in the UK and Europe*, vol. 10, no. 3-4, June-August 2000.

Statewatch 2000c

Statewatch, *Monitoring the state and civil liberties in the UK and Europe*, vol. 10, no. 6, November-December 2000.

Steenbergen, Spijkerboer, Vermeulen and Fernhout 1999

Steenbergen, J.D.M., Spijkerboer, T.P., Vermeulen, B.P., Fernhout, R. (eds.), *Internationaal Migratierecht*, Serie Immigratierecht deel 2, Den Haag, Sdu Uitgevers, 1999.

Steendijk 2001

Steendijk., L., 'The Application of Human Rights Standards to Asylum Cases: the Dutch Example', *European Journal of Migration and Law*, No. 2, 2001, p. 185-198.

Stenberg 1989.

Stenberg, G., *Non-Expulsion and Non-Refoulement*, Uppsala University, Swedish Institute of International Law, Studies in International Law, Volume 9, Uppsala, Iustus Förlag, 1989.

Sunday Observer 2004

*Sunday Observer*, "Lankans arrested in Suez Canal deported", 28 March 2004 (available on: www.sundayobserver.lk).

Swart 1978

Swart, A.H.J., *De toelating en uitzetting van vreemdelingen*, Deventer, Kluwer, 1978.

UNHCR 1968.

UNHCR (United Nations High Commissioner for Refugees), *Background Note on the Safe Country Concept and Refugee Status*, EC/SCP/68.

UNHCR Handbook

UNHCR (United Nations High Commissioner for Refugees), *Handbook on procedures and criteria for determining refugee status under the 1951 Convention and the 1967 Protocol relating to the status of refugees*, HRC/IP/4/Eng/REV.1, Reedited, Geneva, January 1992, UNHCR 1979 (available on: www.unhcr.org).

UNHCR 1979

International protection (SCIP), *Note on asylum*, EC/SCP/12, 1979.

UNHCR 1994

UNHCR (United Nations High Commissioner for Refugees), *Position on Readmission Agreements, 'Protection Elsewhere' and Asylum Policy*, August 1994.

UNHCR 1995

UNHCR (United Nations High Commissioner for Refugees), World Refugee Survey, 1995

UNHCR 2001a

UNHCR (United Nations High Commissioner for Refugees), *Global Consultations Process and Selected Records of the Ministerial Meeting 12-13 December 2001 in Geneva*, "Background paper No. 1, Legal and practical aspects of the return of persons not in need of international protection", May 2001.

UNHCR 2001b

UNHCR (United Nations High Commissioner for Refugees), *Global Consultations Process and Selected Records of the Ministerial Meeting 12-13 December 2001 in Geneva*, "Background paper No. 2, "The application of the "safe third country" notion and its impact on the management of flows and on the protection of refugees", May 2001.

UNHCR 2001c

UNHCR (United Nations High Commissioner for Refugees), *Global Consultations Process and Selected Records of the Ministerial Meeting 12-13 December 2001 in Geneva*, "Background paper No. 3, Inter-State agreements for the re-admission of third country nationals, including asylum seekers, and for the determination of the State responsible for examining the substance of an asylum claim", May 2001.

UNHCR 2001d

UNHCR (United Nations High Commissioner for Refugees), *Global consultations on international protection, Refugee protection and migration control: perspectives from UNHCR and IOM*, EC/GC/01/11, 31 May 2001.

UNHCR 2001e

UNHCR (United Nations High Commissioner for Refugees), *NGO Background paper on the refugee and migration interface*, Geneva, 28-29 June 2001.

UNHCR 2001f

UNHCR (United Nations High Commissioner for Refugees), *Summary observations on the Commission proposal for a Council Directive on minimum standards on procedures for granting and withdrawing refugee status (COM(2000) 578 final*, 20 September 2000), July 2001.

UNHCR 2003a

UNHCR (United Nations High Commissioner for Refugees), *2003 Global refugee trends, overview of refugee populations, new arrivals, durable solutions, asylum-seekers and other persons of concern to UNHCR*, Population Data Unit/PGDS, Division of operational support, UNHCR Geneva, 15 June 2004.

UNHCR 2003b

UNHCR (United Nations High Commissioner for Refugees), *Asylum levels and trends in industrialised countries, January to September 2003*, Population Data Unit/PGDS, Geneva, 28 November 2003 (available on: www.unhcr.org).

UNHCR 2003c

UNHCR (United Nations High Commissioner for Refugees), Working Paper, *A revised "EU prong" proposal*, UNHCR Geneva, 22 December 2003.

Vedsted-Hansen 1999

Vedsted-Hansen, J., "Non-admission policies and the right to protection: refugees' choice versus states' exclusion?", in: Nicholson, F., Twomey, P. (eds.), *Refugee rights and realities: Evolving international concepts and regimes*, Cambridge, Cambridge University Press, 1999.

Vermeulen 1999

Vermeulen, B.P., "De refoulementverboden", in: Steenbergen, J.D.M., Spijkerboer, T.P., Vermeulen, B.P., Fernhout, R. (eds.), *Internationaal Migratierecht*, Serie Immigratierecht deel 2, Den Haag, Sdu Uitgevers, 1999.

Villiger 1985

Villiger, M.E., *Customary International Law and Treaties, A Study of their Interactions and Interrelations with Special Consideration of the 1969 Vienna Convention on the Law of Treaties*, Dordrecht, Martinus Nijhoff Publishers, 1985.

Weis 1979

Weis, P., *Nationality and statelessness in international law*, second edition, Alphen aan den Rijn, Sijthoff & Noordhoff, 1979.

Weis 1995

Weis, P., *The Refugee Convention 1951, the travaux préparatoires analysed, with a commentary by dr. Paul Weis*, Cambridge international documents series, Volume 7, Cambridge University Press, Cambridge, 1995.

De Witte 2000

Witte, B. de, "The role of institutional principles in the judicial development of the European Union legal order", in: F. Snyder (ed.), *The Europeanisation of law, The legal effects of European integration*, Oxford, Hart Publishing, 2000.

World Bank 2003

World Bank, *International conference on migrant remittances: development impact, opportunities for the financial sector and future prospects*, *Report and Conclusions*, organised by the Department for International Development of the World Bank and the International Migration Policy Programme, London, 9-10 October 2003.

WSWS 2004

WSWS (World Socialist Web Site), *Spain and Morocco agree to rail tunnel under Gibraltar Strait*, 5 January 2004 (available on: www.wsws.org).

Zwaan 2003

Zwaan, K. *Veilig derde land, de exceptie van het veilige derde land in het Nederlands asielrecht*, University of Nijmegen, Nijmegen, 2003.

## Primary Materials

### *EU Law*

### Primary legislation

Charter of Fundamental Rights of the European Union, signed and proclaimed by the Presidents of the European Parliament, the Council and the Commission on 7 December 2000, *OJ* 2000/C 364/0118, 18 December 2000.

Treaty establishing the European Community, references to the text consolidated after the Treaty of Nice, *OJ* C 325, 2002.

Treaty on European Union, references to the text consolidated after the Treaty of Nice, *OJ* C 325, 2002.

Draft Treaty establishing a Constitution for Europe, *OJ* 2003/C 169/01, 18 July 2003.

### Secondary legislation (including proposals)

*(by publication date)*

Directive 95/46 of 24 October 1995 on the protection of individuals with regard to the processing of personal data and on the free movement of such data, *OJ* L 281, 23 November 1995, p. 31.

Council Recommendation of 30 November 1994 concerning a specimen bilateral readmission agreement between a Member State and a third country, *OJ* C 274, 19 September 1996, p. 20.

Council recommendation of 24 July 1995 on the guiding principles to be followed in drawing up protocols on the implementation of re-admission agreements, *OJ* C 274, 19 September 1996, p. 25.

Council Resolution of 20 June 1995 on minimum guarantees for asylum procedures of the European Union, *OJ* C 274, 19 September 1996.

Common strategy of the European Union of 4 June 1999 on Russia, *OJ* L 157, 24 June 1999, p. 1.

Council Decision 1999/437/EC of 17 May 1999 on certain arrangements for the application of the Agreement of 18 May 1999 between the European Union and Iceland and Norway concerning the latters' association with the implementation, application and development of the Schengen *acquis*, *OJ* L 176, 10 July 1999, p. 31.

Council Decision 1999/468/EC of 28 June 1999 laying down the procedures for the exercise of implementing powers conferred on the Commission, *OJ* L 184, 17 July 1999, p. 23.

Proposal for a Council Directive on minimum standards on procedures in Member States for granting and withdrawing refugee status, COM(2000) 578, 20 September 1999.

Initiative of the Republic of Finland with a view to the adoption of a Council Regulation determining obligations as between the Member States for the readmission of third country nationals, *OJ* C 353, 7 December 1999, p. 6.

EU common strategy of 11 December 1999 on Ukraine, *OJ* L 331, 23 December 1999, p. 1.

Council Regulation No 99/2000 of 29 December 1999 concerning the provision pf technical assistance to the partner States in Eastern Europe and Central Asia, *OJ* L 12, 18 January 2000, p. 1.

Council Regulation No 2666/2000 of 5 December 2000 on assistance for Albania, Bosnia and Herzegovina, Croatia; the Federal Republic of Yugoslavia and the Former Yugoslav Republic of Yugoslavia, *OJ* L 306, 7 December 2000, p. 1.

Council Regulation No 2698/2000 of 27 November 2000 amending Regulation (EC) 1488/96 on financial and technical measures to accompany (MEDA) the reform of economic and social structures in the framework of Euro-Mediterranean partnership, *OJ* L 311, 12 December 2000, p. 1.

Council Directive 2001/40/EC of 28 May 2001 on the mutual recognition of decisions on the expulsion of third country nationals, *OJ* L 149, 2 June 2001, 34.

Proposal for a Directive on the conditions of entry and residence of third country nationals for the purpose of paid employment and self-employed economic activities, *OJ* C 332 E, 27 November 2001, p. 248.

Amended proposal for a Council Directive on minimum standards on procedures in Member States for granting and withdrawing refugee status, COM(2002) 326 final, 3 July 2002.

Regulation 343/2003 of 18 February 2003 establishing the criteria and mechanisms for determining the Member State responsible for examining an asylum application lodged in one of the Member States by a third-country national, *OJ* L 50, 25 February 2003, p. 1.

Amended proposal for a Council Directive on minimum standards on procedures in Member States for granting and withdrawing refugee status Council Doc. 15198/03, 4 December 2003.

Proposal for a Regulation laying down general provisions establishing a European Neighbourhood and Partnership instrument, COM(2004) 628, 29 September 2004.

Regulation of 10 March 2004 establishing a programme for financial and technical assistance to third countries in the areas of migration and asylum (*Aeneas* Regulation), *OJ L 80*, 18 March 2004, p. 1.

Council Decision 2004/573/EC of 29 April 2004 on the organisation of joint flights for removals from the territory of two or more Member States of third-country nationals who are subjects of individual removal orders, *OJ* L 261, 6 August 2004, p. 28.

Amended proposal for a Council Directive on minimum standards on procedures in Member States for granting and withdrawing refugee status, Council Doc. 14203/04, 9 November 2004.

Proposal for a Directive of the European Parliament and of the Council on common standards and procedures in Member States for returning illegally staying third-country nationals, COM(2005) 391 final, 1 September 2005.

Council Directive 2005/85/EC of 1 December 2005 on minimum standards on procedures in Member States for granting and withdrawing refugee status, *OJ* L 326, 13 December 2005, p. 13.

**Agreements**

Convention of 19 June 1990 applying the Schengen Agreement of 14 June 1985 between the governments of the States of the Benelux Economic Union, the Federal Republic of Germany and the French Republic, on the gradual abolition of checks at their common borders, *OJ* L 239, 22 September 2000, p. 1.

Convention determining the State responsible for examining applications for asylum lodged in one of the Member States of the Community, signed in Dublin on 15 June 1990, *OJ* C 254, 1997.

Agreement of 18 May 1999 between the European Union and Iceland and Norway concerning the latters' association with the implementation, application and development of the Schengen *acquis*, *OJ* L 176, 10 July 1999, p. 36.

Political Dialogue and Cooperation Agreement between the European Community and its Member States and the Andean Community and its Member countries (Bolivia, Colombia, Ecuador, Peru and Venezuela), 15 December 2003, CE/AND/en (available on: www.europa.eu.int/comm/external_relations).

Political Dialogue and Cooperation Agreement between the European Community and its Member States and Costa Rica, El Salvador, Guatemala, Honduras, Nicaragua and Panama (Central America), 15 December 2003, CE/AM-CENTR/en 1 (available on: www.europa.eu.int/comm/external_relations).

Agreement between the European Community and the Government of the Hong Kong Special Administrative Region of the People's Republic of China on the readmission of persons residing without authorisation, *OJ* L 17, 24.1.2004, p. 25.

Agreement between the European Community and the Government of the Macao Special Administrative Region of the People's Republic of China on the readmission of persons residing without authorisation, *OJ* L 143, 30.4.2004, p. 99.

Agreement between the European Community and the Democratic Socialist Republic of Sri Lanka on the readmission of persons residing without authorisation - Declarations, *OJ* L 124, 17 May 2005, p. 43.

Agreement between the European Community and the Republic of Albania on the readmission of persons residing without authorisation - Declarations, *OJ* L 124, 17 May 2005, p. 22.

Agreement on Partnership and Cooperation establishing a Partnership between the European Communities and their Member States, of the one part, and the Russian Federation, of the other part, L/CE/RU/en.

## Cases and Opinions

*Commission v. Council* (ERTA), Case 22/70, [1971] ECR 263

*Van Duyn v Home office*, Case 41/74, [1974] ECR 1337, 1351.

*Opinion 1/94, Competence of the Community to conclude international agreements concerning services and the protection of intellectual property*, 15 November 1994, [1994] ECR I-5267.

## Commission of the European Communities

*(by document date)*

SEC(91) 1857 final

*Communication from the Commission to the Council and the European Parliament on the right of asylum*, 11 October 1991.

SEC(91) 1855 final

*Commission Communication to the Council and the European Parliament on immigration*, 23 October 1991.

COM(94) 23 final

*Communication from the Commission to the Council and the European Parliament on immigration and asylum policies*, 23 February 1994.

SEC(2000) 522

*Commission staff working paper, Revisiting the Dublin Convention: developing Community legislation for determining which Member State is responsible for considering an application for asylum submitted in one of the Member States*, 21 March 2000.

COM(2000) 755 final

*Communication from the Commission to the Council and the European Parliament, Towards a common asylum procedure and a uniform status, valid throughout the Union, for persons granted asylum*, 22 November 2000.

COM(2000) 757

*Communication from the Commission to the Council and the European Parliament on a Community Immigration Policy*, 22 November 2000.

COM (2001) 672 final

*Communication from the Commission to the Council and the European Parliament on a common policy on illegal immigration*, 15 November 2001.

SEC(2001) 1338

Framework for preparatory actions B7-667 in 2001 (available on: www.europa.eu.int/comm/justice_home).

SEC(2002) 1979

Framework for preparatory actions B7-667 in 2002 (available on: www.europa.eu.int/comm/justice_home).

COM (2002) 175

*Green Paper on a Community return policy on illegal residents*, 10 April 2002.

SEC(2002) 412 final

*Proposal for a Council Decision concerning the signing of the Agreement between the European Community and the Government of the Special Administrative Region of the People's Republic of China on the readmission of persons residing without authorisation*, 18 April 2002.

COM(2002) 564 final

*Communication from the Commission to the Council and the European Parliament on a Community return policy on illegal residents*, 14 October 2002.

EU-Russia Joint Statement on Kaliningrad 2002

Tenth EU-Russia Summit, *Joint Statement of the European Union and the Russian Federation on transit between the Kaliningrad region and the rest of the Russian Federation*, 11 November 2002 (available on: www.europe.eu.int/comm/external_relations).

COM(2002) 703 final

*Communication from the Commission to the Council and the European Parliament on integrating migration issues into the European Union's relations with third countries, I. Migration and development, II. Report on the effectiveness of financial resources available at Community level for repatriation of immigrants and rejected asylum seekers, for management of external borders and for asylum and migration projects in third countries*, 3 December 2002.

COM(2003) 104 final

*Communication from the Commission to the Council and the European Parliament, Wider Europe – Neighbourhood: A new framework for relations with out Eastern and Southern Neighbours*, 11 March 2003.

COM(2003) 151 final

*Proposal for a Council Decision concerning the signing of the Agreement between the European Community and the Government of the Macao Special Administrative Region of the People's Republic of China on the readmission of persons residing without authorisation*, 31 March 2003.

COM(2003) 323 final

*Communication on the development of a common policy on illegal immigration, smuggling and trafficking of human beings, external borders and the return of illegal residents*, 3 June 2003.

SEC(2003) 255 final

*Proposal for a Council Decision concerning the signing of the Agreement between the European Community and the Democratic Socialist Republic of Sri Lanka on the readmission of persons residing without authorisation; Proposal for a Council Decision concerning the conclusion of the Agreement between the European Community and the Democratic Socialist Republic of Sri Lanka on the readmission of persons residing without authorization*, 21 March 2003.

COM(2003) 339

Commission staff working paper, *Albania, Stabilisation and Association report 2003*, 26 March 2003.

Press release IP/03/768

*Eleventh EU-Russia Summit, St. Petersburg 31.05*, 28 May 2003

COM(2003) 336 final

*Communication from the Commission to the Council, the European Parliament, the European Economic and Social Committee and the Committee of the regions on immigration, integration and employment*, 3 June 2003.

SEC(2003) 815

*Commission staff working paper, Intensified cooperation on the management of migration flows with third countries, Report by the Commission's Services on the implementation of the Council conclusions on intensified cooperation on the management of migration flows with third countries of 18 November 2002*, 9 July 2003.

COM(2003) 790 final

Proposals for Council decisions concerning the singing and conclusion of the Memorandum of Understanding between the European Community and the National Tourism Administration of the People's Republic of China on visa and related issues concerning tourist groups from the People's Republic of China, 15 December 2003.

Press release IP/04/196

*European Union signs landmark tourism accord with China today in Beijing*, 12 February 2004.

Press release IP/04/243

*The Commission welcomes the adoption of a programme of financial and technical assistance to third countries in the area of migration and asylum*, 19 February 2004.

COM(2004) 373 final

*Communication from the Commission, European Neighbourhood Policy, Strategy Paper*, 12 May 2004.

EU-Russia Joint Statement 2004

Eleventh EU Russia Summit, *Joint Statement on a Common Economic Space (CEP)*, St. Petersburg, 31 May 2004.

COM (2004) 412 final

*Communication from the Commission to the Council, the European Parliament, the European Economic and Social Committee and the Committee of the regions, Study on the links between legal and illegal immigration*, 4 June 2004.

MEDA NIP Morocco 2005-2006

*EUROMED Partnership Morocco, National Indicative Programme 2005-2006*, 29 June 2004 (available on: www.europa.eu.int/comm/external_relations).

COM(2004) 656 final

*Communication from the Commission to the Council and the European Parliament, Recommendation of the European Commission on Turkey's progress towards accession*, 6 October 2004.

SEC(2004) 1201

*2004 Regular report on Turkey's progress towards accession*, 6 October 2004 (also available in Council Doc. 13244/04, 8 October 2004).

SEC(2004) 1349

*Commission staff working paper, Annual report on the development of a common policy on illegal immigration, smuggling and trafficking of human beings, external borders, and the return of illegal residents*, 25 October 2004.

Press release IP/04/1113

*European Commission and Hong Kong SAR step up cooperation against illegal immigration*, 20 September 2004.

Aeneas Call for Proposals for 2004

*Aeneas Programme, Financial and technical assistance to third countries in the field of migration and asylum, Guidelines for grant applicants responding to the Call for Proposals for 2004*, Budget line 19.02.03 (available on: www.europa.eu.int/comm/).

SEC(2004) 374/2

*Commission Staff Working Paper, Albania Stabilisation and Association report 2004* (available on: http://ec.europa.eu/enlargement/pdf/albania/cr_alb_en.pdf).

COM(2005) 184 final

*Communication from the Commission to the Council and the European Parliament, The Hague Programme: Ten priorities for the next five years, The partnership for European renewal in the field of freedom, security and justice*, 10 May 2005.

COM(2005) 352 final

*Communication from the Commission to the Council on the monitoring and evaluation mechanism of the third countries in the field of the fight against illegal immigration*, 28 July 2005.

COM(2005) 390 final

*Communication from the Commission to the Council, the European Parliament, the European Economic and Social Committee and the Committee of the regions, Migration and development: Some concrete orientations*, 1 September 2005.

MEMO/05/351

*Readmission agreements*, 5 October 2005.

Press release IP/05/1263

*EU-Russia relations: next steps towards visa facilitation and readmission agreement*, 12 October 2005.

PRES/05/273

*2686th meeting GAER Council, Brussels, 7 November 2005*, 7 November 2005.

Press release IP/05/1467

*European neighbourhood: A year of progress*, 11 November 2005.

Press release PRES/05/308

*Fifth meeting of the EU-Morocco Association Council (Brussels, 22 November 2005)*, 22 November 2005.

COM(2005) 621

*Communication from the Commission to the Council and the European Parliament on Priority actions for responding to the challenges of migration: First follow-up to Hampton Court*, 30 November 2005.

SPEECH/05/754

Frattini, F., European Commissioner responsible for Justice, Freedom and Security, *EU and the Western Balkans : Visa, Asylum and Immigration*, European Policy Center Conference, *Brussels, 30 November 2005*, 2 December 2005.

COM(2005) 669

*Communication from the Commission, Policy plan on legal migration*, 21 December 2005.

Aeneas Call for Proposals 2005

*Aeneas Programme, Guidelines for grant applicants responding to the Call for Proposals for 2005, Budget line 19.02.03*, EuropeAid/122 511/C/ACT/MULTI (available on: www.europa.eu.int/comm).

SPEECH/06/30

*Migration, External Relations and the European Neighbourhood Policy*, 24 January 2006.

COM(2006) 26 final

*Communication from the Commission to the European Parliament and the Council, Thematic programme for the cooperation with third countries in the areas of migration and asylum*, 25 January 2006.

Press release IP/06/82

*Commission simplifies external cooperation programmes*, 25 January 2006.

MEX/06/0201

*Midday express of 2006-02-01*, 1 February 2006.

The EU's relations with Pakistan

*The EU's relations with Pakistan* (available on: www.europa.eu.int/comm/external_relations/pakistan)

The EU's rclations with Russia

*The EU's relations with Russia* (available on: www.europe.eu.int/comm/external_relations)

Commission work-programme 2006

*Commission actions expected to be adopted: 02/06 – 12/06* (available on: www.europa.eu.int/comm).

Commission reference document for Aeneas 2004 - 2006

*Reference document for financial and technical assistance to third countries in the area of migration and asylum, AENEAS Programme 2004 – 2006* (available on: www.europa.eu.int/comm).

**Council of the European Union**

*(by document date)*

PRES/93/202

Press release, *Agenda of the 1710th Council session (Justice and Home Affairs, Brussels, 29 and 30 November 1994, Readmission*, 25 November 1993.

PRES/93/209

Press release, *1710E session du conseil, Justice et affairs interieures, Bruxelles, les 29/30 novembre 1993, Accords de readmission avec les pays tiers*, 30 November 1993.

Council Doc. 12509/95

*Draft conclusions approved by the Council and the Representatives of the Governments of the Member States meeting within the Council* (standard readmission clause – Community agreements), 8 December 1995.

Council Doc. 4272/96

*Council conclusions on clauses to be inserted in future mixed agreements* (standard readmission clause – mixed agreements) 22 January 1996.

Council. Doc. 9809/98

*Draft strategy paper on immigration and asylum*, 1 July 1998 (available on: www.proasyl.de).

Press release 431 – Nr: 13677/98

Press release, *General Affairs Council meeting of 5-6 December 1998, Asylum and Migration Task Force – Conclusions* (High level Working Group on Asylum and Migration), 6 December 1998.

Council Doc. 6101/99

*Specimen action plans and future procedure for drawing up such plans; Information for the European Parliament*, 18 February 1999.

Council Doc. 7669/99

Readmission Agreements concerning third-country nationals, 26 April 1999.

Council Doc. 7707/99

Nordic Joint Advisory Group on Refugee Policy, *Analysis of the institute concerning readmission agreements – including an assessment of whether it is expedient to conclude such agreements, or whether there are other possibilities of influencing a country of origin to readmit third country nationals and own nationals*, 27 April 1999.

Council Doc. 7609/1/99

Summary report of Member States' contributions on readmission questions, 3 May 1999.

Press release 168 – Nr: 8654/99

Press release, *Justice and Home Affairs Council meeting of 27-28 May 1999, Conclusions on "re-admission agreements – consequences of the entry into force of the Amsterdam Treaty"*, 27 May 1999.

Council Doc. 7668/1/99

*Monitoring the implementation of instruments adopted by the Council concerning illegal immigration, re-admission, the unlawful employment of third-country nationals and co-operation in the implementation of expulsion orders – Summary report of the Member States' replies to the questionnaire launched in 1998*, 14 June 1999.

Council doc. 10338/3/98

*Draft standard readmission agreement between the European Community and a third country*, 9 July 1999

Council Doc. 11042/99

*Expulsion working party, readmission*, 23 September 1999.

Council Doc. 11424/99

*HLWG Action Plan for Afghanistan*, 30 September 1999.

Council Doc. 11425/99

*HLWG Action Plan for Iraq*, 30 September 1999.

Council Doc. 11426/99

*HLWG Action Plan for Morocco*, 30 September 1999.

Council Doc. 11427/99

*HLWG Action Plan for Somalia*, 30 September 1999.

Council Doc. 11428/99

*HLWG Action Plan for Sri Lanka*, 30 September 1999.

Council Doc. 13409/99

*Consequences of the Treaty of Amsterdam on readmission clauses in Community agreements and in agreements between the European Community, its Member States and third countries - Adoption of a Council decision* (1999 standard readmission clause), 25 November 1999.

Council Doc. 13888/99

*Strategic Committee on Immigration, Frontiers and Asylum* (selection first readmission countries), 7 December 1999.

Council Doc. 6720/00

*Recommendations for Council Decisions authorising the Commission to negotiate readmission agreements between the European Community and - Sri Lanka – Morocco – Pakistan – Russia = 'Schengen Relevancy'*, 6 March 2000.

Council Doc. 7637/00

*Readmission policy*, 6 April 2000.

Council Doc. 8939/00

*Adoption of the Action Plan for Albania and the region; Implementation of the Action Plans for Afghanistan and the region, Iraq, Morocco, Somalia and Sri Lanka*, 30 May 2000.

Council Doc. 7653/00

*European Union priorities and policy objectives for external relations in the field of Justice and Home Affairs*, 6 June 2000.

Council Doc. 13993/00

*High Level Working Group on Asylum and Migration Report to the European Council in Nice*, 29 November 2000.

Council Doc. 12790/3/01

*Catalogue of recommendations for the correct application of the Schengen acquis and of best practices - removal and readmission*, 7 January 2002.

Council Doc. 5018/02

*Catalogue of recommendations for the correct application of the Schengen acquis and best practices; Frontiers + Removal and Readmission*, 17 January 2002.

Press release 6247/02 (Presse 30)

*2409th GEAR Council meeting, Brussels, 18/19 February 2002*, 19 February 2002.

EU Schengen Catague 2002

*EU Schengen catalogue for external borders control, removal and readmission: recommendations and best practices*, February 2002 (available on: www.europa.eu.int).

Council Doc. 7990/02

*Criteria for the identification of third countries with which new readmission agreements need to be negotiated - Draft conclusions*, 16 April 2002.

Council Doc. 9433/02

*Modification of the terms of reference of the High Level Working Group on Asylum and Migration (HLWG)*, 30 May 2002.

Council Doc. 7886/1/00

*HLWG draft Action Plan for Albania and the neighbouring region*, 6 June 2002.

Council Doc. 9723/02

*Co-operation in the common management of migratory flows*, 7 June 2002.

Press release 9620/02 (Presse 175)

*2436th Justice and Home Affairs Council meeting of 13 June 2002, Measures to be applied to prevent and combat illegal immigration and trafficking in human beings by sea*, 13 June 2002

*OJ* C 142, 14 June 2002, p. 23.

*Proposal for a comprehensive plan to combat illegal immigration and trafficking of human beings in the European Union.*

Council Doc. 9917/3/02

*Co-operation with third countries of origin and transit to jointly combat illegal immigration*,18 June 2002.

Council Doc. 10525/1/02

*Road Map for the follow-up to the conclusions of the European Council in Seville - Asylum, Immigration and border control*, 11 July 2002.

Council doc. 12625/02

*Readmission agreements*, 10 October 2002.

Press release 12945/02 (Presse 315)

*2459th GAER Council meeting, Luxembourg, 22 October 2002, Council conclusions on Kaliningrad*, 22 October 2002.

Council Doc. 13609/02

*Readmission agreements - Possible Appointment of a Committee*, 29 October 2002.

Council Doc. 13754/2/02

*Draft Council conclusions on intensified cooperation on the management of migration flows with third countries*, 11 November 2002.

Council Doc. 13894/02

*Draft Council Conclusions on intensified cooperation on the management of migration flows with third countries*, 14 November 2002.

Council Doc. 13909/1/02

*European Union action plan to combat terrorism – Updat of the roadmap*, 14 November 2002.

Council Doc. 14528/02

*Readmission agreements – New negotiating mandates*, 20 November 2002.

Council Doc. 14673/02

*Proposal for a return action programme*, 25 November 2002.

Press release 14817/02 (Presse 375)

*2469th Justice and Ho,me Affairs Council meeting - Brussels, 28-29 November 2002*, 29 November 2002.

Council Doc. 15215/02

*Afghanistan return plan*, 4 December 2002.

Council Doc. 7831/1/03

*Proposal for a Council Decision concerning the conclusion of the Agreement between the European Community and the Democratic Socialist Republic of Sri Lanka on the readmission of persons residing without authorisation*, 9 April 2003.

Council Doc. 8927/03

*Communication from the Commission to the Council and the European Parliament: Integrating migration issues in the European Union's relations with third countries - Draft Council conclusions on migration and development* (GAERC Conclusions of 19 May 2003 on migration and development), 5 May 2003.

Council Doc. 10447/03

*Council Conclusions on Wider Europe – New Neighbourhood*, 12 June 2003.

Council Doc. 11490/1/03

*CIVIPOL Feasibility study on the control of the European Union's maritime borders - Final report*, 19 September 2003.

Press release 13747/03 (Presse 308)

*2538th Council meeting – Justice and Home Affairs – 6 November 2003*, 6 November 2003.

Council Doc. 15292/03

*Council Conclusions on the monitoring and evaluation mechanism of cooperation of third countries in the field of the fight against illegal immigration*, 25 November 2003.

Press release 14492/1/03 REV 1 (Presse 320)

*Economic and Financial Affairs Council meeting, 25 November 2003*, 25 November 2003.

Council Doc. 15995/03

*Strategic Committee on Immigration, Frontiers and Asylum, 10 December 2003, Summary of conclusions*, 15 December 2003.

Council Doc. 5139/04.

*Agreement between the Government of the Federal Republic of Germany and the Government of the Russian Federation on facilitating travel by nationals of the Federal Republic of Germany and of the Russian Federation*, 8 January 2004.

Council Doc. 5455/04

*Strategic Committee on Immigration, Frontiers and Asylum 13 January 2004 – Summary of conclusions*, 19 January 2004.

Council Doc. 6144/04

*Framework Preparatory Action on Return*, 10 February 2004.

Council Doc. 6293/04

*High Level Working Group on Asylum and Migration, 6 February 2004, Summary of conclusions*, 12 February 2004.

Council Doc. 10375/04

*Council Conclusions on elements for establishing preparatory actions for a financial instrument for return management in the area of migration*, 9 June 2004.

Council Doc. 10601/04

*Relations with Russia - Council Report on the implementation of the Common Strategy of the European Union on Russia*, 16 June 2004.

Council Doc. 11035/04

*Agreement between the Government of the Italian Republic and the Government of the Russian Federation to facilitate the issue of visas to nationals of the Italian Republic and to nationals of the Russian Federation*, 30 June 2004.

Council Doc. 11071/04

*Relations with Russia*; 2 July 2004.

Council Doc. 11251/04

*List of "A" items for 2596th meeting the GAER Council, Brussels, Monday 12 July 2004*, 9 July 2004.

Council Doc. 11555/04

*Visa Working Party/Mixed Committee, 8-9 July 2004, Summary of conclusions*, 16 July 2004.

Press release 11161/04 (Presse 219)

*2600th Council meeting – Justice and Home Affairs Council - Brussels, 19 July 2004*, 19 July 2004.

Council Doc. 13578/04

*Draft Council Conclusions on the priorities for the successful development of a common readmission policy*, 27 October 2004.

Council Doc. 12289/04

*Agreed minutes of the EC-Turkey Sub-Committee no. 8 on Customs, Tax, Drugs and Money Laundering, Ankara, 15 December 2003*, 9 September 2004.

Press release 15061/04 (Presse 333)

*Fourteenth EU-Russia Summit – The Hague, 25 November 2004*, 25 November 2004.

Council Doc. 12709/04

*A common visa policy*, 22 September 2004.

Council Doc. 16054/04

*The Hague Programme for strengthening freedom, security and justice*, 13 December 2004.

Council Doc. 5001/05

*JHA External Relations Multi-Presidency Programme*, 3 January 2005.

Council Doc. 5614/05

*Council Decision on the signing of the Agreement between the European Community and the Republic of Albania on the readmission of persons residing without authorisation*, 15 February 2005.

Council Doc. 6513/05

*Adoption of a Council Decision concerning the signing of an Agreement between the European Community and the Republic of Albania on the readmission of persons residing without authorisation*, 21 February 2005.

Council Doc. 12361/05

*Council Decision concerning the conclusion of the Agreement between the European Community and the Republic of Albania on the readmission of persons residing without authorisation*, 4 October 2005.

Council Doc. 14769/05

*Council Conclusions of 21 November 2005 on migration and external relations*, 21 November 2005.

Council Doc. 15446/05

*Council Strategy for the external dimension of JHA: Global freedom, security and justice*, 6 December 2005.

Council Doc. 13278/06

*Council Decision authorising the Commission to negotiate with the former Yugoslav Republic of Macedonia a readmission agreement between the European Community and the former Yugoslav Republic of Macedonia*, 29 September 2006.

Council Doc. 15465/06

*Council Decision authorising the Commission to negotiate with the Republic of Serbia a readmission agreement between the European Community and the Republic of Serbia, Council Decision authorising the Commission to negotiate with the Republic of Montenegro a readmission agreement between the European Community and the Republic of Montenegro, Council Decision authorising the Commission to negotiate with Bosnia and Herzegovina a readmission agreement between the European Community and Bosnia and Herzegovina*, 17 November 2006.

Council Doc. 16537/06

*Draft Council Decision authorising the Commission to negotiate with the Republic of Moldova a readmission agreement between the European Community and the Republic of Moldova*, 11 December 2006.

Council Doc. 9312/07

*Council Decision on the signing of the Agreement between the European Community and Ukraine on readmission of persons*, 5 June 2007.

Council Doc. 11505/04 EXT 1 MIGRA 63 RESTREINT UE

*Report on the priorities for the successful development of a common readmission policy*, 3 July 2007.

Council Doc. 11998/07

*Proposal for a Council Decision concerning the signing of the Agreement between the European Community and Bosnia and Herzegovina on readmission*, 20 Juily 2007.

Council Doc. 12001/07

*Proposal for a Council Decision concerning the signing of the Agreement between the European Community and the former Yugoslav Republic of Macedonia on readmission*, 20 July 2007.

Council Doc. 12000/07

*Proposal for a Council Decision concerning the signing of the Agreement between the European Community and the Republic of Montenegro on readmission*, 20 July 2007.

Council Doc. 12002/07

*Proposal for a Council Decision concerning the signing of the Agreement between the European Community and the Republic of Serbia on readmission*, 23 July 2007.

### European Parliament

*(by document date)*

Committee on Citizens' Freedoms and Rights, Justice and Home Affairs, Mollar J.S.H (rapporteur), *Report on asylum-seekers and migrants – action plans for countries of origin or transit: High Level Working Group (C5-0159/1999 - C5-0160/1999 – C5-0161/1999*

*– C5-0162/1999 – C5-0163/1999 – C5-0164/1999 – C5-0165/1999 – C4-0133/1999 – 1999/2096(COS))*, session document A5-0057/2000 PE 285.869/DEF, 29 February 2000.

*European Parliament Resolution of 30 March 2000, European Parliament resolution on asylum-seekers and migrants – action plans for countries of origin or transit: High Level Working Group (C5-0159/1999 – C5-0160/1999 – C5-0161/1999 – C5-0162/1999 – C5-0163/1999 – C5-0164/1999 – C5-0165/1999 – C4-0133/1999 – 1999/2096(COS)), A5-0057/2000, OJ C 378*, 29 December 2000.

Committee on Citizens' Freedoms and Rights, Justice and Home Affairs, Watson R.G. (rapporteur), *Report on the proposal for a Council decision on the signing of the Agreement between the European Community and the Government of the Special Administrative Region of the People's Republic of China on the readmission of persons residing without authorization (SEC(2002) 412 – C5-0263/2002 – 2002/0092(CNS))*, session document A5-0381/2002 final, 7 November 2002.

Committee on Citizens' Freedoms and Rights, Justice and Home Affairs, Ludford S. (draftsman), *Opinion on the Cooperation Agreement between the EC and the Islamic Republic of Pakistan*, session document PE 311.031, 12 September 2002.

Committee on Foreign Affairs, Human Rights, Common Security and Defence Policy, Cushnahan J.W. (rapporteur), *Draft report on the Proposal for a Council Decision on the Cooperation Agreement between the European Community and the Islamic Republic of Pakistan on Partnership and Development*, session document PE 341.360, 3 April 2004.

Committee on Citizens' Freedoms and Rights, Justice and Home Affairs, Pinto S.S. (Rapporteur), *Report on the proposal for a Council Decision concerning the signing of the Memorandum of Understanding between the European Community and the National Tourism Administration of the People's Republic of China on visa and related issues concerning tourist groups from the People's Republic of China (ADS)*, European Parliament, session document A5-0101/2004 final, 23 February 2004.

Committee on Citizens' Freedoms and Rights, Justice and Home Affairs, Pinto S.S. (rapporteur), *Report on the proposal for a Council Decision concerning the signing of the Agreement between the European Community and the Macao Special Administrative Region of the People's Republic of China on the readmission of persons residing without authorisation*, session document A5-0096/2004, 28 February 2004.

Commissie burgerlijke vrijheden, justitie en binnenlandse zaken, Klamt E. (rapporteur), *Verslag over het voorstel voor een Besluit van de Raad betreffende de sluiting van de overeenkomst tussen de Europese Gemeenschap en de Democratische Republiek Sri Lanka inzake de overname van personen die zonder vergunning op het grondgebied verblijven*, sessie document A6-0048/2004, 29 November 2004.

Committee on Civil Liberties, Justice and Home Affairs, Kreissl-Dörfler, *Draft report on the Amended proposal for a Council Directive on minimum standards on procedures in Member States for granting and withdrawing refugee status*, session document PE 357.562v02-00, 11 May 2005.

## Presidency of the European Union

(*by meeting date*)

Presidency Conclusions, Luxembourg European Council of 28 and 29 June 1991 (available on: www.europarl.europa.eu).

Presidency Conclusions, Edinburgh European Council of 12 December 1992 (available on: www.europarl.europa.eu).

Presidency Conclusions, Tampere European Council of 15 and 16 October 1999 (available on: www.europarl.europa.eu).

Presidency Conclusions, Santa Maria de Feira European Council of 19 and 20 June 2000 (available on: www.europarl.europa.eu).

Presidency Conclusions, Laeken European Council of 14 and 15 December 2001 (available on: www.europarl.europa.eu).

Presidency Conclusions, Seville European Council of 21 and 22 June 2002 (available on: www.europarl.europa.eu).

Presidency Conclusions, Thessaloniki European Council of 19 and 20 June 2003 (available on: www.europarl.europa.eu).

Presidency Conclusions, Brussels European Council of 16 and 17 October 2003, Council Doc. 15188/03, 25 November 2003.

Presidency Conclusions, Brussels European Council of 16 and 17 December 2004, Council Doc. 16238/1/04, 1 February 2005.

Presidency Conclusions, European Council meeting in Brussels of 15 and 16 December 2005, DOC/05/4.

## *Other Materials*

### Treaties and Declarations

Universal Declaration of Human Rights, adopted and proclaimed by General Assembly resolution 217 A (III) of 10 December 1948.

European Convention for the Protection of Human Rights and Fundamental Freedoms, Council of Europe of 4 November 1950, *ETS* no. 155.

Convention Relating to the Status of Refugees, adopted by the United Nations Conference of Plenipotentiaries on the Status of Refugees and Stateless Persons on 28 July 1951, 189 *UNTS* 137.

Convention relating to the status of stateless persons of 6 June 1960, 360 *UNTS* 117.

International Covenant of Civil and Political Rights, adopted by the General Assembly of the United Nations on 19 December 1966, 999 *UNTS* 171.

Protocol No. 4 of the European Convention for the protection of human rights and fundamental freedoms of 2 May 1968, *ETS* no. 46.

International Convention on the elimination of all forms of racial discrimination of 4 January 1969, 660 *UNTS* 195.

Organisation of African Unity Convention governing the specific aspects of refugee problems in Africa, adopted by the Assembly of Heads of State and Government on 10 September 1969, 1001 *UNTS* 45.

Vienna Convention on the law of treaties of 24 May 1969, 1155 *UNTS* 331.

Cartagena Declaration on Refugees, Adopted at the *Coloquio Sobre la Proteccíon Internacional de los Refugiados en Américan Central, México y Panamá: Problemas Jurídicos y Humanitarios*, Cartagena, Colombia, 19-22 November 1984, Annual Report of the Inter-

American Commission on Human Rights, OAS Doc. OEA/Ser.L/V/II.66/doc.10, rev. 1, at 190-93 (1984-85).

Convention against Torture and Other Cruel, Inhuman or Degrading Treatment or Punishment, adopted by the General Assembly of the United Nations on 10 December 1984, 1465 *UNTS* 85.

Draft articles on Responsibility of States for internationally wrongful acts, adopted by the International Law Commission at its fifty-third session (2001), Official records of the General Assembly, Fifty-sixth session, Supplement No. 10 (A/56/10), chp.IV.E.1, November 2001; endorsed by UNGA Resolution 56/83, 12 December 2002.

Agreement between the government of the United Kingdom of Great Britain and Northern Ireland and the Government of the Republic of Albania on the readmission of persons and Protocol for the implementation of the Agreement, Tirana, 14 October 2003, Albania No. 1 (2004), Cm 6267, Crown copyright (available on: www.fco.gov.uk).

## Cases

*European Court/Commission of Human Rights*

*X v. Government of Sweden*, 30 June 1959, Application No. 434/58, 28 ILR 242 (1959).

*X v. Belgium*, Appl. No. 7752/76, 15 December 1977.

*Ireland v. United Kingdom*, 18 January 1978, Series A, 25.

*X v. the Federal Republic of Germany*, Appl. No. 8100/77, 6 October 1978.

*Giama v. Belgium*, Appl. No. 7612/76, 17 July 1980.

*W v. Ireland*, Dec. Adm. Com. Ap. 9360/81, 28 February 1983, D&R 32.

*X v. the Netherlands*, Appl. No. 10400/83, 14 May 1984.

*X v. the Netherlands*, Appl. No. 10798/84, 5 March 1986, *RV* 1986, 94.

*Berrehab v. The Netherlands*, 21 June 1988, Series A, 138.

*Soering v. United Kingdom*, 7 July 1989, Series A, 161.

*Cruz Varas v. Sweden*, 20 March 1991, Series A, 201.

*Vilvarajah v. United Kingdom*, 30 October 1991, Series A, 215.

*Drozd and Janousek v. France and Spain*, 26 June 1992, Series A, 240.

*Amuur v. France*, 25 June 1996, Reports 1996-III.

*Akdivar and Others v. Turkey*, 16 September 1996, 21893/93 [1996] ECHR 35.

*Ahmed v. Austria*, 17 December 1996, Reports 1996-VI.

*H.L.R. v. France*, 29 April 1997, Reports 1997-III.

*D. v. United Kingdom*, 2 May 1997, Reports 1997-III.

*Bahaddar v. the Netherlands*, 19 February 1998, Reports 1998-I.

*Selmouni v. France*, 28 July 1999, Reports 1999-V.

*T.I. v. United Kingdom*, 7 March 2000, Decision, Reports 2000-III.

*Jabari v. Turkey, Judgement*, 11 July 2000, Reports 2000-VIII.

*Bensaid v. the United Kingdom*, 6 February 2001, 33 EHRR 10.

*Al-Adsani v. the United Kingdom*, 21 November 2001, Reports 2001-XI.

*Bankovic et al v. Belgium and 16 other States*, 12 December 2001, Reports 2001-XII.

*Öcalan v. Turkey*, 12 March 2003, Appl. no. 46221/99.

*International Court of Justice*

*North Sea Continental Shelf* cases, Judgement, ICJ Reports 1969.

*Military and Paramilitary Activities in and against Nicaragua*, Judgement, ICJ Reports 1986.

*Benelux*

Benelux Gerechtshof 15 April 1992, *RV* 1992, 65.

HR 11 June 1993, *RV* 1993, 63.

*National courts*

The Hague appeals court, 29 October 1987, *RV* 1987, 94.

UK Court of Appeal, *R. v. Secretary of State for the Home Department, ex parte Adan; ex parte Subaskaran; ex part Aitseguer*, [1999] 4 All ER 774.

UK House of Lords, *R. v. Special Adjudicator ex parte Ullah* [2004] UKHL 26.

U.S. Supreme Court, *Sale v. Haitian Centers Council* (Inc. 509 U.S. 155 (1993)).

**Benelux**

Decision M/P (67) 1

Beschikking M/P (67) 1 van de Ministeriële Werkgroep voor het personenverkeer betreffende de verwijdering en de overname van personen", 28 July 1967, *Trb.* 1978, 171

**European intergovernmental cooperation**

Resolution on a harmonised approach to questions concerning host third countries, London, 30 November and 1 December 1992, SN 4823/92.

*Ad Hoc* Group on Immigration, Report from the Ministers responsible for immigration on the harmonisation of immigration and asylum policies to the European Council in Maastricht, WGI 930, SN 4038/91, 3 December 1991.

**Council of Europe**

Recommendation No. R (84) 1 regarding the Protection of persons satisfying the criteria in the Geneva Convention but who are not formally recognised as refugees, adopted by the Committee of Ministers of the Council of Europe on 25 January 1984.

Recommendation No. R (98) 15 of the Committee of Ministers to Member States on the training of officials who first come into contact with protection seekers, in particular at border points of 15 December 1998.

**Documents of the UNHCR Executive Committee**

EXCOM Conclusion No. 22 (1981)

United Nations High Commissioner for Refugees Executive Committee No. 22 (XXXII) 1981, *Protection of asylum-seekers in situations of large-scale influx.*

EXCOM Conclusion No. 25 (1982)

United Nations High Commissioner for Refugees Executive Committee Conclusion No. 25 (XXXIII) 1982, *General.*

EXCOM Conclusion No. 58 (1989)

United Nations High Commissioner for Refugees Executive Committee Conclusion No. 58 (XL) 1989, *Problems of refugees and asylum-seekers who move in an irregular manner from a country in which they had already found protection.*

EXCOM Conclusion No. 79 (1996)

United Nations High Commissioner for Refugees Executive Committee Conclusion No. 79 (XLVII) 1996, *General.*

EXCOM Conclusion No. 85 (1998)

United Nations High Commissioner for Refugees Executive Committee Conclusion No. 85 (XLIX) 1998, *Conclusion on international protection.*

# Index

## Immigration and Asylum Law and Policy in Europe

1. E. Guild and P. Minderhoud (eds.): *Security of Residence and Expulsion*. 2000 ISBN 90-411-1458-0
2. E. Guild: *Immigration Law in the European Community*. 2001 ISBN 90-411-1593-5
3. B. Melis: *Negotiating Europe's Immigration Frontiers*. 2001 ISBN 90-411-1614-1
4. R. Byrne, G. Noll and J. Vedsted-Hansen (eds.): *New Asylum Countries?* Migration Control and Refugee Protection in an Enlarged European Union. 2002 ISBN 90-411-1753-9
5. K. Groenendijk, E. Guild and P. Minderhoud (eds.): *In Search of Europe's Borders*. 2003 ISBN 90-411-1977-9
6. J. Niessen and I. Chopin (eds.): *The Development of Legal Instruments to Combat Racism in a Diverse Europe*. 2004 ISBN 90-04-13686-X
7. B. Bogusz, R. Cholewinski, A. Cygan and E. Szyszczak (eds.): *Irregular Migration and Human Rights: Theoretical, European and International Perspectives*. 2004 ISBN 90-04-14011-5
8. H. Battjes: *European Asylum Law and International Law*. 2006 ISBN 90-04-15087-7
9. Elspeth Guild and Paul Minderhoud (eds.): *Immigration and Criminal Law in the European Union: The Legal Measures and Social Consequences of Criminal Law in Member States on Trafficking and Smuggling in Human Beings*. 2006 ISBN 90-14-15064-1
10. Georgia Papagianni: *Institutional and Policy Dynamics of EU Migration Law*. 2006 ISBN 90-04-15279-2
11. Elspeth Guild and Anneliese Baldaccini (eds.): *Terrorism and the Foreigner: A Decade of Tension around the Rule of Law in Europe*. 2006 ISBN 90-04-015187-7
12. Steve Peers and Nicola Rogers (eds.): *EU Immigration and Asylum Law: Text and Commentary*. 2006 ISBN 90-04-15374-8
13. Prakash Shah (ed.): *Law and Ethnic Plurality: Socio-Legal Perspectives*. 2007 ISBN 978-90-04-16245-7
14. Bruno Nascimbene, Massimo Condinanzi and Alessandra Lang: *Citizenship of the Union and Free Movement of Persons*. 2008 ISBN 978-90-04-16300-3
15. Evelien Brouwer: *Digital Borders and Real Rights: Effective Remedies for Third-Country Nationals in the Schengen Information System*. 2008 ISBN 978 90 04 16503 8
16. Nils Coleman: *European Readmission Policy:Third Country Interests and Refugee Rights*. 2008 ISBN 978-90-04-16554-0

**Martinus Nijhoff Publishers – Leiden • Boston**